READING

THE

WORD OF GOD

IN THE

PRESENCE

OF GOD

A HANDBOOK FOR BIBLICAL
INTERPRETATION

VERN S. POYTHRESS

:: CROSSWAY®

WHEATON, ILLINOIS

Trade paperback ISBN: 978-1-4335-4324-1
ePub ISBN: 978-1-4335-4327-2
PDF ISBN: 978-1-4335-4325-8
Mobipocket ISBN: 978-1-4335-4326-5

Library of Congress Cataloging-in-Publication Data

Poythress, Vern S.
  Reading the word of God in the presence of God : a handbook for
  biblical interpretation / Vern S. Poythress.
    pages cm
  Includes bibliographical references and index.
  ISBN 978-1-4335-4324-1 (tp)
  1. Bible—Hermeneutics. I. Title.
BS476.P688   2016
220.601—dc23   2015005319

Crossway is a publishing ministry of Good News Publishers.

VP		25	24	23	22	21	20	19	18	17	16
15	14	13	12	11	10	9	8	7	6	5	4	3	2	1

To my wife, Diane

Contents

Part V

ISSUES WITH LANGUAGE

Part VI

REDEMPTIVE-HISTORICAL INTERPRETATION

Part VII

ASSESSMENT

Part VIII
EXAMPLES

APPENDICES

Tables and Illustrations

Tables

Illustrations

Part I

INTRODUCTORY PRINCIPLES FOR INTERPRETATION

1

Foundations for Interpretation

This book is a practical handbook to help people grow in skill in interpreting the Bible. It illustrates the process of interpretation by considering the stages through which a Bible student may travel in the course of studying a passage in the Bible. Even beginners can use the early stages of our approach (up through chapters 4–6), because we have designed the explanations to make sense to beginners and to be usable. In later chapters we add more complexity, so that beginners can continue to advance. As more details are added, pastors and advanced students may also find helpful insights.

Our approach should also interest experts, because it differs from what has become standard among many biblical scholars (see appendix A). We endeavor to appreciate how communion with God forms the central axis in every stage of interpretation—the beginning, the middle, and the end. We want to interpret the Bible in a way that has its basis in the Bible itself, in the Bible's instruction about loyalty to God. Both beginners and more mature students can profit from thinking through how to interpret the Bible more faithfully.

This handbook shares much with biblical interpretation that took place in the Reformation and before. The Enlightenment and its fruits have resulted in additional benefits through common grace. But much that has taken place in the modern West has corrupted the process of interpreting the Bible. We must rethink how we work, rather than passively accept the standards and procedures that are now common in the academic world in the West. At the same time, we can profit from positive insights found in modern thinking about interpretation. This handbook has endeavored to use both ancient and modern insights, but only after sifting good from bad, and placing positive insights in the larger framework of a biblically based worldview.

Loving God

So let us begin.

Jesus indicates how we ought to live with wholehearted love for God:

> You shall love the Lord your God with all your heart and with all your soul and with all your mind. This is the great and first commandment. And a second is like it: You shall love your neighbor as yourself. On these two commandments depend all the Law and the Prophets. (Matt. 22:37–40)

If we love the Lord our God with all our heart and soul and mind, we will be interested in learning more about him. And the Bible is the primary source for knowledge of God.[1] Thus, loving God motivates serious study of the Bible. When we study the Bible, we should be loving God in the midst of our study. What implications does loving God have for the *way* we study the Bible? Amid our studying, we will be asking God to enliven our hearts, to enliven and clarify our minds, to sanctify our attitudes, to teach us, and to empower us to receive and obey what we study. We will also be praising him and loving him and enjoying him and marveling over who he is amid every aspect of our study. We will be repenting of sins when the Bible reveals how we have sinned.

So what does it look like to study in this way? We will endeavor to work out details in good time. But first we need to consider briefly some foundational questions: the nature of love, the nature of God, our own nature, and the nature of our needs. These are deep ques-

[1] The Bible comes to us in contexts that the Lord has given us in his providence. The contexts include many modern contexts: our social contexts, our previous spiritual history, our personal struggles, our church, words from Christian friends, the preaching that we hear in church, and the other means of grace (such as prayer and the Lord's Supper). Each of these contexts can function at times as either a help or a hindrance (we can even pray or receive the Lord's Supper in a disobedient way). We cannot here explore all these influences in detail.

tions. We will consider them only in a brief way, leaving it to other books to work out the foundations in a more thorough way.[2] We are condensing our discussion of the foundations so that we can give more attention to how their implications work out in the actual practice of Bible study.

The Centrality of Love

First, let us consider the centrality of love in responding to God. In addition to what Jesus says about love, the apostle Paul indicates that all the commandments of God can be summed up in the second of the two great commandments, the commandment to love your neighbor as yourself:

> for the one who loves another has *fulfilled the law*. For the commandments, "You shall not commit adultery, You shall not murder, You shall not steal, You shall not covet," and *any other commandment, are summed* up in this word: "You shall love your neighbor as yourself." Love does no wrong to a neighbor; therefore love is *the fulfilling of the law*. (Rom. 13:8–10)

> For *the whole law is fulfilled* in one word: "You shall love your neighbor as yourself." (Gal. 5:14)

In a sense, God is our closest "neighbor," so this commandment implies loving God as well as our human neighbors.

God's will can also be summed up in the first and great commandment, to love God, because loving God implies loving your neighbor as well:

> If anyone says, "I love God," and hates his brother, he is a liar; for he who does not love his brother whom he has seen cannot love God whom he has not seen. And this commandment we have from him: whoever loves God must also love his brother. (1 John 4:20–21)

The Bible also indicates that if we love God, we will keep his commandments:

---

[2] There are many resources. I would refer readers especially to Vern S. Poythress, *God-Centered Biblical Interpretation* (Phillipsburg, NJ: Presbyterian & Reformed, 1999), and then to other books that John Frame and I have written (see bibliography).

For this is the love of God, that we keep his commandments. (1 John 5:3)

If you love me, you will keep my commandments. (John 14:15)

Among the commandments is the commandment to love your neighbor. So it makes sense that loving God is the "great and first command- ment." By implication, it encompasses all the other commandments of God and sums up our entire duty to God. Therefore it also sums up our duty when we interpret the Bible.

Redemption

How can we love God with all our heart? In our fallen condition, as children of Adam, we are in rebellion against God and in slavery to sin: "Truly, truly, I say to you, everyone who practices sin is a slave to sin" (John 8:34). At heart, we hate God rather than loving him. God himself has to rescue us. That is why he sent Christ into the world:

> In this the love of God was made manifest among us, that God sent his only Son into the world, so that we might live through him. In this is love, not that we have loved God but that he loved us and sent his Son to be the propitiation for our sins. Beloved, if God so loved us, we also ought to love one another. (1 John 4:9–11)

Other books explain God's redemption through Christ.[3] Here, we will explore how his redemption affects our interpretation of the Bible.

God as Trinity

We can love God only if God himself empowers us. This empowerment begins when we are born again through the Holy Spirit:

> Truly, truly, I say to you, unless one is born of water and *the Spirit*, he cannot enter the kingdom of God. That which is born of the flesh is flesh, and that which is *born of the Spirit* is spirit. Do not marvel that I said to you, "You must be born again." (John 3:5–7)

---

[3] See especially J. I. Packer, *Knowing God* (Downers Grove, IL: InterVarsity Press, 1993); John M. Frame, *Salvation Belongs to the Lord: An Introduction to Systematic Theology* (Phillipsburg, NJ: Presbyterian & Reformed, 2006).

This principle is confirmed by other verses that indicate that God takes the initiative:

> We love because he first loved us. (1 John 4:19)

> Being therefore exalted at the right hand of God, and having received from the Father the promise of the Holy Spirit, he [Christ] has poured out this [the Holy Spirit at Pentecost] that you yourselves are seeing and hearing. (Acts 2:33)

The Holy Spirit empowers us to love: "The fruit of the Spirit is love . . ." (Gal. 5:22). Loving God leads in turn to communion with him: "If anyone loves me, he will keep my word, and my Father will love him, and we will come to him and make our home with him" (John 14:23). Jesus says that both he and his Father will dwell with anyone who loves him. In the context of this verse, he also indicates that the Holy Spirit will dwell with believers (v. 17). Communion with God is communion with the one true God who is three persons and whose communion with us takes place through the mediation of the Son in the power of the Holy Spirit.[4] This communion takes place only with those who belong to Christ, who are united to him by faith.

Since the Bible is God's word, his own speech to us,[5] his speech functions as one way in which he has communion with us. Through his word, God works sanctification: "Sanctify them in the truth; your word is truth" (John 17:17). God's communion with us always harmonizes with his own character. We have communion with our *Trinitarian* God. So we can think about how his Trinitarian character affects our communion with him.

As we have indicated, when we are united to Christ and trust in him, God the Father, God the Son, and God the Holy Spirit come to dwell in us, and this indwelling expresses God's communion with us. The work of the Holy Spirit is particularly prominent in this indwelling. Romans 8, in teaching about the Spirit's indwelling, calls him "the Spirit of God"

---

[4] Vern S. Poythress, *Logic: A God-Centered Approach to the Foundation of Western Thought* (Wheaton, IL: Crossway, 2013), chapter 15.

[5] See Benjamin Breckinridge Warfield, *The Inspiration and Authority of the Bible*, ed. Samuel G. Craig, with an introduction by Cornelius Van Til (Philadelphia: Presbyterian & Reformed, 1948); John M. Frame, *The Doctrine of the Word of God* (Phillipsburg, NJ: Presbyterian & Reformed, 2010); J. I. Packer, *"Fundamentalism" and the Word of God: Some Evangelical Principles* (Grand Rapids, MI: Eerdmans, 1958).

and "the Spirit of Christ" (Rom. 8:9). The Father and the Son make their home in a Christian specifically through the Holy Spirit.

We experience fellowship with Christ as we are buried and raised with him, according to Romans 6:3–11. We experience his lordship and control both through his commandments and through having his work applied in our lives. By God's work we begin to love him and to express our love in faithful obedience.

The lordship of Christ over our lives expresses the lordship of God the Father as well. God the Father, as Creator and sustainer, represents the ultimate source of authority. He makes moral claims on our lives. His claims have relevance when we are studying the Bible.

Perspectival Triads

The lordship of Christ has implications for the process of interpretation. John M. Frame, by meditating on the biblical teaching on God's lordship, has summed up the nature of God's lordship using three overlapping themes: authority, control, and presence.[6] He uses and expounds these themes in understanding God's lordship over all creation and all history. But the themes also apply to God's lordship over the lives of believers. When we have communion with God through Christ, we experience his lordship as he applies Christ's work of salvation to us.

Frame also indicates that the three categories of lordship reflect the work of the three distinct persons of the Trinity. Authority belongs to the Father, control to the Son, and presence to the work of the Holy Spirit.[7] Since, however, the three persons of the Trinity indwell one another, and since they all act in all of God's works in the world, the three categories of lordship function as perspectives on one another, rather than being separable. And even though we can associate one distinct person of the Trinity more closely with one category, all three persons are active in all the aspects of lordship.

Each perspective on lordship points to the other two and presupposes the other two. For example, if we start with the perspective of control, we can see that God's control implies control over my loca-

---

[6] John M. Frame, *The Doctrine of the Knowledge of God* (Phillipsburg, NJ: Presbyterian & Reformed, 1987); John M. Frame, *The Doctrine of God* (Phillipsburg, NJ: Presbyterian & Reformed, 2002), 21–115.
[7] John M. Frame, "Backgrounds to My Thought," in *Speaking the Truth in Love: The Theology of John M. Frame*, ed. John J. Hughes (Phillipsburg, NJ: Presbyterian & Reformed, 2009), 16.

tion and my heart, which means that God is present with me. Control implies control over standards for authority, and so implies that God has ultimate authority. If we start with presence, we are dealing with the presence of God, who also makes present his moral standards, and therefore makes present his ultimate authority. His power to be present represents a form of power and therefore of control.

The interlocking and interpenetration of the perspectives on lordship reflect the inexhaustible mystery of the Trinity, which we can never understand completely. God understands himself completely because he is God (1 Cor. 2:10). We as creatures can understand truly and genuinely, as God gives us ability and reveals himself through Christ. But we never come to understand him exhaustively and we never dissolve all mystery. The mysteries concerning God only deepen as we deepen our understanding. They should stir up our awe and praise, rather than frustration.

When God acts, he expresses his authority, control, and presence. All three—authority, control, and presence—come to expression when he speaks to us in Scripture. So these perspectives on lordship describe how we have communion with God in our reception of Scripture. By specifically thinking about these perspectives as we read, we may stir up our hearts to praise and to stand in awe of him, and at the same time remind ourselves that Scripture contains mysteries. The ultimate mystery of God himself always remains.

We can further explore what it means to listen to Scripture by using a second triad of perspectives, namely the triad consisting in the normative, situational, and existential perspectives. John Frame has developed this second triad of perspectives for analyzing ethics.[8] The normative perspective focuses on the norms for ethics, which are summarized in God's commands. Parts of Scripture with explicit commands are further explained and deepened by the surrounding Scriptures that contain other kinds of communication. The situational perspective focuses on our situation, and asks how we may best promote the glory of God in our situation. Loving our neighbor offers one

---

[8] John M. Frame, *The Doctrine of the Christian Life* (Phillipsburg, NJ: Presbyterian & Reformed, 2008); an earlier and shorter explanation can be found in John M. Frame, *Perspectives on the Word of God: An Introduction to Christian Ethics* (Eugene, OR: Wipf & Stock, 1999); Frame, "Backgrounds to My Thought," 16.

way of glorifying God. So as an aspect of the situational perspective, we may ask how we may best express love for our neighbors and how we may best help and bless them. Finally, the existential perspective focuses on the people in the situation and their motivations. The primary motivation should be love.

These three perspectives, when rightly understood, interlock and reinforce one another. Each functions as a perspective on all of ethics. Rightly understood, each not only points to the others but even encompasses them. For example, the normative perspective starts with God's commands. But God's commands include the command to love, and so this perspective tells us to pay attention to motivations and attitudes. Thus it encompasses the existential perspective, which focuses on motivations and attitudes. Next, suppose that we start with the existential perspective. We start with the emphasis on loving God. If we love God, we will keep his commandments, and so we also have to pay attention to the commandments, which involves the normative perspective. Loving our neighbors means paying attention to how we may bless them in their circumstances, and so leads to the situational perspective on their circumstances. If we start with the normative perspective, the commandments of God imply that we should pay attention to the circumstances in order to act wisely. So the normative perspective leads to the situational perspective.

In sum, we may profitably consider Scripture using Frame's perspectives, because Scripture itself invites us to reflect on aspects of God's lordship and aspects of our obligations to God.

Unity and Diversity in Humanity

To appreciate more fully what it means to listen to God's word in the Bible, we have to consider who we are as *recipients* of God's word. So let us consider our humanity. The reality of God's Trinitarian nature has implications for our understanding of humanity. We are made in the image of God (Gen. 1:26–27). God is one God in three persons. He has unity and diversity in himself. We as human beings are creatures, not the Creator. But we also have unity and diversity, though unity and diversity operate on a different level and in a different way than with God himself. (For example, we do not have the ultimate mutual indwelling or "coinherence" belonging only to the persons of the Trinity in their relation to each other.)

The unity of humanity consists in the fact that we are all human—we are all made in the image of God, and we share common ways of thinking, speaking, and acting. But we also show diversity. Each of us is a distinctive human being, unlike anyone else in details. Sin makes diversity contentious, but a certain kind of harmonious diversity was present with Adam and Eve before they sinned. And redemption brings back harmonious diversity: diversity in the church blesses every member of the body of Christ. The church is one body with many members (1 Corinthians 12). We have a diversity of gifts, which in their diversity bring health and growth to the one body (see also Eph. 4:1–16).

This diversity among human beings expresses itself in how we understand the Bible. We find ourselves at different stages of growth. Not everyone pays attention to exactly the same verses or the same aspects of the verses. Not everyone understands with equal depth or acuity. We can also see diversity in the human authors of the Bible. The four Gospels—Matthew, Mark, Luke, and John—have fascinating differences in emphasis. They have four distinct human authors, though we should be quick to add that it was God who raised up these four authors in their distinctiveness, and the distinctions express God's will and receive God's authorization. The Gospels did not arise merely from human individuality, in a way independent of God.[9]

Unity and diversity show themselves in our study of Scripture as well. Some people memorize more Scripture than others. Some people find themselves drawn to the Psalms, while others pore over Matthew or Romans or Revelation. God equips some people with gifts of teaching (Rom. 12:7; 1 Cor. 12:28–29; Eph. 4:11), and they explain Scripture to others or write commentaries that help others. Some people have the gift of helping (1 Cor. 12:28; see Rom. 12:7), and their practical acts of helping bring home the implications of Scriptural passages that talk about practical service.

When all the people in the church are following Christ, all their efforts work together to build up the church, which is the body of Christ

---

[9] Vern S. Poythress, *Symphonic Theology; The Validity of Multiple Perspectives in Theology* (reprint; Phillipsburg, NJ: Presbyterian & Reformed, 2001), 47–49.

(1 Cor. 14:12; Eph. 4:12–16). But the church as a whole suffers when some members suffer (1 Cor. 12:26). This interaction of unity and diversity expresses God's plan for the church and for the members in the church—for every Christian believer.

The unity and diversity in the church have a role when we consider studying the Bible. We have already mentioned the gift of teaching. Teachers play a leading role in guiding the whole church into understanding the Bible more deeply and faithfully. Not everyone is a teacher, so we have a diversity here. The whole church profits from godly and gifted teachers, so the church has a unity as well. All believers grow in knowing Scripture in common ways, because the Bible is the word of God, from the Father through the Son in the power of the Holy Spirit. Believers share doctrines in common (Eph. 4:5: "one Lord, one faith, one baptism").

But we meet diversity as well. In the first century of the church, and in some cultures of the world even today, some of the believers cannot read, or do not have access to a printed Bible of their own. They rely on hearing from others, perhaps as the Bible is read in a church meeting or as they listen to a radio or a TV or a recording that has a reading from the Bible. Even in situations where believers have access to the Bible and other aids such as concordances, Bible atlases, and commentaries, we must reckon with diversity in the body of Christ. Not everyone will read and study according to the same exact pattern.[10]

Means of Growth

The Bible prescribes one central "method" for learning: Christ himself is "the way, and the truth, and the life" (John 14:6). Christ is the "method." But of course he is a person, not a mechanical list of steps. When we hear the word *method*, we may think of a fixed series of steps that guarantees a particular outcome. For example, we follow the instructions for putting together a new bookcase; and if we follow them carefully, we obtain a finished bookcase. Or, the recipe for cooking muffins leads to tasty muffins.

Christ as a person is actually the opposite of having a "method" in this sense, because we cannot reduce the person of Christ to a mechani-

---

[10] On the use of multiple perspectives from multiple human beings, see Poythress, *Symphonic Theology.*

cal method, nor can we as human beings guarantee beforehand merely by our own will or power that we will always be faithful to Christ and his lordship as we study his word. Precisely because we do not have a simple, fail-safe "recipe" for interpretation, a recipe that would work independently of our religious commitment and our spiritual health and our moral obedience, it is all the more important that we affirm that Christ is the *way*. He is the way to eternal life, the way to understanding God. We may add that he is also the way to understanding Scripture, because we need him and the power of his Spirit to arrive. We can never reduce any human person, let alone Christ, to a list of steps. Personal interaction creates rich relationships, including surprises.

God has made the world with regularities in it. We have regular ways of multiplying numbers. People, as we said, are much richer, and the text of Scripture is much richer, but here too we may speak of regularities. Scripture itself indicates that the word of God, now contained in Scripture, has been designed by God himself as a key means for our growth in knowing him:

> *Sanctify* them in the truth; your word is truth. (John 17:17)

> For I have given them the *words* that you gave me, and they have received them and have come *to know in truth* that I came from you; and they have *believed* that you sent me. (John 17:8)

> Your word is a *lamp* to my feet
>   and a *light* to my path. (Ps. 119:105)

> All Scripture is breathed out by God and *profitable* for teaching, for reproof, for correction, and for *training in righteousness*, that the man of God may be complete, equipped for every good work. (2 Tim. 3:16–17)

Accordingly, theologians have described reading and listening to Scripture as a *means of grace*. A means of grace is a means or a path by which God gives grace and blessing to those who seek him. The study of Scripture stands alongside other means of grace: prayer, the sacraments (baptism and the Lord's Supper), and fellowship with God's people. All the means of grace reinforce one another.

In addition, we may say that God has established ways for engaging the means of grace that Scripture itself is. Because of what Scripture is, God has established ways or paths that believers may travel to receive and absorb Scripture properly, in communion with God who gave it and who continues to speak it. We must only add, to balance what we have already said, that the ways and paths for studying Scripture offer a unity amid the diversity of different readers and reading strategies. We do observe a diversity in human reception of the Bible. But there is also a fundamental unity in how people ought to approach the Bible: they should all submit unreservedly to God who speaks. Neither unity nor diversity reduces to the other; but at their best they presuppose and fortify each other.

In short, Christian growth begins by being born again by the Spirit of God. It continues as we grow in holiness and in conformity to Christ. One of the main means of spiritual growth that God uses is the Bible, which is his word.

2

Principles for Interpreting the Bible

We could develop a whole book-length discussion of doctrinal principles that we ought to presuppose as we study the Bible. But in this book we intend to move quickly toward practicing biblical interpretation. So we will explain some important principles only briefly, leaving it to other books on theology to develop these principles more extensively[1] and to show how they spring from the Bible's own view of God, man, and its own role.

God Speaking

The Bible is God's speech in written form. So we should think about what it means for God to speak. God's speech has several forms.

1. God speaks eternally in the Word, the second person of the Trinity (John 1:1). God the Son is the Word spoken. God the Father is the speaker. John 1:1 does not mention the Holy Spirit explicitly, but other passages (for example, Ezek. 37:10, 14) compare the Holy Spirit to the breath of God taking his word to its destination.[2]

2. God speaks to create and to govern the world. In Genesis 1 we see repeated instances where God speaks to bring about his work of creation:

---

[1] Poythress, *God-Centered Biblical Interpretation* (Phillipsburg, NJ: Presbyterian & Reformed, 1999), contains a sketch of such principles, but it could be further expanded. John Frame's *Systematic Theology* (Phillipsburg, NJ: Presbyterian & Reformed, 2013) expands on doctrinal principles.
[2] Vern S. Poythress, *In the Beginning Was the Word: Language—A God-Centered Approach* (Wheaton, IL: Crossway, 2009), chapter 2.

And God said, "Let there be light," and there was light. (Gen. 1:3)

By the word of the Lᴏʀᴅ the heavens were made,
    and by the breath of his mouth all their host. (Ps. 33:6)[3]

God's speech continues to govern the world in providence:

he [the Son] upholds the universe by the *word* of his power. (Heb. 1:3)

This speech displays the authority of God the Father, the control by God the Son who is the Word, and the presence of the Holy Spirit (who in Gen. 1:2 hovered over the face of the waters).

3. God spoke orally to human beings, in theophanies (Gen. 17:1; Ex. 20:18–19) and through prophets as his spokesmen (Ex. 20:19, 21).

4. God wrote his word. He did so directly with the tablets at Mount Sinai, which were "written with the finger of God" (Ex. 31:18). Later, he committed his word to writing through human spokesmen who did the actual writing (Deut. 31:24–26).

5. Finally, at the climax of history, God spoke through the incarnate Son (Heb. 1:1–2).

6. God now speaks to us through the Bible, which God has given us as the permanent deposit of his word. John 21:25 indicates that not all God's spoken words have been recorded in Scripture:

Now there are also *many other things that Jesus did.* Were every one of them to be written, I suppose that the world itself could not contain the books that would be written.

In accordance with the pattern established in Deuteronomy 31:9–13, 24–29, God has provided for the gradual accumulation of a group of authoritative texts, written with his authority, that would serve for the permanent guidance of his people. The Bible is the completed collection of these infallible texts. It is called the *canon* of Scripture, because it is the standard for our instruction.[4] It is God's permanent communication to us.

---

[3] See also Psalm 148:5–6; Romans 4:17; 2 Corinthians 4:6; Hebrews 11:3; and 2 Peter 3:5.
[4] On the canon, see Herman Ridderbos, *Redemptive History and the New Testament Scriptures* (Phillipsburg, NJ: Presbyterian & Reformed, 1988); and Michael J. Kruger, *Canon Revisited: Establishing the Origins and Authority of the New Testament Books* (Wheaton, IL: Crossway, 2012).

Three Aspects of Speaking

God's communication involves God as author, the Bible as the text that he communicates, and us as the recipients. In the archetypal communication of the Word of God in the Trinity, we have God the Father as author, God the Son as the Word communicated, and the Holy Spirit as the one associated with the destiny of the Word. These three aspects of communication coinhere, and can function as perspectives on one another. No one aspect can be strictly isolated. Likewise, when God communicates to us in Scripture, the three aspects function like three perspectives.[5] If we start with God as author, his intention in authorship leads to paying attention to the text of the Bible and to the recipients. He intended to write the text that was produced, and he intended to address the recipients to whom his communication was directed. So both text and recipients belong to his intention. If we start with the text, its interpretation requires that we pay attention to God as author. And the text addresses recipients, sometimes directly (Galatians goes to the Galatian churches), but always at least indirectly, by way of implication.

We can accordingly consider interpretive principles that focus on God, on the Bible itself, or on the recipients. But these three foci are not strictly isolated. All of them have implications for all three aspects of biblical communication.

God

If we are going to appreciate what God says, we must know God and grow in knowing him. What we know about him feeds into our understanding of what he says.

1. God is Lord over all things. So we must take into account his lordship as we study. We may use Frame's triad of authority, control, and presence as one summary of his lordship.

2. God is Creator, while we and everything else in the world are creatures. The Bible makes a distinction between the Creator and his creatures. God as Creator is Lord, while his creatures are subjects and ought to submit to his lordship. This distinction implies that we must listen to God when we read the Bible, and not imagine that we can listen

---

[5] Poythress, *In the Beginning Was the Word*, chapter 4.

merely to our own ideas that arise while reading. Some false religions claim that each human being is really divine in his core. If this were so, we could gain understanding merely by listening to this inward, allegedly "divine" self. But that is antithetical to God's way that he reveals in Scripture.

In sum, the Creator-creature distinction leads to rejecting pantheistic mysticism, where readers think that they are themselves divine and listen for the "divine" within them rather than really listening to the Bible. We should also reject Platonic reminiscence, which says that knowledge consists in remembering what the soul already knows from eternity past. We reject rationalism, which makes our own rationality the final standard for sifting what we will accept in the Bible. We reject autonomous hermeneutics, which says that we must first work out how we interpret texts using our own autonomous ideas, before we come to any particular text.

3. God is immanent. He is present in the whole world. He is also especially present, with his offer of redemption in Christ, as we read Scripture. Much modern thinking assumes or alleges that God (if there is a God) is absent when we read Scripture. But he is not, and it makes a difference. We meet God, not merely a text that substitutes for God.

4. God has planned history and brings about his plan in time (Eph. 1:11). History has purpose, and God has designed in particular that our study of the Bible should have a purpose. The Bible serves *his* goals, not whatever goals we may devise out of our own hearts. In particular, we are not supposed to be studying the Bible merely to acquire information, but for our spiritual good—for our salvation. We are looking forward to "new heavens and a new earth in which righteousness dwells" (2 Pet. 3:13). God gives us the Bible as a means that aids us and empowers us in moving toward that goal.

The Bible

Now let us consider some basic principles about the Bible.

1. The Bible is God's own word, so that what the Bible says, God says.

2. God governs the whole world through his divine speech, which specifies and controls what happens (Heb. 1:3). The Bible indicates that

God speaks to govern the world, but we do not hear this speech; we only see its effects (for example, Ps. 33:6, 9; 147:15–18). The Bible, by contrast, is the word of God, designed by God to speak specifically to *us* as human beings. All divine speech, whether directed toward governing the world in general or directed toward us as human beings, has divine character. In particular, it displays God's lordship in authority, control, and presence.

3. God speaks his words to us in *covenants* (Gen. 9:9; 15:18; 17:7; Ex. 19:5; etc.). A "covenant" is a solemn, legally binding agreement between two parties. In this case, the two parties are God and human beings. In the Old Testament, God's covenants with human beings show some affinities with ancient Near Eastern suzerainty treaties.[6] These treaties show five elements, which also appear either explicitly or by implication in God's covenants in the Old Testament (table 2.1):

Table 2.1: Comparing Treaties and Covenants

Hittite Suzerainty Treaties	Exodus 20
Identification of the suzerain	"I am the Lᴏʀᴅ . . ." (Ex. 20:2)
Historical prologue	"who brought you out of the land of Egypt" (Ex. 20:2)
Stipulations	The Ten Commandments (Ex. 20:3–17)
Sanctions (blessings and curses)	"The Lᴏʀᴅ will not hold him guiltless . . ." (Ex. 20:7; see also v. 12)
Recording and passing on	"the two tablets" (Ex. 31:18; Deuteronomy 31)

These five points have correlations with John Frame's triad for lordship, the triad consisting in authority, control, and presence. The identification of God proclaims his transcendent *authority*, and the stipulations as norms imply his *authority* over the people. The historical prologue shows how he has exercised his *control* in past history. The blessings and curses indicate how he will exercise his *control* in the future. His identification also proclaims his *presence*, and the recording and passing on of the covenantal words imply his continuing *presence* with the people.

---

[6] Meredith G. Kline, *The Structure of Biblical Authority* (Grand Rapids, MI: Eerdmans, 1972).

4. All the Bible is the *covenantal* word of God. That is, the idea of *covenant* offers us one perspective on the Bible. The New Testament proclaims the gospel concerning the death, resurrection, and ascension of Christ. The apostle Paul characterizes his entire ministry as a ministry of the "new covenant" (2 Cor. 3:6). So all of Paul's writings are covenantal words in a broad sense. At the Last Supper, Jesus inaugurated "the new covenant" (Luke 22:20; 1 Cor. 11:25). The other apostles and New Testament writers function to convey the words of the new covenant to us.

When the Bible uses the word *new* to describe the new covenant, it clearly presupposes an older one. The new covenant fulfills the Abrahamic covenant (Gal. 3:7–14) and the Davidic covenant (Acts 2:30–36), but the Mosaic covenant is principally in mind when the New Testament implies a covenant that is "old" (Heb. 8:8–13). The Mosaic covenant also contains, in Deuteronomy 31, explicit instructions for preserving canonical covenantal documents and explicit instructions about future prophets (Deut. 18:18–22). The entirety of the Old Testament consists in divinely authorized additions to the initial Mosaic deposit, so it fits into the covenantal structure inaugurated with Moses. The entire Old Testament is covenantal in character.

Thus both the New Testament and the Old Testament can be viewed as covenantal in a broad sense. Indeed, the traditional names, in which they are called "Testaments," signify their covenantal character ("testament" is a near synonym for "covenant" in later theological usage, which builds on Heb. 9:15–16).

Accordingly, all the Bible shows the character of God's lordship, including authority, control, and presence. As usual, the three aspects of lordship are perspectivally related. They interlock, and they imply each other. The interlocking implies that we cannot neatly separate them. We cannot have God's presence without having him affect us in control, and without having him speak specifically in authority, especially through stipulations. This interlocking excludes wordless mysticism, according to which a deeper union with God goes beyond words and ignores them. Certainly our fellowship with God in Christ, through the Spirit, includes matters "too deep for words" (Rom. 8:26). But that does not mean that words become devalued. The apostle Paul uses plenty of words in Romans.

Likewise, we cannot have the authority and stipulatory meanings of Scripture without God's presence and without the effects of his control. This interlocking excludes a merely academic or informational treatment of Scripture. The Scripture contains information—plenty of it. But when we meet the information, we are also meeting God in his presence and control. We are truncating the fullness of Scripture if we deny God's presence. Any alleged "scientific" treatment of Scripture, which claims to aim at mastery and control of its meanings rather than submitting to fellowship with God in his presence, already denies and undermines its actual character.

5. The Bible is a single book, with God as its author. It does of course have multiple human authors. But its unity according to the divine author implies that we should see it as a single unified message, and should use each passage and each book to help us in understanding others. Because God is faithful to his own character, he is consistent with himself. We should therefore interpret each passage of the Bible in harmony with the rest of the Bible.

6. The Bible is God-centered. It not only has God as its author, but in a fundamental way it speaks about God as its principal subject. It does so even in historical passages that do not directly mention God, because the history it recounts is history governed by God.

7. The Bible is Christ-centered.[7] Covenants mediate God's presence to us, and at the heart of the covenants is Christ, who is the *one* mediator between God and men (1 Tim. 2:5). Christ, as the coming servant of the Lord, is virtually identified with the covenant in Isaiah 42:6 and 49:8.[8] In Luke 24, Jesus teaches the apostles that all of the Old Testament Scriptures are about him and his work (Luke 24:25–27, 44–49). Understanding how the Old Testament speaks about Christ is challenging, but in view of Jesus's teaching it cannot be evaded. Fortunately, we have the New Testament to aid us. It contains not only teachings that help us to understand the Old Testament as a whole, but many quotations from the Old Testament that illustrate Jesus's claims in Luke 24.

---

[7] Edmund P. Clowney, *Preaching and Biblical Theology* (Grand Rapids, MI: Eerdmans, 1961); Clowney, *Preaching Christ in All of Scripture* (Wheaton, IL: Crossway, 2003); Clowney, *The Unfolding Mystery: Discovering Christ in the Old Testament* (Colorado Springs: NavPress, 1988); Dennis E. Johnson, *Him We Proclaim: Preaching Christ from All the Scriptures* (Phillipsburg, NJ: Presbyterian & Reformed, 2007).
[8] Vern S. Poythress, *Logic: A God-Centered Approach to the Foundation of Western Thought* (Wheaton, IL: Crossway, 2013), chapter 15.

8. The Bible is oriented to the history of redemption. God caused the Bible's individual books to be written over a period of centuries. God's later speech builds on earlier speech, and further unfolds the significance of his plan for history. God's redemption takes place in history. Christianity is not merely a religious philosophy, a set of general truths about God and the world. At its heart is the gospel, the good news that Christ has come and has lived and died and has risen from the dead, and now lives to intercede for us. God has worked out our salvation by coming in the person of Christ and acting in time and space. The message of what he has done now goes out to the nations (Matt. 28:18–20; Acts 1:8).

9. Christ's first and second coming are central to history. God's work of redemption came to a climax in the work of Christ on earth, especially in his crucifixion, death, resurrection, and ascension. Christ now reigns at the right hand of the Father (Eph. 1:20–21). We look forward to the future consummation of redemption when Christ returns.

10. God's work of redemption interweaves word and deed. We see this interweaving even during his work of creation:

Word: God said, "Let there be light."
Deed: And there was light.
Word: And God saw that the light was good [similar to verbal evaluation]. (Gen. 1:3–4)

Word: "Let us make man in our image . . ."
Deed: So God created man in his own image, . . .
Word: And God said to them, "Be fruitful and multiply . . ."
     (Gen. 1:26–28)

Likewise, Jesus's words interpret his deeds and vice versa:

If I am not doing the works of my Father, then do not believe me; but if I do them, even though you do not believe me, *believe the works*, that you may know and understand that the Father is in me and I am in the Father. (John 10:37–38)

In the book of Acts, the miracles and the growth of the church help unbelievers to grasp the implications of apostolic preaching, and vice versa:

Philip went down to the city of Samaria and proclaimed to them the Christ. And the crowds with one accord paid attention to *what was being said* by Philip when they heard him and *saw the signs* that he did. For unclean spirits, crying out with a loud voice, came out of many who had them, and many who were paralyzed or lame were healed. (Acts 8:5–7)

The Recipients

Some of the books of the Bible indicate that they were originally written to particular recipients, such as the church at Corinth, Philippi, or Colossae. But God, who knows the end from the beginning (Isa. 46:10), also had us in mind:

> For whatever was written in former days was written for our instruction, that through endurance and through the encouragement of the Scriptures we might have hope. (Rom. 15:4)

We enrich our understanding when we keep in mind both sets of recipients. For both the original recipients and the larger body of the people of God, several principles hold true.

1. *Man made in the image of God.* We are made in the image of God, so that we have the capacity for understanding God, both through general revelation in the world that God made (Rom. 1:18–25; Ps. 19:1–6) and through the special revelation in Scripture.

2. *The fall.* The fall into sin has corrupted mankind, so that in deep and complex ways we evade and fight against what God says.

3. *Redemption.* God provided in Jesus Christ the definitive and full remedy for our rebellion. Through the Holy Spirit he applies this remedy to those who trust in Christ for salvation.

4. *The presence of sin.* Though believers are renewed by the Holy Spirit (John 3:1–8), those who remain in this life still have sin in them, and sin distorts their response to God, including the mental and intellectual aspects of their response.

5. *Continued growth.* Within this life we grow in sanctification but never reach sinless perfection. We continue to stand in need, corporately and individually, of biblical teaching, reproof, correction, and training in righteousness (2 Tim. 3:16–17).

6. *Interaction of foci.* Our growth in communion with God includes growth in knowing God and knowing the Bible as his word. In this growth, we profit from interaction between three interlocking foci: (1) theology, as a summary of the teaching of the Bible as a whole; (2) interpretation of individual passages of the Bible (sometimes called "exegesis"); and (3) hermeneutics, the study of principles for and practice of interpretation.[9] Troubles can arise if we absolutize any one of the three foci, refusing to let it be informed by insights from the others.

Traditional Roman Catholicism provides an example concerning the danger of absolutizing theology. Certain church pronouncements, namely deliverances of councils and *ex cathedra* deliverances from the pope, have become within Roman Catholicism irreformable pieces of theology. Their irreformability produces the danger that particular passages of Scripture no longer have their own voice but get molded automatically into conformity to preexisting theology. (Of course, if a person actually believes the Roman claims about its infallibility in doctrine, this conformity seems to him to be a good thing. But if, as I believe, the claims of infallibility are wrong, they are also disastrous for biblical interpretation.)

We might think that spiritual health can be enhanced only by promoting attention to individual passages. And if everything were healthy in our use of individual passages, that would be true. But sin can creep in here as well. For example, Arians have appealed to John 14:28, "the Father is greater than I," to conclude that the Son of God is only a creature and not the eternal God. But such an interpretation is not correct. Other passages of Scripture, including John 1:1 and 20:28, protect us from erroneously interpreting this one passage, because those other passages indicate that Jesus is fully God. From these passages we derive our overall theology, which summarizes the teaching of the Bible. Good theology leads us to reject the Arian interpretation of John 14:28, and to look at the passage more carefully to see what it really means in the context of the Gospel of John. Jesus is speaking about his submission

---

[9] These three foci have a correlation with the normative, situational, and existential perspectives, respectively. Systematic theology, as a summary of what God says, sets forth norms for our belief and action, and so naturally correlates with the normative perspective. Individual passages offer themselves within the pages of the Bible as an aspect of our situation, and so have a correlation with the situational perspective. Hermeneutics describes how we go about growing in theology and in understanding individual passages, and so has a correlation with us as persons who have the task of interpretation. It has a correlation with the existential perspective. As usual, the three perspectives interlock and interpenetrate. When understood expansively, theology can become a perspective on all of our study of Scripture; and the same holds for exegesis and hermeneutics.

to the Father in carrying out the work of redemption on earth (note the first part of 14:28, and verse 31). Verse 28 is thus not speaking about the nature of Christ's divinity as such, and is quite compatible with the theology of the rest of the Bible.

As an example of dominance by hermeneutics, we may take the case of Rudolf Bultmann. Bultmann worked out a complicated hermeneutics of "demythologization," which led to finding only a message about existential authenticity in the New Testament. His hermeneutical system was destructive not only because of its distorted conclusions, but also because it threatened to be irreformable. Any biblical teaching that challenged it was reinterpreted before the challenge could be seriously weighed.

We have considered more extreme examples of theological dominance, exegetical dominance, and hermeneutical dominance. But the dangers afflict us all. In more subtle ways, any of us can "read in" his favorite theology where it does not really belong. Or we can uncritically accept a certain traditional or comfortable interpretation of a particular text. Or we can refuse to ask critical questions about our hermeneutical principles and practice.

Because we are sinners, and because sin has a tendency to make excuses and conceal itself, we cannot always easily detect subtle sins. They even creep into our practice of studying the Bible. Studying the Bible works fruitfully for us when we are ready to listen to all three aspects—theology, exegesis, and hermeneutics—and let them correct each other. In doing so, we need to have the Lord give us the humility to see sins and failings quickly. But of course there is an opposite danger, a danger to which the modern atmosphere of "tolerance" may tempt us: we might use an appeal to "humility" to excuse ourselves from standing boldly for the truth when we need to. Who will deliver us from these twin sins? Ultimately, only Jesus our Savior (Rom. 7:24–25).[10]

7. *Human relationships.* God designed us to live in human relationships as well as in relationship to him. Accordingly, we learn from others, including unbelievers (who receive insights by virtue of common grace). This learning aids us in our own understanding of the Bible (though we must be cautious, because sin infects both us and others).

---

[10] Vern S. Poythress, "Christ the Only Savior of Interpretation," *Westminster Theological Journal* 50 (1988): 305–321.

8. *Tradition.* Our learning from others includes learning from past generations. The Bible itself is infallible in its teaching; later generations are not. We must sift through the views of later generations using the Bible as our standard. But the later generations and their teachings should not be ignored. People through many generations have received gifts from the Spirit. And other generations and other cultures are valuable to us because they may help us to see the limitations that belong to the culture and the assumptions with which we have grown up. The wisdom of past generations is *tradition.* Tradition can be both a blessing and a curse. We receive a blessing when we profit from the wisdom of previous generations:

> Hear, my son, *your father's instruction,*
>   and forsake not *your mother's teaching.* (Prov. 1:8)

On the other hand, we can be cursed when we give uncritical allegiance to tradition, and cling to it when it is in tension with God's word:

> So for the sake of *your tradition* you have made void the word of God. (Matt. 15:6)

> For you have heard of my former life in Judaism, how I persecuted the church of God violently and tried to destroy it. And I was advancing in Judaism beyond many of my own age among my people, so extremely zealous was I for the *traditions of my fathers.* (Gal. 1:13–14)

9. *Use of human resources.* The principles concerning tradition apply when we use lexicons, grammars, commentaries, dictionaries, and other resources to help in interpreting the Bible. The resources offer help because they contain wisdom from the past. They can also on occasion ensnare us, because they may be corrupted by sin and its intellectual effects. In subsequent chapters we will often include at the end of the chapter a list of further resources. Readers need to recognize that even the best human resources may contain subtle deficiencies. And sometimes the deficiencies are more serious. Any human resource must be used with care, and with an understanding of its fallibility.[11]

---

[11] More about the deficiencies of some present-day resources can be found in the appendices in this book, and then in Vern S. Poythress, *Inerrancy and Worldview: Answering Modern Challenges to the Bible* (Wheaton, IL: Crossway, 2012).

3

Complementary Starting
Points for Interpretation

Now we begin to consider in more detail ways in which we may study the Bible. We consider both simple approaches and those that are more complex. The simple approaches of reading and listening are important, both because they form the starting point for more complex reflections and because people with all levels of skill can practice them. The Westminster Larger Catechism emphasizes reading Scripture and especially listening to preaching:

> Q. 155. How is the Word made effectual to salvation?
> A. The Spirit of God maketh the *reading*, but especially the *preaching* of the Word, an effectual means of enlightening, convincing, and humbling sinners; of driving them out of themselves, and drawing them unto Christ; of conforming them to his image, and subduing them to his will; of strengthening them against temptations and corruptions; of building them up in grace, and establishing their hearts in holiness and comfort through faith unto salvation.[1]

In addition to reading and listening, we should include Bible memorization and meditation, which Scripture itself encourages.[2] Psalm 1 says of the blessed man,

---

[1] The Westminster Larger Catechism (1648), online at http://www.reformed.org/documents/wlc_w_proofs /index.html, accessed November 5, 2012.
[2] Donald S. Whitney, *Spiritual Disciplines for the Christian Life* (Colorado Springs: NavPress, 1991), chapters 2–3.

His delight is in the law of the LORD,
and on his law he *meditates* day and night. (Ps. 1:2)

Similarly,

I have *stored up* your word in my heart,
that I might not sin against you. (Ps. 119:11)

I will *meditate* on your precepts
and fix my eyes on your ways. (Ps. 119:15)

This Book of the Law shall not depart from your mouth, but you shall *meditate* on it day and night, so that you may be careful to do according to all that is written in it. For then you will make your way prosperous, and then you will have good success. (Josh. 1:8)

People in the Western world have become so busy and so surrounded by a barrage of information that most of them no longer memorize passages or books of the Bible, and they do not know how to slow down to meditate. There is no easy solution for this deficiency. People must come to grips with what is important in God's eyes, and reorder their time and priorities accordingly. Memorization is work, but it is spiritually profitable in the long run.

Three Perspectives on Interpretation

Let us now consider ways of studying the Bible that involve more explicit focus. As we saw, God calls on us to "love the Lord your God with all your heart and with all your soul and with all your mind" (Matt. 22:37). The commandment applies to all our life, and so by implication to all our study of the Bible. We may love and serve God as we study, or we may fail to love and serve him. Study is an ethical task. God is Lord, and our study is subject to his norms. We can use Frame's three perspectives for ethics that we introduced earlier, namely the normative, situational, and existential perspectives.

The normative perspective leads naturally to focusing on the Bible's teaching as a whole, because that teaching as a whole gives us our norms. The norms include communication in the form of commandments, commandments that demand our obedience. But other kinds of communication also make demands on us. We ought to believe what God says, and search out what we still do not understand. God has spoken once and for all, in the completed canon of Scripture. When we focus on this once-for-all character of Scripture, we are using what we may call a *once-for-all* approach. Systematic theology summarizes what the Bible as a completed canon teaches. So we can associate the normative perspective with an approach to the Bible similar to systematic theology. The once-for-all approach is akin to a systematic theological approach.

Next, consider the situational perspective. The situational perspective can lead to each person focusing on his present-day situation, and asking what the Bible says about his situation. This focus is helpful, because James and other passages of the Bible stress the importance of applying God's word and acting on it: "But be doers of the word, and not hearers only, deceiving yourselves" (James 1:22). "What good is it, my brothers, if someone says he has faith but does not have works? Can that faith save him?" (James 2:14). The situational perspective can also lead to focusing on the situations in which God caused the Bible to be written, and how he then had it transmitted to us over time. This focus leads to considering the situation surrounding each book in the Bible: its language, its social and historical context, its human author and audience, and the larger line of the history of redemption that leads from the past up to the present, according to God's design. Thus, this approach focuses on history, and especially the history of redemption. We may also designate this approach as a *transmission* approach, because it focuses on how God transmits his word through time.

Third, we may use the existential perspective. This perspective leads to each person focusing on himself as a conscious receiver of the word of God. God is speaking to each person in the moment when he reads. God is speaking even if the person resists his word and does not profit from it. This third perspective thus emphasizes present personal experience of God's word. We may call this approach a *present-time* approach because of its focus on the present.

In fact, thinking in terms of perspectives is particularly appropriate when we are studying a passage of the Bible. No matter how many times we come back to the same passage, no matter how many questions we ask, and no matter what *kinds* of questions we ask, we are dealing with the same passage. Each way of studying the passage functions as a perspective on the passage. In each case, though some one aspect of the passage may be the primary focus, the passage as a whole, including its context, has to be taken into account if we are to do justice to what it says.

In this case, we are using the three perspectives on ethics. Each of these three perspectives is appropriate in studying the Bible. In principle, they harmonize, because God speaks his normative teaching once for all in Scripture (focus on systematic theology); God governs history so that his speech travels forward in time (the transmission approach, with its focus on redemptive history); and God governs each individual here and now, so that individuals hear the voice of God (the present-time approach).

Any one of these approaches, if used by itself, can become lopsided. If we use the once-for-all approach, we might neglect to notice the developments over time, and we might neglect our personal obligation in the present. If we use the transmission approach, we might neglect the unity of Scripture and the fact that God designed it to address us in the present. If we use the present-time approach, we might neglect to reflect on what God has done in the past.

But as usual, perspectives when rightly understood point to each other and even include each other. If we start with the transmission approach, it includes at one end of the transmission the point at which God's word impinges on us as readers. So it includes in principle the present-time approach. It also reckons with the fact that God as Lord of history designed the whole process so that all the earlier writings of Scripture would accumulate into a completed canon, and therefore it includes the once-for-all approach.

Suppose, on the other hand, that we start with the once-for-all approach. When we actually examine the contents of biblical teaching, the contents include teaching about history, about the fact that God had a redemptive plan from the beginning and that he is working it out in time. The Bible also indicates how the work of Christ brings this history to its climax (Heb. 1:1–3). So the once-for-all approach in principle includes the transmission approach. And it includes the present-time approach, since in passages like Romans 15:4 the Bible explicitly teaches, once and for all, that God continues to speak to new readers through what he wrote long ago.

Using the Present-Time Approach

In this handbook we will focus primarily on the present-time approach to the Bible. The other two approaches just mentioned include it by implication, since their initial focus leads to acknowledging God's presence in speaking the message of the Bible today. But the present-time approach has value, especially for those who want to study the Bible more closely and methodically. It reminds us that we cannot dispense with God or ignore his presence anywhere in the process of our study. If we follow a "method," we can make the mistake of treating the method as if it worked "by itself." We might begin to act as if we did not need to pay attention to our spiritual relationship to God—at least not until after we had finished using the method.

The present-time approach uses a perspective, namely the existential perspective, that focuses on each reader as a recipient. So we expect that it will perspectivally include the other two approaches. That is to say, if we follow the approach properly, in obedience to God who is present with us, it should lead to and even include the other two approaches. Does it?

God who speaks to us now, in the present, tells us now in the present, through Scripture, that all of Scripture is breathed out by God and is profitable (2 Tim. 3:16–17). So in responding to God now, we have to take responsibility to treat the Bible according to what God says now, and view it as a finished deposit or canon that permanently teaches the church. We use it as a source for systematic theology. Therefore, we must affirm the validity of the once-for-all approach.

In addition, God tells us now through the Bible that he spoke to his people "long ago, at many times and in many ways" (Heb. 1:1). He instructs us that over the ages he has been concerned not only with us now but also with previous generations ("our fathers"; Heb. 1:1). So he implies that we should think about what he said back then and why. God enlarges our hearts by showing how he is God through all the ages and not just here and now. Understanding his work through the ages actually encourages and strengthens our hearts now, which is part of the effect that he intends Scripture to have now. So the present-time approach includes perspectivally the transmission approach.

Resources

Further discussion of the once-for-all approach, the transmission approach, and the present-time approach can be found in:

Poythress, Vern S. *God-Centered Biblical Interpretation*. Phillipsburg, NJ: Presbyterian & Reformed, 1999. Chapters 9–10.

Part II

SIMPLE STEPS IN
INTERPRETATION

4

Three Simple Steps in Interpretation

We can use the present-time approach to Bible study in simpler or in more complex ways. In the simplest form, we sit down and read the Bible with a focus on the fact that God is present and speaks to us through what we read. We can also consider more complex forms, in which we can distinguish distinct foci or perspectives that we may employ over a more extended time. In the rest of this handbook, we will illustrate progressively more complex approaches. We will apply these approaches to one main passage, 1 Samuel 22:1–2, so that readers may see how to work with a specific sample text. (In the final chapters we will also illustrate how our approach can be used with other passages: Prov. 10:1; Ps. 4:8; and Amos 1:3.)

Three Kinds of Questions

The first layer of added complexity is still relatively simple. We consider a three-step approach to studying the Bible. The three steps are observation, elucidation, and application. I learned this three-step approach from InterVarsity Christian Fellowship when I was a college undergraduate. We find its current form in a booklet by Jack Kuhatschek and Cindy Bunch, *How to Lead a LifeGuide Bible Study*.[1] This booklet uses the term *interpretation* instead of the term *elucidation* to describe the

---

[1] Jack Kuhatschek and Cindy Bunch, *How to Lead a LifeGuide Bible Study*, 3rd ed. (Downers Grove, IL: InterVarsity Press, 2003), chapters 6–7.

second of the three steps, the step in between observation and application. But the word *interpretation* can be used more broadly to cover the entire process of studying a text, not simply the middle step of elucidation. I use the word *interpretation* in this broader sense. So I am introducing the term *elucidation* as my preferred label for Kuhatschek and Bunch's second step.

Observation answers the question, "What does the text *say?*" *Elucidation* answers the question, "What does it *mean?*" *Application* answers the question, "What does it mean to *me?*"[2] (See table 4.1.)

Table 4.1: Three Steps: Observation, Elucidation, and Application

Steps	Type of question	Question for 1 Samuel 22:1-2
Observation	What does it *say*?	Who joined David?
Elucidation	What does it *mean*?	How did David take responsibility for the people?
Application	What does it mean to *me*?	How might I honor God, as I absorb this meaning?

Kuhatschek and Bunch's booklet instructs leaders of group Bible studies on how to prepare questions beforehand about a passage, so that the group can focus on the passage and learn effectively. The questions follow a natural progression, beginning with simple observation questions that invite each person in the group to notice what is actually there in the passage, and to notice details as well as overall themes. The leader gradually moves toward questions of elucidation, which ask the group to reflect on the meaning of what is there. And once they see the meaning, they ask themselves how to apply it to their lives in their beliefs, their attitudes, and their behavior.

Three Steps for 1 Samuel 22:1–2

Below is an example, based on 1 Samuel 22:1–2. It includes prayer and reading in its introductory phase, before proceeding to the main part of the study.

---

[2] Ibid., 31.

I. Pray and ask the Lord to be present and to illumine the study.

II. Look at surrounding parts of the book: 1 Samuel 18:6–9; 20:31; 21:10–15. (For the passage 22:1–2, it may be important to understand why David did what he did.)

III. Read the passage:

David departed from there and escaped to the cave of Adullam. And when his brothers and all his father's house heard it, they went down there to him. And everyone who was in distress, and everyone who was in debt, and everyone who was bitter in soul, gathered to him. And he became commander over them. And there were with him about four hundred men. (1 Sam. 22:1 2)

IV. Consider some questions:

A. Observation questions:

1. Where did David go?
2. Who joined him?
3. What kind of people were they?
4. What was David's relation to the people with him?

B. Elucidation questions:

1. Where did David come from and why?
2. What caused David to be in danger? (hint: see preceding context; see 1 Sam. 18:6–9)
3. Why might people be motivated to come and join David?
4. What does the passage show about people's view of David?
5. What does it show about David taking responsibility?
6. What does it show about David's leadership?
7. What was God's plan for David's future? (hint: see 1 Sam. 16:1–2, 13)
8. What do we see about community life around David?
9. How does the passage show God's care for David and for the community?
10. What does the passage foreshadow about a future greater son of David? (hint: see Acts 2:30–31)

C. Application questions:

1. How is Christ's care for you reflected in David?
2. In what ways does the passage foreshadow your relation to Christ? Other people's relation to Christ? What

does the passage imply about how your relation to
Christ should develop?

3. In what ways does David serve as an example for you?

4. In what ways do the people around David serve as an
example for you?

5. What does the passage suggest about your relation to
those in distress?

6. In what ways does the passage prefigure the church?

7. In what ways might the passage prefigure the relation of
the church to outsiders, and what does it imply for your
attitude toward outsiders?

Using the Questions

A person may study the Bible by himself for his personal benefit, or he
may study in order to prepare for leading a group or giving a presentation
or a sermon. For any of these goals, a person may ask himself the three
types of questions, concerning observation, elucidation, and application.

To study a passage more fully, a person may prepare a worksheet,
with four columns on a single sheet of paper or on a word processor. He
then fills the far left-hand column with the text of the passage, spreading
the passage out within the column so that it fills the whole column (or,
for longer passages, a person can use the left-hand column of multiple
pages). To the right of the far left-hand column are three other columns.
These columns have space that will contain observations, elucidations,
and applications, respectively. Then the student adds comments on the
passage in the other three columns. Fig. 4.1 shows how the worksheet
might look at the beginning, and fig. 4.2 how it might look after a person fills it out completely.

The Value of Three Steps

Breaking the study of the Bible into three steps, rather than seeing it as
all one process of interaction, has an advantage. We all have weaknesses
and biases in how we look at Scripture. The three steps help people not
to overlook one or more aspects of interpretation as they hurry to get
to their favorite part. One person loves application, and tends to leap
into it without taking time to think through what the passage is really

Fig. 4.1: Three-Steps Worksheet

Text: 1 Sam. 22:1-2	Observation	Elucidation	Application
David departed from there and escaped to			
the cave of Adullam. And when his brothers and all his father's house heard it, they went down there to him.			
And everyone			
who was in distress, and everyone who was in debt,			
and everyone who was bitter in soul, gathered to him.			
And he became commander over them.			
And there were with him			
about four hundred men.			

saying. Another person avoids application, and tends to think and think and think without ever acting on the message. By contrast, James tells us that we should make sure that we act on what we hear: "But be doers of the word, and not hearers only, deceiving yourselves" (James 1:22; see also vv. 23–27). Still another person reads and reads, without asking himself about what it means or how it applies. He remains largely on the level of observation. The division into three steps encourages people to look at the passage in several ways, and not to neglect aspects that they tend to minimize.

Fig. 4.2: Three-Steps Worksheet, Filled Out

Text: 1 Sam. 22:1-2	Observation	Elucidation	Application
David departed from there and escaped to	What is the importance of David? From where? Why "escaped"? Escaped from what?	David is anointed to be king. From Achish and Gath. Threat of Achish or of Saul killing him.	See God's hand in David's life and mine. God delivers me from danger, spiritual and sometimes physical.
the cave of Adullam. And when his brothers and all his father's house heard it, they went down there to him.	Where? Why a cave? Sons of Jesse or another meaning? Who else besides brothers? Why?	Good hiding place. Protects from bad weather. Probably literal brothers. Father, mother, cousins?, servants? Were they afraid that Saul would hold them hostage or otherwise exploit them?	God gives me refuges. God gives me companions. God gives me family (literal and/or spiritual). My family may support each other in suffering.
And everyone	Literally everyone, or characteristic pattern?	Characteristic (cf. Matt. 3:5).	
who was in distress, and everyone who was in debt,	What kind of distress? Why the parallel "everyone" and several categories?	Any kind of difficult circumstances. Several categories show David as refuge for many distresses.	Will the church and I attract others? Go to God in distress, and welcome others in distress. Help in debt.
and everyone who was bitter in soul, gathered to him.	What kind of bitterness? What kind of inwardness? Why go to David?	Now inward rather than outward trouble. Various kinds. Maybe various reasons—rebellion, discontent, start new life, get hope, get place of meaningful service.	Help for inward troubles. We gather around Jesus the Messiah. Jesus was exalted to God, and is Lord.
And he became commander over them.	Did David volunteer, or did others suggest it, and why? Commander for what?	David was already known for leadership in battle (1 Sam. 18). So logical for people to offer service to him as leader.	God gives us fellowship with Christ and with each other.

Figure continued on next page

Text: 1 Sam. 22:1-2	Observation	Elucidation	Application
And there were with him	In the cave? How were they together?	We don't know details. Cave may be central, and some lodged nearby.	
about four hundred men.	Is the number four hundred important? Why?	A significant number recognize his leadership, but this anticipates much more as he later becomes king. Pointing forward to Christ.	In growing numbers. God shows his wisdom in planning and working for us from long ago.

Resources

There are a large number of introductory helps and introductory texts for Bible study, too numerous to mention.

The classic introduction to the three-step approach is found in:

Kuhatschek, Jack, and Cindy Bunch. *How to Lead a LifeGuide Bible Study.* 3rd ed. Downers Grove, IL: InterVarsity Press, 2003.

More thorough expositions of entry-level Bible study can be found in:

Sterrett, T. Norton, and Richard L. Schultz. *How to Understand Your Bible.* Downers Grove, IL: InterVarsity Press, 2010.
Wald, Oletta. *The New Joy of Discovery in Bible Study.* Rev. ed. Minneapolis: Augsburg-Fortress, 2002.
———. *The New Joy of Teaching Discovery.* Minneapolis: Augsburg Fortress, 2002.

Particular focus on application can be found in:

Doriani, Daniel M. *Putting the Truth to Work: The Theory and Practice of Biblical Application.* Phillipsburg, NJ: Presbyterian & Reformed, 2001.
———. *Getting the Message: A Plan for Interpreting and Applying the Bible.* Phillipsburg, NJ: Presbyterian & Reformed, 1996.

5

The Three Steps as Perspectives

Kuhatschek and Bunch's booklet addresses people who may never have led a group Bible study before. So it tries to give simple descriptions and has much to say about how to interact with a group. But the same format can apply to an individual who is studying the Bible by himself. For 1 Samuel 22:1–2, he can use the questions that we offered above, or he can think up his own questions as he interacts with the passage. Thus, the three steps offer a pattern for either individual Bible study or group study.

Viewing the Steps as Perspectives

Though the study method we are describing has a natural progression from observation to elucidation to application, the three steps interact with each other. In fact, a closer analysis shows that the steps are not neatly separable but are more like perspectives. They imply each other.

In a sense, we are trying to *observe* what the passage says and implies all the way through the process. The observations at the beginning may be simpler and remain more "at the surface," but we need to be observing the text and not just our own ideas all the way through the study. Elucidation means *observing* what the text means, and application means *observing* what it implies for me.

Similarly, all three steps are forms of elucidation. Even simple observations during the first step of observation require us to understand the sentences that make up the text, and this understanding already involves a preliminary kind of elucidation. The step of application is an *elucidation* of how the text has implications for me.

Finally, all three steps are forms of application. Application as a whole includes not only how I may decide to act on the basis of the passage, but also what I decide to believe it says and what I decide to believe it means. In a broad sense, dealing with the questions of observation and elucidation involves *applying* the text to my mind and my beliefs, and making sure that I *apply* the text to my mind by getting into my mind what the text says and means. I as an individual have an inextricable role in the process. I am doing the observing and elucidating. If so, my personal involvement already constitutes an *application*—an application to *me*. Moreover, when a Christian studies the Bible, the Holy Spirit who indwells him is active in making *application* to him in every stage of the process.

The same principles apply if we are thinking of a group Bible study instead of an individual study.

Applying the Normative, Situational, and Existential Perspectives

We can see a correlation between this three-step approach to Bible study and John Frame's three perspectives on ethics. The application step clearly has a close relation to the existential perspective. In application, I am looking at myself and asking how the passage invites or demands personal change—existential change. The existential perspective on a text asks how I apply it. Now, since the existential perspective functions as a perspective on all of ethics, it also functions as a perspective on the ethics of interpreting texts, including any passage in the Bible. Thus, all three steps can be viewed from the existential perspective. That is what we did when we considered all three steps as forms of application.

Next, the second step, the step of elucidation, has a correlation with the normative perspective. Whatever God says is authoritative for us. He speaks 1 Samuel 22:1–2, so this passage along with the rest of the Bible is authoritative for us. It is normative. But how it is normative depends on what it means. We must believe what it asserts, and obey what it commands, and take to heart what it conveys by way of encouragement or exhortation. That is to say that its meanings are normative for us.

Hence, the step of elucidation is like a normative perspective on the text. Since the normative perspective functions as a perspective on the whole of ethics, it covers every aspect of interpretation, including what we have called observation and application. The application must be not whatever we want it to be according to our own sinful desires, but according to what God purposes.

Finally, the first step, the step of observation, has a correlation with the situational perspective. In observation we make a concerted attempt to pay attention to informative aspects of the text as it stands on the page, and the page is part of our "situation" in a broad sense. We find out details of our situation by observing which words are on the page, in which order, and how they form specific sentences. Since the situational perspective functions as a perspective on the whole of ethics, it covers every aspect of Bible study, including elucidation and application. In all three stages we continue to interact with information external to us, as recorded on the page. And of course at the heart of our "situation" is God, the most important person in our situation, who speaks to us as we are interacting with the passage on the page.

A Benefit of Perspectives

What difference does it make whether we consider the three steps as perspectives? Our perspectival approach is one approach alongside others. If we want, we can leave to one side reflections about perspectives, and simply go ahead happily with the three steps. We do not need conscious awareness of perspectives in order to study the Bible faithfully. I nevertheless think there is a benefit in thinking about perspectives: we can use it to remind ourselves about the centrality of God.

At the beginning we observed that we need to love God. In all our lives we must love God, and so we should love God in interpretation. We must love God when we observe; we must love him when we elucidate the meaning of a biblical text; we must love him when we apply the Bible. How? With all our heart and all our soul and all our mind. We must serve him and praise him and glorify him in all things. This principle of love is the central principle of ethics. It is the central principle in the three perspectives on ethics, but it comes to the fore especially in the existential perspective.

The principle of love is therefore central in the present-time approach to studying the Bible. It has to be central in each of the three steps. Receiving Scripture properly means receiving it as the word of God—God speaks the Scripture to us here and now, and in speaking he is present with us and confronts us with his glory, majesty, holiness, and love. We should therefore be continually applying the Scripture as we read, by praising and magnifying our God. All study is application in this sense. In all three steps we are interacting with God. God has given us this text in accessible form, and he provides us with the simple information that we confront in the observation questions. We should have an attitude of gratitude as well as of submission.

When we engage in elucidation, we interpret the meanings with the question in mind, "What does God mean?" Everything that we know about God comes into play, and we aim at understanding a meaning that will further display his glory.

When we come to application, we must think of ourselves as servants of God who are responsible to him continually for what we do in response to his word. We acknowledge also that God sees our hearts and inspects our responses. He is our judge, our king, and our rewarder. When we contemplate his holiness, we might well respond with a plea for mercy. Indeed, mercy has come to us through Christ. What a relief, and what a cause for celebration! The comforting exhortations in Hebrews apply to us:

> For we do not have a high priest who is unable to sympathize with our weaknesses, but one who in every respect has been tempted as we are, yet without sin. Let us then with confidence draw near to the throne of grace, that we may receive mercy and find grace to help in time of need. (Heb. 4:15–16)

> He [Jesus] holds his priesthood permanently, because he continues forever. Consequently, he is able to save to the uttermost those who draw near to God through him, since he always lives to make intercession for them. (Heb. 7:24–25)

These principles from Hebrews apply to the entire process of interpretation, because in interpretation we approach God through hearing him speak.

In any one of the three steps, or in any part within them, we live as servants of Christ in the presence of God through the power of the Holy Spirit. If we lose sight of God's presence, or think that we can dispense with him, we are dishonoring him in our interpretation, however much we may think we are accumulating intellectual insights for ourselves.

We should not be polarizing or dichotomizing between an intellectual reception of Scripture and a spiritual reception. Rightly understood, the two sides harmonize. The Holy Spirit, along with the Father and the Son, created our mind along with every other aspect of our being. We ought to love God *with all our mind* (Matt. 22:37). Using our mind in this way is spiritual, because it is empowered by the Holy Spirit. But we interpret in a spiritual fashion only if we are using our mind in conformity with the experience and knowledge of the presence of God. The three steps offer a useful tool for proceeding in our study of the Bible. But the tool does not substitute for *us*. *We* have to respond with heart and soul and mind.

The Bible calls for a thoughtful response for many reasons. For one thing, not everything in the Bible applies to us in the same way. The commandment to love our neighbor has a direct application to all times and circumstances in which we have neighbors. But what about the instructions in Leviticus 11 about eating clean but not unclean foods? How do they apply to us? These instructions about food are directed specifically to the "people of Israel" (Lev. 11:2). The larger redemptive context shows that they function to separate Israel as a holy people from the surrounding nations. They have a symbolic function, symbolizing the contrast between holiness and unholiness. The coming of Jesus means that their literal observance is now obsolete (Mark 7:19).

This one passage in Leviticus 11 illustrates a broader principle. Every individual passage in the Bible should be interpreted in the larger context of the whole instruction of the whole Bible.

Still other principles have relevance in a group Bible study. In a group, we need to be practicing love toward our neighbors who are in the study along with us. So the principle of loving our neighbor has an integral role as well. Again, loving God and loving neighbor are not in tension with each other: "Whoever loves God must also love his brother" (1 John 4:21).

An additional benefit of understanding the perspectival relationship between the steps is that we avoid the temptation to regard one step as isolated from the others. And we do not worry about whether we have transgressed some "boundary" that would rigidly separate the steps. We allow ourselves to be full persons as we interact, and we allow our thoughts at one stage to influence and flow into the thoughts at other points in the process.

Mystery

In addition, the interlocking of perspectives can usefully remind us to stand in awe of God, whose knowledge surpasses ours. When we encounter God, we are never in charge. We never master a passage. All its aspects interlock, and all the questions that we can ask interlock. We never get to the bottom, to a place where we can make perfectly transparent to ourselves how the pieces get sorted out, each into its appropriate bin. The use of a "method," even as simple a method as three steps of questions, can tempt us to think that we have a guarantee: we tell ourselves that, if we use the method properly, we will achieve our goal. And the goal in this case is to know the meaning of the passage. We think we can master meaning, if we succeed in staying loyal to the method.

Over against this reliance on "method," I propose reliance on God and his mercy. In this, I aim to call us toward a fuller rather than a lesser engagement of our minds—with our hearts and souls. Using our minds fully includes recognizing the unfathomable mysteries in interpretation, rather than thoughtlessly (mindlessly!) establishing a false confidence in our ability to master meaning without the help of God's presence and mercy.

Perspectives on Preparation for the Three Steps

In our discussion of the three steps, we also mentioned some preparations. In either a group study or an individual study, people can begin with prayer. They can also look at the surrounding passages in the book of the Bible that they are studying. Before entering into the questions about the passage, they can read it. We have thus considered the possibility of having some preparatory actions before we come to the three steps.

These actions as well as the questions can be considered a part of the study. And they can be expanded into perspectives. For example, a group or an individual may begin with prayer. But should we be in an attitude of prayer all the way through the study? We can also pray in the middle of the study. It may or may not be awkward to pause in a group study for prayer. But an individual in private study can stop at any time to pray. If he meets a difficulty, he may ask the Lord for help. If he receives some exciting insight or some heartfelt comfort, he may thank the Lord. In a broader sense, the whole study should take place with a prayerful attitude—of expectation, of petition, of openheartedness, and of thanksgiving.

So here now are the preparatory actions that a person might take:

I. Pray
   A. Thank the Lord for giving his word
   B. Ask him to send the Holy Spirit to empower and enlighten
   C. Ask him to make us willing to receive his word in humility
II. Look at surrounding parts of the book of the Bible in which the passage is embedded
III. Read the passage
IV. Use the three steps
   A. Observation
   B. Elucidation
   C. Application

Reading the passage can be considered a form of observation. So we may reorganize the outline:

I. Pray
II. Look at the rest of the book
III. Use the three steps
   A. Observation
     1. Read
     2. Continue to observe, using questions
   B. Elucidation
   C. Application

We can see a correspondence between prayer and the existential perspective. In prayer we are expressing our own attitudes through thanksgiving, and we are asking the Lord to prepare our hearts to receive his word. Looking at the rest of the book means looking at the *situation* in which the passage sits. We are using the situational perspective. And looking at the passage itself corresponds to the normative perspective. What the passage says is normative for us. Thus the three main points, labeled I, II, and III, offer three perspectives on the process of studying a passage. Within the third point (III) we have a further breakdown into situational (observation), normative (elucidation), and existential (application) perspectives. Thinking of the stages as perspectives helps to remind us that the entire process should be prayerful (I), the entire process should take into account the rest of the book (II), and the entire process should seek to receive what God says in the passage under study (III).

Since we can treat the stages I, II, and III as perspectives, we will proceed in subsequent chapters to "fold them in" to the three main steps, A, B, and C. Prayer can and should run through the entire process. And we can give focal attention to related passages as part of the step III.B. (Elucidation). That is to say, the step we have called *elucidation* can be understood expansively (treated as a perspective). Elucidation then includes taking into account how other passages throw light on the one we are studying.

Resources

On perspectives:

Frame, John M. "A Primer on Perspectivalism." 2008. Internet publication, http://www.frame
    -poythress.org/frame_articles/2008Primer.htm, accessed January 26, 2012.

Poythress, Vern S. *Symphonic Theology: The Validity of Multiple Perspectives in Theology.*
    Reprint. Phillipsburg, NJ: Presbyterian & Reformed, 2001.

6

Correlation:
Comparing Passages

We can expand from the three steps of interpretation to more elaborate forms of interpretation. Since each step offers a perspective on the whole, we can elaborate any one of the steps as much as we choose. As a first form of elaboration, let us focus on the second step, the step of elucidation.

The Role of Other Passages
In our earlier discussion of elucidation, we concentrated on understanding the passage itself, in distinction from other passages of the Bible. This concentration is appropriate. But other passages help us to understand the one on which we are concentrating.

Again we may take 1 Samuel 22:1–2 as our example:

> David departed from there and escaped to the cave of Adullam. And when his brothers and all his father's house heard it, they went down there to him. And everyone who was in distress, and everyone who was in debt, and everyone who was bitter in soul, gathered to him. And he became commander over them. And there were with him about four hundred men.

What are its main correlations with other passages?

Other passages may fill in details about a topic like David's leadership. David's leadership has a role in 1 Samuel 22:1–2, but does not receive full elaboration there. Other passages also help us to understand the past events that form a background for our passage. For example, it helps us to know from 1 Samuel 16:1–2 and 16:13 that God had rejected Saul from being king of Israel, and that he had commissioned Samuel to anoint David as Saul's successor. First Samuel 18:6–9 indicates that Saul was jealous of David, and Saul eventually pursued David to try to kill him. Taken all together, 1–2 Samuel and 1–2 Kings contain a multigenerational history of Israel's kings, and they note the special role of God's promise to David and his descendants. They help to answer the question of why we should be particularly interested in a detail in David's life such as 1 Samuel 22:1–2. Finally, the Bible as a complete canon shows us where the history of kingship is headed, namely to find its climax in Christ the King, descended from David (Matt. 1:1–17; 2:5; Isa. 11:1–10).

As originally conceived, the three-step approach of Kuhatschek and Bunch recommends working with only *one* passage during a whole study session, while leaving other passages to the side. For group Bible studies, such a restriction helps the group maintain its focus. It also allows newcomers to participate without having to know about the rest of the Bible. If we are doing a private individual study instead of a group study, following Kuhatschek and Bunch's advice encourages us to maintain our concentration on particular verses, and to try to absorb them thoroughly, rather than flitting around many passages.

At a practical level, the practice of restricting our study to one passage functions well in many cases, but with 1 Samuel 22:1–2 it already shows some of its limitations. Can we really appreciate this one passage fully without understanding how it fits into a larger history of Israel's kings? David's coming to the cave of Adullam in verse 1 makes sense only if we know about his fears that Saul will pursue him and kill him. Accordingly, as part of the study process, we can add a preliminary stage where the individual or the group would at least read a few verses earlier in 1 Samuel that supply some background. (In chapters 4–5 of this book, such a stage was labeled step II, "Look at surrounding parts . . ." or, "Look at the rest of the book.")

Correlation as an Extra Step

But why should we confine this attention to other passages to a preliminary stage? Clearly we may, if we wish, include it as an extra step, a fourth step, in the middle of the process of interpretation. Let us call this fourth step *correlation*, because in this step we examine the correlation between the verses in our chosen passage and other verses throughout the Bible. To engage in correlation, we need to know something about the passage on which we are initially focusing, in order to discern which other passages have important correlations with it. So the step of correlation can fit in as the third step out of four:

    A. Observation
    B. Elucidation
  *C. Correlation
    D. Application

Elucidation in the fullest sense includes not only attention to the meaning of our passage, but also attention to the relation of its meanings to other passages. So "correlation" can actually be included as a subdivision within "elucidation":

    A. Observation
    B. Elucidation
       1. Examination of one passage
     *2. Correlation
    C. Application

Two Kinds of Correlation

For a more thorough analysis, we may distinguish two kinds of correlation. The first kind, *topical* correlation, links passages that address the same topic or overlapping topics. The second kind, *temporal* correlation, links passages dealing with successive times, by paying attention to how God works out in time his plan for the history of creation, redemption, and consummation. We may call this second kind of correlation a focus on *redemptive history*, which studies how our passage fits into the entire plan of God for redemption, a redemption that takes place in time.

We may illustrate using our chosen passage, 1 Samuel 22:1–2. Under topical correlation we may study all the passages in 1–2 Samuel that illustrate David's leadership. We may also note contrasts between David's leadership and Saul's, and—earlier still—contrasts between Samuel and David or between Samuel and Saul. We may also note the contrasts between David's leadership on the one hand and Absalom's leadership or Joab's on the other. We may range more broadly and consider Noah, Abraham, Joseph, Moses, Joshua, and the judges of the book of Judges, or, going forward in time, Solomon and the kings of the divided monarchy. At the period of time mentioned in 1 Samuel 22:1–2, David leads mostly in military ways. So we may look particularly at David's military deeds, especially against the Philistines, and David's mighty men (2 Samuel 23). More broadly, we may also look at the leadership offered by prophets and priests as well as kings. The theme of God's preservation of David and care for him is not explicit in 1 Samuel 22:1–2, but it is definitely a theme in 1–2 Samuel as a whole (see 2 Sam. 23:5), and so is illustrated in 22:1–2. This theme has a close relationship to God's promise to David, and to the broader sweep of God's promises in the whole Bible.

We can see how this attention to topics can deepen our understanding of application. God's care for David reminds us of God's care for us in Christ. God's promises to David remind us of his promises to us.

We can also consider the topic of people in distress, as mentioned in verse 2: "everyone who was in distress, and everyone who was in debt, and everyone who was bitter in soul." People's struggles with various kinds of distress receive some attention from time to time in 1–2 Samuel and 1–2 Kings. But we find this theme also in the law of Moses, in its provisions for the poor and widows, and in the later prophets, in their criticisms of oppression. God's care for distressed people in David's times reminds us of his care for us when we are in distress, and how we ought in turn to care for others in their distresses.

Now consider the second kind of correlation, correlation through redemptive history. How does 1 Samuel 22:1–2 fit into the entire outline of redemptive history? First Samuel 22:1–2 is one episode in the life of David. David has been anointed to be the king of the people of God. As such, he foreshadows the coming of Christ the great King. Prophecy promises that the great king will be a descendant of David. David's victories over the Philistines establish freedom and well-being for God's people on a physical and political and military level. Christ comes to accomplish the climactic victory over Satan and his hosts and the power of sin. He establishes freedom and well-being for God's people, first on a spiritual level, but finally, in the new heaven and the new earth, on a comprehensive plane.

We can also travel backward in time before David. We can consider the order of creation before the fall of man. It was "very good," according to Genesis 1:31. But God also intended that it would lead to something even better, at the end of the process in which man fulfilled his calling. An endpoint of consummation was already planned. The fall disrupted this goal, but God promised redemption, beginning with Genesis 3:15. Christ is the offspring of the woman who has bruised the serpent's head. Before him, Noah and Abraham and Joseph and Moses and David were shadowy forerunners of what Christ would accomplish. In 1 Samuel 22:1–2, David is the latest of a whole line of leaders who protect and bless those under their representative headship.

Perspectives on Correlation

We have distinguished two kinds of correlation, correlation in topic and correlation in history, in order to remind ourselves to pay attention to both, and not let one kind alone occupy all our attention. Yet we cannot really separate the two kinds. Studying redemptive history means studying the *topic* of redemption and the *topic* of temporal development. Redemptive history thus forms one aspect of topical correlation.

Conversely, each topic that we study has a history of its development and exposition in Scripture. The topic of distress, for example, begins its unfolding with the "distress" of the fall into sin and the subsequent curses. Distresses in the time of David, distresses in the time of Christ, and distresses today all play out in the wake of this initial distress. Thus the study of each topic forms a subdivision within the study of redemptive history.

We may say, then, that redemptive history offers a *perspective* on topics. Conversely, topics offer a perspective on redemptive history.

A Triad of Perspectives: Particle, Wave, and Field

In fact, when we take the two kinds of correlation together with the initial attention to a single passage, these three kinds of study offer three interlocking perspectives on the passage. The attention to the passage in its uniqueness and integrity results from a *particle* perspective, where we consider each text as a distinct unit. Each text is a particle-like whole, which is distinct from every other unit. We ask, "What does this passage tell us by its unique structure and contents?" The attention to redemptive history results from a *wave* perspective, according to which we focus on movement in time or gradual change. God's work in history *develops over time*, in a movement or wave of organic growth. The attention to topics results from a *field* perspective, according to which we focus on relationships between passages. In this case, the relationships are relationships arising from sharing a common topic.

As usual, the three perspectives interlock. They imply one another and in a sense include one another. To compare passages, we must first have multiple passages, each one of which is a unit, a particle. Thus the field perspective, which relates passages, presupposes the particle perspective, where we focus on one passage at a time. In addition, each unit has an origin in time and constitutes a development: it is also a wave. Thus the particle perspective, which focuses on a single unit, presupposes the wave perspective, which describes the unit "in motion." And each unit is distinguished and marked out for what it is partly through its relationships to other units. The unit means what it means and functions as it functions within a larger plan of God, into which it fits and to which it relates. Thus the particle perspective presupposes the field perspective, according to which units are related to other units. Each perspective, when considered in depth, leads to the others.

We may also say that we have chosen these three perspectives partly because, like the other triads that we have used, they image or mirror aspects of Trinitarian coinherence. The Father has a comprehensive plan for all time, and the stability of this plan invites us to think of it as a unified whole. We obtain the particle perspective. The Son executes the plan of the Father in time and space, and his work is spread out and develops in time during his incarnation on earth. The focus on development in time leads to the wave perspective. The Holy Spirit unites us to Christ and his benefits. He brings about our relationship to the Father and the Son. This relational aspect in his work leads to thinking in terms of a *field* perspective or relational perspective.[1]

The Father, the Son, and the Holy Spirit are one God, and dwell in each other in coinherence. This Trinitarian character of God is mysterious to us; it is the ultimate mystery. Derivatively, by analogy, the three perspectives—particle, wave, and field—interlock with each other and coinhere. This coinherence too is mysterious. Ultimately, in contemplating a triad of perspectives, we interact with a display of the character of God, who reflects his character in the mystery that we confront. We may honor God's presence in his works by giving thanks to him and praising him for the richness of his display of his character. He displays his character not only when he accomplishes specific works such as the protection of David, but also when he created the world and constituted it to be what it is, in its many aspects. God also displays his character in the constitution of each passage in its uniqueness, its temporal relatedness, and its topical relatedness.

In particular, God raised up David to be leader of four hundred men at this point in history. He wrote his word in 1 Samuel to indicate the significance of his work in David. The significance resides in (1) the uniqueness of this event; (2) the relations in time to a whole program of successive leaders pointing forward to Christ; and (3) the relations to everything concerning the topic of leadership and the benefits or oppressions of those under leadership. We understand the significance of the one event partly through observing its relations to other events, and we understand each event partly because it is itself distinct and unified as a whole.

In the previous chapter we observed that the three simple steps—observation, elucidation, and application—enjoy perspectival relations with each other. The same remains true when we break up the middle step, elucidation, into three smaller perspectives: (1) examination of one passage, (2) correlation in redemptive history, and (3) correlation in topic. Each of these three "smaller" perspectives functions as a perspective on

---

[1] Vern S. Poythress, *In the Beginning Was the Word: Language—A God-Centered Approach* (Wheaton, IL: Crossway, 2009), chapter 7.

elucidation, which functions as a perspective on observation and application. So each step functions as a perspective on the whole.

The Structure for Interpretation

By splitting the step of elucidation into three smaller perspectives, we obtain the following outline for interpretation:

A. Observation
B. Elucidation
    1. Focus on one passage
    *2. Redemptive-historical correlation
    *3. Topical correlation
C. Application

Because of the key role of Christ in all of God's redemptive work, and because Christ is anticipated in the Old Testament, we ought to devote particular attention to seeing the relation of each passage to Christ. Often, we best accomplish this goal if we reorder the tasks, so that earlier topical study can aid us in seeing redemptive-historical correlations. Thus we may use the following order:

A. Observation
B. Elucidation
    1. Focus on one passage
    *2. Topical correlation
    *3. Redemptive-historical correlation
C. Application

In subsequent chapters we will include more details under these headings. (An outline including all the details is provided in chapter 29.)

The Steps as Perspectives

Since each of the steps offers a perspective on the whole, they all function together and help to deepen one another. For example, understanding the general theme of people in distress within the Old Testament can serve to alert us to the fact that distresses of all kinds have resulted directly or indirectly from the fall. God's salvation ultimately must work out an answer to "distress" of every kind. It follows that, when Christ comes at the climax of history, he works to relieve distress in the form of healing diseases, casting out demons, welcoming tax collectors and prostitutes, dying for our sins, and being raised to justify us (Rom. 4:25).

Conversely, suppose that we start with understanding how Christ fulfills the Old Testament promises of redemption, and in particular the promises made concerning David and his descendants. This linkage with David helps us to recognize that analogies between David's kingship and Christ's kingship form an integral part of God's overall plan for history. We are not inventing imaginary linkages or letting our imaginations work irresponsibly. Given the linkage obtained from redemptive-historical reflection, we come to the text in 1 Samuel 22:1–2 and notice that the topic of people in distress and the topic of David's leadership fit neatly into God's program of redemption leading forward to Christ. So the redemptive-historical insight helps us deepen our understanding of the topical correlations.

Thus, both a topical perspective and a redemptive-historical perspective offer insight, and each helps to deepen the other. Given this interaction of perspectives, any one "order" for the steps is somewhat artificial. In practice, we may find ourselves cycling back and forth several times among the different perspectives.

Resources

Topical study of the Bible can begin with study of parallel passages, such as can be found using the system of cross-references that appear in a column within a reference Bible:

The Holy Bible: English Standard Version. Wheaton, IL: Crossway, 2001. Use an edition that is a "reference Bible" or "study Bible." The *ESV Study Bible* provides not only cross-references but also much more material, in the form of notes and special articles: *ESV Study Bible*. Wheaton, IL: Crossway, 2008.

Novum Testamentum Graece: Nestle-Aland. (Greek Edition.) Edited by Erwin Nestle and Kurt Aland. Various editions. Note cross-references in the margin.

Topical Bibles and Bible dictionaries and encyclopedias may also help in locating passages that discuss a topic:

Kohlenberger, John R., III. *Zondervan NIV Nave's Topical Bible*. Grand Rapids, MI: Zondervan, 1992. The best topical concordance.

Joy, Charles R. *Harper's Topical Concordance of the Bible*. New York: HarperCollins, 1989. Not as comprehensive as Kohlenberger's, but independently produced and so of independent value.

Bible encyclopedias:

Bromiley, Geoffrey W., ed. *The International Standard Bible Encyclopedia*. 4 vols. Rev. ed. Grand Rapids, MI: Eerdmans, 1995.
Marshall, I. Howard, A. R. Millard, J. I. Packer, and D. J. Wiseman, eds. *New Bible Dictionary*. 3rd ed. Downers Grove, IL: InterVarsity Press, 1996.
Ryken, Leland, James C. Wilhoit, and Tremper Longman, III, eds. *Dictionary of Biblical Imagery*. Downers Grove, IL: InterVarsity Press, 1998.

Systematic theologies can also help in locating passages that touch on the topics of systematic theology.

Word-based concordances can also be used, but there are difficulties, because it is easy to neglect the word-concept distinction, to be discussed in chapter 17.

Works of "biblical theology" orient us to the flow of redemptive history:

Clowney, Edmund P. *Preaching and Biblical Theology*. Grand Rapids, MI: Eerdmans, 1961.
———. *The Unfolding Mystery: Discovering Christ in the Old Testament*. Colorado Springs: NavPress, 1988.
Vos, Geerhardus. *Biblical Theology: Old and New Testaments*. Edinburgh/Carlisle, PA: Banner of Truth Trust, 1975.

Part III

ISSUES WITH TIME

7

Transmission

We saw earlier (chapter 3) that the present-time approach that we are using includes in principle the other two main approaches—the transmission approach and the once-for-all approach. Within the overall framework of the present-time approach, we now proceed to develop more explicitly the way in which it can include the transmission approach.

We can pay attention to time and history under the focus on redemptive history, which we have included as step B2 within the three-step approach to interpretation. Redemptive history has to do with the large-scale function of time and history in the plan of God. But we can also explore time and history at a smaller scale, as they affect the actual transmission of the message of one book of the Bible, or one part of a book. That narrower focus is closer to what we have in mind at this point.

If we focus on a single passage, such as 1 Samuel 22:1–2, we ask how God brought it to us so that it becomes accessible to us now, as we have it before our eyes and read it. (Or we may listen to an audio recording or a reading out loud.) Since we are focusing on a single passage, and what God says to us through it, we are using a particle focus on the integrity of this passage. Our work falls naturally under step B1, "one passage." We are considering the study of transmission of a particular passage as one aspect of studying the passage.

God's Communication to Us

In the present-time approach that we are using, we begin with a focus on God speaking to us here and now as we read 1 Samuel 22:1–2. How does he speak to us? He uses as his central means a message written in a book. We may grow in praising God by thinking about how he does this. His use of a means invites us to praise him for how he did it through the means that he chose. Through thinking about the means, we may also refine our understanding of how God wants us to understand the message. The message and the means go together; each tacitly interlocks with the other. So how does the written passage 1 Samuel 22:1–2 come to us?

At an elementary level, we can consider three aspects in the process of communication. God is the author, the text is the message, and I as a reader am the recipient. In some ways, written communication has distinctive characteristics of its own, because the author need not be physically present. But in many ways it also has characteristics in common with oral communication, in which a speaker utters a speech to an audience. God is a speaker from all eternity, since God speaks the Word who is the second person of the Trinity, and this speaking is an eternal speaking. God speaks the eternal Word through the Holy Spirit, who is like the breath of God. The original or archetypal speech is Trinitarian. The Bible also indicates that the Holy Spirit is a receiver of the speech of God:

> When the Spirit of truth comes, he will guide you into all the truth, for he will not speak on his own authority, but whatever he *hears* he will speak, and he will declare to you the things that are to come. (John 16:13)

When God made man, he made him "in the image of God" (Gen. 1:27). Our speech imitates God's speech, but on the level of a creature. God also speaks to human beings, as he did at the beginning in Genesis 1:28: "Be fruitful and multiply and fill the earth and subdue it, and have dominion . . ." Our speech and our writing have three aspects, in imitation of God's Trinitarian character. Speaking involves a speaker, a speech, and an audience. Writing involves an author, a text, and readers.

Since the persons of the Trinity enjoy coinherence, we should not be surprised that speaking and writing among human beings enjoy a derivative coinherence. A speaker is a speaker only if he says something, namely a speech. And he says something in order to communicate to someone (an audience), even if in the exceptional case of a soliloquy the audience is himself.

Conversely, a speech implies the existence of a speaker who speaks it. Otherwise, it is merely sounds in the air—noise, without a personal purpose to make us realize that it has meaning. And an audience is an audience only if it is listening to someone speaking a speech. Speaker, speech, and audience offer three perspectives on the process of oral communication. Similarly, author, text, and reader offer three perspectives on the process of written communication.[1] (See table 7.1.)

Table 7.1 Aspects of Verbal Communication

	Origin	Process	Destination
Trinitarian Communication	God the Father	God the Son (the Word)	God the Holy Spirit
Divine speech	God as speaker	speech to us	human hearers
Human speech	(human) speaker	speech	audience
Human writing	author	text	reader(s)

The triad of author, text, and reader is a perspectival triad, because each of the three not only implies the others but also demands in the long run that we pay attention to the others. How can we understand a text without thinking about the purposes of the one who wrote it? How can we understand an author without reading his text? How can we understand either one without becoming readers? Moreover, if we are sensitive readers, we will ask ourselves how the author and the text intend to affect those who read.

Literary Context for Speech and Writing

Speech takes place within a context. Even God's eternal speech takes place in the context of God in his Trinitarian nature, according to which

---

[1] Vern S. Poythress, *In the Beginning Was the Word: Language—A God-Centered Approach* (Wheaton, IL: Crossway, 2009), 33–34.

each person is an ultimate "context" for the relation of the other two. By analogy, when God speaks to us, he governs contexts and expects us to take them into account.

The particular text in 1 Samuel 22:1–2 comes with a literary context, namely the rest of the book of 1 Samuel. First Samuel fits together with Second Samuel. First and Second Samuel together fit in with the other books of the Bible into a single book, the whole Bible in its present form. (In this case, the Bible that I have at hand is an English language version, the English Standard Version [ESV].) The modern binding into one physical book involves a human decision, to bind up the whole Bible rather than the Old Testament alone, or only the books that the Jews call the "former prophets" (Joshua, Judges, 1–2 Samuel, and 1–2 Kings), or only 1–2 Samuel, or only 1 Samuel by itself.[2] But in this case the modern human decision helps to remind us that God himself designed the biblical canon to constitute a single whole, permanently available to the people of God.

We may also note how texts group together within the Old Testament. First and Second Samuel belong together as a larger literary whole, dealing with the transition from the period of the judges to the end of David's kingship. First and Second Samuel also belong together with 1 and 2 Kings, which continue the historical record into the period of David's son Solomon and the succeeding kings of Israel and Judah. We can also see a link backward to the books of Joshua and Judges, which provide information about the history of God's people Israel from the time of the conquest under Joshua through the time of the judges. If we want to go still further back, we can include Genesis through Deuteronomy.

Context of Transmission

When we ask questions about how the text of 1 Samuel 22:1–2 comes before us, we can also look at the temporal developments in transmitting the text. The Bible as a whole gives us an understanding of history and God's plan for history. Within this plan, we come to understand that God is now presenting us with a text that he originally caused to

---

[2] Early editions of the King James Version included some apocryphal books, like 1 Maccabees, without implying that these books had divine authority.

be written down centuries ago. Since then, scribes have copied and re-copied it, so that we have Hebrew manuscripts that include 1 Samuel 22:1–2. And then these Hebrew manuscripts get compared, leading to modern printed editions of the Hebrew text. Translators undertake to translate the Hebrew found in the printed editions, and so we get the Bible in English (such as the ESV).

Thus, understanding 1 Samuel 22:1–2 involves two contexts, namely the literary context and the context of transmission. Altogether, we have three possible foci for study and reflection: the text of 1 Samuel 22:1–2 itself; the literary context for this text (1 Samuel and 2 Samuel, and also the whole Bible); and the context of its transmission through time. These three foci offer us three perspectives, which are related respectively to the particle, field, and wave perspectives.

An Enhanced Outline of Interpretation

We can add these details to our previous outline of steps for interpretation. The focus on the text itself, on its literary context, and on its transmission context, all fall under the focus of one passage. So here is the enhanced list of steps (with the newly added steps starred):

A. Observation
B. Elucidation
   1. One passage
      *a. The text
      *b. The literary context
      *c. The transmission context
   2. Topical correlation
   3. Redemptive-historical correlation
C. Application

From a certain logical point of view, we can regard the text as logically prior to the literary context and the transmission context surrounding it. In practice, however, it is often expedient to study the literary context and the transmission context *prior to* a detailed consideration of the text itself. Since each of the three areas—text, literary context, and transmission context—offers a perspective on the others, the order is not vital. Nevertheless, for ease of use we offer an alternate order:

A. Observation
B. Elucidation
   1. One passage
      *a. The literary context
      *b. The transmission context
      *c. The text
   2. Topical correlation
   3. Redemptive-historical correlation
C. Application

Further Analysis of Transmission

Within the total process of transmission, we can distinguish stages: the beginning, the middle, and the end. The process starts at the beginning, when God caused 1 Samuel to be written. It reaches an end with the ESV Bible that I have in front of me. In between lies a process of transmission spanning centuries. The beginning, middle, and end belong together according to the plan of God. God, who knows the end from the beginning (Isa. 46:10), planned from the beginning that I would eventually receive this text and be able to profit from it. He had me (and others) in mind when he wrote 1 Samuel centuries ago. Conversely, I enjoy the endpoint only because God accomplished his work at the beginning point and all along through the middle.

The three points in time constitute a plot structure that coheres according to God's plan: (1) planning and initiation with a goal in mind; (2) work toward the goal; and (3) achievement.[3] As usual, these phases offer perspectives on each other, united by the purpose of God. If we wish, we can also see here a way in which God reflects his Trinitarian nature through his acts in time. All three persons of the Trinity participate in all of God's acts within the world. But we may nevertheless see a correlation in terms of prominent roles. God the Father is the planner, corresponding to the beginning; God the Son is the executor, corresponding to the middle; and God the Holy Spirit is the consummator, corresponding to the end.

Within this process, each of the stages involves smaller acts of communication. (1) At the beginning, God communicates in writing to the

---

[3] Poythress, *In the Beginning Was the Word*, chapters 13 and 24.

immediate recipients of 1 Samuel. We have (a) God as author (working through a human author), (b) the autographic text as text, and (c) ancient Israelites as potential readers (or hearers of an oral reading). (2) In the middle, we have scribes writing to scribes, which involves scribal authors, scribal texts, and scribal readers. (3) At the end, we have translators, publishers, and printers. The translators undertake to translate from Hebrew to English on the basis of the best available Hebrew text. We can produce a schematic outline of the process:

(1) God writes through a human author
    (a) Author: God through human author
    (b) Text: autograph of 1–2 Samuel
    (c) Readers: Israelites
(2) God providentially supervises the text's voyage, that is, its transmission in the middle period
    (a) Authors: scribes
    (b) Texts: scribal copies
    (c) Readers: later scribes
(3) God sees to it that I receive what he says
    (a) Author: ESV translation team
    (b) Text: ESV of 1 Samuel
    (c) Reader: me (and others)

We could break down this analysis into still smaller phases. But we must leave to other books the detailed study of transmission in the middle period. For the benefit of beginners, we will include a brief explanation: The detailed study of transmission is called *text criticism*. The term *criticism* has unfortunate unintended connotations for beginners. Here it is used as a technical term. It does not mean that people are criticizing the Bible; rather, they are using a self-conscious critical awareness as they study the texts that we now have.

Research specialists investigate the Hebrew manuscripts that have survived until now, and ancient translations like the Septuagint (Greek) translation. The surviving Hebrew manuscripts agree with each other remarkably. But here and there specialists find small differences. By weighing all this evidence the specialists endeavor to discern what exact Hebrew letters were in the autographic text.

In some cases uncertainties remain. But such marginal uncertainties are no worse in principle than other kinds of uncertainties about the Bible. Scholars find uncertainties about the meaning of some rare ancient Hebrew or Greek words, or uncertainties about the meaning of a sentence, or uncertainties about why certain sentences have been included within a given paragraph within the text. God can use these uncertainties positively, to remind us of our creaturely limitations, and to remind us to trust him rather than our own mastery.[4]

God has made sure that the important teachings in the Bible occur more than once, in more than one form. By reading widely in the Bible and asking for the Spirit's illumination, we come to understand more and more, and God provides us enough knowledge to guide our lives, while leaving us with remaining limitations in order to humble our pride.

Since God controls the whole world, he also controls the entire process leading to our modern access to his word. Because of the central role that God designed for his word, he has given special providential oversight to the transmission of copies of Scripture. The Westminster Confession of Faith summarizes it:

> The Old Testament in Hebrew (which was the native language of the people of God of old), and the New Testament in Greek (which, at the time of writing of it, was most generally known to the nations), being immediately inspired by God, and, by His *singular care and providence*, kept pure in all ages, are therefore authentical; so as, in all controversies of religion, the Church is finally to appeal unto them. But, because these original tongues are not known to all the people of God, who have right unto, and interest in the Scriptures, and are commanded, in the fear of God, to read and search them, therefore they are to be translated into the vulgar [common] language of every nation unto which they come, that, the Word of God dwelling plentifully in all, they may worship Him in an acceptable manner; and, through patience and comfort of the Scriptures, may have hope. (1.8; italics mine)

---

[4] See Vern S. Poythress, *Inerrancy and the Gospels: A God-Centered Approach to the Challenges of Harmonization* (Wheaton, IL: Crossway, 2012), chapter 15.

The Text of 1 Samuel 22:1–2

We can apply these principles to 1 Samuel 22:1–2. We can obtain the basic necessary information about these verses from the standard reference work for the Hebrew text, *Biblia Hebraica Stuttgartensia.*[5] The information there shows two variations in the text of 22:1–2. In verse 1, most Greek manuscripts and one edition of the Aramaic Targum omit the word "all" (Hebrew כל). However, the manuscripts in Hebrew all include it. In effect, the variation amounts to saying "his father's house" instead of "*all* his father's house." The omission of "all" is probably a later variation. A scribe may have thought that it was improbable that literally *everyone* in David's father's house would have heard about David's escape. But in the autograph the word *all* is probably used more loosely. Mark 1:5 says that "*all* the country of Judea and *all* Jerusalem were going out to him [John the Baptist]." We understand that "all" means "a great many." The word *all* in 1 Samuel 22:1 functions to include a larger group besides David's brothers. Not merely his brothers but his father and mother (see 22:3), nephews, nieces, and servants would potentially be included.

In addition, verse 2 contains one variation. Hebrew manuscripts vary in the spelling for the Hebrew word underlying the English translation "in debt." The Hebrew is *noše'* or *noseh* (נֹשֶׁה ,נֹשֶׁא, or נוֹשֶׁא ,נוֹשֶׁה). All the spellings have the same meaning.

Outline of Steps

We can now insert our analysis of transmission into the overall outline for steps in interpretation.

    A. Observation
    B. Elucidation
        1. One passage
            a. The literary context
            b. The transmission context
                *(1) God writes through a human author
                    (a) Author: God through human author
                    (b) Text: autograph of 1–2 Samuel
                    (c) Readers: Israelites

---

[5] *Biblia Hebraica Stuttgartensia* (Stuttgart: Deutsche Bibelstiftung, 1977).

   *(2) God providentially supervises the text's voyage, that
    is, the transmission in the middle period
    (a) Authors: scribes
    (b) Text: scribal copies
    (c) Readers: later scribes
   *(3) God sees to it that I receive what he says
    (a) Author: ESV translation team
    (b) Text: ESV of 1 Samuel
    (c) Reader: me (and others)
  c. The text
 2. Topical correlation
 3. Redemptive-historical correlation
C. Application

The Focus of Divine Authority

Does the process of transmission imply that all stages in transmission
are equally authoritative? No. We must leave the details to books that
discuss text criticism, the canon of Scripture, and the divine inspiration
of the original writing. But we may say a few words. Consider two key
examples: the Ten Commandments, written on stone by the finger of
God (Ex. 31:18; Deut. 9:10), and the additional written material that
Moses was told to deposit beside the ark (Deut. 31:24–29). These passages show that divine authority belongs to the original document. But
God's people can subsequently wander away from the document in disobedience (Deut. 31:27–29). It does not take much inference to see that
failure could enter the process even in copying. So we may conclude that
the later copies and translations from the copies represent the word of
God, because they express the same message. But when we have questions about details, God intends that we should regard the later copies
and translations as conveying his message *from* the original, which means
that we should still look toward the original for the most exacting detail.[6]

Resources

Wegner, Paul D. *A Student's Guide to Textual Criticism of the Bible: Its History, Methods, and
 Results.* Downers Grove, IL: InterVarsity Press, 2006.

---

[6] Thus, the later copies and translations are authoritative as perspectives on the original.

8

Original Contexts

Our reflection on transmission has included attention to the starting point of transmission, the point when God originally wrote 1 Samuel. Understanding God's large-scale plans should deepen our confidence in him. He has governed all of history so far; through his providential work he has brought about the transmission of Old Testament texts, so that I (and others) would be able to read 1 Samuel.

Benefits and Hazards of Attending to Original Context

Studying the original context of 1 Samuel 22:1–2 can tempt some people to forget or lay aside the reality of God's presence today. But it need not. Through God's speech to us today, in 1 Samuel, he makes it evident that he did not begin speaking just today! He spoke to people long ago. He spoke to those to whom he originally wrote 1 Samuel. He is saying to us now, today, that he spoke to them, and through the text of 1 Samuel he invites us to understand that he has larger purposes than *merely* speaking to us directly. We are not the center of the world! So we may grow spiritually by reflecting on what God's speech today tells about his speech back then.

This interaction between earlier and later speech also helps us to be alert to the fact that we ourselves as readers are prone to read the Bible in our own favor, according to our pet prejudices. We hear what we want to hear. And among the things that we want to hear, in the sense of an unsanctified "want," is that God is merely speaking to us now. We would rather not have to take the trouble to think through the fact that God long ago said things to other people in other times that suited what they needed to hear, not necessarily only what we need to hear now.

What God says to us now harmonizes with what he said to the early Israelite readers of 1 Samuel. He is the same God. So paying attention to what he said back then offers a way of checking our own tendency to make ourselves the center, and to hear only what we want to hear. Instead, we begin to hear that in 1 Samuel 22:1–2 God is saying to us now, "I said what I said back then to the people back then." Of course he designed what he said to have relevance to us, and he caused it to be recorded and transmitted in order that it might actually reach us. But if we are going to absorb it profitably and sensitively, we want to acknowledge the depth and magnificence of his purposes in the text, purposes that include the ancient Israelites as well as us.

For example, why in the world should we care whether David "escaped to the cave of Adullam," or whether "everyone who was in distress" came to him (22:1–2)? What difference does it make to us? If we are self-centered and immature in our understanding of God and the Scriptures, we may not care. With a rebellious heart we may tell ourselves that we do not need all this irrelevant information. We dispense with the Bible, or at least with the Old Testament, and follow some idea that we think will give us some immediate spiritual benefit.

Or maybe, if we are not so foolish as to give up reading the Bible, we look for some fancy way of pressing it into our mold to give us spiritual benefit. As an example, let us consider a hypothetical modern reader, whom we may call Tammy. Tammy reads everything as if it were merely written to her today and *not* to the Israelites. She ignores the fact that the passage says, "David" and "the cave of Adullam." She acts as if it said "me" and "my home." As she makes mental substitutions like that, she can pretend that she herself is now in the passage directly. She can read the passage as if it were talking directly about her receiving her brothers and her father's house. She then interprets "brothers" and "her father's house" as meaning her fellow Christians. She concludes that she ought to welcome everyone who comes to her in distress. And so on.

What do we say about such a reading of the passage? Well, God is gracious to us all. We need his grace. None of us *deserves* to receive a proper understanding of the Bible or to profit from it. When we receive benefit, we receive it because God is gracious to us for the sake of Christ, who bore our sins and intercedes for us. So, by the grace of God, even Tammy's kind of reading can lead to spiritual benefit. But the benefits get limited because of the self-centered focus underneath. Such a reading is not ideal. It is not loving the Lord your God with all your heart.

So we have to pay attention to the fact that it says, "David" and "the cave of Adullam." Not us. Not our home country. God is saying, here and now to us, that he cared for David, took charge of his life, and gave him a cave to stay in. It happened long ago. That idea of "long ago" is part of what God is saying, here and now. This reflection confirms what we said before, that the present-time approach implicitly includes the transmission approach, where we pay attention to the reality "long ago." God cares about us, here and now, enough to display his greatness to us in the fact that he transmitted a message concerning events three thousand years ago, and told us about his care and reliability three thousand years ago. God is still the same God today, and that already means encouragement for us today.

Suppose that we keep thinking about long ago. Suppose that we think about David rather than just ourselves and delay our desire to get a present-day spiritual lesson out of the passage. We may realize that David was the anointed king, the future king of Israel. His suffering (by being like a kind of outlaw in a cave) led eventually to his glory, his recognition and open establishment as king. Christ the greater descendant of David is now the anointed king ("Christ" means "anointed"). He went from suffering to the present glory of his enthronement at the right hand of the Father:

> "Was it not necessary that the Christ should *suffer* these things and enter into his *glory*?" And beginning with Moses and all the Prophets, he interpreted to them in all the Scriptures the things concerning himself. (Luke 24:26–27)

Christ is the final, humble, compassionate king. Long ago, God was crafting in David a humble, compassionate, *suffering* king. And he taught the people back then to hope for a greater descendant of David to come. Do we admire God for his wisdom? Do we glory in Christ our Savior? Do we love the Lord our God with all our heart? We at least come closer to obeying that commandment when we exercise the patience to allow God to say what he really does say: "David"; "the cave of Adullam." And we exercise patience in thinking through why God would give us information like that. Before God's presence, he calls on us to think about the past, about David. And he calls us to think about what he was saying and doing back then and there.

So, in the presence of God, let us proceed to admire what he tells us now about what he did in the past. At the same time, let us not travel to the opposite extreme, and treat the Bible as if it were merely an antiquarian message about what happened "back then." God is addressing us here and now through his words.

Society

We can look not only at the text of 1 Samuel 22:1–2, but also at its contexts. We have already talked about literary contexts. But there are other ancient contexts, the contexts of the communication from God to Israel. One such context is the society—Israelite society. It is not a modern society. So we have challenges. But God is involved in all societies, not merely our own. So again we can learn humility and learn something about the breadth of God's plan and his compassion.

In the case of a historical narrative like 1 Samuel 22:1–2, we have two main social contexts: the context at the time when 1 Samuel was originally written as a whole book, and the context at the time when David was living in the cave of Adullam. David lived in the cave of Adullam when he was still fairly young, before he became king. First Samuel was written later, since it takes us up to the time when Saul died (1 Samuel 31).

So when was 1 Samuel written? We do not know for sure. To try to get more information, we can do some "detective" work. What we now know as 1 Samuel and 2 Samuel was originally one book. Up until the sixteenth century AD, the Hebrew manuscripts included 1–2 Samuel as one continuous book, the book of Samuel. The ancient Greek translation, the Septuagint, divided it into two books, which we now know as 1 Samuel and 2 Samuel.

Since 1–2 Samuel was originally one book, the original would have been written sometime after the last events mentioned in 2 Samuel, near the end of David's life. The writing could have taken place right then, before the events mentioned in 1 Kings 1. Or it could have taken place at some later point.

How much later? We do not know. It is another one of those uncertainties with which God leaves us. It is plain from the opening lines of some of the prophetic books that God can provide specific information about time when he wishes. Amos, for example, received his prophecies "in the days of Uzziah king of Judah and in the days of Jeroboam the son of Joash, king of Israel, two years before the earthquake" (Amos 1:1). But God does not furnish equivalent information for 1–2 Samuel.

We can still make some intelligent guesses. First Samuel fits into a continuous record in Scripture that goes from the days of Samuel to the time of the exile to Babylon, which is mentioned in 2 Kings 25. The record begins with 1 Samuel, and continues with 2 Samuel, 1 Kings, and 2 Kings. God may have caused the whole of 1–2 Samuel and 1–2 Kings to be written by a single human author at the time of the exile (the period 586–538 BC), just after the conclusion of the events recorded in 2 Kings.[1] (In this case, Jeremiah the prophet might possibly have been the human author.)

Or the entire work of 1–2 Samuel and 1–2 Kings could have been written successively, over a number of generations, using a number of human authors. Samuel himself could have supplied information about the events up until the time of his death (1 Sam. 25:1). Nathan the prophet could have written about events up until the reign of Solomon. And so on. First Chronicles 29:29–30 talks about early documentary records made by the prophets Nathan and Gad:

> Now the acts of King David, from first to last, are written in the Chronicles of Samuel the seer, and in the Chronicles of Nathan the prophet, and in the Chronicles of Gad the seer, with accounts of all his rule and his might and of the circumstances that came upon him and upon Israel and upon all the kingdoms of the countries.

---

[1] See, e.g., Ralph W. Klein, *1 Samuel*, Word Biblical Commentary, vol. 10 (Waco, TX: Word, 1983), xxx.

Both Nathan and Gad were alive at the conclusion of 2 Samuel (1 Kings 1:10–11; 2 Sam. 24:11), so either one could have been commissioned by God to write 1–2 Samuel.

The completed work including all of 1–2 Kings would nevertheless have come into being only at or after the time of exile mentioned in 2 Kings 25.

David Tsumura points out that 1 Samuel 27:6 gives significant information: "Therefore Ziklag has belonged to the kings of Judah to this day."[2] Tsumura observes that Ziklag would not have actually been controlled by Judah after the campaign of Shishak king of Egypt (925 BC, in the days of Rehoboam; see 1 Kings 14:25; 2 Chron. 12:5, 9). This information suggests that 1–2 Samuel was written *before* Shishak's campaign.

The primary social context for 1 Samuel is the context into which God wrote. God as master of effective communication takes into account the contexts into which he speaks.[3] We understand him more accurately when we take into account these contexts. So the context is significant. But we are not sure when 1–2 Samuel reached its present form. Conceivably it could have been written or revised (from earlier work by Samuel or Nathan the prophet or Gad the seer) in the last days of David (1 Kings 1:1). It could have been written in the days of Solomon's reign or Rehoboam's reign, as Tsumura's reasoning suggests. Or the entire corpus composed of 1–2 Samuel and 1–2 Kings could have been composed under divine inspiration at the time of the exile, based on earlier sources. The later composition could still have left in place the key information in 1 Samuel 27:6. The key verse would indicate not that the kings of Judah actually *controlled* Ziklag the whole time up until the exile, but that the kings of Judah, rather than the king of Gath, had official legal rights to the city.

The lack of explicit information about the time of composition of 1–2 Samuel is an indication from God that the exact time of composition is not crucially important for understanding what God says. What God says is relevant to all subsequent times.

---

[2] David Toshio Tsumura, *The First Book of Samuel* (Grand Rapids, MI: Eerdmans, 2007), 18.
[3] Vern S. Poythress, *Inerrancy and Worldview: Answering Modern Challenges to the Bible* (Wheaton, IL: Crossway, 2012), chapter 11; Poythress, *In the Beginning Was the Word: Language—A God-Centered Approach* (Wheaton, IL: Crossway, 2009).

In addition, since God speaks in 1 Samuel about David's life, he invites us to see the meaning of his work in the context of the society of David's time, the time when the kingship in Israel is being inaugurated. This context then informs the meaning of the events described in 1 Samuel. In particular, David's escape to the cave of Adullam makes sense when we take into account the threat within the circumstances of David's life from Achish, king of Gath, and from Saul, king of Israel. The gathering of people in distress and in debt says something about the social troubles of that time period.

We also have a specific location to which we should pay attention: the cave of Adullam. Adullam is mentioned in Joshua as one of the cities belonging to the tribal inheritance of Judah (Josh. 15:35). According to Klein's commentary, it "is usually identified today with Khirbet esh-Sheikh Madhkur, . . . midway between Gath and Hebron."[4] The identification is uncertain, but the cave was probably in the vicinity of the town of Adullam.

Modern Approaches

We should consider these social and historical contexts as we stand in the presence of God. How do we proceed? The growth of modern sociology and social anthropology represents both a potential benefit and a potential danger. These disciplines promise to aid people who are considering the nature of society and social structures. And they do provide some beneficial insights by virtue of common grace. But the modern disciplines in their usual form also tacitly assume that God is absent from society.[5] According to this impersonalist assumption, society runs by purely horizontal interaction among human beings. The result may be that the Bible is treated as if it were trapped within a purely human context, to which God is irrelevant. The interpretation of Scripture is bound to suffer from the influence of this viewpoint. And, taken to an extreme, it implies that Scripture itself is merely a human product, not divine.[6]

---

[4] Klein, *1 Samuel*, 222.
[5] See William W. Klein, Craig L. Blomberg, and Robert L. Hubbard, *Introduction to Biblical Interpretation*, rev. and expanded ed. (Nashville/Dallas/Mexico City/Rio de Janeiro: Nelson, 2004), 84–87.
[6] Vern S. Poythress, *Redeeming Sociology* (Wheaton, IL: Crossway, 2011); Poythress, *Inerrancy and Worldview*, chapters 15–18.

Even with the best of principles, we can go only so far in reconstructing and imagining what Israelite society was like. We do not know all the details. And we do not need to know, because human nature is fundamentally the same, and there will be likenesses between societies. We learn more when we recognize some of the differences, but even with limited knowledge we can understand Scripture in a manner sufficient to instruct us and sufficient for us to continue to grow in the presence of God.

For example, we can understand that people in distress and in debt in David's time were in some respects like people in distress and in debt in modern times. We may also reckon with differences. In Western societies, a powerful person who wants to eliminate or neutralize another person whom he perceives as a threat seldom goes after the person's family. But the family was tighter and had a more significant social role in ancient Israelite society.[7] So, within Israelite society, there was a real danger that Saul, in his enmity toward David, might threaten David's family. We can see how David's brothers and "father's house" might be inclined to join him to avoid danger from Saul.

These social connections help interpretation to move toward application. By envisioning how people lived then, we get ideas about similar situations now, and then similar applications now.

Sources

We may include within our examination of context the possibility of earlier written sources being used in the composition of 1 Samuel. God indicates in the Bible that in ancient times other written records existed, including what were probably official court records about the histories of the northern and southern kingdoms (2 Sam. 1:18; 1 Kings 11:41; 14:19, 29; etc.). As we observed, 1 Chronicles 29:29 also mentions material from Samuel, Nathan, and Gad:

> Now the acts of King David, from first to last, are written in the Chronicles of Samuel the seer, and in the Chronicles of Nathan the prophet, and in the Chronicles of Gad the seer.

---

[7] We can see similar effects today in some societies in the Middle East or in Asia. If a person becomes a follower of Christ or becomes a political dissident, some people from the majority culture may attack not only him but also his family.

The human author of 1–2 Samuel may have been Nathan or Gad. Or, under God's guidance, some other human author of 1–2 Samuel may have used information from earlier sources. We do not know.

It is also possible that a human author at the time of Solomon or at the time of the exile used an earlier work, written by Samuel or Nathan or Gad or some other person, who had compiled a history that extended through only part of the earlier period of 1 Samuel. On the basis of detailed study of the original Hebrew text in 1–2 Samuel and 1–2 Kings, specialists may try to detect stylistic differences or differences in themes or emphases that make them think that they have clues as to when and how people composed earlier texts that lie behind the present text. And in some cases their guesses may be right. But we have no way of knowing for sure.

We have what God says in the text of 1 Samuel. Some of the written sources behind 1 Samuel, if they existed, may have been inspired by God in their own time. In addition, there would have been inspired oral communication through prophets like Samuel, Nathan, and Gad. But God intends us to listen to what he wrote for us (1 Samuel), which has its own meanings and its own integrity. Speculation about sources helps little. For one thing, it is speculative (we are guessing; we do not really know). In addition, the sources do not influence the meaning of the text that we have. The meaning is found by reading the text, not by traveling backward to its sources.[8]

If we had them available, such sources might still throw light on the general social and historical context. But that information would be like any other information from the ancient Near East; it is potentially helpful, but it does not dictate the meaning of the finished text. The finished text means what God means in speaking through it. His meanings may be either the same as or different from the sources. It is completely up to him how he speaks.

History

We may also consider the *historical* context of 1 Samuel. Again we have two contexts. One context is the time of David. The other is the time

---

[8] See appendix D; and Vern S. Poythress, *Inerrancy and the Gospels: A God-Centered Approach to the Challenges of Harmonization* (Wheaton, IL: Crossway, 2012), chapter 16.

when 1–2 Samuel was written in its present form. Both time periods are relevant, since God writing to Israelites at a later time intends them to understand what he was doing in the time of David.

History is about movement in time, governed providentially by God for his purposes. The narrative in 1 Samuel begins during the last part of the time of the judges, when "there was no king in Israel" (Judg. 21:25). God raises up Samuel as the last judge (1 Sam. 7:15). At God's direction, Samuel presides over the transition to the time of the kings, beginning with Saul and then David. Saul, the king after the people's heart, falters and fails, while David, the king after God's heart, establishes the people under the blessing of his rule. Yet even the time of David is not without its blemishes. After Solomon's kingship the kingdom splits and then goes through ups and downs, terminating in the exile of the northern kingdom of Israel in 722 BC and the southern kingdom of Judah in 586 BC.

God invites us to see the episode recorded in 1 Samuel 22:1–2 in the light of the forward-moving character of events throughout the time of David's life. And God also invites us to see that David's life is not the end of the story. More kings come after David, as we find in 1–2 Kings. God cares for David. After David's death, God leaves him a "lamp" (1 Kings 11:36; 2 Kings 8:19), in the form of descendants on the throne in Jerusalem. God also blesses the people through good kings, and the blessing in 1 Samuel 22:1–2 toward those in distress presages the continuing pattern of blessing through good kings. But it is all inadequate, and near the end of 2 Kings it gets thoroughly depressing, as the kings of Judah spiral downward into unfaithfulness.

God also invites the readers in later times to see the meaning of their own previous history, including the history of David and the history of the episode at the cave of Adullam. Israelites later on in the time of the monarchy could learn the crucial importance of David and God's care for David. Israelites who went into exile must have struggled about whether God was really God, and if so why he had abandoned them to exile. First Samuel through Second Kings shows how the exile was a fulfillment of the curses of Deuteronomy 27–28 and the prediction of Deuteronomy 29. God is faithful to both his promises and his curses, and the exile is a curse on account of the accumulation of Israelite treachery and disobedience. David himself suffered a kind of "exile" when he lived in the cave of Adullam. God's care for David therefore has implications for the people of Israel who went into exile to Assyria and later to Babylon.

In this context, 1 Samuel 22:1–2 serves as a reminder of God's past faithfulness to David, and not only to David but also to those in distress. God is the same God during the monarchy and during the exile, the God who is "merciful and gracious, slow to anger, and abounding in steadfast love and faithfulness" (Ex. 34:6). Past history reminds later Israelite readers—and us today as well—that past history is relevant for our understanding of our own history, because God is working in each of our lives and each of our circumstances.

The larger vista of history includes the reality that history in the Old Testament is moving forward to Christ. We can see this reality in the case of David, because David is the ancestor of Christ. God promised David not only that he would become king but also that he would have a line of descendants who were kings. This entire line would lead forward to Christ (Isa. 11:1–9; Ezek. 34:23–24; Mic. 5:2; Matt. 1:1–17). We have already touched on the fact that the Bible is Christ-centered in discussing redemptive history (chapter 6; part B3 in the steps of interpretation). The focus on Christ the center belongs most suitably in step B3. But a focus on immediate historical events, within the life of David, naturally leads to reflecting on a larger context that includes wider vistas of history. We understand the smaller pieces in the light of the larger, and vice versa. We can be comfortable with this interaction, since it illustrates again the interpenetration of perspectives, in this case the perspective of narrow historical focus and the perspective of broad historical focus (redemptive history).

Examining Society and History in the Presence of God

As we indicated already, we should be reflecting on society and history as we live in the presence of God. Living now in the presence of God should encourage us to understand the presence of God in David's society and in David's history. God is the same God back then. If we recognize God's presence, we cannot be content to proceed with social and historical analysis as if this analysis were religiously neutral or as if it could dispense with God.

We may illustrate the analysis of society by considering the people "in distress" who came to David. An impersonalist analysis, using the framework of modernist reductionistic sociology and anthropology, might see here a typical case of disgruntlement and the formation of a political and social group based on common antagonism to the status quo. There may be considerable truth in such an analysis. But it skews the picture by tacitly eliminating God and trying to treat society as merely a structure of horizontal relations among human beings. Instead, we should be asking about God's work among these people. Yes, they had human circumstances of distress. God was present and called them to come to David for relief. Seeing God's urging helps us to understand present-day searches for relief among distressed people. They may or may not seek relief in a good way. But we remember how Jesus had compassion on the multitudes, even though they did not yet have faith in him. "Come to me," he says (Matt. 11:28). We see the events in 1 Samuel 22:1–2 in a different light when we view society as a whole in the light of God's presence.

A similar issue arises when we consider the history of David's life. Does David's life and his relation to Saul simply represent one more instance of political maneuvering, as a modern secular historian might see it? Or do we see God's hand in David's life? Did God preserve David's life from the threat of Saul? Did God provide him with the cave of Adullam as a refuge, and did God give him followers? Once we see the hand of God in David's life, we see its significance not merely as a lesson in earthly politics but as an example of God's grace. And we see its connection with the broader issue of salvation. God saves us by bringing us into fellowship with Christ, forgiving our sins, renewing our hearts, and justifying us by faith. This central meaning of salvation includes God's commitment in Christ to care for us *comprehensively*. It includes caring for our bodies and giving us daily bread and giving us companionship. David's life has spiritual resonances with our lives. And of course it has resonance with the life of Christ, who is the final David.

We should also consider God's involvement when we analyze the social and historical circumstances at the time when 1 Samuel was written. Suppose that it was written in the time of Solomon's kingdom. God was present to the Israelites of that period. He was saying to them that he was still the same God that he proved to be in the life of David. Or suppose that we think that 1 Samuel belongs together with 2 Samuel and 1–2 Kings, and that it achieved its final form when it was joined to 2 Samuel and 1–2 Kings. This final form would have come at the time of the exile. In that case, God was present with the exiles to say through the life of David that he still maintained his commitment to them, not merely to David. If they found themselves "in distress" or "bitter in soul," they could seek refuge in God and hope for the coming of a final descendant of David. God addressed their social situation of distress. And he revealed himself as one who was moving history forward to the time when he would raise up Christ as the final descendant of David who would fulfill all the promises (2 Cor. 1:20).

Perspectives on the Text in Its Environment

In addition to focusing on the social environment and on the historical sequence of the *events*, we may focus on the *text itself* as an act of communication. We then have three complementary foci for study: (1) the text as an act of communication; (2) the social environment of the text; and (3) the historical environment of events moving forward in time. We can include these three foci as subdivisions within the overall outline for interpretation that we are developing:

   c. The text
       (1) The text as act of communication
       (2) The social contexts
       (3) The historical contexts

These three foci correspond respectively to the particle, field, and wave perspectives. The text is a single writing, which is like a particle. The text exists in a multitude of relationships with its social environment, and the study of relationships constitutes a field-like focus. Finally, the text exists as part of a sequence of events leading from the past history of David and the monarchy to the future, including the future promises of a Messiah. The sequence of events is wave-like in character.

As usual, these three foci are perspectivally related. God issues the text in a manner that takes into account the human contexts of those to whom he speaks. God intends that the text have an influence on real people in real circumstances. And so understanding God's purposes for the text includes understanding how God intends it to interact with the people in their circumstances, both social and historical. Conversely, study of the social circumstances logically includes studying the text both as clue to the circumstances and as one part of the total social and historical picture. Yet this perspectival relation does not mean that we level out the difference between the text and its environment. God's speech carries his authority. God providentially governs the society and its history, but the society and history as such do not have the divine authority of his speech. His word governing the universe (Heb. 1:3) governs society and history but is not identical with it.

Outline of Steps

If we insert our three foci into the overall outline of steps, we obtain the following (with the newly added lines starred):

A. Observation
B. Elucidation
   1. One passage
      a. The literary context
      b. The transmission context
         (1) God writes through a human author
            (a) Author: God
            (b) Text: autograph of 1–2 Samuel
            (c) Readers: Israelites
         (2) God providentially supervises the text's voyage, that is, the transmission in the middle period
            (a) Authors: scribes
            (b) Text: scribal copies
            (c) Readers: later scribes
         (3) God sees to it that I receive what he says
            (a) Author: ESV translation team
            (b) Text: ESV of 1 Samuel
            (c) Reader: me (and others)
      c. The text
        *(1) The text as act of communication
        *(2) The social contexts

         *(3) The historical contexts
  2. Topical correlation
  3. Redemptive-historical correlation
C. Application

Actually, we could organize the outline in more than one way. In principle, we can apply the three foci—on the text itself, on its social environment, and on its historical environment—to *any stage* in the process of transmission. For example, we may consider how social pressures in the Roman Empire, together with waves of Roman persecution of the early church, resulted in the confiscation and destruction of some copies of New Testament manuscripts. The social and historical circumstances of the Roman Empire affected the middle period of scribal transmission. Or we can consider the challenges involved in our modern circumstances, from the modern social structures and historical events that surround us.

For convenience, we choose to consider the modern environment primarily under the heading "C. Application." We consider the ancient environment for the autographic text under the heading "B.1.c. The text" rather than under the transmission context ("B.1.b.(1) God writes through a human author"). We inevitably find some overlap between headings, because each of the headings in the end presents a perspective, which can potentially expand to include the whole.

In the process of refining our headings, we have made more precise what we mean by "The text" in B.1.c. We focus on the autographic text, not the copies and translations.

Resources

Atlas:

Currid, John D., and David P. Barrett. *Crossway ESV Bible Atlas*. Wheaton, IL: Crossway, 2010.

Old Testament:

Borowski, Oded. *Daily Life in Biblical Times*. Atlanta: Society of Biblical Literature, 2003.
Merrill, Eugene H. *Kingdom of Priests: A History of Old Testament Israel*. 2nd ed. Grand Rapids, MI: Baker, 2008.

New Testament:

Bruce, F. F. *New Testament History*. Garden City, NY: Doubleday, 1980.
Ferguson, Everett. *Backgrounds of Early Christianity*. 3rd ed. Grand Rapids, MI: Eerdmans, 2003.

In addition, the introductory sections within commentaries on individual books of the Bible will usually contain valuable information on the historical and cultural setting. A survey of commentaries can be found in:

Carson, D. A. *New Testament Commentary Survey*. Grand Rapids, MI: Baker, 2007.
Longman, Tremper, III. *Old Testament Commentary Survey*. Grand Rapids, MI: Baker, 2007.

9

Original Communication

Let us consider further the original act of communication, when 1 Samuel was originally written. God raised up a human author to write 1–2 Samuel. The human author may have used sources. If the sources were extensive, some scholars may choose to speak of an "editor" rather than an "author." But whatever we call him—author or editor—he took responsibility for producing what he wrote.[1] In addition, God superintended what the author wrote. Whatever the details of the process of research and writing, the product has divine authority as well as the authority of its human author.

The text of 1–2 Samuel, as produced by God through a human author, represents an act of communication. God and a human writer write a text to readers. In the long run, according to God's intention, the readers include us: "For whatever was written in former days was written for *our* instruction, that through endurance and through the encouragement of the Scriptures we might have hope" (Rom. 15:4). But if we are focusing on the ancient text, we may focus on the original readers. Since not everyone had the ability to read in ancient times, we may include within the company of the original readers those who would have the text read out loud to them.

---

[1] It is also theoretically possible that in some cases a "team" of "editors" worked together (as in Prov. 25:1, "the men of Hezekiah"). God does not give us the details. For the sake of simplicity we will speak about the "human author" of 1 Samuel. The decisive element was that the Holy Spirit worked through human beings so that the final product was inspired; it was fully God's speech.

We have three foci: author, text, and readers. These three involve one another, as we saw in chapter 2. The text is not a meaningless object, but the product of authorial intentions. So it points to the author. At the same time, the author's intentions get expressed in the text. Among these intentions are intentions to change the beliefs and attitudes and behavior of the readers. So the text at least tacitly invites us to reflect on how the author intends the readers to respond. If we start with the reader, we see that the reader is reflecting on a text, and faithful readers are trying to discern what the author wanted to tell them. Rightly understood, the foci on author, text, and readers form three perspectives, each of which includes the others. If we add these three foci to our outline of steps for interpretation, we obtain the following:

(1) The text as act of communication
   (a) Authorial intention
   (b) Textual expression
   (c) Readers' impression

We can insert these three elements into the overall outline. We obtain the following list (with the added lines starred):

A. Observation
B. Elucidation
   1. One passage
      a. The literary context
      b. The transmission context
         (1) God writes through a human author
            (a) Author: God
            (b) Text: autograph of 1–2 Samuel
            (c) Readers: Israelites
         (2) God providentially supervises the text's voyage, that is, the transmission in the middle period
            (a) Authors: scribes
            (b) Text: scribal copies
            (c) Readers: later scribes
         (3) God sees to it that I receive what he says
            (a) Author: ESV translation team
            (b) Text: ESV of 1 Samuel

        (c) Reader: me (and others)
   c. The text
     (1) The text as act of communication
       *(a) Authorial intention
       *(b) Textual expression
       *(c) Readers' impression
     (2) The social contexts
     (3) The historical contexts
  2. Topical correlation
  3. Redemptive-historical correlation
C. Application

Have we repeated ourselves? The triad of original author, text, and reader occurs at two points: B.1.b.(1), under the transmission context, and B.1.c.(1), under three views of the text. These two are perspectivally related. But we still find it convenient to make a distinction between the two occurrences. Under the topic of transmission we are thinking of the first stage among many stages that proceed through time to bring the text before our eyes. We are thinking about processes that take place in succession in time. By contrast, under the topic of the text itself, we are focusing on the three perspectives on textual meaning, as a stable whole.

The Presence of God in Communication

In chapter 2 we indicated that God participates in an original, archetypal communication. God the Father speaks his Word, who is God the Son. The Holy Spirit is like the breath of God. This original communication forms the ultimate foundation for the subordinate acts of communication in which God speaks to human beings. Every speech of God to human beings expresses God's intention. We can associate God's intention and his authorship particularly with the person of God the Father, who is the preeminent source for God's plan (see John 5:30). In particular, the authorial intentions in 1 Samuel 22:1–2 reside in God the Father.

God's intentions as author get expressed in a verbal text, which expresses his wisdom. The original Word is God the Son. Subordinate words express his wisdom. Since all wisdom resides preeminently in

Christ (Col. 2:3; 1 Cor. 1:30), we may associate God the Son especially with the meaning of textual expressions from God. First Samuel 22:1–2 as a textual whole expresses God's wisdom, which is found in God the Son.

The recipients of God's speech in the Bible are human beings. But God does not leave these human beings to their own resources. He sends the Holy Spirit to open their minds and interpret what they read:

> So also no one comprehends the thoughts of God except the Spirit of God. Now we have received not the spirit of the world, but the Spirit who is from God, that we might *understand* the things freely given us by God. (1 Cor. 2:11–12)

The Spirit who "searches everything, even the depths of God" (1 Cor. 2:10) functions as the divine "recipient" of God's word, standing with us to enable us to understand. Within this life our understanding remains incomplete and tainted by sin. God does not endorse every human interpretation—in fact, some interpretations are radically mistaken. Yet through the work of the Spirit we can have genuine understanding of what we need to know. And the understanding by the Holy Spirit himself is perfect. This principle of understanding applies to 1 Samuel 22:1–2. The Holy Spirit understands it perfectly, though we do not.

So we have three ways of approaching the meaning of 1 Samuel 22:1–2. The text represents (1) the Father's intention, (2) the Son's expression of wisdom, and (3) the Spirit's reception or interpretation. All three persons of the Trinity are God, and have comprehensive understanding. Their understanding is one, because there is only one God. But we can also see a differentiation, due to the distinction of persons. Each person of the Trinity understands as a distinct person. So we cannot reduce the meaning to author alone, or text alone, or reader alone. All three persons of the Trinity interact at the divine level of divine persons. Subordinately, we may conclude that author, text, and reader interact at the human level as well.[2]

---

[2] Note the difference between our approach and the many secular approaches to meaning, which attempt to reduce meaning to authorial intention, or to textual expression, or to reader impression (see appendices B and C).

Avoiding Interpretive Mistakes

In the normal course of affairs, people without formal training in hermeneutics almost automatically take into account all three aspects in communication: author, text, and reader. In many cases communication succeeds well enough for practical purposes. But it sometimes fails, either through carelessness or bias or loss of crucial information. Theories in hermeneutics can come in to urge us to take special care. But the theories themselves can contain their own biases.

For example, one kind of approach, after observing that no reader exactly duplicates an author's ideas, gives up on authors and locates meaning wholly in the readers. The difficulty here is that people can easily conclude that all readers have a right to their own interpretations. However, readers can have biases. For 1 Samuel 22:1–2, we can imagine a reader who thinks that because David was a righteous man, he would have collected around him only supporters who were as righteous as he. But that is unrealistic. We can imagine another reader who goes to the opposite extreme and pictures the situation with David's followers as little better than a gang of malcontents and good-for-nothings.

A second kind of approach may focus on the text but treat it in isolation from both author and readers. The text becomes a "literary artifact." But almost any text, when ripped out of context, can sponsor more than one meaning. For example, 1 Samuel 22:1–2, apart from author and literary context, could be seen as part of a manifesto for rebellion against authority, or an approved example that might be intended to exhort us to make friends with malcontents, or a disapproved example to warn us against associating with malcontents.

A third kind of approach tells us to focus on the author. But unless we further explain *how* we focus on the author, we open the door to someone who speculates about what was in the author's mind but did not get expressed in the text. So, for example, a Marxist analyst might postulate that the author writes as he does in 1 Samuel 22:1–2 because he is filled with Marxist discontent. He wants to show us that Israelite political powers have oppressed people and led them to join David. Or, conversely, a Marxist might see the author as one who supports the political status quo, and is writing about David's followers in order to discredit rebellion. He wants us to see that the type of people who rebel are disreputable. Focus on the author, when not further defined, can tempt us to "psychologize the author" and invent many things that we think would have gone on in his mind. But we are just speculating unless we discipline ourselves to follow the text, not what is behind the text.

The distinction between author, text, and reader also becomes important in the context of discussions of what *inspiration* means. Does God inspire authors, or texts, or readers? God does *illumine* readers by sending the Holy Spirit and opening their hearts and minds to receive what he says. But that does not make readers infallible. Some forms of neoorthodox thinking about inspiration make illumination the essence of inspiration: the Bible is "inspired" because from time to time God uses it to "inspire" readers with holy thoughts or to meet him in a personal encounter. According to this viewpoint, the Bible on the shelf is not really inspired, but becomes inspiring in the moment when God uses it with respect to one particular reader.

This view contains a grain of truth in what it affirms, namely that God does use the Bible to communicate to modern readers. But it is false in what it denies. Contrary to this neoorthodox viewpoint, the Bible is already breathed out by God and is therefore the inspired word of God (2 Tim. 3:16) before any particular human reader takes it up.

Liberal and modernist views of inspiration have sometimes located inspiration in the author and not in the text. They may say that God gave inspiring ideas to prophets and apostles, but left it to the unaided powers of these fallible men to write down the ideas in whatever words they found best. According to this view, 1 Samuel 22:1–2 as a text would represent only the expression of a human author. Only the ideas behind the text (which of course we cannot directly access) would actually be "inspired." Second Timothy 3:16 contradicts this view by indicating that the "Scripture" (Greek *graphe*), the written text, is breathed out by God. Likewise Jesus indicates that "not an iota, not a dot, will pass from the Law until all is accomplished" (Matt. 5:18), thereby referring to features of the written text. We rightly affirm that the Holy Spirit worked in a special way in the human authors (2 Pet. 1:21), but the text, not simply the author, has the Holy Spirit's authority.[3]

---

[3] For a full defense of the biblical doctrine of inspiration, see John M. Frame, *The Doctrine of the Word of God* (Phillipsburg, NJ: Presbyterian & Reformed, 2010). What we say here needs to be nuanced by the discussion about the primacy of the autograph.

Part IV

ISSUES WITH
AUTHORSHIP

10

Dual Authorship

Now let us turn to consider the question of authorship. Who is the author of 1 Samuel 22:1–2? First Samuel never identifies its human author. We assume that there was one—an author or "editor" who took human responsibility for the canonical text. In addition, God was the primary, divine author.

Questions about Authorship

If we have two authors, what is the relation between them? Second Peter 1:21 describes the relationship by indicating that the primary, divine author "carried along" the secondary, human author: "For no prophecy was ever produced by the will of man, but men spoke from God as they were *carried along* by the Holy Spirit."[1] This work of the Holy Spirit is mysterious—we know only a little about it. We can see from the different books in Scripture that inspiration from the Spirit could have different textures in the case of different individual human authors. The author of the book of Revelation received visions (Rev. 1:10–20; 22:8). The author of Luke and Acts conducted historical research (Luke 1:1–4). The apostle Paul saw a vision of Christ when he was first converted (Acts 9:3–8), and God gave him other special

---

[1] Second Peter 1:21 speaks about "prophecy," which in its broadest compass includes both oral prophecies (e.g., Elijah, Elisha, Amos's oral preaching) and written prophecies ("no prophecy of *Scripture* . . ."; 2 Pet. 1:20). The principle of God's speaking through human agents applies to both oral and written discourse. It is generalizable to the whole Old Testament—and indeed the New Testament as well.

experiences afterwards (Acts 26:16; 2 Cor. 12:1–7), but he apparently wrote his letters in a normal state of consciousness. In his letters he indicates that he is an apostle of Christ, and as such he has a commission to write with divine authority, as a person who has digested the meaning of Christ's work (1 Cor. 14:37; 1 Thess. 2:13).

We see the role of the human author most vividly in the case of Moses. The Lord originally spoke with an audible voice from the top of Mount Sinai. The people were terrified, and asked God to appoint Moses as intermediary (Ex. 20:18–21; Deut. 5:22–33). God was pleased to do this (Deut. 5:28–29).

The Relation of Two Intentions

If we have two authors, divine and human, do we also have two distinct intentions, divine and human? Do we have the intention of God side by side with the intention of Moses, or the intention of God alongside the intention of Paul? And if we have two intentions, what is the relation between them?

People have proposed more than one answer. Some people have maintained that one intention virtually swallows up the other. For instance, the divine intention could swallow up the human intention, so that neither the human author nor his intention make any difference. People with this view imply that we should listen to God's voice and ignore any human intermediary. But God, by appointing an intermediary, seems to imply that we *should* listen to the intermediary. The need for taking into account the intermediary becomes especially clear when the intermediary speaks of himself in the first person, as the apostle Paul does, and as Moses does in his speeches in Deuteronomy.

Other people have maintained that the human intention swallows up the divine intention. According to this view, God intends merely to communicate whatever the human intermediary intends. God purposely limits himself to the capacity of the human author or human speaker. This view might seem reasonable until we try to apply it. Then we may realize that it is virtually impossible to square this view with the fact that when God had 1–2 Samuel written long ago, he already had us in mind (Rom. 15:4). God is addressing us, whereas a human author is limited in his capacity to envision a many-generational audience. Even if he does envision multiple generations, he does not envision each of us modern readers in our individuality. God speaks to us personally, as one who knows us by name. If, by contrast, we limit the idea of intention to human intention, our recipe virtually removes the presence of God from his speech.

In addition, from time to time human spokesmen draw attention to the fact that they themselves are not speaking merely from the standpoint of their limited human capacity. For example, when the apostle Paul identifies himself as an apostle of Christ at the beginning of his letters, he implies that we should take into account his commission from Christ. Therefore, we should read what he says as coming from Christ and not merely from himself as a private individual with merely human opinions or merely human authority.[2] Similarly, the book of Isaiah begins,

> The vision of Isaiah the son of Amoz, which he *saw* concerning Judah and Jerusalem in the days of Uzziah, Jotham, Ahaz, and Hezekiah, kings of Judah. (Isa. 1:1)

The key word *saw* indicates that Isaiah had a divine source for his message. If we have any doubts about the source, the book of Isaiah further explains God's commissioning of the author in chapter 6.

Thus, both Isaiah and Paul point away from themselves as merely private, limited individuals, and point toward the Lord as the source both of their authority and of their messages. We can summarize by saying that they as human beings intend for us to receive their messages as the messages of the Lord. Their intention includes pointing away from their own finite intention to a divine intention. It is as if they said, "My message means what it means according to the intention of the Lord."

This pointing to divine intention becomes particularly clear in cases where an Old Testament prophet admits that he does not understand the full meaning of what he has seen or heard: Daniel 8:27; 12:8;

---

[2] This implication remains, of course, in those cases where Paul's letters mention another participant at the beginning: Sosthenes (1 Cor. 1:1); Timothy (2 Cor. 1:1; Phil. 1:1; Col. 1:1; Philem. 1); Silvanus and Timothy (1 Thess. 1:1; 2 Thess. 1:1); and "all the brothers who are with me" (Gal. 1:2). In Galatians 1:2, it may be that the participation of "all the brothers" means little more than that they join Paul in spirit in the opening greeting, "Grace to you and peace . . ." Or it may mean that they concur with the contents of the letter and are joining in prayer with Paul for its effectiveness (compare 2 Thess. 3:1). Or they may have supported the writing in a more active way. Whatever active or ancillary role these fellow servants played in the composition of the respective letters, the authentication by Paul implies the divine authority of the product. Paul takes responsibility for it. And if Paul does so as an apostle, he points to the authority of Jesus Christ, whose apostle he is.

Zechariah 4:4, 13–14; 6:4. A prophet can confidently pass on a description of what he has seen or heard, with the intention that it should mean to its recipients whatever the Lord means by it. Likewise, Luke could record and pass on parables of Jesus, with the intention of having those parables mean whatever Jesus intended them to mean. His intention is to express Jesus's intention, whatever Jesus's intention might have been. Luke could do such a thing without having fully comprehended every aspect of Jesus's intentions and meanings.

Consciousness of Inspiration

Were the human writers consciously aware of working under divine power? Did they know that their writings would be included in the canon of Scripture? Does it matter whether they did?

The directions that Moses gave in Deuteronomy 31 about depositing the law (vv. 24–26) and about periodic public reading (vv. 9–13) suggest that he understood the permanent function of what he wrote. John, the human author of Revelation, describes his book as "prophecy" (1:3; 22:7) and includes a warning about adding or subtracting words from it (22:18–19). His warning picks up the language of Deuteronomy 4:2 and 12:32, thereby indicating that it has the same divine authority as the Old Testament law. With many other books of the Bible, however, including the book of 1–2 Samuel, we have no direct record about what the human author thought about his own work.

I do not think it makes much difference. Yes, what we know about a human author's perception of his role may give us a slightly different understanding about the texture of what he says. But conscious awareness is not everything. Biblical teaching on inspiration indicates that the Holy Spirit was present, whether or not the author was fully *conscious* of it. As 2 Peter 1:21 says, "Men spoke from God as they were *carried along by the Holy Spirit.*" Human cooperation with the Holy Spirit implies that the human authors intended, at the deepest level, to cooperate, and so in their human actions they point at least indirectly to the meanings of the Holy Spirit.[3] They did not need self-consciously and

---

[3] I regard Caiaphas's prophecy in John 11:49–53 as an exception. Caiaphas was directly opposed to God's intention. God communicated his meaning in spite of Caiaphas. But in the case of Scripture the human intermediaries were "*holy* prophets" and "*holy* apostles and prophets" (Acts 3:21; Eph. 3:5). They had the spiritual desire to honor God (cf. 1 Pet. 1:10–11).

analytically to "work everything out" about their cooperation—in fact, they could not, because there is mystery to it. Thus it is unnecessary for us to work it out ourselves. We do not need to worry about how much they were conscious of.

Jesus as the Final Prophet

We may understand the use of human intermediaries more fully by reflecting on Jesus as the final intermediary, the "one mediator between God and men" (1 Tim. 2:5). Hebrews 1:1–2 indicates that Jesus is the final and climactic prophet:

> Long ago, at many times and in many ways, God spoke to our fathers by the *prophets*, but in these *last* days he has *spoken* to us by his *Son*, whom he appointed the heir of all things.

Jesus as the incarnate Son is God and man in one person. When he speaks, God speaks. So his speech offers the climactic instance of God's intention. At the same time, when Jesus speaks, he speaks also as a human being, the final prophet. He fulfills the pattern in which God speaks through a *human* intermediary. His speech offers the climactic instance of human speech and human intention. His divine intention represents intention according to his divine nature. His human intention represents intention according to his human nature. He has two natures, divine and human, and they remain distinct and unconfused. According to his divine nature, he speaks with omniscience. According to his human nature, he speaks in accordance with the finite knowledge of his human nature. We cannot reduce the one side to the other. We confront great mystery.

At the same time, he speaks as *one* person, the person of Christ, who existed with the Father from before the foundation of the world. His two natures are united in one person. Therefore we ought not to separate the two intentions, divine and human, just as we ought not to confuse the two.

Through Christ's atoning death and life-giving resurrection, he has triumphed over sin and death and accomplished reconciliation with God for those who believe in him. Because of sin, no human being can stand in God's presence apart from Christ's atoning mediation. The principle applies even to special prophetic figures like Moses, Isaiah (Isa. 6:5–7), and Paul (Acts 22:16). If so, Christ is present as mediator *whenever* God uses a human intermediary to speak to human beings. This conclusion agrees with what we observed earlier concerning covenantal speech. Christ as the heart of the covenant stands between God and us every time God speaks to us in Scripture. In addition, as we have indicated, Christ as God is the Word himself.

Perspectives on Authorship

We may therefore consider the issue of authorship from three perspectives, not merely two. The three perspectives are (1) God's authorship; (2) authorship through Christ the atoning mediator; (3) human authorship. Correspondingly, we have three foci for intentions: (1) God the Father's intention; (2) the intention of Christ as mediator, particularly now as he sits at the right hand of the Father, as God and man in one person; (3) intention from the human writer, moved by the intention of the Holy Spirit.

These three are *perspectives*, because each presupposes the others, each points to the others, and each includes the others. God's intention includes the fact that we should pay attention to his human agents and their intentions. Conversely, the human intention is to affirm the intention of the Holy Spirit. In addition, God intends that we should pay attention to the intention of Christ the mediator. Christ the mediator is God, and therefore points us to the divine intention. As man, Christ the mediator stands with the human writer, reconciling him to God, purging him from sin, and enabling him to function as one renewed in the image of Christ in his humanity.[4]

Integrating Authorship into the Process of Interpretation

If we wish, we can integrate attention to authorship into the entire process of interpretation, by distinguishing the three foci on authorship, as illustrated by the starred entries in the following list:

---

[4] For further reflections on dual authorship, see Vern S. Poythress, "Divine Meaning of Scripture," *Westminster Theological Journal* 48 (1986): 241–279; Poythress, "Dispensing with Merely Human Meaning: Gains and Losses from Focusing on the Human Author, Illustrated by Zephaniah 1:2–3," *Journal of the Evangelical Theological Society* 57/3 (2014): 481–499.

A. Observation
B. Elucidation
   1. One passage
     a. The literary context
     b. The transmission context
       (1) God writes through a human author
         (a) Author: God
         (b) Text: autograph of 1–2 Samuel
         (c) Readers: Israelites
       (2) God providentially supervises the text's voyage, that is, the transmission in the middle period
         (a) Authors: scribes
         (b) Text: scribal copies
         (c) Readers: later scribes
       (3) God sees to it that I receive what he says
         (a) Author: ESV translation team
         (b) Text: ESV of 1 Samuel
         (c) Reader: me (and others)
     c. The text
       (1) The text as act of communication
         (a) Authorial intention
           *((1)) Divine intention
           *((2)) Christ's mediatorial intention
           *((3)) Human intention
         (b) Textual expression
         (c) Readers' impression
       (2) The social contexts
       (3) The historical contexts
   2. Topical correlation
   3. Redemptive-historical correlation
C. Application

How readers interpret a text depends on who they think the author is and what they think are the author's intentions, given what they know about the author. Thus the distinction of authors leads in principle to a distinction between three kinds of reading: reading for divine intention, reading for mediatorial intention, and reading for human intention. But, as usual, rightly understood, these distinctions constitute three perspectives rather than three separated kinds of reading, as if they simply proceeded side by side without interacting with one another. The meaning of textual expression also depends on the source of the text, so the perspectival distinctions can apply to textual expression as well:

A. Observation
B. Elucidation
   1. One passage
      a. The literary context
      b. The transmission context
         (1) God writes through a human author
            (a) Author: God
            (b) Text: autograph of 1–2 Samuel
            (c) Readers: Israelites
         (2) God providentially supervises the text's voyage, that is, the transmission in the middle period
            (a) Authors: scribes
            (b) Text: scribal copies
            (c) Readers: later scribes
         (3) God sees to it that I receive what he says
            (a) Author: ESV translation team
            (b) Text: ESV of 1 Samuel
            (c) Reader: me (and others)
      c. The text
         (1) The text as act of communication
            (a) Authorial intention
               *((1)) Divine intention
               *((2)) Mediatorial intention
               *((3)) Human intention
            (b) Textual expression
               *((1)) Divine expression
               *((2)) Mediatorial expression
               *((3)) Human expression
            (c) Readers' impression
               *((1)) Impression from God
               *((2)) Impression from covenantal mediator
               *((3)) Impression from human source
         (2) The social contexts

        (3) The historical contexts
   2. Topical correlation
   3. Redemptive-historical correlation
C. Application

Since the incarnation of Christ presents us with deep mystery, we confront mystery in the issues with respect to authorship of Scripture, mystery that we will never penetrate fully. We should acknowledge that we are servants hearing God's word. We can never "master" God. Nor can we master his word, or masterfully control the nature of its authorship or authorial intentions. "Speak, LORD, for your servant hears" (1 Sam. 3:9).

11

Difficulties with Authorship

The approach that we have developed for dealing with divine and human authorship may seem obvious to some readers. We are saying that we should pay attention to both the divine author and the human author, and we should see their intentions as overlapping. In fact, they are perspectives on one another.

In the process, we acknowledge mystery about the relationship of the two authors. Many ordinary Christian readers of the Bible accept mystery. They do their reading well, even without explicitly and self-consciously reflecting on the issue of authorship. Guided by the Holy Spirit, they do the right thing almost instinctively. But people can make mistakes, and we need to look at some of them.

Strange Meanings

As an example, we can consider Philo of Alexandria, an ancient Jewish interpreter who ingeniously found Platonic and Stoic philosophy in the Old Testament. Philo concentrated on interpreting the books of Moses (Genesis–Deuteronomy), but we can illustrate how his method would apply to 1 Samuel 22:1–2 as well. Here is how a Philonic interpretation of our passage might go:

> "David departed from there and escaped to the cave of Adullam."
> "David" means "beloved" and stands for the soul of man as the part that we should most value. David's departure stands for the journey

of the soul. He departs from Achish, a Philistine king, who stands for the dominion of sin. David comes to the cave of Adullam, which is the place of God's refuge from the corruptions of the world. Adullam in Greek is Odollam, which allegorically means the way (*odos*) of light (*lampō*, to shine). He receives enlightenment of the soul through the light of God's truth.

"And when his brothers and all his father's house heard it, they went down there to him." His brothers and all his father's house stand for the affections. The wise man brings all his affections under the illumination of the truth in his soul.

"And everyone who was in distress, and everyone who was in debt, and everyone who was bitter in soul, gathered to him." David's followers stand for the disorders in human life. The disorders come under the dominion of the soul, which is now enlightened and brings order and relief to a person's life.

Philonic interpretation seems outlandish to many modern people. But an ancient interpreter could defend it by saying that God intended these meanings as spiritual meanings in addition to the literal meanings lying on the surface. This kind of appeal to God's meanings can produce strange results.

So does Philo's problem arise from concentrating on the divine author and ignoring the human author? It might seem so. But further reflection shows that such a focus on the divine author is not actually the real source of the troubles. Theoretically, an appeal to the *human* author could produce equally strange results. The human author of 1–2 Samuel is unknown to us. If Philo could postulate that the divine author meant to communicate Platonic philosophy, he is equally free to postulate that an unknown human author meant to communicate such philosophy. Why not?

Though a person like Philo could attribute Platonic meanings to a *human* author, he would probably be less likely to do so. The attribution is more tempting in the case of a divine author, precisely because the divine author's writings are authoritative. If Philo's interpretation persuades people, the divine author seems to give authority to Platonic ideas that are actually Philo's. As a result, Philo's own ideas become authoritative, which obviously has an attraction for sinful pride. At the same time—and this may be the more important motive for Philo—his interpretation raises the status of a biblical writing in the eyes of those who already admire Platonic philosophy. It allegedly shows the compatibility of Scripture and the God of Scripture with the best of the Greek world. It builds an apologetic bridge.

Still, the same Philonic motives could in theory arise in dealing with a merely human author. The hidden intentions of a human author are really not any more accessible hermeneutically than the intentions of a divine author.

Divine Use of the Human

Suppose a person concentrates on divine authorship. What did God intend? God intended to speak *through* a human author. So, rightly understood, a focus on divine authorship includes reckoning with a human author. But some people are tempted to ignore this aspect of divine authorship. They read in strange meanings, meanings almost unrelated to the original literary, social, and historical contexts. These meanings, they may think, are more worthy of God, and more "spiritual." What they fail to realize is that the human heart, which is "deceitful above all things" (Jer. 17:9), can covertly project its own desires onto God, trying to make God into a mouthpiece for what it already desires or already thinks it knows. Such an approach may feel "spiritual," but it is actually rebellious beneath the surface.

Philo swallowed a lot of Platonic and Stoic philosophy. He saw their philosophic themes as worthy subjects for God to address, while the sweatiness and bodily discomforts of literally living in a cave were not worthy of much attention.

The ancient church struggled with Platonism and Stoicism and asceticism. These influences tempted readers to see in the Bible reflections of themes from Platonism or Stoicism or asceticism that they already thought they knew to be true.

Many modern cults claim to honor Scripture but read into it the favorite teachings of the cult leader. The cult leader has allegedly discerned what God really means to say in Scripture, and historical interpretations of the church through the ages have got it wrong.

In the time of the Reformation, many Roman Catholics understood the meaning of Christianity through the eyes of tradition. In the West the Bible was available to only a few, and only in Latin (until Erasmus published the Greek New Testament and others undertook to translate the Bible into the vernacular). Roman Catholicism tended to make the official pronouncements of the church, together with a diffuse sense of "tradition," into the voice of God. Then, even when Scripture became more accessible for reading, people could try to make the divine voice say whatever they already supposedly "knew" was the official church doctrine.

We may see similar difficulties during the time of Jesus's life on earth. Jesus rebuked the religious leaders because they mistreated the word of God for the sake of their traditions (Matt. 15:1–9). He said to the Sadducees, "You are wrong, because you know neither the Scriptures nor the power of God" (Matt. 22:29). The Sadducees did not fail because they were untaught or had never read the Old Testament. They were religious experts. They nevertheless failed to understand God.

So what do we conclude? Should we give way to postmodern skepticism about finding any stable meaning? No. Jesus's rebuke to the Sadducees implies that they were *guilty* for not knowing the Scripture. He thus implies that God has spoken clearly and made himself accessible through Scripture. A person can come to know the Scripture and know God. Why? God has made provision for us in Scripture, and climactically in Christ himself. But we have to submit ourselves to God's way, and listen humbly to what he says in Scripture, rather than imposing on Scripture ideas that come from our own hearts.

Remedy in Man or in God?

Modern scholars frequently think that we can avoid these difficulties by paying attention to the human author. But the history of post-Enlightenment interpretation shows that scholars can attribute multiple outlandish views to the *human* authors of Scripture and their sources. The basic problem is the human problem of sin. We have deceitful hearts. People inject into the Bible the meanings that they want to hear. They thereby show their pride. In effect, they are telling God what he ought to say, rather than humbly seeking him.

How will we ever root out pride unless we come to God himself, through Christ, to receive spiritual healing? The remedy is not the human author! It is communion with God. The typical advice from many modern scholars goes in exactly the opposite direction from what it needs to be. They are saying, go to the human author. God in Scripture says to go to God, through Christ who is "the way, and the truth, and the life" (John 14:6).

We should also acknowledge the importance of the *clarity* of Scripture. God indicates that the Bible is designed to teach the "simple," not merely those whose learning or advanced sanctification already qualifies them: "the testimony of the LORD is sure, making wise the *simple*" (Ps. 19:7; compare Prov. 1:4). Many proud interpreters are not satisfied with what ordinary people can receive from the Bible. They want an extra, secret meaning. The ancient Platonist can show how he can get Platonic philosophy out of the Bible by finding an alleged extra layer of "spiritual" meaning. The modern cult leader will give his followers meanings that everyone else has missed. The modern scholar may find sources behind the Bible with messages not directly revealed in the surviving text.

The Bible's teaching about its clarity is itself both clear and subtle. The most important teachings are accessible to all. But not everything is equally easy. The Bible contains difficulties: "There are some things in them [the letters of the apostle Paul] that are *hard to understand*, which the ignorant and unstable twist to their own destruction, as they do the other Scriptures" (2 Pet. 3:16). The Westminster Confession of Faith presents a balanced summary:

> All things in Scripture are not alike plain in themselves, nor alike clear unto all; yet those things which are necessary to be known, believed, and observed for salvation, are so clearly propounded, and opened in some place of Scripture or other, that not only the learned, but the unlearned, in a due use of the ordinary means, may attain unto a sufficient understanding of them. (1.7)

Focusing on the Human Author

Can we completely exclude fanciful interpretations by focusing on the human author? Actually, no. If human authors are writing *without* the superintendence of a primary divine author, they are in some measure unstable and unreliable. Some hermeneutical theorists have postulated that a human author completely controls his meanings. And there is some truth here: we are responsible for what we say. But the ideal of complete control is a simplification. Authors who are merely human may have lapses. They may fall into depression. They may in a moment of anger write things that they later regret. They may sometimes be of a double mind.[1]

The difficulties mount because we as readers have imperfect knowledge of a human author. He may be basically good and generally reliable, but is it possible that one particular written product produced on one particular day was an exception? How do we know for sure?

We can illustrate how interpretations multiply by using our usual example of 1 Samuel 22:1–2. In this case, we know nothing about the human author except what we can infer from the text and from the rest of 1–2 Samuel (and 1–2 Kings, if we think that these come from the same author). If we ignore the reality of divine inspiration, none of these texts, nor all of them taken together, will tell us definitively whether the author is historically reliable. Did he embellish 1 Samuel 22:1–2, or invent the whole story from scratch, in order to suggest that David was an attractive figure who easily drew followers? On the other hand, if we turn to God as the divine author, we can confidently draw the conclusion that what we have is historically reliable, because God is reliable in a way that human authors often are not.

The problems with focusing merely on a human author do not end with the issue of historical reliability. Even if the report is historically reliable, we can raise all kinds of questions about its implications. Does the author intend to make a political statement that would support or undermine the Davidic monarchy? Does he intend his mention of the various discontented people in verse 2 to suggest that *all* earthly kingdoms are going to have an underbelly of sad human suffering? Or does he intend to suggest that Saul's work as king fell short? It is easy to read this or that intention into the text, depending on how we picture the details about the human author.

---

[1] In fact, every human being who struggles with sin has some double-mindedness. His indwelling sins incline him to one meaning, while indwelling grace, either common grace or special grace, inclines him to other meanings. And the two aspects may combine in one text. See Vern S. Poythress, *In the Beginning Was the Word: Language—A God-Centered Approach* (Wheaton, IL: Crossway, 2009), chapter 20.

We can also raise some of the questions that came up earlier about deeper implications of meaning. Do the physical forms of distress in verse 2 open the door to deeper and broader reflections about suffering in general and the unsatisfactory character of life in a fallen world? Does David's escape have implications for how we understand God's providence, his providential care for David, and his broader plan for David's descendants, including the coming Messiah? How many of these implications does the human author intend? Can we tell? Taken together, the books 1–2 Samuel and 1–2 Kings include as a theme that God left a "lamp" for David (1 Kings 11:36; 2 Kings 8:19). Just what does this theme imply, in the mind of the human author? Maybe he had thought about it a lot, and the texts that we have represent the tip of a deep iceberg. Or maybe not. We cannot plumb human intention to the bottom. "The inward mind and heart of a man are deep" (Ps. 64:6). "For who knows a person's thoughts except the spirit of that person, which is in him?" (1 Cor. 2:11).

We have already mentioned the danger of psychologizing an author, if we try to construct speculatively everything that is going on in his mind as he writes. So shall we focus on the text instead of the author? But do we read the text only on the surface, for a kind of minimal meaning? Or do we read it for its more subtle implications? And if so, how do we know which possible implications we should follow, except by reconstructing an author's thoughts?

I do not think that we as human beings can achieve definitive mastery of what a human author is doing, let alone a divine author. But, paradoxically, we are in a better position for understanding the divine author, because we can know a lot about him. In a case like 1–2 Samuel, we know almost nothing about the human author, but because we have the whole canon of Scripture, we can know a lot about the divine author. We can confidently infer that God was concerned not only to tell us about David but also to enable us to see his care through the ages, leading from David to Jesus as David's greatest descendant. God knows the end from the beginning, so God already had his plan in mind during the days of David, and during the days when 1–2 Samuel was written. He invites readers both then and now to read what he says in the light of the fact that it fits into a larger plan.

So even when 1–2 Samuel was first written, it would be legitimate for readers to understand 1 Samuel 22:1–2 in the light of God's promises to David and his descendants (2 Sam. 7:8–16). Early readers would not be able to infer all the details that we now know on the basis of the New Testament. But they could understand that God had more that he was going to do and say, building on what he had done during the life of David. Thus it is appropriate even for an early reader to see 1 Samuel 22:1–2 as having pertinence for the future development of kingship. More ultimately, it has pertinence for the saving reign of God, which he would exercise in a definitive way in the future through David's descendant (Ezek. 34:20–24). Readers could be confident about these things because they could know about the purposes of God. They need not speculate about how far these things were visible or consciously in the mind of the human author of 1–2 Samuel.

Advantages of Focusing on the Divine Author

In sum, if an interpreter determines to concentrate wholly on a human author, and ignore the divine author, he plunges into uncertainties and speculation, because he knows too little about the human author. And if we ignore the fact that God guided the human authors of Scripture, we have no guarantee that the human authors were stable in their conceptions and their writing. By contrast, if an interpreter keeps in mind the divine author, he receives many answers as he grows spiritually, and he grows in confidence in understanding God's meanings.

In addition to these more ordinary advantages, we may mention again what is crucial. We must love God with all our mind. We must serve and worship him. He is present and comes to us when we read Scripture. To try to forget or suppress his presence is to twist the purpose of Scripture, to express ingratitude, and to turn away from life to death. How can we expect to understand Scripture if, at the beginning, we insist on treating Scripture as something that it is not, namely a merely human document from a merely human author?

It is regrettable and dangerous that we live in a time and at a cultural moment when most of Western scholarly study of the Bible follows the route of virtually exclusive focus on human authors. The mainstream of biblical scholarship does not believe in divine authorship at all. Many scholars outside of the mainstream still believe in divine authorship somewhere in the back of their minds, but they may nevertheless partly lay aside what they believe for the sake of a method that takes human authorship in isolation. They may say to themselves that they will come to consider divine authorship eventually. Perhaps, after analyzing what they regard as "the human meaning," they will come to the topic of application. They will then consider what God wants them to do with this human meaning that they have in hand.

But they cannot practice faithfulness to God by building faithful application on top of unfaithful acts in all their previous work. No. We must be living in the presence of God from the beginning, and engage the Bible as his word from the beginning, or we will never have him rightly at the conclusion.[2]

Affirming Context

A focus on divine authorship has sometimes led people to neglect social, historical, and literary contexts. People regard the Bible as if it were a book dropped from heaven in one piece, with no relation to Israel in the time of David, or to the hardness of heart in Isaiah's time. But we have already in previous chapters emphasized ways in which God acts in contexts. His speech and his deeds take these contexts into account. To begin with, he governs all contexts, whether social, historical, literary, or linguistic. They are not alien to him, and they are not a straitjacket that hems him in or prevents him from speaking the way he otherwise would speak. He speaks just as he pleases. In speaking to Israel, God takes into account the social context in which he himself has placed them. He speaks in Hebrew as a language that he himself has given as a gift to human beings. He speaks through a human author whom he himself has raised up.

All these uses of contexts have as their more fundamental background the final, archetypal context in God himself. Before there ever was a world with which God would interact, it was always true that the Father loves the Son in the context of the Holy Spirit as the expression of his love (John 3:34–35). God the Father sends forth his Spirit like

---

[2] See also appendix A, on redeeming scholarly interpretation.

a breath in the context of God the Son, the Word. The persons of the Trinity act with respect to contexts, and their actions take into account the context offered by the other persons.

So, once God has created a world with human beings in it, it makes sense that he should interact with them within contexts that he uses and takes into account. The use of context does not limit God, because he ordained all the contexts. And the most ultimate context is himself, in his Trinitarian nature.

How does context work with 1 Samuel 22:1–2? First Samuel 22:1–2 has contexts—literary, social, historical, and linguistic—which God takes into account. He expects us as recipients to understand that he is communicating one text, namely 22:1–2, in a manner that interacts with the contexts. The interaction takes place in accord with how he has ordained literary communication, society, history, and language to work. God is present in every cranny of the world that he has created, and his presence there harmonizes with his special presence as he speaks to us in 1 Samuel 22:1–2.

Part V

ISSUES WITH
LANGUAGE

12

Basic Linguistic Structures

We have looked at social and historical contexts for a passage of Scripture. We have looked at the context of authors—the divine author and the human author. We now focus on the text itself. But we should keep in mind that the text goes together with author and reader in a seamless communication. The text expresses the intention of the author(s) and includes the purpose of impressing itself upon readers.

Language

Texts make sense because they use elements of language. And these elements make sense against the background of previous knowledge of language on the part of authors and readers. First Samuel 22:1–2 now exists for us in translation—English translations in particular. In autographic form it was written in Hebrew. To understand the particulars of the Hebrew text, we have to use knowledge of Hebrew. We use knowledge both of individual words that appear in 1 Samuel 22:1–2, and knowledge of structures—how words fit into clauses and sentences and paragraphs and discourses, and how words and clauses and so on serve to communicate from one person to another.

When we are operating using our mother tongue, we usually do not think about the role of language, but it is there. God gave human beings the gift of language. How we interpret depends on assumptions about language, even when we do not consciously make those assumptions explicit.

We can admire the intricacies of language, and praise God for his wise provision for us, even if we are just using our native language. But it becomes more important to appreciate how language works when we are dealing with a second language that we know imperfectly. Readers who just want to read the Bible in English may, if they wish, ignore this chapter and subsequent chapters dealing with language. They are depending on God's provisions for language when they read in English, but they usually do not need to worry about it. On the other hand, readers who want to study the Bible in its original languages—Hebrew, Aramaic, and Greek—have a greater need to understand explicitly how languages work, in order wisely to assess issues about languages that they understand imperfectly.

A full discussion of language and its use would require a lot of space and would take us away from our focus on interpreting a particular text like 1 Samuel 22:1–2. We must direct readers elsewhere for such a discussion.[1] But we must keep in mind the presence of God as we think about language. As usual, we are not "off duty" as disciples of Christ when we study language. God is present in a special sense with the text of the Bible, because it is his word. But in a broader sense he is present everywhere in the universe (Jer. 23:24). He is present in particular in every bit of ordinary language, because it is his gift. The gift reflects the divine Giver, because the archetype or original form of language is in God himself, in the Word who is God (John 1:1). All reflection on language and all use of language can become an occasion for praising him. Language is not a religiously neutral "tool" that we use, a tool from which we excise the mysteries of divine presence.

The issue is important because bad assumptions about language corrupt the practice of interpretation. And bad assumptions have indeed come into secular thinking about language. Secular thinking wants to eliminate the presence of God, both for the sake of alleged "objectivity"

---

[1] Vern S. Poythress, *In the Beginning Was the Word: Language—A God-Centered Approach* (Wheaton, IL: Crossway, 2009); Poythress, "A Framework for Discourse Analysis: The Components of a Discourse, from a Tagmemic Viewpoint," *Semiotica* 38-3/4 (1982): 277–298, http://www.frame-poythress.org/wp-content/uploads/2012/08/semi.1982.38.3-4.277.pdf, DOI: 10.1515/semi.1982.38.3-4.277, accessed December 29, 2012; Poythress, "Hierarchy in Discourse Analysis: A Revision of Tagmemics," *Semiotica* 40-1/2 (1982): 107–137, http://www.frame-poythress.org/wp-content/uploads/2012/08/semi.1982.40.1-2.107.pdf, DOI: 10.1515/semi.1982.40.1-2.107, accessed December 29, 2012. ("Tagmemics" is a linguistic approach with distinctively Christian and Trinitarian roots. It emphasizes the role of human participants and the rich, multidimensional character of language, in contrast to reductionistic approaches that hope to explain language with some minimal system.)

and for the sake of the rigor of "scientific" analysis. But it is hardly "objective" or "scientific" to misconstrue in a foundational way the nature of what you are studying, by suppressing the reality of its roots in God.

We want to work free from corruptions in the history of experts' views of language. And that is not easy, because the corruptions extend a long way back. I propose to help the process by using perspectives on language. The use of perspectives can remind us of the roots of perspectives in God who is Trinitarian. And they can caution us to avoid a false sense of godlike mastery of language, because a perspective is, after all, a perspective. We know truth, but we do not know it exhaustively.

Unit, Hierarchy, and Context

We may begin by using a triad of perspectives that we have already introduced: particle, wave, and field. Language has "particles" in the form of stable units, such as letters (for written language), words, and clauses. The words *David, departed, from,* and *there* are all stable units in English. The entire clause, *David departed from there,* is also a stable unit. The Hebrew text of 1 Samuel 22:1–2 shows different units, characteristic of Hebrew rather than English, but there are still units, both words and clauses. We tacitly rely on the stability of these units whenever we interpret, either in Hebrew or in English. The stability comes from God, who has established and sustains all the regularities of all natural languages. (He also superintends the changes in languages over time.) God's stability, his faithfulness, is displayed in language, and should stimulate our gratitude.

Second, language has "waves" in the form of the dynamic movement of communication. In reading, we move along from the word *David* to the word *departed* and the word *from* and so on. Oral communication shows the movement even more obviously, because oral communication unfolds gradually in time. It is a process. Writing is a process, and reading and more complex forms of interpretation of written texts are processes. The processes have smoothness to them, but they also include structure, namely the structure of *hierarchy*. Letters make up words; words make up clauses; clauses make up sentences; sentences make up paragraphs; paragraphs make up whole discourses, like the book of 1–2 Samuel as a larger discourse. Discourses can make up a series of volumes, as when we consider 1–2 Samuel and 1–2 Kings as successive volumes comprising a larger work.

It should go without saying that we depend on God for the coherence of processes. God is Lord of history with its movements in time. He is Lord over the movements in language as well. The inclusion of words in clauses and larger units is ordained by God as part of his plan for each language of the world. It is important that we acknowledge his presence here, because twentieth-century secular thinking about language sometimes argues that language is like a prison from which we cannot escape. Supposedly, because we are trapped in the prison, we cannot see the world as it really is. If we grant that assumption, language is also a prison from which even God cannot escape when he chooses to use it. This kind of assumption undermines confidence in Scripture and in God's ability to inspire a text that we can trust. God says what he wants to say, not what he is "constrained" to say by the alleged "prison" of language.

Finally, we consider the field perspective, which concentrates on relationships. The pieces of language have significance in *relation* to one another. All the words of English belong to *English*. For example, the word *departed* is the past tense of the English verb *depart*. We can identify it as "past tense" because of the suffix, -*ed*. Those who know English know that the suffix -*ed* is a regular marker of past tense in English; its use with the verb *depart* has a relation to its use with many other verbs. Its use also has a relation to the fact that verbs can appear in other tenses besides the past tense.

In the same verse we meet the word *went*, which is the past tense of the verb *go*. The verb *go* is an exception to the general pattern for past tense, according to which we form a past tense by adding the suffix -*ed*. We can still recognize that the verbal form *went* is in the past tense, and that it functions in a manner analogous to all the past-tense verbs formed by adding -*ed*. Likewise, a single word like *who* has a meaning in relation to English as a system of language. The same sound sequence, now spelled *hu'* in a transliteration of Hebrew, has a different meaning in Hebrew: it means *he* (third person masculine singular personal pronoun). We depend on systematic relationships in the use of tenses and systematic relationships in the use of pronouns whenever we use language. We are depending on God, who has established and who sustains these relationships.

Interlocking Perspectives

As usual, the three perspectives (focusing on units, hierarchy, and contextual relations) interlock, rather than being independent of one another. Units can be identified only when they exist in contrastive relationships to other units (that is, when they are clearly distinguishable from other units; see chapter 14). For example, the word *went* is a unit in relation to other verbs in English. We learn units by hearing and seeing them in the context of communication, where they appear in hierarchies. To say that the unit *went* is a verb is to imply that it can appear in specific roles in clauses, which are larger units in a hierarchy. Thus the understanding of a unit presupposes some understanding of hierarchy.

Conversely, hierarchies presuppose units, because they are composed of units. And they presuppose relationships. For example, all transitive clauses (with subject, verb, and object) have a common structure in relationship to one another. Relationships in language are relationships among units and relationships within the context of hierarchies. Thus they presuppose units and hierarchies.

This interdependence frustrates people who desire a kind of "scientific" mastery of language. Experiments in physics or chemistry may physically isolate a system in order to focus on one particular phenomenon and avoid interference from the environment. But language innately involves complex, multidimensional, interlocking pieces and structures and relationships. We cannot really "isolate" any piece, though we can focus on it and may pretend for the sake of simplification that it could be isolated.

First Samuel 22:1–2 represents a complex structure, with units, hierarchies, and systematic relationships. When we study it, we deal not only with the words and clauses that are immediately present in the text, but also with the web of relationships to the Hebrew or English language. The web of relationships offers the context in which the units and hierarchies have meaning. This web exists even when we are only using it tacitly, without thinking about what we are using. But in times of reflection, such as what we are doing now, we may focus explicitly on the web of relationships. Even then, we cannot simultaneously focus on everything. We are not God.

If we are native speakers of English and we are studying a text in English, we usually take for granted all of our accumulated knowledge of English. Because the Bible was originally written in Hebrew, Aramaic, and Greek, we can gain extra insight by looking at its texts in the original languages. But we are not native speakers, and so we find ourselves learning painfully some of the different ways in which different languages function. And because of our imperfect knowledge, we keep having to look things up for more information about the language we are studying. In such a situation, we run the danger of underestimating the full complexity of language and the full extent of its various forms of interlocking. When we are using our native language, we run an analogous danger of not appreciating the complexity, because we take it for granted.

Whether we study with our native language or another language, we never achieve "scientific mastery," in the sense of being able to master bits that we can cleanly isolate. We must trust. We should be trusting God: (1) that he has crafted language, including the specifics of Hebrew and English; (2) that we can understand truly without understanding exhaustively; and (3) that we can know something without knowing everything. God sustains a world and the systems of languages in the context of his exhaustive knowledge. He guarantees that the structures and relationships and meanings in the periphery, where we are not focusing, support our understanding of that on which we do focus. But we are fallible; we can go astray. We go astray most when we do not trust him!

Developing an Outline

We can add three distinct foci, foci on units, hierarchies, and systemic linguistic contexts, to our previous outline of interpretation.

A. Observation
B. Elucidation
   1. One passage

    a. The literary context
    b. The transmission context
    c. The text
       (1) The text as act of communication
          (a) Authorial intention
          (b) Textual expression
            *((1)) Units
            *((2)) Hierarchies
            *((3)) Systemic linguistic contexts
          (c) Readers' impression
       (2) The social contexts
       (3) The historical contexts
  2. Topical correlation
  3. Redemptive-historical correlation
C. Application

13

Understanding Linguistic Subsystems

Within the topic of linguistic contexts we can explore three subcontexts or subsystems that operate in every language. We are going to look at these subcontexts because appreciating their interlocking roles helps us to understand analytically how people go about finding meanings in text, particularly texts in other languages.

Types of Resources

Every language offers to language users three elements: (1) resources for talking about the world, including imaginary or hypothetical worlds, and resources for talking about oneself and one's attitudes as well; (2) resources for sending communication through a physically based channel or medium; and (3) internal resources for indicating the structural relations between language pieces or units belonging to communication.

The Referential Subsystem

We could illustrate using Hebrew or Aramaic or Greek from the Bible, but for the sake of simplicity and clarity we will use examples from English. Consider the word *departed* in 1 Samuel 22:1. The word *depart* in an English dictionary has built into it a meaning of physical movement (though it can also be used in metaphorical ways in which there is no physical movement). This meaning offers a resource that enables the writer of 1 Samuel 22:1 to use the word *departed* to refer to a particular instance of physical movement in the world, when David left Gath.

The totality of these resources within English make up what we might call a subsystem of meanings, or a *semological subsystem* or a *referential subsystem*. We call it a *subsystem*, rather than just a miscellaneous collection, because the resources have to provide a systematic range of resources for all kinds of things that we might want to say. The verb *departed*, when used to refer to movements in past time, has links with an analogous word *depart*, used to refer to movements in the present time or a general pattern of customary movement at various times. The word *departed* also has relationships to other verbs of motion, such as *left, exited, went, ran, walked, traveled, rode,* and so on. The word *departed* also has relationships to nouns such as *departure, exit, journey, egress,* and *passage.* (Semanticists have labeled a collection of words of related meaning a *semantic domain* or *semantic field.*)

The Graphological and Phonological Subsystems

Second, each language has to have resources for using a physically based medium of communication. In the case of sign language, the medium may be hand gestures and sight. But ordinary human languages all use the medium of sound, as produced by the vocal apparatus and interpreted through the ear. Some languages in addition have a writing system, involving the medium of recorded physical marks and sight. The written word *departed* illustrates the use of the writing system. The word *departed* is composed of eight letters in a fixed order, *d + e + p + a + r + t + e + d*. If we focus on oral communication, the word *departed* consists in a sequence of sounds, called *phonemes*: *d + ə + p + ä + r + t + ə + d* (where the symbol *ə* stands for a very short, neutral vowel).[1]

The totality of resources for written communication in a language forms the *graphological subsystem*; the totality of resources for oral communication forms the *phonological subsystem*. Both of these subsystems are not mere miscellaneous collections, but provide *sys-*

---

[1] In my dialect of English, the same word *departed* can also be pronounced with a longer vowel in the first syllable: *dēpärtəd.*

tematic resources. The graphological subsystem, for example, must provide written symbols that can be easily written and reproduced and distinguished from one another; and it must have enough distinct symbols so that readers can reliably distinguish different words from each other.[2]

The Grammatical Subsystem

Third, language has resources for expressing complex ideas by putting together pieces in specified ways. The resources indicate structure. What we have in mind is usually called *grammar*. Every language has *grammar* that indicates in regular ways how pieces fit together and modify each other.

The word *departed* can illustrate grammar. The word *departed* is composed of two pieces, the root *depart* and the suffix *-ed*. The suffix indicates past tense. In English, this suffix functions as the regular way for indicating the past tense of a verb, but there are exceptional cases like the past tense *went* of the verb *go*. The suffix *-ed* and its variants (like *came* as past tense for *come*) provide regular resources for indicating a structure that attaches the meaning "past time" to a specific verb in a specific clause and sentence.

Or consider a sentence like "The boy fed the dog." It shows a word order in which the subject *the boy* comes first, then the predicate *fed*, then the object *the dog*. In English, the regular word order of subject, predicate, object is a grammatical structure that helps to indicate what is the subject and what is the object corresponding to a particular predicate (where the "predicate" designates the role usually played by a verb or verb phrase). This word order constitutes a grammatical regularity of a grammatical structure. Grammar provides *systematic* resources for talking about past, present, and future times, and for identifying subjects and objects in relation to predicates. Accordingly, grammar is properly described as a *subsystem*—the *grammatical subsystem*.

---

[2] Many languages, including English, contain instances of *homonyms*, distinct words that sound alike (*sight* and *site* and *cite*), and *homographs*, distinct words that are spelled alike (present tense and past tense of the verb *read*). These phenomena are exceptions. Homonyms and homographs can usually be distinguished using the context of their occurrence. But if there were too many potential ambiguities of this kind, communication would become problematic.

Interlocking

Note that we have used the word *departed* to illustrate all three sub-systems—the referential subsystem, the graphological subsystem, and the grammatical subsystem (or four subsystems, if we include the pho-nological subsystem as an alternative to the graphological subsystem). Not only the word *departed* but every word in English, and every clause and sentence as well, belongs to *all three* subsystems, not just one. The joint working of the subsystems and their interlocking is essential for the fruitful functioning of language. When people communicate, they are simultaneously saying things about the world (invoking the referential subsystem), using a medium (invoking the graphological or phonological subsystem), and using structured organization to indicate relationships (invoking the grammatical subsystem). How can they say anything without a medium or without organization? And how can there be grammatical organization without something based on a me-dium that can be organized? And why bother organizing it or using a medium unless one wants to say something?

In a sense, what we have called *subsystems* are artificial, simplify-ing abstractions that invite us to focus temporarily on one aspect of the whole, namely the whole of language. The aspects exist only in relation to the whole. Yet it is still true that we use the different as-pects, and that we can partially distinguish the subsystems from each other. In the referential subsystem, the word *departed* enjoys relations to other words with related meanings. In the graphological subsystem, the word *departed* enjoys relations to the alphabet and to spellings. In the grammatical subsystem, the word *departed* enjoys relations to grammatical constructions that involve many verbs and many clause types that show common patterns. We have here three distinct types of relationships. But the relationships exist only because there are units like the word *departed* and people communicating in English, and these words and communications invoke all three subsystems simultaneously.

The three subsystems are partially distinguishable, but not really separable. We can imagine a graphological sequence with no discernible grammar or reference: glab sed flombly. We can imagine English gram-mar without much discernible reference: "'Twas brillig, and the slithy toves did gyre and gimble in the wabe."[3] But such things are artificial.[4] Referential meaning, phonology or graphology, and grammar normally function together, simultaneously. Since they cannot be isolated, they are not strictly "masterable."

Roots in the Trinity

Why these three subsystems? We could answer on a simple, practical level by observing that communication requires a subject matter, a medium, and an internal structure. But we can also see deeper roots. All of reality bears the impress of being structured by God's word, which is multifaceted. In particular, the perspectival triad of particle, wave, and field is pertinent. Suppose that we apply those three perspectives to language as a system of resources. We can see that the particle perspective naturally focuses on the stable content of communication, which has correlations with the referential subsystem. The wave perspective focuses naturally on communication as a process, which leads to attention to the medium that structures the process. The nature of the oral medium means that communication is spread out in time, while the nature of the written medium means that communication is spread out in space (on the page). Thus the wave perspective correlates with the phonological or graphological subsystem. Finally, if we use the field perspective, we focus on relationships. The grammatical subsystem is innately relational, in that it provides structure that organizes the pieces.

We know that man is made in the image of God. Man speaks because first of all God speaks, as the archetypal speaker. Using this analogy, we may see how the three subsystems have a more direct foundation in God's Trinitarian nature. In God's archetypal speech, the Father is the source of the content; the Son as the Word represents articulate expression of the content. The Holy Spirit is like the breath of God. In this respect, the Holy Spirit as the breath of God offers the archetype for human ectypal use of breath, or alternative media such as

---

[3] Lewis Carroll, "Jabberwocky," in *Through the Looking Glass, and What Alice Found There* (many editions; Mineola, NY: Dover, 1999). Even in this example there are some hints of referential meaning. In the construction "'Twas brillig," we can guess that *brillig* is some kind of weather or atmospheric condition. The nonsense word *slithy* suggests associations with slimy, slithery, slippery. The word *gyre* is a real word in English, meaning to "move in a circle or spiral" (*Merriam-Webster's Collegiate Dictionary*, 11th ed. [Springfield, MA: Merriam-Webster, 2007]).

[4] Moreover, even such artificialities depend for their appreciation on our regular background experience of multiple instances of meaningful pieces of language, in this case the English language.

writing. The Holy Spirit is the divine foundation for the phonological and graphological subsystems. The Father as the source of content is the foundation for the referential subsystem, which provides resources for content. The Son as the articulate Word offers the divine foundation for the articulations in grammatical subsystems.

The foundations for the three subsystems in the Trinity testify to the revelatory presence of God in all language, which is not only his gift but a gift structured according to the nature of the Giver. The Trinitarian origin confirms the fact that the three subsystems interlock and that they cannot be isolated or mastered by human beings.

Differences between Languages

People who learn a second language know that languages differ in striking ways. They have differing phonological subsystems, grammatical subsystems, and referential subsystems (vocabularies differ). Hebrew differs from Greek, and Greek from English. Hebrew differs from Aramaic as well, although there are tantalizing analogies between Hebrew and Aramaic because they belong to a common larger language grouping, the Semitic languages.

How do we travel between languages? By translation. We are all made in the image of God, and our common likeness to God makes it possible to translate between languages. On the day of Pentecost in Acts 2, the apostles communicated the gospel in many languages, by means of a miracle of speaking in tongues. The miracle signifies that the good news about Christ is going to go out "to the end of the earth," including all the peoples in all the languages of the earth (Acts 1:8; Rev. 7:9). Subsequently, the gospel goes out primarily in the Greek language, which was the common language of the Roman Empire. But the picture in Acts implies that translation will be part of the total process, and indeed translation of the Bible and its message is still going on to this day, to bring the gospel to every tribe and every language group.

In this book we cannot explore the details about translation. But we should recognize that it has an integral role in God's purposes for the salvation of the nations, the people groups. It utilizes the linguistic structures that we are exploring.

Processes with the Subsystems

We have indicated that the three subsystems—referential, graphologi-cal/phonological, grammatical—function together. Yet in the process of communication, we can observe a certain priority of attention and movement from one to another aspect. Human speakers and writers start with ideas. They often have an experience in which ideas get fleshed out and developed in the course of speaking and writing. Frequently a writer starts out with only a general idea or a not-fully-developed idea, and the process of writing forces him to think it through.

Yet we can still say that, in a rough way, writers move from ideas or expressions of ideas, including grammatical expression, and from there to production of marks on a page. That is, they move from focusing on aspects involving primarily the referential subsystem to those involving the grammatical subsystem and then the graphological subsystem. We can take 1 Samuel 22:1–2 as a specific example. The human author may have started with the idea, "God wants me to indicate that David left Achish, king of Gath, and went from there to the cave of Adullam." He was focusing on referential content. Then he moved to grammar. If he had been writing in English, he would have chosen the specific word *depart* in the past tense, with the form *departed*. He would choose that form out of awareness of how one writes a simple historical narrative in English. But he wrote in Hebrew. He chose a specific verb, with the root *hlk* ("go"), and a specific grammatical form of the verb (imperfect with waw-consecutive), the normal grammatical form to use in the backbone of narrative about past events. He moved to a focus on the graphologi-cal system as he wrote the letters one by one on the document.

God as the divine author knows the end from the beginning (Isa. 46:10). He knows not only the content of what he will say, but exactly how he will say it. Yet we can still see a kind of logical "movement." God the Father has a plan for what he will say—he has content. God the Son as the Word of God represents the articulation of the plan, the "grammar," metaphorically speaking. The Holy Spirit, functioning like the breath of God, carries God's word in the medium of breath. The Trinitarian speech of God is thus the archetype for the movement from focusing on the referential subsystem ("content") to the grammatical subsystem ("ar-ticulation") to the graphological or phonological subsystem ("breath").

Receiving the word of God reverses the process. As readers, we start with marks on a page: we start with observations focusing on the graphological subsystem. But when we have learned to read, we do not stay there. We go from the graphological subsystem to the grammatical subsystem and to the referential subsystem, and we do so smoothly, so that we hardly think about the fact that the graphological subsystem exists. Of course it does, but we look through it to grammar and to meaning.

When we are studying a text in an unfamiliar language, we move more slowly. We have to learn new alphabets for Hebrew and for Greek. Once we have learned the graphological subsystems for these languages, we stop thinking about them most of the time. But they can come to the surface when the manuscripts differ (a text-critical problem, involving differences in lettering), or when we detect a phonological or sound effect in a written text. The biblical texts were originally written at a time when reading out loud was common, and we can sometimes see plays on similar sounds (alliteration, assonance, and other associations with similar-sounding words).

Though we meet with phenomena that draw direct attention to sound and writing, as a general principle sound and writing are in the service of meaning. We use the letters to discern the grammar, and the grammar to discern the meaning. Again, 1 Samuel 22:1 may serve as an example. We move from letters on the page, $d + e + p + a + r + t + e + d$, to recognizing a word *departed* with the grammatical past tense marker *-ed*. We move from grammar to reference as we discern that the text is using the past tense as part of a historical narrative concerning events that happened in the past, and that are set in relation to events described in the preceding and following pieces of text in 1 Samuel. The same process occurs if we are studying the Hebrew of 1 Samuel 22:1, only it is more laborious.

Common linguistic aids come in as we make the transition from writing to meaning. Lexicons for Hebrew, Aramaic, and Greek allow us to travel from written sequences of letters to lexical entries to meanings for the entries. Reference grammars allow us to travel from grammatical constructions to the meanings of those constructions.

For the sake of readers who would like an example, let us illustrate with a case from 1 Samuel 22:1. The Hebrew word underlying the English word *departed* is *wayyēlek* (וַיֵּלֶךְ). The interpreter starts with the letters, which belong to the graphological subsystem. The sequence of letters enables him to identify a grammatical form, namely the waw-consecutive imperfect of the verb *hlk* (הלך). Under the root *hlk* (הלך), the Hebrew lexicon by Brown, Driver, and Briggs[5] lists several possible meanings, the first of which is for persons. Since in context David is the subject of the verb and is a person, we arrive at the meaning *go, proceed, move, walk*. By supplying the phrase "from there," the context indicates that the movement is a case of departure, making the translation *depart* appropriate (so ESV, KJV, NASB). In doing a translation, the interpreter has moved from grammatical information about the verb root to a focus on the referential subsystem, and within that subsystem to the idea of movement that is a departure.

The interpreter is not through, however, because he also should pay attention to the grammatical form of the verb. He consults a reference grammar (we choose Waltke-O'Connor).[6] The grammar indicates that the waw-consecutive imperfect (or "waw-relative plus prefix conjugation") has several functions, among which the most common is chronological succession (Waltke-O'Connor, section 33.2.1). This function fits the context of 1 Samuel 22:1. In the context of narrating past events, it translates as "departed," with past tense in English: "And David departed . . ." The interpreter has used the grammar to obtain information about the referential force of the use of the waw-consecutive imperfect, and has ended with a conclusion about the function in relation to the referential subsystem.

Our description is painfully elaborate. As an interpreter gains skill in using the lexicons and grammars, he proceeds more naturally in understanding how the lexicons and grammars allow him to move from graphology to referential meaning.

Using Contexts

In using both lexicons and grammars, the principle holds that context has a decisive function. A word or a grammatical piece can often take

---

[5] Francis Brown, S. R. Driver, and Charles A. Briggs, *A Hebrew and English Lexicon of the Old Testament with an Appendix Containing the Biblical Aramaic*, with corrections (Oxford: Oxford University Press, 1953).
[6] Bruce K. Waltke and M. O'Connor, *An Introduction to Biblical Hebrew Syntax* (Winona Lake, IN: Eisenbrauns, 1989).

multiple meanings, depending on context. Which meaning it has in any particular occurrence is indicated by context, both the immediate linguistic context, the larger literary context, what we know about the author, and so on. In principle, all the contexts that we have talked about are relevant, and wise readers weigh all the information that they can collect. Even then, because of limited knowledge, either of an ancient language or an ancient author or an ancient social or historical context, we may not always reach a confident decision about details.

Our exploration of the complexities of language can remind us of the challenges. At the same time, we should remember the principle of the clarity of Scripture: the things essential for salvation are set down plainly in various places in the Bible, so that we can be confident about them. And when the information about language and context comes together in a happy manner, we can also at many points be confident even about some details. The interlocking of the three subsystems makes it possible to travel from graphical marks to meaning.

Steps in Interpretation

If we like, we can add to our steps in interpretation the distinction between subsystems, as follows:

- A. Observation
- B. Elucidation
    - 1. One passage
        - a. The literary context
        - b. The transmission context
        - c. The text
            - (1) The text as act of communication
                - (a) Authorial intention
                - (b) Textual expression
                    - ((1)) Units
                    - ((2)) Hierarchies
                    - ((3)) Systemic linguistic contexts
                        - *((a)) Referential subsystem
                        - *((b)) Grammatical subsystem
                        - *((c)) Graphological subsystem
                - (c) Readers' impression

(2) The social contexts

(3) The historical contexts

2. Topical correlation

3. Redemptive-historical correlation

C. Application

Challenges in Using Extrabiblical Resources

Those who have knowledge of the original languages may use the added precision that can be obtained from examination of the original-language biblical texts. In order to derive full benefit from the original languages, we often need to use the resources found in lexicons and grammars that describe the languages in detail. These technical books are all fallible. Fortunately, in many respects they prove accurate. They have been written by people with gifts and abilities in the area of language and linguistics, and they are the product of common grace. They prove generally reliable partly because they remain a step away from the interpretation of particular verses and the interpretation of the teaching of the Bible as a whole. They are technical in nature, rather than being directly focused on biblical teaching. The nature of their focus diminishes the temptations to distort the Bible's content.

Yet they may still show problems. For example, in the list of resources that will be given below, Brown, Driver, and Briggs's lexicon makes reference on occasion to nineteenth-century Pentateuchal source theory (JEDP), but these references can simply be ignored. As noted below, the most recent edition of the standard Greek-English lexicon for New Testament Greek (edited by Danker) shows problems due to the influence of modern agenda. In addition, subtle, deeper problems creep into lexicons and grammars due to defective models about the nature of language. We will touch on this last concern in the next chapter.

Resources

For word meanings in the Old Testament, the standard resources are two major lexicons:

Brown, Francis, S. R. Driver, and Charles A. Briggs. *A Hebrew and English Lexicon of the Old Testament with an Appendix Containing the Biblical Aramaic*. With corrections. Oxford: Oxford University Press, 1953.

Koehler, Ludwig, and Walter Baumgartner. *The Hebrew and Aramaic Lexicon of the Old Testament*. Rev. Walter Baumgartner and Johann Jakob Stamm. Leiden/New York: Brill, 1994–2000.

They both have their strengths and weaknesses. I advise the use primarily of Brown, Driver, and Briggs, because it is much less expensive to acquire.

For New Testament Greek, the standard lexicon is Danker's revision of Bauer's lexicon:

Danker, Frederick William, ed. *A Greek-English Lexicon of the New Testament and Other Early Christian Literature*. Chicago: University of Chicago Press, 2000.

This third English edition is inferior in some ways to the second edition:

Bauer, Walter. *A Greek-English Lexicon of the New Testament and Other Early Christian Literature*. Translated by William F. Arndt and F. Wilbur Gingrich. 2nd English ed., rev. and augmented by F. Wilbur Gingrich and Frederick W. Danker. Chicago: University of Chicago Press, 1979.

For discussion of the difficulties with the 3rd ed. (2000) of Bauer's lexicon, see:

Poythress, Vern S. "How Have Inclusiveness and Tolerance Affected the Bauer-Danker Greek Lexicon of the New Testament (BDAG)?" *Journal of the Evangelical Theological Society* 46/4 (2003): 577–588. http://www.frame-poythress.org/how-have-inclusiveness-and-tolerance-affected-the-bauer-danker-greek-lexicon-of-the-new-testament-bdag, accessed January 1, 2013.
———. "Extended Definitions in the Third Edition of Bauer's Greek-English Lexicon." *Journal of the Evangelical Theological Society* 45/1 (2001): 125–131. http://www.frame-poythress.org/extended-definitions-in-the-third-edition-of-bauers-greek-english-lexicon/, accessed January 1, 2013.

For lexicons not affected by political correctness, one may consult the 2nd edition of Bauer (1979), or:

Thayer, Joseph H. *Greek-English Lexicon of the New Testament*. Peabody, MA: Hendrickson, 1995.
Liddell, Henry George, Robert Scott, Henry Stuart Jones, and Robert McKenzie. *A Greek-English Lexicon*. 9th ed. With a rev. supplement. Oxford: Oxford University Press, 1996.

For grammatical issues, the standard Hebrew grammar is:

Gesenius, Wilhelm. *Gesenius' Hebrew Grammar*. 2nd English ed. Rev. E. Kautzsch and A. E. Cowley. Oxford: Clarendon, 1980.

It is, however, difficult to use, so for a more accessible grammar, see:

Waltke, Bruce K., and M. O'Connor. *An Introduction to Biblical Hebrew Syntax*. Winona Lake, IN: Eisenbrauns, 1989.

For Aramaic, the standard is:

Rosenthal, Franz. *A Grammar of Biblical Aramaic*. Wiesbaden: Harrassowitz, 1995.

For Greek grammar:

Burton, Ernest DeWitt. *Syntax of the Moods and Tenses in New Testament Greek*. Reprint of the 3rd ed. (1900). Grand Rapids, MI: Kregel, 1976.

For issues not covered in Burton:

Wallace, Daniel B. *Greek Grammar Beyond the Basics: An Exegetical Syntax of the New Testament*. Grand Rapids, MI: Zondervan, 1996.

Note that Brown-Driver-Briggs, Gesenius, Joseph H. Thayer's Greek-English Lexicon, and Burton are available for free download on the Internet, because the copyrights have expired (at least for the earlier editions).

14

Units in Contrast, Variation, and Distribution

Now let us turn our attention from linguistic subsystems to linguistic *units*. Why? Even if we as interpreters are not consciously focusing on units, we depend on them in the process of interpretation. We use what we see about words, clauses, sentences, and paragraphs. So it is fruitful to see how they function. In addition, fallacies can arise from misconstruing how units work. Fallacies can crop up particularly in dealing with words.

Linguistic units come in various sizes. Each individual written letter is a unit. A written word is a unit. Most languages have clauses, sentences, and paragraphs as units. Careful interpretation takes account of all the sizes and types of units.

Interlocking with Subsystems

At times, units sort themselves into distinct subsystems. A single written letter like the letter *d* in the word *departed* belongs to the graphological subsystem. But it is not a distinct unit within either the grammatical or the referential subsystem. The suffix *-ed* in the word *departed* is a grammatical unit called a *morpheme*, which indicates past tense. But it is not a single unified graphological unit. Rather, it is two units, *e* and *d*, side by side. The word *departed*, on the other hand, functions as a unit in all three subsystems. It is a word belonging to the grammatical subsystem and functioning like many other verbs. It is a graphological word separated by spaces on both sides. And finally, it is a semological or referential term that, in context, refers to an event of physical motion in David's life.

What we have called a *unit* is more technically a piece of language recognizable as a distinctively functioning whole by native speakers of a language. Its identification depends on insiders' knowledge and experience.[1] For example, an insider knows that the word *departed* is an English word, while an outsider who does not know English would not know whether it is a word or a nonsense string of letters.

Structure of a Unit

Units in language have structure. A close analysis, using the particle, wave, and field perspectives, can distinguish three interlocking aspects in the structure of a unit, which are called *contrast, variation,* and *distribution.*[2]

First, using the particle perspective, we focus on a unit's distinctiveness, its being a "thing" that is stable and distinguishable from neighboring units. The *contrast* of the unit, or more elaborately its *contrastive-identificational features,* function to identify it as the unit that it is and to distinguish ("contrast") it from other units. Consider the word *departed.* Its spelling and its tense and its meaning all identify it as a distinct unit, and distinguish it from other verbs. The contrasts include contrasts that function in each of the three subsystems: it has contrastive spelling, the spelling $d + e + p + a + r + t + e + d$, which distinguishes it from other words with different spellings. This contrast functions in the graphological subsystem. It has contrastive grammar, in being marked as past tense and in forming the past tense in the regular way using the morpheme *-ed.* It has contrastive meaning within the referential subsystem. It designates a motion, and more specifically a motion away from a previous stable location.

Second, using the wave perspective, we focus on change and varia-

---

[1] The principle of insider identification can be generalized beyond language to culture (Vern S. Poythress, *In the Beginning Was the Word: Language—A God-Centered Approach* [Wheaton, IL: Crossway, 2009], 151).
[2] See Kenneth L. Pike, *Linguistic Concepts: An Introduction to Tagmemics* (Lincoln/London: University of Nebraska Press, 1982), 41–65.

tion in a unit—how much change could there be, while we still have the unit with which we started? The change could be either change in time or change in space. The word *departed* is the same word if pronounced fast or slow, or written with all caps (DEPARTED), or written in various fonts. It could even be mispronounced or misspelled and still be identifiable (*deeparted*). *Variation* is the term describing the allowable range of change within which a unit remains the "same" unit from an insider's point of view. Typically, the ability to identify a unit fades off gradually rather than failing suddenly.

Third, using a field perspective, we focus on the *relation* of a unit to the environments in which a unit customarily sits. Words typically sit in the environment of other words. And we do not have just any words in any order. The word *departed* is a verb, and as such expects a subject nearby ("David departed"). Perhaps we may find an indication of source ("from there") or goal ("to the cave of Adullam"). The name for the patterning of the environment is *distribution*. The particular occurrence of the word *departed* in 1 Samuel 22:1 has as its distribution the surrounding clause, "David departed from there," which in turn has a distribution in a sentence, "David departed from there and escaped to the cave of Adullam."[3] The underlying linguistic units in Hebrew have their own contrasts, variations, and distributions, which may be quite different from those in English.

We can analyze a unit either as in a single occurrence (say, in 1 Sam. 22:1) or in the general pattern of its occurrences within a language. Thus, instead of looking just at 1 Samuel 22:1, we could look at all the potential occurrences of the word *departed* in English, within various clauses and sentences. We would see a characteristic pattern for the distribution of the word within clauses.

Interlocking

As we might expect, contrast, variation, and distribution interlock with one another. They presuppose each other. In any description of variation we must use contrastive features to define the variation itself. We

---

[3] At a more fine-grained, technical level, we can also distinguish several different kinds of distribution. See Vern S. Poythress, *Redeeming Philosophy: A God-Centered Approach to the Big Questions* (Wheaton, IL: Crossway, 2014), chapter 12; Pike, *Linguistic Concepts*, 60–65.

must also use contrastive features of distribution in order to define distribution. Distribution includes the possibility of variation in the environment in which a unit sits. Each contrastive feature that characterizes a unit displays within itself variation and distribution.

Working with an Example

As an illustration, consider first an example from English. We have the word *departed* in 1 Samuel 22:1. The distinctiveness of this word, and its distinctive spelling, express contrastive-identificational features. The features allow us to look up the word *depart* in a dictionary. In Merriam-Webster's dictionary we find several meanings:

> *vi* . . . **1 a** : to go away: LEAVE **b** : DIE **2** : to turn aside: DEVIATE ~ *vt*
> : to go away from : LEAVE *syn* see SWERVE[4]

The special abbreviations *vi* and *vt* indicate that the word *depart* functions as both an intransitive verb (*vi*) and a transitive verb (*vt*). The distinction concerns distribution: is the verb followed by a direct object? The use with a direct object is unusual: "depart this life," or "depart the premises." The more common use of *depart* is intransitive. In 1 Samuel 22:1 we have an intransitive use, without direct object. This distributional information leads us to focus on the meanings 1a, 1b, and 2 given for the intransitive form.

Each of these meanings has its contrastive features, and together the three meanings show the range of variation in the meaning of the word. The context of occurrence in 1 Samuel 22:1 quickly leads to picking meaning 1a, since the meaning "die" (1b) requires a special context, and the meaning "turn aside" (2) would be expected in a context where a person departs from a path or a plan rather than from a place. The meaning "turn aside" usually suggests a focus on a choice to take some alternative different from the initial way with which a person began. Native speakers of English normally decide quickly on the right meaning, so quickly that they do not consciously realize that the word *depart* allows other meanings in other contexts.

Does the particular meaning *to go away* or *leave* come from the

---

[4] *Merriam-Webster's Collegiate Dictionary*, 11th ed. (Springfield, MA: Merriam-Webster, 2007).

word *depart* or from the context? How do we answer? The interpreter uses information from both. We could argue that the word *depart* is ambiguous among three meanings, 1a, 1b, and 2, and that the ambiguity is eliminated by context. Or we could argue that the word in itself has only a broad meaning, *go away*, and that the specific variations are a product of context rather than of the word itself. To *die* is to go away from this life, and to *deviate* is to go away from the correct way. According to this point of view, the specific coloring is not "built into" the word itself, but is added by context.

How do we tell what comes from the word and what comes from the context? We are confronting the interlocking of contrast, variation, and distribution. The three distinct meanings are variations in a single word *depart*, which still has its contrasts with other words. Each distinct submeaning contrasts with the other two. And distribution indicates which submeaning is active.

But there may be ambiguous distributional contexts, where, for example, the context does not indicate clearly whether the meaning is "go away" from a metaphorical "place" or "deviate" from a path. Suppose someone says that "Joe departed from the principle of loving one's neighbor." Did Joe "depart" by building on the principle? Did he live his life in a way that started from the principle as a foundation? Or did he "deviate" from the principle by violating it? The two possible meanings are almost opposite, since in one case Joe is following the principle and in the other case he is violating it.

But what makes the difference? Is the difference in the "meaning" of *depart*? In both cases he "goes away" from the principle. Do we have two different kinds of "going away"? Maybe. But could we also say that in the two cases he goes away in two different *directions*, in the direction of obedience or in the direction of disobedience? So would the difference not be in "going away" but in the "direction," a direction that is simply not indicated in the word *depart*, but only inferred from context? So when we infer obedience or disobedience, do we do so because such a meaning is "in" the word *depart*, or because the meaning is "in" the context, or both?

It seems impossible to answer definitively, precisely because our conclusions depend on the interaction between the word *depart* and its context. The word *depart* has a potential to imply either obedience or disobedience in various contexts. One context "activates" the implication of obedience. Does it do so because the context indicates that the word *depart* now has that more specialized meaning? Or does the word *depart* only have the vague, broad meaning "go away," to which the context adds more specificity?

Does our answer depend on our viewpoint? We can choose, if we wish, to impute specificity either to the word *depart* or to the context. Either way, the specificity belongs to the whole sentence or paragraph, once we get enough information to remove the ambiguity.

Meaning Developing in Time

Now consider the meaning 1b, DIE. This meaning is more specialized: "depart from this life." We can see how such a specialized meaning could have arisen over time. Cultures are always looking for euphemisms for death. So at some point someone says for the first time, "Joe departed from this life." Perhaps after such an expression has been used several times, someone else uses it without the extra explanation; he simply says, "Joe departed." The context nevertheless makes it evident that the new expression is short for "Joe departed from this life." Eventually, this new kind of use of the word *departed* becomes a kind of common expression or idiom, so that people recognize the meaning, "die" without much trouble or much explicit indication from context.

Let us look at the process of developing this specialized meaning, "die." At what point in the process does the word *depart* acquire a new, distinct meaning, as opposed to being only an elliptical form of the expression "departed from this life," as a full expression whose meaning depends vitally on the explanatory phrase "from this life"? When does the meaning become "part" of the word *depart* as opposed to being "part" of the context? Meaning as a contrastive feature of the word *depart* interlocks with meaning found in distribution. We can also say that distinct distributional contexts for the word result in *variation* in details of meaning.

Other Examples

The complexities that we have seen with the word *departed* occur repeatedly in natural languages. We can see one case of such complexity if we consider the underlying Hebrew word in 1 Samuel 22:1 instead of the English word *departed*. The Hebrew is *wayyēlek* (וַיֵּלֶךְ), from the root *hlk* (הלך). The lexicon gives the following meanings:

I. lit.[eral]
  1. of persons,
     a. *go, proceed, move, walk* . . .
     b. *depart, go away* . . .
     c. less oft.[en] where Eng.[lish] idiom requires or prefers *come,* . . .
     d. with modifiers: . . .
  2. Also of animals, in similar meanings and combinations: . . .
  3. in like manner of inanimate things, . . .
  4. The Inf.[initive] abs.[olute] is often used . . .
  5. In combination with other verbal forms: . . .
II. Fig.[urative]
  1. *pass away, die* . . .
  2. *live* ('*walk*'), in general . . .
  3. of moral and religious life . . .
  4. other fig.[urative] uses . . .[5]

How many distinct meanings do we have here? Is each subcategory a distinct meaning? Or, at the other extreme, do we have only one broad meaning, "go," with variations due to what is added from context? At one level of specificity, persons and animals "go" in a different manner (meanings I.1. and I.2.), since persons typically go by walking on their two feet, and animals go on all fours (or six or eight!). But is this difference "built in" to the Hebrew word for "go," or is it information about persons and animals that we get not from the word for "go" but from the subject of the verb, which indicates who or what is going, and by implication how many limbs are being used in the process? The word interacts with its context.

In some cases we may be confident that we have two distinct meanings. For example, consider the word *house* in 1 Samuel 22:1: "all his father's *house*" (Hebrew בֵּית, *bēyt*). Because of context, we know that

---

[5] Francis Brown, S. R. Driver, and Charles A. Briggs, *A Hebrew and English Lexicon of the Old Testament with an Appendix Containing the Biblical Aramaic*, with corrections (Oxford: Oxford University Press, 1953), under the root הלך.

it means the people of his [David's] father's *household*, as distinct from a "house" as a physical structure in which people live (*domicile*). But even here the two meanings, *household* and *domicile*, are closely related, so that one leads to the other. In other cases, such as the word *depart*, we may wonder whether we should conceptualize the variation in use as exhibiting primarily one broad meaning or as having several submeanings. If we start with one broad meaning, the broad meaning receives differentiation that context adds, while if we start with the several submeanings, we still have to say that they have their specificity distinguished by context.

Generalizing

What we have seen for words applies not only to words but also to grammatical functions like tense. For example, does the imperfect tense in Greek have one broad function, which context then further differentiates? Or does it have many, related functions, "built in" to the tense but distinguishable only through context?

We can also apply the analysis of contrast, variation, and distribution to whole clauses ("David departed from there"), sentences, paragraphs, and larger units. Each unit has some specific function, with contrastive-identificational features. At the same time, each unit is not infinitely specific—it allows variation. And each unit comes within a larger literary context and a context of communication (distribution).

We may endeavor to make a simple summary by saying that each unit makes a specific contribution, because it has *contrast*. It allows a range in interpretation, because it has *variation*. And its function is influenced by its context in *distribution*. These three—contrast, variation, and distribution—interlock. All display the presence of God. All are informative, but none is masterable.

Contrast, variation, and distribution are always present in language. But we do not always need to be consciously aware of them. Native speakers of English confidently interpret 1 Samuel 22:1–2 in English without consciously thinking through the details about the functions of each word, phrase, clause, and sentence. If we study a passage like 1 Samuel 22:1–2 in the original language, we must sometimes slow down, and we may puzzle over an unfamiliar word, or an unfamiliar use of a familiar word, or an unfamiliar grammatical construction, or a theologically puzzling meaning expressed in a familiar grammatical construction. But we also know that even in cases like this not everything is a problem. As a person grows in understanding Hebrew or Greek, many words become familiar, and he does not look up each of them. He does not find a need to look up each grammatical construction. Many aspects of interpretation become semiautomatic, even in a second language. The student looks up information only when he senses a problem. Thus, he is not consciously aware of all the ways in which language functions in contrast, variation, and distribution, or ways in which it functions in the three subsystems (referential, graphological/phonological, and grammatical).[6]

Moreover, God is present in contrast, variation, and distribution, even when we are not consciously aware of him. By taking time to reflect on our dependence on him in one particular case, with a word like *departed*, we may encourage in ourselves and in others an attitude of praise, thanksgiving, awe, and submission to his ways.

Steps in Interpretation

We can add the triad of contrast, variation, and distribution to our steps in interpretation, as follows:

A. Observation
B. Elucidation
  1. One passage
    a. The literary context
    b. The transmission context
    c. The text
      (1) The text as act of communication
        (a) Authorial intention
        (b) Textual expression
          ((1)) Units
            *((a)) Contrast
            *((b)) Variation

---

[6] On tacit aspects of knowledge, as contrasted with aspects in focal awareness, see Michael Polanyi, *The Tacit Dimension* (Garden City, NY: Anchor, 1967); Polanyi, *Personal Knowledge: Towards a Post-Critical Philosophy* (Chicago: University of Chicago Press, 1964).

     *((c)) Distribution
    ((2)) Hierarchies
    ((3)) Systemic linguistic contexts
      ((a)) Referential subsystem
      ((b)) Grammatical subsystem
      ((c)) Graphological subsystem
   (c) Readers' impression
   (2) The social contexts
   (3) The historical contexts
  2. Topical correlation
  3. Redemptive-historical correlation
 C. Application

Further Challenges

Lexicons and grammars characteristically organize their discussions of kinds of construction and kinds of meaning by providing lists of alternatives. The above discussions of the words *depart* and *house* and the underlying Hebrew words display examples of these organized lists, and similar lists occur in the analysis of grammar. Difficulty arises because the presentation of a list may tempt students to think of the various items on the list as completely isolated from each other, or else as completely flowing into each other and undifferentiated. Neither is true, because contrast and variation interlock.

  In addition, the list can tempt readers to ignore the influence of distribution—the context of a sentence or paragraph or larger unit (though lexicons and grammars often provide in their detailed notes information about the occurrence of meanings within distributional contexts). Through its structure, the list can tempt people to ignore the ways in which literal and figurative uses or connotations can interlock rather than being completely separate.

  In spite of the liabilities, lexicons and grammars continue to use the simplified format of a list, because it is convenient and pragmatically effective, even though it is a simplification. But a larger history of philosophy of mind and philosophy of language also contributes to the difficulty, because philosophy of language has often attempted to reduce language to one dimension or to simplify it in order to claim to master language. The heritage of Plato and Aristotle lies in the background, as well as more recently the heritage of twentieth-century structural linguistics. Language is richer than these approaches admit, because it reflects in its depths the wisdom of the Trinitarian God. We cannot further explore these depths here.[7]

Resources

Pike, Kenneth L. *Linguistic Concepts: An Introduction to Tagmemics.* Lincoln/London: University of Nebraska Press, 1982.

---

[7] See Poythress, *In the Beginning Was the Word.* On Plato, see ibid., appendix D; on Aristotle, see Vern S. Poythress, *Logic: A God-Centered Approach to the Foundation of Western Thought* (Wheaton, IL: Crossway, 2013), chapters 17–25 and appendix F2; on structural linguistics, see Poythress, *In the Beginning Was the Word,* appendices E and F.

15

Meaning

What is meaning? What is the meaning of 1 Samuel 22:1–2? We have already seen that we can focus on meaning from the perspective of the author(s), the text, or the readers (chapter 9). We can also analyze meaning in terms of focus on contrast, variation, and distribution (chapter 14).

The Focus of Meaning on the Referential Subsystem

Let us recall from chapter 13 that communication in language simultaneously uses three linguistic subsystems: the referential subsystem, the grammatical subsystem, and the graphological subsystem (replaced by the phonological subsystem in oral communication). Of the three subsystems, meaning has associations primarily with the referential subsystem. The graphological and grammatical subsystems also contribute to meaning indirectly, by interaction with the referential subsystem. Historically, discussions about meaning have often distinguished meaning from "form," where "form" includes grammatical or graphological "form" or both. For example, the word *departed* has the grammatical form of a past-tense verb, and the graphological "form" of a fixed sequence of letters, $d + e + p + a + r + t + e + d$. The word *departed* means that someone (in our context, David) goes away. In addition, the past tense (within a larger context) indicates that the action of going away took place in the past in relation to the time at which the author wrote the text. These features, concerning an agent acting (David), an action (going away), and a time period (past) function primarily with the referential subsystem. This meaning, of David going away, has contrast, variation, and distribution. The linguistic unit *departed* has contrast, variation, and distribution within all *three* linguistic subsystems. But when we focus on meaning, we also focus on contrast, variation, and distribution within the referential subsystem in particular.

The Meaning of Meaning

So what is "meaning"? Up to now, we have been using the word *meaning* in a fairly ordinary way. The English word *meaning*, like any word of English, has its own contrast, variation, and distribution. It has a range of uses and, we might say, a range of "meanings." If we are just considering the word *meaning* as a word in English, it is not yet a technical term in some hermeneutical or literary theory about "meaning." A theory may choose to develop or define a special, technical sense for the word *meaning* (and some theories do). A theory could, for example, attempt to define meaning as "authorial intention," or "textual expression of sense," or "impressions on the readers." But, as we have seen, these three approaches actually function as perspectives on one another rather than being rigidly isolatable. Any one of the three approaches may serve as a starting point, provided that we understand that it leads to the other two rather than excludes them.

If we want to move toward some technical definition of meaning, we could employ some secular theory of meaning that endeavors to provide a fixed "metaphysics" of meaning. E. D. Hirsch, for example, argues that meaning is a "willed type." But the underlying metaphysics is problematic (see appendix B).

We will continue to employ a multiperspectival approach. First, when people use the word *meaning* they may have in focus a minimal or "surface" meaning. Meaning is what we as interpreters would naturally include in a paraphrase. According to this perspective, all paraphrases of 1 Samuel 22:1–2 express "the same meaning" as the original text. Here is an example of a paraphrase of 22:1:

> David the son of Jesse went away from Gath and fled to the opening in the rock that is called Adullam. And when his brothers and his father's family found out, they joined him.

When two paragraphs paraphrase each other, they are "saying the same thing," at least roughly. But are they saying *exactly* the same thing? Usually not. There are tiny differences. And sometimes, on closer inspection, the differences are not so tiny. In the case of our paraphrase, the substitute wording includes the extra expression "the son of Jesse." The longer expression "David the son of Jesse" obviously refers to the same person as the shorter expression "David." So they are roughly equivalent. But the longer expression includes more information, namely that this David is Jesse's son. It *adds* meaning to the whole paragraph. The meaning that it adds is of course found elsewhere in 1 Samuel (16:1–3, 18–19, and elsewhere). So it is understandable why an interpreter might add this information if he is trying to explain the passage to someone who has not read 1 Samuel as a whole. The paraphrase draws out information that can legitimately be found in 1 Samuel. But it does not exactly represent the information that is found in verse 22:1.

As a second meaning of "meaning," we can include in our word *meaning* not only ordinary paraphrases, but also explanations that include many implications drawn from what is said explicitly. So here is an extended paraphrase that draws out implications:

> In the providence of God, David the son of Jesse left Gath and the company of Achish, king of Gath. Achish and Saul, who was king of Israel, were both potential dangers to David's life, so he had to find a safe place where they could not easily find him. He came to the cave called Adullam. Maybe his brothers and his father's family also felt unsafe. So when they heard that David had left Gath, they came to him. They probably came from Bethlehem, which is higher above sea level than the cave of Adullam. They had to travel down in elevation to get to where he was.

We can include even more if we allow ourselves to use more information from the literary context:

God had rejected Saul from being king, and had instructed Samuel to anoint David as his replacement. So God was committed to caring for David and protecting him until the time when he became king. David feared that he was in danger in the presence of Achish, king of Gath, so he left there. In the providence of God, David came to the cave of Adullam, where he had shelter and where it was more difficult for Achish or Saul to come after him to kill him. In those days, families and clans held together, and David's father's family might be in danger from Saul on account of David. Because they saw the danger, or maybe just because they wanted to express their solidarity with David, his brothers and his father's family left where they were, probably Bethlehem, and went down to join David. God thereby showed how he was caring not only for David but also for his family, and it seems probable that God also encouraged David through his being able to see his family members.

This provision for David was one step in a larger process. The provision of the cave of Adullam facilitated the events in the next verse, 22:2, where other people joined David. Verse 2 in connection with verse 1 explains some of the processes, superintended by God, through which David began his years of leading a band of followers in various places in the wilderness. In these events God showed not only care for David as an individual, but also care for his people Israel, for the benefit of whom he was raising up David as a warrior to protect and deliver them and as a king to govern them.

First Samuel 22:1–2 exists in relation to the larger context of 1–2 Samuel and 1–2 Kings. We can infer many things from the text together with its context. There is no sharp boundary between the contribution from the text and from its context, since they function together. How much "meaning" we attribute to the text and how much we attribute to text plus context depends on what exactly we want to mean by "meaning." The important point is to see that we can learn by paying attention to the relation of the text to its implications and its context.

Paraphrases versus Authority

We should also be aware of the issue of authority. When we draw out more implications, we run greater danger of bringing in interpretations that are not actually faithful to what God says. God is the final authority. His meanings are authoritative. Our interpretations of his meanings are derivative. Some are legitimate, but not all. So, like the Bereans in Acts 17:11, we should be "examining the Scriptures daily to see if these things were so."

An interpretation of 1 Samuel 22:1 needs careful inspection when it draws on other parts of 1 Samuel or other parts of the Bible, because the complexity of the inferences increases. The complexity of the *relationships* between multiple passages also increases when we draw on more passages.

It is right, then, that we receive confidently a relatively "straight" translation of a single verse. We do not worry greatly over a small difference in translation that makes little difference in meaning.

Consider then the following parallel "explanations" of 1 Samuel 22:1:

David departed from there and escaped to the cave of Adullam. (ESV)

So David departed from there and escaped to the cave of Adullam. (NASB)

David therefore departed thence, and escaped to the cave Adullam. (KJV)

David left Gath and escaped to the cave of Adullam. (NIV)

So David left Gath and took refuge in the cave of Adullam. (HCSB)

All of the translations offer something reasonable. But some use a more interpretive rendering that relies on the context. The word "so" in NASB and HCSB and "therefore" in KJV pay attention to the threat from Achish in 1 Samuel 21:12–15. They infer that David's departure was a response to the threat or to Achish's irritation in 21:14–15. The NIV and HCSB bring in the word "Gath," which comes from 21:10, 12, and which replaces the word "there" in the ESV and NASB (and "thence" in the KJV). This importation of the name of the city is an interpretative rendering, since the original Hebrew offers only a term meaning "there." The HCSB offers the expression "took refuge," which adds to the idea of "escape" the idea of a positive refuge. So we see some interpretation beyond a minimum. But all of these renderings are much less venturesome than the interpretive expansions that give much more explanation and that are likely to be found in commentaries.

With more expansive interpretations, it is appropriate for us to do what the Bereans did: we examine the Scriptures to see whether the interpretations derive legitimately from the texts. Some of the inferences are legitimate. They actually follow from the passage as a whole or from the whole of 1–2 Samuel or from the whole Bible. But they need checking. Both straight translations and complex inferences should base themselves on the original text, which has direct divine authority. The inferences have derivative authority when they are solidly based on the text. But instances involving complex inferences may in many cases have to remain tentative.

Meaning, Impact, and Import

We can further expand our appreciation for meaning by using once again the perspectival triad of particle, wave, and field perspectives. People use the word *meaning* in several ways. But in many uses, at least, they have in mind a stable, propositionally summarizable whole. Meaning, so construed, is like a stable particle. It remains the same through time. The idea of stability applies fully when we are dealing with Scripture. The stability through time has its foundation in God, who is faithful and who remains the same through time. God knows the end from the beginning (Isa. 46:10). What he knows about what he means with a text and what he knows that he will do with the text throughout all of history is the same through all time.

In addition to this focus on meaning as stable content, we can use the wave perspective and focus on *process*. We suggest using a distinct word, *impact*, to designate what we notice when we focus on process. A text like 1 Samuel 22:1–2 changes readers. Readers change in an obvious way by coming to know the content. So knowing the content, or *meaning*, is in this respect an aspect of impact. But we may also reflect on the process of change in the people themselves. Readers change, perhaps by gaining admiration of David, or gaining admiration of God's providence. Or a reader's heart warms toward entrusting his own life to God, as he sees how God dealt with David's life. Or a reader's heart turns toward entrusting himself to Christ, as he realizes, in the process of thinking about 1 Samuel 22:1–2, that it points typologically to Christ as the final king in the line of David. In looking at *impact*, we focus on such changes.

Impact, as a valid focus, has its foundation in God, who rules history and who exercises his control in the process of changing people's lives through his word. As with other kinds of inferences and more indirect effects from God's words, ideas about impact invite Berean-like testing and examination. Impacts on readers vary. Readers respond in many ways to texts, including biblical texts. Some responses are good in the sight of God, but not all.

Finally, we may use the third perspective, the field perspective, and focus on relationships between meanings. This focus is similar to, even overlapping with, the earlier foci on literary context in B.1.a. and on topical correlation in B.2. We ask what we can learn by considering 1 Samuel 22:1–2 *in relation* to many other texts, the rest of 1–2 Samuel, or all of 1–2 Samuel and 1–2 Kings, or even all of the canon of Scripture. We can introduce a third term, *import*, to designate the product of this focus. Import includes what we have already called *meaning*, but adds to it what we find out from relationships between meanings of individual texts. God designed all the individual texts to function together, as coherent speech of God, and so the legitimate inferences from relationships also belong to his intention with respect to the canon as a whole.

When God wrote 1 Samuel 22:1–2, he already knew what else he would commission to have written, in all the rest of the canon. He already had a design for the ways in which readers would learn from interacting with many individual texts taken together. The comprehensive wisdom of his plan implies that *import* is a valid perspective on 1 Samuel 22:1–2 or on any other text of Scripture.

The idea of import, when expanded even further, encompasses the entirety of God's plan. Every particular text in Scripture exists in relationship to God's comprehensive plan. Since God is the author, the text presupposes his plan and at least indirectly points to it. The text invites us to reckon with God's plan, and with all the relationships between the text in its particularity and the plan in its full expanse. Import, in an expansive sense, includes all the relationships—import is infinite.

But in contemplating God's plan we have to reckon also with our human limitations. We do not know all of God's plan, but only what he has chosen to reveal to us in Scripture. In addition, of course, we may attempt to get hints and draw conclusions from what we see in God's providential control of the world. But God's providential control over the whole world does not give us more *verbal instructions* about meaning. So the meaning of God's providential acts remains in many respects mysterious (Eccles. 8:17).

Once again, Berean-like examination is appropriate. God knows all relationships, in all their various significances. But we as human beings do not. We as interpreters may twist Scripture not only if we twist the meaning of an individual passage but also if we twist our understanding of the relations between two or more passages. For example, we may observe a connection between two distant verses due to the fact that the same word occurs in each of the two verses. But many times a connection based merely on the recurrence of a single word is incidental. It is *merely* verbal.

For example, 2 Chronicles 21:20 has the same English word *departed* as does 1 Samuel 22:1. The key part of 2 Chronicles 21:20 reads, "He *departed* with no one's regret." It is talking about Jehoram king of Judah, who "departed" from this life. Underlying the English, the Hebrew word for *departed* is the same in 1 Samuel 22:1 and 2 Chronicles 21:20. But in their contents the two verses have little to do with each other. One is about David going from Gath to the cave of Adullam. The other is about Jehoram dying.

Now suppose, hypothetically, that a person nevertheless treats the verbal connection between the two verses as if it were a strong connection. He may *wrongly* infer that the same word means *exactly* the same thing in the two places. He may press even further and claim that Jehoram merely hid himself and did not die. (But the preceding verse 19 says explicitly, "He died in great agony.") Furthermore, a person may claim to discover some new doctrine by building multiple inferences from one incidental relationship between two passages. Such interpretations involve misconstrual of relationships between verses.

God in his comprehensive knowledge knows not only all the relationships, but all possible *misconstruals* of relationships—all possible blunders. But of course he does not *approve* of them. In this context it is important to have our anchor in what is *clear* in Scripture, and to move out from there with a sense of our finiteness and our lingering temptations to intellectual sins. The Westminster Confession of Faith has a summary that exhibits balance between clarity on main points and caution elsewhere:

> All things in Scripture are not alike plain in themselves, nor alike clear unto all; yet those things which are necessary to be known, believed, and observed, for salvation, are so clearly propounded and opened in some place of Scripture or other, that not only the learned, but the unlearned, in a due use of the ordinary means, may attain unto a sufficient understanding of them. (1.7)

Interlocking

As usual, meaning, impact, and import interlock, and offer perspectives on one another. God intended that readers should read a single text, 1 Samuel 22:1–2, with its textual environment in mind. And so all the inferences that readers legitimately draw by comparing texts are in a sense contained in God's intention for the one text, 1 Samuel 22:1–2. If God intended them, they are part of the "meaning," stable for all time, though this divinely intended meaning does not become accessible to human readers all at once. God also intended its implications to unfold gradually in time, which means that impact is an aspect of meaning. And what unfolds in time in terms of impact includes not only meaning in a narrower sense, but the full import. So import is implicated in impact.

The interlocking of meaning, impact, and import suggests that, though we can temporarily focus on meaning, we cannot isolate it from impact and import. As usual, we cannot master it.

Meaning has a close connection both with contrastive features of units and with the referential subsystem. We could add it to our outline under either of these headings:

((1)) Units
    ((a)) Contrast
        *a1. Meaning
        *a2. Impact
        *a3. Import
    ((b)) Variation
    ((c)) Distribution

16

Figurative Language

How do we deal with figurative language in the Bible? How do we discern when we are reading figurative language, and how do we interpret its meaning? The issue is important, because misjudgments about figurative language can make a big difference.

The Importance of Judgments about Figures of Speech

Real events in history are significant. God is a God who acts in history. He brought about our salvation through the life, death, and resurrection of Jesus Christ. We look forward to the second coming of Christ, when our redemption will be complete. The Bible describes real events, rather than offering merely figurative fiction. People distort and evaporate the main message of the Bible if they turn these historical events into merely figurative, symbolical expressions of philosophical principles.

Bible students who have seen this kind of distortion can understandably become suspicious about *all* figurative language. But the real problem with the evaporation of history does not lie in piecemeal mistakes in interpreting a few individual passages. People evaporate history by making false claims about the genre of whole books of the Bible (on genre, see chapter 19). For example, people may try to convert the Gospels from historical accounts into mere symbols of spiritual truth, or into allegedly "mythological" representations of the meaning of human life.[1] This conversion of the Gospels into symbolism is neither naive nor innocent. It has to suppress obvious as well as subtle indications that the Gospels intend to tell us what happened in space and time.

In reaction to the evaporation of history, it might seem that the safest course is to take everything literally, not figuratively. But such a course will not work. In John 10:7 Jesus says, "I am the door of the sheep." No one thinks that Jesus is saying that he has a handle or hinges or that he is made out of wood. We recognize that he is using a figure of speech. In fact, a good deal of the Bible is poetry, and poetry typically contains many figures of speech. For example, poetry makes up the larger part of Job, Psalms, Proverbs, Song of Solomon, Isaiah, and Hosea through Malachi. In addition, Jesus spoke in parables, which are figurative stories. Even prose passages may build on analogical relations between God and human beings. We say that God is the king of the universe, but he is not a king on the same level as a human king. God is our Father, but not in the same way as a human father. So such language is in a sense figurative.

In addition to all these examples, the Old Testament contains records about symbolical institutions that depict beforehand the meaning of the redemption that will eventually come through Christ. For example, the animal sacrifices depict beforehand the final sacrifice of Christ. But animal sacrifices are not on the same level as Christ's sacrifice. David as king of Israel gives us a picture beforehand of Christ, who is a descendant of David and comes as the final king, who now rules over all (Eph. 1:21–22). But David is not a universal king in the way that Christ is. David was not capable of ruling over people's hearts, but ruled only over external relationships. The Old Testament examples that point to Christ are so important that they deserve a separate discussion, which we will undertake later on (chapters 23–27).

Principles about Figurative Language

All the capabilities of language come to us as gifts of God. These capabilities include capability both for simple description of events in

---

[1] On the historical character of the Gospels, see Vern S. Poythress, *Inerrancy and the Gospels: A God-Centered Approach to the Challenges of Harmonization* (Wheaton, IL: Crossway, 2012), chapters 4–5, and the larger body of literature by evangelicals about the Gospels.

time and for figurative expressions. When God speaks in Scripture, he uses all the capabilities masterfully. We should not despise figurative language, as if it were "inferior" to simple description. God himself in Scripture frequently uses poetic language, and that in itself shows us that it is valuable and not inferior.

We need to resist the modern atmosphere that tells us otherwise. In our modern context many people are heavily influenced by the prestige of science and its achievements. They may begin to think that only precise, literal, scientific description is ultimate. Figures of speech are then treated as *mere* adornment, or even as false to the nature of reality.

In fact, God has built the world so that analogies and possibilities for metaphor abound. Scientific analysis offers only one perspective out of many. Some of the most fundamental analogies express God's relationship to human beings, as when he tells us that he is king or father. Some analogies, like king and father, are easier to digest. Others, like the statement that God is "my rock" (Ps. 18:2), are more startling, but we can still work out what they mean.

All analogies within this world have their ultimate foundation in divine language: "In the beginning was the Word" (John 1:1). The Word, as the second person of the Trinity, is the ultimate expression of the character of God. He is "the exact imprint of his nature" (Heb. 1:3) and therefore the ultimate "analogy" in relation to God the Father. God himself is therefore the ultimate starting point for thinking about all kinds of analogies within language. God authorizes both literal and figurative language in Scripture. And, subordinately, he gives us the possibility of using both literal and figurative language in our own human communication.[2]

Kinds of Figurative Language

What kinds of figurative language can we expect? First, we should note that, though we can roughly distinguish literal from figurative language, the boundary is not sharp. For one thing, live metaphors can gradually become dead metaphors over time. The first time that someone said, "He departed from this life," the expression exhibited a metaphorical

[2] Vern S. Poythress, *In the Beginning Was the Word: Language—A God-Centered Approach* (Wheaton, IL: Crossway, 2009), chapter 34.

extension of the notion of "departure" as a physical movement. But after continual reuse, speakers of English begin to recognize that "depart" has the meaning "die" as one of its senses. Its use to describe death ceases to be a lively metaphor, but becomes just another instance of one sense of the word *depart*.

We have another reason to see the boundary between literal and figurative as fluid when we deal with descriptions of God. When we say that God is a king, do we speak metaphorically? Since God is not a king on the same level as a human king, the expression is in a sense metaphorical in comparison to a "literal" human king. But why do human kings exist? God made man in his image. And one aspect of the nature of imaging is that human beings can receive authority and exercise authority over other human beings—they can become kings. The ultimate king is God. The subordinate, derivative kings are human beings. So is human kingship a "metaphor" for God's original, "literal" kingship? In a sense, yes. It depends on what we consider foundational.

God is the original king, who always exists. From that standpoint, human beings are kings only by metaphorical derivation from that original kingship. On the other hand, we may choose to start from the standpoint of common, earth-centered thinking, and from the standpoint of immediate visibility. We start with a human king, and in our own mind we think of this king as "literal," because it is where we start within our conscious thinking. Both ways of thinking, if done reasonably, acknowledge the reality of a relationship between God as king and a human being as king. Both should also acknowledge that God is the ultimate *source* for kingship. So the two ways of thinking harmonize with one another. They are two perspectives on the same reality.

We can also recognize different ways in which language may build on analogical relationships within the world. Literary people distinguish different kinds of figurative language: metaphor, simile, synecdoche, metonymy, personification, hyperbole, sarcasm. They can also study larger literary forms such as allegories, which rely on extensive analogical relationships. Classifications of different kinds of figurative language are useful up to a point, because they help us to become familiar with the possibilities and adjust to them when we come across them in our reading. But I have doubts as to whether any classification could be complete, or whether the boundaries between different forms can be made perfectly precise.

Later we will discuss the subject of typology. Events and institutions in the Old Testament often have symbolical dimensions, which serve to point forward to the final redemption that God accomplished through Christ. In such cases, symbolical depth exists *in addition to* the obvious level of physical objects and visible events in the Old Testament. Symbolical depth does not compete with physicality, but builds on it.

The main principle should be clear: God, who gives us language, is master of it. We should be open to the full range of ways in which he may choose to address us. We should come to the Bible with no special bias in favor of language with physical reference, or in favor of figurative language. We should be ready to treat each text in the Bible according to the way in which God intends it to function. We treat as figurative whatever he intends to function as figurative. And we accept a reference to physical realities in whatever texts refer to such realities. In addition, with symbolical events and institutions, we should be prepared to discern both a physical object and a symbolical significance (as in the case of animal sacrifice). The two exist as aspects of a complex whole.

In many cases, the contexts contain clear indications as to whether a particular piece of language is figurative, and in what way it is figurative. But we may also come across more difficult cases, where we must exercise patience. We may sometimes have to say that we do not know for sure. The difficulties in Scripture are also there by God's design, and may serve as an occasion to grow in humility.[3]

Context for Figurative Language

Figurative language has its meaning in connection with larger contexts. The larger literary context can provide clues as to whether a particular sentence or expression is figurative, and in what way it may be figurative. Influence can also come from a surrounding historical or cultural environment. For example, animal sacrifice made more sense within an

---

[3] Poythress, *Inerrancy and the Gospels*, chapter 15.

Israelite environment because surrounding cultures practiced animal sacrifice (and sometimes even human sacrifice) to appease the gods. Animal sacrifice in Israel had positive significance as an expression of a personal relationship to God, and it symbolized reconciliation to God. Both the personal relationship and the idea of reconciliation were analogous to the relationships that surrounding cultures tried to establish with false gods. At the same time, God's teaching about animal sacrifice indicated that sacrifice ought to be offered to the one true God. This teaching untwisted the ideas of false religions, which were confused by polytheistic thinking.

The assessment of figurative language in a book of the Bible, and the assessment of symbolical institutions such as animal sacrifice, must take into account the associated cultural knowledge of the time in which the book was written. To a modern American, animal sacrifice might seem repulsive and bloody. But in ancient Israel it had associations with the need to be reconciled to God. God established the institution of animal sacrifice in Israel, and gave instructions in the Bible about it, in order that it might communicate to the Israelites in harmony with its meaning of symbolizing reconciliation with God.

Similar examples show ways in which the ancient cultural context provides a meaning different from a modern context. To a modern American, the mention of a locust perhaps produces an association with other insects that are mainly loathsome pests. To a biologist, on the other hand, it might stir up scientific interest. To an ancient Israelite, locusts in large numbers caused devastating destruction of crops, which threatened famine as an aftermath (Joel 1). But locusts could also be a tasty food (Lev. 11:22; Matt. 3:4).

To a modern American, the "heart" is the center of emotion. In ancient Israelite culture, the "heart" is the center of a person's entire being; emotions are associated with the kidneys and intestines (KJV "bowels"). We therefore have to make appropriate adjustments when we come across nonphysical uses for the words for heart, kidneys, and intestines in the Bible.[4]

---

[4] It should be clear that the ordinary use in Scripture of Hebrew-language analogues to our words for *heart* or *bowels* does not imply a literalistic, quasi-scientific "theory" about how thinking or emotions operate, any more than a modern reference to the "heart" in the expression "it broke his heart" propounds a theory about emotional heartbreak or has a connection with the physical organ.

In many cases in the Bible, when we deal with figurative language, we must make adjustments to the kind of associations that made sense within the cultures of the time.

Resources

Ryken, Leland, James C. Wilhoit, and Tremper Longman, III, eds. *Dictionary of Biblical Imagery*. Downers Grove, IL: InterVarsity Press, 1998.

17

Words and Concepts

Now we turn to an issue closely related to meaning, namely the interpretation of words in relation to concepts.

Justification and Faith

We may begin with an illustration. James 2:24 says that "a person is justified by works and not by faith alone." Romans 3:28 says that "one is justified by faith apart from works of the law." Do these verses contradict each other? The problem does not disappear if we look at the verses in the original language, namely Greek. The key words *justified*, *faith*, and *works* are the same in the two verses, not only in English but also in Greek.[1]

In the time of the Reformation, John Calvin discussed these verses in the context of disputes over the nature of justification. Calvin recognized that, though the two verses use the same words, the verses do not mean the same thing when they use those words.[2] A distinction in meaning exists both for the word *faith* and for the word *justified*.

The apostle Paul in Romans 3:28 has in mind true faith, the kind of faith that trusts in Christ for salvation. James is discussing someone who "*says* he has faith" (James 2:14), but whose life contradicts his claim. James also uses as an example someone who believes "that God

---

[1] In Greek, the grammatical forms differ in ways appropriate to the context in each verse.
[2] John Calvin, *Institutes of the Christian Religion*, trans. Henry Beveridge (Grand Rapids, MI: Eerdmans, 1970), 3.17.11–12.

is one" (v. 19). Monotheism by itself is not saving faith. "The demons believe" (v. 19), but obviously not in the sense that they have saving faith in Christ. Thus "faith" in the crucial verses in James can denote a minimal form of belief, or pretended belief, without substance. By contrast, in Romans 3:28 Paul has in mind genuine trust in Christ.

In addition, Paul and James do not mean the same thing with the word *justified*. In the context in Romans 3, Paul has in mind God's declaration that sinners are forgiven and that they are righteous in God's sight, a righteousness based on what Christ has done to turn away God's wrath (note the language about "propitiation" and "blood" in verse 25). James, by contrast, is speaking about the *manifestation*, not the imputation, of righteousness.[3] Abraham's righteousness was demonstrated through the sacrifice of Isaac (James 2:21); Abraham had already received God's declaration of righteousness at an earlier point in time, through his faith (Gen. 15:6).

Our point here is not to discuss or defend the Reformation doctrine of justification by faith. Rather, we are illustrating that a difference exists between the word *faith* on the one hand and the theological concept of "saving faith" on the other. Likewise, a difference exists between the word *justified* (as an English word) and the theological concept of "justification by faith." A concept is not the same thing as a word.[4] Calvin defends the theological concept of justification by faith in a series of eight chapters in the *Institutes*.[5] The chapters appeal to a wide range of biblical teachings, using many verses with many different words. Calvin does not make the mistake of building the doctrine of justification by faith on the word *justified* alone. As Calvin's discussion of James 2 shows, he also avoids the mistake of supposing that the same word must mean the same thing in each verse where it occurs. In our own terminology, words like *faith* and *justified* and their Greek analogues have contrast, variation, and distribution. In particular, the *variation* in use and the *variation* in meaning prohibit a naive approach in which we suppose that a single word in some magical way contains

---

[3] Ibid., 3.17.12.
[4] Discussion of the distinction between word and concept in biblical interpretation received its initial impetus largely from James Barr, *The Semantics of Biblical Language* (London: Oxford University Press, 1961); see also Moisés Silva, *Biblical Words and Their Meaning: An Introduction to Lexical Semantics* (Grand Rapids, MI: Zondervan, 1994).
[5] Calvin, *Institutes*, 3.11–18.

the whole body of biblical teaching that Calvin takes eight chapters to expound.

Word and Concept: Illustrations

What, then, is the difference between a word and a theological *concept*? It depends on what we mean by a *concept*. There is more than one way in which people might want to use the word *concept*.

Rather than going directly to a definition of a "concept," let us first consider some more examples. The Bible teaches that there is only one true God (Mark 12:29; 1 Cor. 8:4). It also indicates, especially in the Gospel of John, that God exists in three persons, each of whom is distinct from the other two. This teaching about God is called "the doctrine of the Trinity." The word *Trinity* is not found in the Bible. The word *Trinity* denotes a theological concept, a concept that summarizes the Bible's teaching on the subject of God. The Bible's teaching on the subject uses many words in many different passages.

The word *Trinity* is an English word, and at the same time also a technical designation or abbreviation for the entire doctrine of the Trinity, which would take many sentences to expound fully. The word *Trinity* is thus *both* a word *and* a theological concept. Or, if we want to be more precise, we can say that, as a word, it functions to "designate" the entire theological concept.

The situation with the term *Trinity* is fairly clear, because the term has only one main use,[6] and it is not a term that directly appears as a single word within the Bible itself. But what about the term *faith*, or its Greek analogue (*pistis*)? What about the term *justified*, or its Greek analogue (forms of the word *dikaioō*)? The situation here has a greater potential for confusion, because both of these terms (*faith* and *justified*) occur directly in English translations of the Bible. And, as we have seen, they occur with a range of meaning (not the same in James 2 as in Romans 3). The situation becomes still more complex because the two English terms (and earlier in history, corresponding Latin terms)

---

[6] *Webster's Dictionary* reports two other senses: "2 *not cap* : a group of three closely related persons or things"; and "3 : the Sunday after Whitsunday observed as a feast in honor of the Trinity" (*Webster's Ninth New Collegiate Dictionary* [Springfield, MA: Merriam-Webster, 1987]; also http://www.merriam-webster .com/dictionary/trinity, accessed August 28, 2013). The lack of capitalization distinguishes the second sense. The third sense involves a specialized use that clearly derives from the main sense of the word *Trinity* to designate a doctrine. Our discussion leaves to one side these additional senses.

can be closely associated with theological concepts. Calvin expounds the theological concept of *justification by faith alone*. And in doing so, he also employs the theological concept of *saving faith*, which is not the same as mere belief that there is one God.

Regeneration

Let us consider another example of word and concept. We have the English word *born* and the theological concept of *regeneration*. The word *born* in English corresponds roughly to the Greek word *gennaō*. The Greek word *gennaō* can mean "to beget" or "to father, become father to," when used with respect to the father, or "to bear" when used with respect to the mother.[7] It can also be used metaphorically for God producing spiritual children through the power of the Holy Spirit. The famous passage with this meaning is found in John 3: "You must be born again" (v. 7; see also vv. 3, 5, 6, and 8). The fuller expression is "born again," but the word "again" is sometimes omitted (vv. 5, 6, and 8; 1 John 2:29; 3:9; 4:7; 5:1, 4, 18). Starting from the passages in the Gospel of John and 1 John, theologians have defined a theological concept of *regeneration* (the word *regeneration* derives from Latin, *regeneratio*, which means "being born again").

We can proceed to analyze the word *born* more precisely using the perspectives of contrast, variation, and distribution. Contrastively, the word *born* denotes a birthing process, in contrast to many other kinds of processes, such as growing, producing, tending, overseeing, and manufacturing. The word *born* shows variation: it can be used for physical birth, either of human beings or of higher animals; and it can be used for processes metaphorically analogous to physical birth ("a new nation was born"). The word *born* has a distribution. In context, someone or something is born, and if the birth is physical, what is born is a human being or an animal. It is also implied that someone or something is giving birth (the mother; or, for "begetting," the father).

Now we may analyze the concept of *regeneration*. We must be careful. The word *regeneration* is a word in English, but not every occur-

---

[7] Walter Bauer, *A Greek-English Lexicon of the New Testament and Other Early Christian Literature*, trans. William F. Arndt and F. Wilbur Gingrich (2nd ed.; Chicago/London: University of Chicago Press, 1979).

rence of the word has exactly the same meaning or denotation (unlike the word *Trinity*). The word *regeneration* and the cognate verb *regenerate* can be used when a lizard *regenerates* a limb that it has lost. We want to analyze the particular meaning of the word *regeneration* in the context of its use as a technical term in systematic theology, where we talk about "the new birth." And even here, there is variation. Some people might use the term *regeneration* more loosely, to describe any experience of spiritual renewal or spiritual change—whether or not it proves to be a lasting or fundamental change. Or the term *regeneration* could function as an umbrella term that covers every aspect of change involved in becoming a Christian.

Professional theologians in the Reformed tradition have developed a narrow use, in which it designates the initial work of the Holy Spirit that changes a person's heart, so that he no longer has a "stony heart" that resists the good news of Christ. Ezekiel 36 describes the radical change:

> I will sprinkle clean water on you, and you shall be clean from all your uncleannesses, and from all your idols I will cleanse you. And I will give you a new heart, and a new spirit I will put within you. And I will remove the heart of stone from your flesh and give you a heart of flesh. And I will put my Spirit within you, and cause you to walk in my statutes and be careful to obey my rules. (Ezek. 36:25–27)

Ezekiel 36:25–27 does not happen to use the specific language or imagery of "birth." It is nevertheless relevant to the *doctrine of regeneration*, in the eyes of systematic theologians. It talks about substantially the same reality as does John 3:3–8. God by his sovereign power makes people new, radically new in spirit, through the work of the Holy Spirit.

We can now analyze this concept of *regeneration* in terms of contrast, variation, and distribution. *Regeneration* contrasts with staying the same, and it also contrasts with religious experiences of change within false religions, and with experiences within the realm of the Christian religion where a person undertakes to "turn over a new leaf," but where his change is fundamentally his own work rather than the work of the Holy Spirit.

What about variation? Regeneration as the work of the Spirit has mystery to it:

> The wind blows where it wishes, and you hear its sound, but you do not know where it comes from or where it goes. So it is with everyone who is born of the Spirit. (John 3:8)

This mystery prevents us from giving a detailed account of variations. But we can at least see variations in the effects. Each person who is regenerated changes, but his change is not exactly a duplicate of the change in another person who is regenerated. The Holy Spirit works in each individual in a manner that is specific to that individual. In the process, people's personalities as we experienced them prior to their regeneration are not completely obliterated, but rather spiritually changed—subtly perhaps, but nevertheless profoundly. We can see that it is the "same" person but also a person with new life and joy and attitudes. There may also be variation in the time it takes for us to see major changes. One person appears to change suddenly. Another changes just as surely, but the results appear more gradually.

Finally, consider distribution as a perspective on regeneration. Regeneration takes place with a context. God the Father takes the initiative; God the Holy Spirit, sent from Christ, works in power; the person who experiences regeneration has many accompanying experiences: being united to Christ; moving from spiritual darkness to light, from unbelief to faith in Christ, from hostility to God to reconciliation with God, from guilt to forgiveness, from unholiness to holiness. Hearing the gospel goes together with regeneration (1 Pet. 1:23).

The Distinction between Word and Concept

Now we can stand back and consider the relation of the word *born* to the concept of *regeneration*. Clearly, the two are distinct. The word *born* is a word of English, often used with respect to physical birth. In such contexts, it certainly does not *mean* "regeneration." The word *born* has its distinctive contrast, variation, and distribution, all of which are different from the contrast, variation, and distribution of the concept *regeneration*.

Many uses of the word *born* do not automatically evoke the idea of regeneration, unless we ourselves bring in the idea. For example, we watch the birth of a calf. And then, because we know about the biblical teaching on regeneration, we ask ourselves what our observations might suggest about spiritual regeneration. Even in such a train of thought, we are clearly distinguishing between the birth of the calf and spiritual "rebirth" or regeneration. We have to have the distinction in place in order even to consider what analogies we might detect.

When we look at the occurrences of the word *born* or similar words within the Bible, the same distinction holds. Many occurrences describe instances of physical begetting or physical birth. They have a relation to regeneration only by way of analogy.

Even when we confine ourselves to biblical verses that discuss *spiritual* birth, we cannot assume that every verse must contain the full concept of regeneration. Consider 1 Corinthians 4:15: "I became your *father* in Christ Jesus through the gospel." The key Greek word in 1 Corinthians 4:15 is *gennaō*, "beget," the same word used in John 3. The apostle Paul "begat" the Corinthians through the gospel. Paul is talking about the fact that he was the first to proclaim the gospel at Corinth. As a result, the Corinthians became Christians and then were further nurtured in the faith through his preaching (Acts 18:5–11). But this "begetting" or "fathering" does not have exactly the same meaning as when God causes new birth. In 1 Corinthians 4:15, Paul is the agent of "begetting." In John 3, God is the agent of new birth. Of course, the one presupposes the other. When we put together the teaching of the Bible as a whole, we understand that God through the Holy Spirit was at work to give the Corinthians new birth, and that God used Paul in the process. Paul's act of "begetting" presupposed God's act of begetting. But 1 Corinthians 4:15 does not say so explicitly. And we would just confuse things if we tried to force the word "beget" or "father" (or Greek *gennaō*) to have exactly the same function in all the passages.

So the word *born* and the concept of *regeneration* are distinct. Should we therefore go to the opposite extreme, and say that they have no relation to each other at all? Clearly they do have a relation. Even the ordinary meaning of the word *born* has a relation to regeneration, because regeneration is *analogous* to physical birth. In addition, we have some passages, in John 3:3–8 and in 1 John, where the word *born* occurs and where the passages as a whole contribute to the doctrine of regeneration. We can say that in these passages the relation between the word *born* and the concept of regeneration is much closer.

But we must beware of overdoing it. First, we should observe that the doctrine of regeneration or the concept of regeneration comes from *whole passages*, not from the word *born* in isolation. The doctrine has much more content than the word.

Second, other passages, such as Ezekiel 36:25–27, throw light on the doctrine of regeneration, even though they do not happen to use the word *born* or an analogy with birth. We might add to the list Jeremiah 31:31–34, which uses still other kinds of description of renewal: "I [God] will put my law within them, and I will write it on their hearts" (v. 33). Deuteronomy 30:6 says that "the LORD your God will circumcise your heart and the heart of your offspring, so that you will love the LORD your God with all your heart and with all your soul, that you may live."

Third, even with a technical term like *regeneration* in English, the word *regeneration* is still distinguishable from the concept that the word designates. We can see this because the word *regeneration* can also be used in another sense, for a lizard regenerating a limb. It is really the concept that we are after.

Fourth, the concept of regeneration, as a technical concept, needs explaining. Explaining it well takes whole paragraphs. The doctrine of regeneration consists in what we find in the extensive paragraphs of explanation. The term *regeneration* is a convenient shorthand. Each new person who encounters the shorthand must also have the paragraphs if he is going to understand the shorthand. The shorthand does not function like a magic box that automatically opens its contents to anyone who chances upon it.

The shorthand has its advantages, when we want to say something briefly to another person who already knows the shorthand. But it is not advantageous if the person we are addressing does not already know the shorthand. Thus, God was wise when he did not fill the Bible with shorthand. It would have been indigestible to all but an elite few who had already possessed the secret meanings of the shorthand. Instead, God spreads out his instruction by using paragraphs and whole books.

It takes longer, but it is clearer and more effective for the purpose of spreading the good news through all the world and all people groups of the world, including the simple as well as the learned.

Practicing Distinctions in Interpretation

We can develop a simple maxim that will help us in the process of interpretation. The maxim is this: distinguish between words and theological concepts when you study the Bible. Theological concepts are useful as summaries of the teaching of the Bible as a whole. But we can easily miss what a passage is saying if we read in a theological concept where it does not belong. Not every case of being "born" in the Bible is regeneration. That is so obvious that we do not need to tell ourselves to avoid the mistake. But what about when we come to 1 Corinthians 4:15? Because the "begetting" or "birth" in this verse is spiritual in character, it may look as if the verse must be talking about regeneration as a concept. But it is not.

Similarly, James 2:24 is not talking about the concept of justification by faith as the apostle Paul expounded it in Romans 3–4 and Galatians 3. It may *look* as if James is saying the same thing. "After all," someone says, "he is using the same words. What else could it mean?" He could still mean something different from the theological concept. Look and see. And when you look, remember that words like *justified* and *faith* and *works*, when they appear in the Bible, are not technical terms that function as mere shorthand for complex theological concepts. They are words, with contrast, variation, and distribution according to what God has ordained. And God's ordination, it turns out, is richer and more complex than what we might naively have believed. He is pleased with variation. He is pleased to *not* just use the Greek word for *justified* in exactly the same way in every location in Scripture. Variation derives from God, the one who exists forever in the mystery of his triune nature.

Temptations with the Original Languages

In most of our discussion, we have concentrated on what happens in English, with English words like *justified*. We have illustrated with English because English illustrations are accessible to English-speaking readers. But the same principle applies to Greek, Hebrew, and Aramaic words. They are not identical to theological concepts. For some of us, the temptation to become confused may be stronger with the original languages than with English, because the original languages are not second nature to us. Because we think we understand God's ways, we may assume that God will use words precisely, and therefore that we will find an identical meaning in each and every occurrence of a word. Surely that is how God would do it. Surely he would do something very special in Hebrew and Greek.

Yes, he did do something very special: he wrote the Scripture, which is his divine word, with divine authority, power, goodness, and truth. And he prepared the languages, Hebrew, Aramaic, and Greek, to be exactly what they were at the time when the biblical writers wrote. It all conforms to his wise plan and control. But does his providential control imply that Hebrew and Aramaic and Greek were designed by him to be weird languages, unlike any other natural languages? Not necessarily.

We may imagine how a person might reason onward if he has pre-conceptions about how God would use language. Perhaps this person concedes that many uses of words in Hebrew, Aramaic, and Greek show typical interlocking of contrast, variation, and distribution. But he still wants an exception. "Surely," he says, "surely God would at least bring in a specially precise use of terms in all the *key* occurrences, the occurrences where crucial doctrines are being expounded."

It seems plausible to many people that he would do it that way. But he did *not*. He did it *his* way. His way displays the glory of his Trinitarian nature as he reflects his archetypal coinherence in the coinherences of contrast, variation, and distribution in language in general and in words in particular, and most especially in the language that he himself uses as he speaks to us in the Bible. It is beautiful; it is wise with infinite wisdom—if only we could see it!

Perspectives on Words and Concepts

How then do we understand the distinction between words and concepts and at the same time their relatedness? We have mostly stayed at the level of particular examples. But it is possible to generalize. The distinction between words and concepts employs several intersecting subordinate distinctions. We have: (1) the distinction between an ordinary-language use of the word *regeneration*, such as when a lizard regenerates a limb, and a technical term, such as the theological use of the term *regeneration*; (2) the distinction between a single word (*regeneration*) and longer discourses—sentences and paragraphs—used to expound a doctrine (John 3:3–8; Ezek. 36:25–27); and (3) the distinction between what a person says (the word *regeneration*) and what he knows (the doctrine of regeneration). Each of these three small distinctions contributes to the overall distinction between the word *regeneration* and the concept of regeneration (that is, the doctrine of regeneration).

We can see how these three distinctions express a focus on systematic language contexts, on hierarchy, and on unit, respectively. (1) The ordinary-language use and the theological use of the term *regeneration* are distinguished by belonging to different parts of the referential subsystem. We distinguish ordinary meaning and technical meaning from one another, and this distinction constitutes one dimension within the referential subsystem. (2) Words fit into sentences and paragraphs by means of hierarchy. The distinction between words on the one hand and sentences and paragraphs on the other functions within hierarchical structure. (3) The word *regeneration* and the doctrine of regeneration (the concept) are both units, the one being a unit in language and the other a unit in thought.

Let us begin with the distinction between knowledge and thought on the one hand and language on the other. This distinction is operative in human life. But it has its roots in God. God is the original knower, the original thinker, and the original speaker. God the Father has his plan and his knowledge. God the Father also speaks. When he speaks, he speaks in accord with his knowledge. He speaks eternally, in God the Son, who is the Word. The Word goes out through the Spirit. Thus, we suggest that the thoughts of God have a close correlation with God the Father, while the word or speech of God has a correlation with God the Son. Thought and speech are in perfect accord, because God is one and is in harmony with himself.

Now consider human thought and speech in their analogies to God's thought and speech. By analogy with God, the human speaker conveys his thoughts through his words to a destination (a human or divine or angelic recipient). We can distinguish our thoughts from our expression in words because, first of all, in God, God the Father is distinct from his Word. The distinction is real, but deep and mysterious. Mystery cannot be eliminated from the word/concept distinction.

Words and concepts are not only distinct but also related. If we refuse to use any words at all, we cannot communicate our concepts effectively! In many situations we use many, many words, belonging to several paragraphs, in order to explain a single concept adequately. But we can also summarize a concept in a single word like *regeneration*, which begins to function as a technical term. Words evoke our awareness of the sentences in which they lie, and the sentences evoke the paragraphs, and the paragraphs evoke the canon of Scripture, and the canon teaches us about creation, providence, and general revelation. Each word in Scripture may evoke our awareness of God who speaks it. And God knows everything, including the doctrine of regeneration. The word *born* can thus evoke the entire doctrine of regeneration, because of the unity of God. We should not isolate the word from various concepts, any more than we simply equate it with a concept.

God the Son, who is the Word, expresses God the Father. By analogy, our words express our thoughts. Other people can actually come to understand our thoughts about regeneration when we use the word *regeneration* to speak to them. But a human recipient who is previously unfamiliar with the technical term *regeneration* is going to need more than the single term if he is going to understand us. So hierarchy comes in: we speak paragraphs. And the referential subsystem comes in: we make a distinction between different ways of using the term *regeneration*. In these moves also we are imitating God, whose utterance in the Word is the archetype.

Multiple perspectives come in when we consider word usage. Will you or I belittle a person who does not know the technical meaning of the word *regeneration*, because he uses it "improperly"? That is, his use is out of accord with our perception of how *we* want it to be used in a technically precise way. Or will we allow that he has a perspective, which may be valid? Let us suppose that he is not denying the doctrine of regeneration, as expressed in Ezekiel 36:25–27. He may be quite content with Ezekiel 36:25–27. Maybe the language concerning a new heart is his preferred way of describing the way in which God renews sinners. It is just that he has never heard of the specialized use of the term *regeneration*. To him *regeneration* means a lizard regenerating a limb.

We do not want to quarrel about words. There is even a Greek word, *logomachia*, meaning "dispute about words," which occurs in 1 Timothy 6:4. (And the corresponding verb occurs in 2 Tim. 2:14.) We do not know all the details about the disputes that Paul is advising against—there is variation. But the thrust of the verses suggests their relevance to modern temptations. Two people can fall into a dispute because they are using the same words with two different meanings. They end up talking past one another, and neither understands what the other person *means*.

On the other hand, sometimes differences in doctrine are important, and it is necessary to engage in discussion, or even in a dispute:

> But some men came down from Judea and were teaching the brothers, "Unless you are circumcised according to the custom of Moses, you cannot be saved." And after Paul and Barnabas had *no small dissension and debate* with them, Paul and Barnabas and some of the others were appointed to go up to Jerusalem to the apostles and the elders about this question. (Acts 15:1–2)

If we do have to enter into a dispute, let us dispute primarily about concepts, that is, about what the Bible teaches, because such teaching is designed by God to make a difference in what we believe and in how we serve God. Moreover, let the dispute in such a case be weighty enough to warrant the attention and energy that we give to it. And let us in humility weigh our own competence as well.[8]

Resources

Silva, Moisés. *Biblical Words and Their Meaning: An Introduction to Lexical Semantics.* Grand Rapids, MI: Zondervan, 1994.

---

[8] Two dangers await us. Some people are perpetually quarreling over doctrine, because they are quarrelsome by nature, or because they have an exaggerated estimate of the importance of their own views about minor points of doctrine. Others—and I think it is becoming more common in the cultural atmosphere of postmodernism—just want to "love" and never dispute. But this second group misses the importance of sound teaching and the dangers to the sheep posed by heretical deviations. We must love God's sheep enough to care about what they are eating spiritually, and to guard them from wolves (Acts 20:29; 1 Tim. 1:19–20; 4:1–5; 2 Tim. 2:23–26).

18

Discourse

A *discourse* is a connected piece of text of any size. But usually the word *discourse* designates a larger-sized text, containing more than one clause. Clauses fit together into sentences and paragraphs, and paragraphs into larger sections and whole books.

Discourse Analysis

Discourses are not random sequences of sentences. They are organized and have structure. *Discourse analysis* studies how pieces of text fit together. But the term *discourse analysis* can mean more than one thing. Some forms of discourse analysis have technical details. We will not take time to enter into all the technical details, but will stay at an introductory level.

Discourse analysis can focus on grammar or reference (that is, meaning content) or both.[1] Grammar provides clues for meaning and reference. Since most biblical interpretation is more interested in meaning and reference, we will concentrate on that aspect.

Discourse analysis can take three interlocking forms: (1) it can focus on the order of the text on the page; (2) it can engage in rearrangement on the basis of topical unities; and (3) it can focus on allusions

---

[1] For a more elaborate classification of foci, see Vern S. Poythress, "A Framework for Discourse Analysis: The Components of a Discourse, from a Tagmemic Viewpoint," *Semiotica* 38-3/4 (1982): 277–298, http://www.frame-poythress.org/wp-content/uploads/2012/08/semi.1982.38.3-4.277.pdf, DOI: 10.1515/semi.1982.38.3-4.277, accessed December 29, 2012.

and multilevel analogies, such as metaphor, metonymy, symbolism, and other figurative devices.

Analyzing Flow

The first form of discourse analysis, which focuses on the order of the text, studies the flow of text from one idea to another and how one idea supports or qualifies another.[2] The support between pieces of text can take the form of a causal relation (cause and effect, purpose, unexpected effect), a logical relation ("hence," "or"), a topical relation (repetition or contrast or filling in detail), or a temporal relation ("after," "before," circumstantial information). Analysis of these supporting relations can take an elaborate form, if desired. But most of the benefits can be reaped simply by asking repeatedly how clauses fit together into larger units, which themselves fit together into still larger ones.

We may take 1 Samuel 22:1–2 as our example. Here is the text, mostly arranged in clauses:

> David departed from there
> and escaped to the cave of Adullam.
> And when his brothers and all his father's house heard it,
> they went down there to him.
> And everyone who was in distress,
> and everyone who was in debt,
> and everyone who was bitter in soul,
> gathered to him.
> And he became commander over them.
> And there were with him about four hundred men.

The text divides naturally into two main parts. The first two clauses are about David alone. The rest are about people who come to him. Among those people there are two subgroups: David's relatives and those in distress of various kinds. So we can analyze the relevant sentences as follows:

---

[2] This focus for discourse analysis is called *rhetorical analysis* in Vern S. Poythress, "Hierarchy in Discourse Analysis: A Revision of Tagmemics," *Semiotica* 40-1/2 (1982): 107–137, http://www.frame-poythress.org/wp-content/uploads/2012/08/semi.1982.40.1-2.107.pdf, DOI: 10.1515/semi.1982.40.1-2.107, accessed December 29, 2012.

David departed from there
    → before and then after →
and escaped to the cave of Adullam.

And when his brothers and all his father's house heard it,
    → cause to effect →
they went down there to him.

    And everyone who was in distress,
        —"and" (addition, a kind of relation based on topic)—
    and everyone who was in debt,
        —"and"—
    and everyone who was bitter in soul,
    → completion (a relation based on topic, in which one part of
        a proposition is completed by another)→
    gathered to him.

And he became commander over them.
    → temporal circumstantial detail →
And there were with him about four hundred men.

We can also ask about the supporting relationships between the major pieces:

David departed from there and escaped to the cave of Adullam.
    → cause to effect →

And when his brothers and all his father's house heard it, they
    went down there to him.
    → "and" (relation based on topic: two different groups come
    to David) →

And everyone who was in distress, and everyone who was in debt,
and everyone who was bitter in soul, gathered to him.
    → cause to effect (David responds) →

And he became commander over them. And there were with him
    about four hundred men.

Fig. 18.1: Tree for Rhetorical Analysis

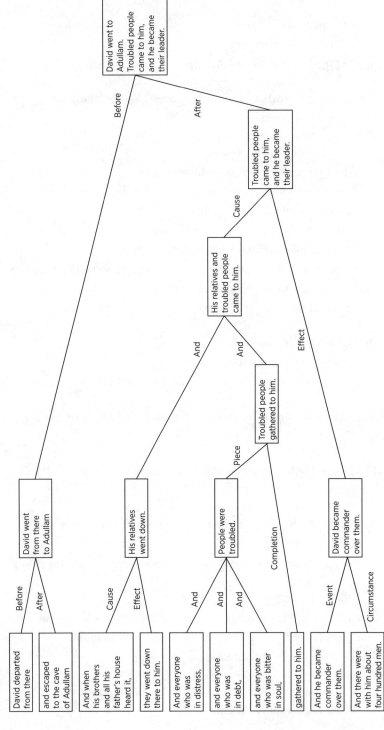

The entire structure can then be analyzed as a tree on its side, where branches link together to indicate larger units of text. (See fig. 18.1.)

We can add to this analysis an assessment of the relative prominence or emphasis that belongs to any one piece. For each time when two or more units come together to form a larger unit, we can ask which of the smaller pieces is more prominent, within the larger context. For example, consider the first part of 1 Samuel 22:1:

> David departed from there
> and escaped to the cave of Adullam.

We consider the two propositions together and see that they form a larger whole, describing David's journey. Within this larger whole, is one of the two propositions more prominent, or do they have equal weight? In this case both propositions contribute in a substantial way to the total picture. David goes *from* one place and *to* another. But the second proposition is still somewhat more prominent. For one thing, in many situations the goal of a movement has more prominence than the starting point. In addition, reaching the goal, together with the idea of "escape," suggests that David has found temporary relief from possible threats from Achish or from Saul. Given the concern for David's safety, this relief has more prominence than the mere fact that he departed from the vicinity of Achish and Gath. The prominence belonging to the second proposition can be marked within a diagram by circling it or by inscribing a special script P (*p*), standing for "Prominence."

David departed from there

and escaped to the cave of Adullam.

or:

David departed from there

and escaped to the cave of Adullam. *p*

In the same way we can add information about prominence to the whole tree that analyzes 1 Samuel 22:1–2. (See fig. 18.2.)

The advantage of this type of analysis is that we can appreciate more

Fig. 18.2: Tree for Rhetorical Analysis, with Prominence

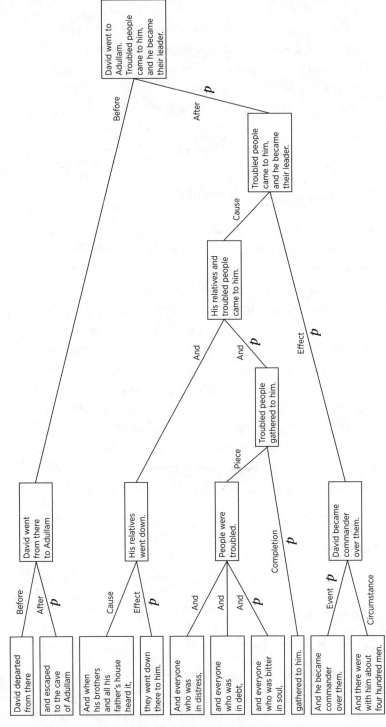

precisely how smaller pieces fit into larger wholes. We can also appreciate ways in which one piece of text supports or reinforces another. These relationships contribute to the overall force of any piece of text. In addition, by asking about prominence we may exercise discernment as to what points are the main points.

Narrative Flow

If we are analyzing narrative discourse, we may also pay attention to an important feature of narrative, the rise and fall of tension. Narrative episodes frequently show a flow that begins with a stable situation and then introduces a problem or tension. The narrative shows an increase in tension toward a climax, and then ends in a resolution that partially or wholly dissolves the tension.

The narrative in 1 Samuel 22:1–2 does not have a lot of tension. But there is some small tension over David's escape from Achish, king of Gath. The tension lies in the question as to whether he will be pursued, and how he will fare. Does the tension resolve when his relatives come to him? It is possible to interpret the narrative in that way. But given the way in which enemies like Achish or Saul could pursue relatives as well as David himself, the second half of verse 1 is better interpreted as actually increasing the tension. Will David's relatives be okay? The situation becomes even more complicated when people in distress come to David. A partial resolution takes place when David becomes commander over them, because the word *commander* suggests military leadership. David now has a fighting band that could resist the threat of an attack.

In more extended narratives, the rise and fall of tension offer important information. The fall of tension, or "resolution," frequently takes the form of a miniature sort of redemption, in a broad sense of the term. If David becomes a commander, and if that word suggests some protection or security, even this event is a small instance of redemptive resolution. The resolution frequently shows us the main point of the story. We will discuss redemptive plots at a later point (chapter 26).

Larger Units in Hierarchy

We may also analyze how 1 Samuel 22:1–2 fits into the larger context of 1–2 Samuel as a whole. First and Second Samuel form a continuous narrative, so a narrative analysis in terms of the tensions involved in good and bad kingship is appropriate. We can also analyze how smaller units fit into bigger ones.[3] David's time in the cave of Adullam fits into a larger sequence of events where he stays at several places. We find that David spends time at Nob (21:1–9), at Gath (21:10–15), at the cave of Adullam (22:1–2), at Mizpeh of Moab (22:3–4), and in the forest of Hereth (22:5). All these times belong to the period where David flees from Saul because Saul is trying to kill him (20:1–42). After 22:5 we have an account of Saul's slaughter of the priests at Nob (22:6–23), which describes Saul's response to David's earlier time at Nob (21:1–9). After chapter 22 come a series of further escapes, including a more extended time in interaction with the Philistines (27:1–30:31).

On a larger scale, the book of 1–2 Samuel divides itself roughly into the time of Samuel (1 Samuel 1–8), the time of Saul (1 Samuel 9–15), the time of Saul versus David (1 Samuel 16–31), and the time of David's kingship (2 Samuel). The time of Saul versus David breaks up into an early period of ambivalence (16–20), the time of David's escapes (21–30), and the time of Saul's death (31). The small piece 22:1–2 is one of David's escapes. In light of the context, we can see that this small piece is primarily about the rise of David but also about the decline of Saul. David repeatedly has to flee because of the permanent break created by Saul's murderous designs. In the whole narrative, the sovereign purpose of God is at work.

In a complex narrative like 1–2 Samuel, there are many forms of tension. In 1 Samuel 1–8, the primary tension concerns the religious allegiance of the priests and the people. In 1 Samuel 9–15, the tension concerns Saul's allegiance to the Lord's word. In 1 Samuel 16–30, the tension stems from Saul's envy and then murderous designs. It is finally resolved only by Saul's death (chapter 31).

Analyzing Topics

A second form of discourse analysis asks what content belongs to a discourse regardless of the order of its flow. We look at topics, themes, and motifs that repeat themselves, either in a small piece or in a whole book or in the Bible as a whole.[4]

---

[3] Consider, for example, the extensive outline provided by David Toshio Tsumura, *The First Book of Samuel* (Grand Rapids, MI: Eerdmans, 2007), 73–81. See also the outline in Joyce G. Baldwin, *1 and 2 Samuel: An Introduction and Commentary* (Downers Grove, IL/Leicester, England: InterVarsity Press, 1988), 45–47.

[4] This focus for discourse analysis is called *motific analysis* in Poythress, "Hierarchy."

In 1 Samuel 22:1–2, the topic of David's movements occurs twice, in the first and second clauses. The topic of David's supporters occurs in the next clauses. The topic of David's leadership, which recurs in the rest of 1 Samuel, is present at the end of verse 2. Topical analysis can pay attention not only to repetitions *within* a smaller passage, but also to topics and themes and motifs that run through whole books. The topic of David's leadership fits into a broad theme in 1–2 Samuel and 1–2 Kings, concerning what type of king Israel has, and what are the consequences of good and bad kingly leadership.

Analyzing Figurative Language

A third form of discourse analysis focuses on figurative language and allusions.[5] It is appropriate especially for poetry, parables, riddles, and other allusive texts. First Samuel 22:1–2 is fairly straightforward prose, so it does not lend itself so obviously to this kind of analysis. However, we know from the larger discussion of kingship in 1–2 Samuel that God's kingship has analogies (and disanalogies!) with human kingship under Saul and David. So we can compare David's leadership with God's kingship. Physical distress also offers analogies with spiritual distress, so we could consider the larger issue of distress of all kinds, against the background of the fall and its effects.

Analysis of discourse offers a perspective, so it is related to all the aspects of analysis that we have already discussed. But discourse structure is closely related to hierarchy, the fitting of smaller pieces of language into larger ones. So it makes sense to list the three forms of discourse analysis under the larger category of hierarchy. We can integrate discourse analysis into our overall outline as follows:

A. Observation
B. Elucidation
   1. One passage
      a. The literary context
      b. The transmission context
      c. The text
         (1) The text as act of communication

---

[5] This focus for discourse analysis is called *analogical analysis* in Poythress, "Hierarchy."

        (a) Authorial intention
        (b) Textual expression
          ((1)) Units
          ((2)) Hierarchies
            *((a)) Discourse flow
            *((b)) Discourse topics
            *((c)) Discourse figures
          ((3)) Systemic linguistic contexts
        (c) Readers' impression
      (2) The social contexts
      (3) The historical contexts
   2. Topical correlation
   3. Redemptive-historical correlation
C. Application

Our previous discussion of figurative language (chapter 16) can fit into the outline under "Discourse figures."

Resources

Because various forms of discourse analysis can include technical detail, we refer readers to details found in a number of resources.

For analysis of flow:

Beekman, John, and John Callow. *Translating the Word of God*, with Scripture and Topical Indexes. Grand Rapids, MI: Zondervan, 1974. Chapters 17–19.

Piper, John. *Biblical Exegesis: Discovering the Meaning of Scriptural Texts*. Internet publication, http://www.desiringgod.org/resource-library/seminars/biblical-exegesis, accessed December 27, 2012. ("Arcing," as taught by Daniel P. Fuller at Fuller Theological Seminary.)

Poythress, Vern S. "Hierarchy in Discourse Analysis: A Revision of Tagmemics," *Semiotica* 40-1/2 (1982): 107–137. http://www.frame-poythress.org/wp-content/uploads/2012/08/semi.1982.40.1-2.107.pdf, accessed December 29, 2012.

———. "Propositional Relations." In *The New Testament Student and His Field*. Vol. 5 of *The New Testament Student*. Edited by John H. Skilton and Curtiss A. Ladley. Phillipsburg, NJ: Presbyterian & Reformed, 1982. Pp. 159–212.

Traina, Robert. *Methodical Bible Study*. Grand Rapids, MI: Zondervan, 2002. (A revision of a 1952 precursor to flow analysis and "arcing.")

For analysis of topics and figurative language:

Poythress, Vern S. "Hierarchy in Discourse Analysis: A Revision of Tagmemics," *Semiotica* 40-1/2 (1982): 107–137. http://www.frame-poythress.org/wp-content/uploads/2012/08/semi.1982.40.1-2.107.pdf, accessed December 29, 2012.

19

Genre

We now consider the topic of *genre*. Genre is significant in interpreting the Bible because it concerns the literary context in which smaller pieces of text occur. Genre has to be taken into account because smaller pieces of text have their meaning in the context of the larger pieces in which they are embedded. We should not treat a poem in the same way as a prose description of history, nor do we treat a fictional story such as a parable of Jesus in the same way as the miracle accounts in the Gospels, which describe real events.

The Meaning of Genre

The *genre* of a piece of text is the kind of literature that it is. In the Bible, we find quite a few distinct genres: historical reports, genealogies, songs, parables, letters, visions, proverbs. Roughly speaking, a genre is "a group of pieces of literature with similar organization or style." We should add that a genre should be seen primarily as an "insider's" category. It describes how an insider or native to a particular language and culture would naturally classify a piece of literature. God sovereignly determines all the genres available in each language and culture. When he caused the books of the Bible to be written, he naturally wrote within the linguistic and cultural context that he had previously shaped. As readers belonging to another culture, we have to make adjustments to genres that were familiar within the original context but may not be immediately familiar to us. Fortunately, the wisdom of God and the commonalities in human nature make such adjustment possible.

As a simple example, consider the letters in the New Testament. In contemporary English culture, we begin a letter with a conventional line, "Dear Mary," or "Gentlemen: . . ." We usually end the letter with another conventional line, "Sincerely," or "Cordially," or "Yours truly," followed by the author's name and perhaps further information about the author. In the Greek-speaking world of the Roman Empire in the first century AD, letters began by identifying the author and then the addressees:

> [Author(s):] Paul and Timothy,
> servants of Christ Jesus,
> [Addressees:] To all the saints in Christ Jesus
> who are at Philippi,
> with the overseers and deacons. (Phil. 1:1)

So when we deal with letters in the New Testament, it helps to understand that they follow the normal pattern for letters of *that* time, not the pattern in *our* time. The same principle holds for other discourses coming from biblical times.

Size and Scope

Genre classifications can apply to both bigger and smaller pieces of text. Consider a particular example, from Matthew 6:24:

> No one can serve two masters, for either he will hate the one and love the other, or he will be devoted to the one and despise the other. You cannot serve God and money.

Matthew 6:24 is a short figurative saying that uses a comparison between master-servant relationships and serving either God or money. It belongs to a larger paragraph that includes a number of sayings about money and purity of service (Matt. 6:19–24). This paragraph belongs in turn to the Sermon on the Mount, which is a sermon. The Sermon on the Mount is one of several sections that contain teachings of Jesus, all of which belong to the Gospel of Matthew as a still larger whole.

In academic biblical studies, the word *genre* is sometimes used only with respect to the largest size of text—whole books. The word *form* is then used for smaller-sized pieces. But the same general principles can be applied to all the sizes. (We choose to use the word *genre* for all sizes.) How a piece of text functions is colored by the genre to which it belongs, and by larger contexts as well.

We should also observe that a genre can be a more expansive or a less expansive grouping of texts. For example, within the Gospels we find a number of episodes where Jesus casts out demons. These episodes belong together under the genre "exorcism stories." The exorcisms are also included within the larger category "miracle stories," and these in turn are included within the still larger category "stories about Jesus's ministry." Each of these groupings of texts forms a "genre."

The text 1 Samuel 22:1–2 is a single unit of text that describes one connected episode in the life of David. So it belongs to the genre "episode in Hebrew Israelite historical narrative." How we interpret it is obviously influenced by the judgment that it is historical narrative, not fiction. Modern Westerners also have to adjust to the fact that ancient Israelite historical narrative is customarily sparse and omits much that we might like to know. For example, Old Testament narratives usually contain little about the "inner psychology" of the characters. When we read 1 Samuel 22:1–2, we might have many questions about David's state of mind. How did David feel when he departed? Was he afraid? Was he relieved when he arrived at the cave of Adullam? Was he depressed because he had nothing better than a cave to live in? Was he glad when his family arrived? Did he welcome the troubled people who came to him, or was he reluctant to take responsibility for them? Did David volunteer to become commander over them, or did other people have to urge him? The passage does not give us answers. Typically, inner character has to be inferred from speech and action.

Cross-Cutting Classifications

The word *genre* in its usual modern meaning has a focus on *formal characteristics* of pieces of text, rather than on their informational content. But we should recognize that pieces of text can be classified by content as well. For example, all the episodes about David belong together because of their common content in being about David. The prose accounts of creation in Genesis 1 and 2 go together with the poetic account in Psalm 104.

In addition, we may classify texts by their authorship. All the letters of the apostle Paul belong together as "Pauline letters." As we indicated earlier, God speaks to human beings in a manner that fits together into contexts, including the context of the human author. So the letters by Paul invite us to interpret them all together, in a manner usually associated with what is called "Pauline theology."

Distribution

A single unit of text such as 1 Samuel 22:1–2 belongs to a collection of texts on the basis of common genre. A genre itself is a linguistic unit, and therefore has contrast, variation, and distribution. The genre *contrasts* with other genres that are distinct groupings. Each example of the genre varies from other examples, and thus illustrates *variation*. And genres are *distributed* in a larger system of genre classification.

It helps at this point if we distinguish three interlocking forms of distribution.[1] Distribution *in class* describes the fact that a given unit of text belongs to a larger class of units that can substitute for it. The class in question is the "substitution class," that is, the class of units that can fit into the same linguistic location as the unit in question. First Samuel 22:1–2 is distributed *in class* with the class of episodes in historical narrative. Distribution in class is closely related to *genre*. The genre is a larger class of pieces in which a given piece is distributed.

Second, distribution *in sequence* describes the fact that a given unit of text fits into a larger hierarchy of units surrounding it in time or space. First Samuel 22:1–2 has a particular location within the entire narrative of 1–2 Samuel, and is surrounded mainly by other episodes from the life of David (and some from the life of Saul). Typically, the fact that a piece of text belongs to a particular genre has a close relationship to how it is qualified for use within a sequence of pieces, to form a larger whole.

---

[1] The distinction is introduced in Kenneth L. Pike, *Linguistic Concepts: An Introduction to Tagmemics* (Lincoln: University of Nebraska Press, 1982), 62–65.

Third, distribution *in system* describes the fact that a given unit of text can be classified in many dimensions, such as its form, its content, or its authorship. We have already touched on this aspect in considering that classifications can cut across each other. For example, Exodus 14 and 15:1–18 represent respectively prose and poetic accounts of Israel crossing the Red Sea. Judges 4 and 5 represent respectively prose and poetic accounts of Barak and Deborah's exploits against Sisera. The classification as prose or poetry cuts across a classification by subject matter or by human authorship.

Profiting from Genre

Studying a piece of text should involve attention to its genre. This study can apply to pieces of text of a smaller or larger size. Assessing the genre of a text makes a difference. We ought not to treat Jesus's parables as if they were historical reports whose main point is to tell us what happened between a shepherd and his one hundred sheep (Luke 15:3–7), or between a master and his servants. The meaning of a parable can be found only when we take into account that a parable functions figuratively. The shepherd stands for God and for Jesus as his representative. The lost sheep stands for a lost sinner.

Conversely, we need to treat historical reports within the Bible as historical rather than fictional. Some skeptical scholarly critics tend to classify anything miraculous as "nonhistorical," because they have a prejudice against miracles. They have a prior commitment that biases them against admitting that miracles occur in history. God cares about what happens in history, because he works out salvation in Christ through Christ's death and resurrection in space and time (1 Cor. 15:12–19). The Gospel of Luke begins with a paragraph that clearly claims to describe what happened (Luke 1:1–4). Therefore, when a book of the Bible describes events, we should assume that it is talking about real events, unless there is some definite evidence to the contrary (such as a special genre like Jesus's parables).

In addition, we need to beware of making genre into a straitjacket. God and his human authors are free to create new genres (e.g., the Gospels) or create new works that go beyond anything that existed before. The book of Revelation is simultaneously a letter (see Rev. 1:4), a prophecy (1:3), and an account of apocalyptic visions (similar to the visions in parts of Ezekiel, Daniel, and Zechariah).

Outline of Study

Within our overall outline for studying texts, this study of genre is a perspective on the text we are studying. It interlocks with all the other foci for study. It falls most naturally under the aspect of contrast, variation, and distribution of the piece of text (B.1.c.(1).(b).((1)).). Usually we think of "genre" as a term applying to larger pieces of text, but the same principles could apply even to individual sentences or individual words. If we wish, we can include the study of genre under the aspect of "distribution":

A. Observation
B. Elucidation
   1. One passage
      a. The literary context
      b. The transmission context
      c. The text
         (1) The text as act of communication
            (a) Authorial intention
            (b) Textual expression
               ((1)) Units
                  ((a)) Contrast
                  ((b)) Variation
                  ((c)) Distribution
                      *c1. In substitution class
                      *c2. In sequence
                      *c3. In system
               ((2)) Hierarchies
               ((3)) Systemic linguistic contexts
            (c) Readers' impression
         (2) The social contexts
         (3) The historical contexts
   2. Topical correlation
   3. Redemptive-historical correlation
C. Application

Resources

Fee, Gordon D., and Douglas Stuart. *How to Read the Bible for All Its Worth*. Grand Rapids, MI: Zondervan, 2003.

Poythress, Vern S. *In the Beginning Was the Word: Language—A God-Centered Approach*. Wheaton, IL: Crossway, 2009. Chapter 23.

Ryken, Leland. *How to Read the Bible as Literature*. Grand Rapids, MI: Zondervan, 1984.

20

Using Commentaries

Commentaries on the Bible provide rich resources that supplement and correct an individual's study of Scripture. All of us have biases and hidden sins. It is easy to overlook some aspect of a passage, and it is easy to distort meaning in favor of pet ideas. When we consult commentaries, they may help us in overcoming our sins and limitations.

So where does the use of commentaries fit into the steps in study that we are exploring? In theory, commentaries could throw light on any of the stages. They are potentially relevant to all, and they may be consulted at any time. But it takes skill to use them wisely.

The Principle of Community

So let us consider what principles are involved. God sends the Holy Spirit to guide us into the truth (John 16:13; see Job 32:8),[1] and this guidance includes a process of overcoming sins and biases. In this process, the Holy Spirit uses means, and one primary means is our fellowship with other people in the church. In a broad sense, the church includes not only those with whom we meet in a single congregation, but also the worldwide church, which includes the people who write scholarly commentaries and practical, pastoral commentaries and study guides for books of the Bible. It includes not only Christians who are

---

[1] In John 16:13 Jesus may be speaking primarily about what the Holy Spirit will do for the apostles. But the principle applies at a subordinate level to all Christian believers.

alive today, but also writers of past generations. These include not only commentary writers, but systematic theologians, church historians (who help us to understand the wisdom and folly of the past in a larger historical context), and specialists in archeology, ancient history, lexicography (dictionary writers), grammar, geography, and others as well. We may also benefit from insights from non-Christians, due to common grace.

There are no simple formulas for appropriating the wisdom of other people. On the one hand, we can learn much and use the labors of others to overcome our individual limitations. On the other hand, other people, like us, are still influenced by sin, and they may lead us astray as well as help us. It is all the more important for us to use the Bible as a standard in sorting through good and bad. This sorting out is a process, because the good that we learn from others serves to deepen our understanding of the Bible, and then our deeper understanding of the Bible enables us to sift good and bad with greater discernment.

Principles for Using Commentaries

Commentaries range from technical focus to pastoral and practical focus. Both have benefits, and the benefits are complementary. During those times when our focus is primarily on elucidation of a single text rather than correlation or application, exegetical commentaries are the most valuable. More technical exegetical commentaries contain information on meanings and on historical background and on literary parallels that might easily escape our notice, and some of this information is very difficult for a nonspecialist to obtain through his own independent investigation.

But there are potential liabilities. First, if a student consults commentaries early in the process, or if he relies on them too intently, it can ruin his own personal interaction with the text, and it can ruin his own evaluation of what the text implies. The commentaries can fill his mind so much that he is no longer reading the text but only listening to the commentaries through the text. He thinks only of those ideas or trains of thought that the commentaries have brought up. The need for evaluation of interpretive options can also be overwhelmed by commentaries. Where commentaries disagree, the student may end up preferring the commentary whose ideas he already prefers. He chooses one because it "sounds good" to him, rather than because it builds the most solidly on what is actually found in the Bible.

For this reason, it is worthwhile for a student to avoid commentaries for the first part of his study. He needs to discipline himself and apply himself to the passage. He can still use lexicons and grammars, which have fewer problems because they are not offering opinions on the passage. Often, by working on a passage himself, a student will notice many features that push him in the direction of solid interpretation. Because he has listened to the passage, he then has some ability to evaluate which commentary opinion is most sound. He consults the commentaries later, in order to make sure that he has not overlooked something, rather than in order to have the commentaries make up his mind for him.

Pastoral and practical commentaries, often written from collections of sermons, have strengths and weaknesses of other kinds. They promote edification and challenge us particularly in the area of application. They are worth reading. But if used too early in the process of interpretation, they too can create an unhealthy dependence. The student can end up reading the text only through the eyes of what the commentary has suggested, and he may miss a very specific application to his life that he might have noticed if he had interacted with the text first and postponed reading the commentaries.

A special form of this danger arises with pastors and pastoral trainees who are preparing to deliver sermons to a congregation or some other group of people. The pastoral commentary or written sermon may seem so good in comparison to the student's own thoughts that he is tempted to preach someone else's sermon rather than his own. Yes, he may put his own touches on it, and put it in his own words, but still the substance is less his own and more that of his source. This approach may appear to work at times, but it is an unhealthy practice for the long run. God meant for his word to come to people primarily through human instrumentality—living, breathing human beings, rather than robotic imitators. What the preacher says should have been digested not only into his own mind, but also into his life, and he should speak as a full person, one person exhorting another heart to heart (note, for example, 1 Thess. 2:1–12; 1 Tim. 4:11–16).

Biases from Modern Culture

A second potential liability arises from cultural and presuppositional influences on commentary writers. As discussed in appendix A, the Enlightenment has brought about a sea change in the attitude toward the supernatural aspect of the Bible. Commentary writers feel the influence of this sea change, even if they partly resist it. Depending on their presuppositions, commentary writers may or may not treat the claims of the Bible as trustworthy. For this reason, commentaries written by authors who are evangelical in theology, who believe in the reality of God and the supernatural, and who believe that the Bible is the genuine word of God, are more trustworthy than commentaries written by mainstream scholars. But the degree of reliability still depends on the individual scholar and on the kind of issue being discussed. Scholars who are evangelical in theology and whose hearts are right with God may still make mistakes. Some are more competent than others for the task.

Mainstream critical scholarship can also serve as a source of some valuable information, because of common grace. But such a source must be critically sifted. The same applies in some ways even to evangelicals. No evangelical is sinlessly perfect. And the world of evangelical scholarship has been influenced both for good and for ill by the winds of scholarship from the mainstream. Many technical evangelical commentaries make it a practice to concentrate almost wholly on the human author, and there are liabilities in such a concentration (see appendix A).

A practical commentary written in the United States in the twenty-first century may include suggestive and penetrating applications to some of the particular issues arising in the United States—say, political issues, or moral issues such as abortion, or the lure of worshiping money or sex. But if the whole culture of twenty-first-century America has a blind spot, for example in an overemphasis on individual self-realization, the culture may influence both the commentary writer and the student studying the commentary. Voices from other cultures or other centuries, not to mention the transcendent voice of God himself in Scripture, can awaken us to such blind spots.

Using commentaries can be like a group Bible study. The insights of each individual benefit everyone. But students need to continue to interact firsthand with the Bible itself, and not merely with what other

people say the Bible says. The Bible is infallible, while the secondary interpretations are not. Each student must labor to do justice both to the
unique character and role of the Bible, and to God's design for mutual
edification in the church.

Role in an Outline of Steps

For practical purposes, I suggest, as a rule of thumb, that students preparing to preach or write on a passage should postpone consulting
commentaries until near the end of the time when they are focusing on
a single passage. In our overall outline, consultation of commentaries
might suitably be added as follows:

A. Observation
B. Elucidation
   1. One passage
      a. The literary context
      b. The transmission context
      c. The text
     *(d. Consult exegetical commentaries)
   2. Topical correlation
   3. Redemptive-historical correlation
C. Application

We have put in parentheses the step in which we consult commentaries, not because it is less important in practice, but because it is not a
distinct "step" in the same way as the other steps. Rather, it invites the
reader to practice all the steps in interaction with the ideas of others.
In the order of steps, we have placed it where it most aptly contributes
to the whole.

Resources

Carson, D. A. *New Testament Commentary Survey*. Grand Rapids, MI: Baker, 2007.
Longman, Tremper, III. *Old Testament Commentary Survey*. Grand Rapids, MI: Baker, 2007.

Part VI

REDEMPTIVE-
HISTORICAL
INTERPRETATION

21

The History of Redemption

We now turn our focus away from issues with language and toward issues relating to the history of redemption. God has one plan and one program encompassing all of history, and the Bible describes how he works out his plan over the centuries. Within this plan, Christ is at the center. The work that Christ accomplished by his life, death, resurrection, and ascension represents the fulcrum-point of history. Therefore we should not be surprised to hear that the Old Testament points forward to him:

> Then he [Jesus] said to them, "These are my words that I spoke to you while I was still with you, that everything written about me in the Law of Moses and the Prophets and the Psalms must be fulfilled." Then he opened their minds to understand the Scriptures, and said to them, "Thus it is written, that the Christ should suffer and on the third day rise from the dead, and that repentance and forgiveness of sins should be proclaimed in his name to all nations, beginning from Jerusalem. (Luke 24:44–47)

Accordingly, in our earlier outline of interpretive steps we have included a step B.3., which focuses on redemptive history and the centrality of Christ:

A. Observation
B. Elucidation

1. One passage
2. Topical correlation
*3. Redemptive-historical correlation
   C. Application

How do we study a passage like 1 Samuel 22:1–2 with a focus on its redemptive-historical correlations?

Attention to Scriptural Teaching

Scripture is a rich source. As usual, no recipe will guarantee that we gather and understand everything that we could learn. We should be asking God himself to teach us. We may learn in particular from New Testament uses of the Old Testament,[1] and from ways in which later parts of the Old Testament use or build on earlier parts. We should also digest the broader principles about history and God's providence. G. K. Beale helpfully summarizes the basic biblical assumptions that inform an understanding of New Testament use of the Old Testament:

1. Corporate solidarity or representation is assumed. [An individual member within a group can be treated as represented by the group or vice versa.]
2. On the basis of point 1 above, Christ is viewed as representing the *true Israel* of the OT *and* the true Israel—the church—in the NT.
3. *History is unified* by a wise and sovereign plan so that the earlier parts are designed to correspond and point to the later parts (cf. Matt. 11:13–14).
4. The age of *eschatological fulfillment* has come but has not been fully consummated in Christ.
5. As a consequence of point 4, it may be deduced that the later parts of biblical history function as the broader context to interpret earlier parts because they all have the same, ultimate divine author, who inspires the various human authors. One deduction from this premise is that Christ and his glory as the end-time

---

[1] We now have some fine resources in G. K. Beale and D. A. Carson, eds., *Commentary on the New Testament Use of the Old Testament* (Grand Rapids, MI: Baker; Nottingham, England: Apollos, 2007); G. K. Beale, *Handbook on the New Testament Use of the Old Testament: Exegesis and Interpretation* (Grand Rapids, MI: Baker, 2012).

center and goal of redemptive history are the *key to interpreting the earlier portions of the OT and its promises*.[2]

Each of Beale's five principles makes sense as we consider a particular passage, such as 1 Samuel 22:1–2.

1. *Corporate solidarity*. First Samuel 22:2 says that David "became commander over them." The band of men forms a corporate whole, and David is their leader and representative. Their well-being depends in many respects on David's well-being, and vice versa. This form of corporate solidarity is natural for a group like David's that is living and acting together. We can see how it is analogous in some ways to the corporate solidarity between the king of Israel and the people of Israel whom he leads. At this point in 1 Samuel, Saul is still king, but the reader who has absorbed 1 Samuel 16 and Samuel's anointing of David knows that God intends David to become king at a later point.

2. *Christ representing true Israel*. Israel the people of God in David's time is intrinsically linked to fulfillment in Christ. So David as their future king is linked to Christ as the climactic future king.

3. *History is unified*. So the events described in 1 Samuel 22:1–2 have an integral role in the plan of God. His plan encompasses both the "short run," the period of 1–2 Samuel where Israelite kingship is established, and the "long run," where the kingship leads to Christ the King, in both his first and his second coming.

4. *The age of eschatological fulfillment has come (in Christ)*. This principle also is important for 1 Samuel 22:1–2, because it says that eschatological fulfillment had not come during David's time or the time when 1 Samuel 22:1–2 was initially written. The events of David's time and their description in 1 Samuel 22:1–2 indicate by their less-than-climactic character that fulfillment is still to come. They point forward.

5. *Later parts of Scripture interpret earlier parts*. God never intended for 1 Samuel 22:1–2 or even the whole book of 1–2 Samuel to stand in isolation or to be the only words he would speak. It is legitimate for us to read 1 Samuel 22:1–2 in the light of later revelation, including the New Testament, because God intended it so from the beginning. For example, we know that Christ the final king of God's people has come,

---

[2] Beale, *Handbook on the New Testament Use of the Old Testament*, 53 (italics his).

and that the saving reign of God, called the "kingdom of God," has come through Christ the King. God invites us to see 1 Samuel 22:1–2 in the light of our additional knowledge. It suggests already that David foreshadows Christ.

Progressive Revelation

Beale's fifth principle, concerning divine authorship and the goal of redemptive history, could be further expanded to make explicit the concept of *progressive revelation*. God works out his plan of redemption in successive phases of history. He also gives revelation to his people in successive phases. God's deeds of redemption fit together, and his words interpret his deeds.

God's *deeds* lead up progressively and organically to the climactic act, the working out of redemption in the life of Christ. Likewise, God's *words* lead up progressively and organically to the climactic word, Christ as the word made "flesh" (John 1:14), and the explications of the meaning of his work by New Testament apostles and other authors commissioned to write in his name and with his authority.

The progressive character in God's deeds and words imply that (1) he does not reveal everything at once, at the beginning, but only gradually; (2) later deeds and words build on and further illumine the significance of earlier deeds and words; (3) the later deeds and words supplement the earlier ones, in such a way that God's people deepen their understanding of God and his plan; (4) the deeds help to interpret the words, and vice versa; and (5) every deed and every word means what it means within a context in which God designs it to fit into a particular stage and moment within the total progress of redemptive history, and in which it has a forward-pointing thrust, toward the climax in Christ and the consummation in the new heaven and the new earth.

These principles apply to 1 Samuel 22:1–2. The original readers of 1 Samuel 22:1–2 could already understand that David had been anointed to be the next king, and that he would be superior to Saul, who was the king after the people's heart. They could understand that David's life as a fugitive in verses 1–2 was temporary. God had more in store for him, but first had him go through times of trial. Because of God's promise in 2 Samuel 7:8–16, the readers could also understand that David was the first of a line of kings. If they took account of the promise of redemption in Genesis 3:15 and later expanded promises, they could also infer that David's kingship functioned as one phase along the road to a future climactic redemption. But they would be limited in their ability to see what the details of this future redemption would look like. They knew that God already had a plan. They could know that what he was saying in 1 Samuel 22:1–2 had significance within that comprehensive plan.

Standing as we do in the period following the first coming of Christ, we can look back and understand more of God's plan and the significance of 1 Samuel 22:1–2. But that fuller significance is fully compatible with what God always had in mind, and what he purposed to tell the earlier readers of the text in 1–2 Samuel.

Thus, we can focus either on the earlier functions of 1 Samuel 22:1–2 for its earlier readers or on its functions for us as later readers—or on both, in their relation to each other. On the one hand, we can say that we as later readers see more meaning or more significance in the passage than what earlier readers could establish within the context of their limited knowledge. God in a sense "added" meaning, in the context of our experience, because we as later readers can compare 1 Samuel 22:1–2 with later Scriptures. In another sense, the meaning is always the same. God intended from the beginning everything that we now receive from the passage. Even earlier readers could appreciate that there was more meaning than what they could presently grasp, because they could know, from what they grasped even then, that the climax was still in the future.

This situation can seem paradoxical. Does 1 Samuel 22:1–2 mean more now than it did then, or does it mean the same? Someone might react by saying, "Make up your mind." But it is not as paradoxical as it seems. We can use an analogy from the communication by an earthly father. Suppose an earthly father teaches his son John 3:16 and explains its meaning. Suppose the son grows up, and even goes to seminary to study the Bible more deeply. The son then recalls at one point how his father, years ago, first taught him about John 3:16. What did the father intend to convey? He intended that the son would understand John 3:16 in a way that a child is capable of. But he also intended that the son would continue to return to the verse, and would understand more and more as time passed. He intended that the boy's understanding would grow. So the father's intention encompassed the earlier understanding, the growth, and the later understanding, all in one unified purpose.

Likewise God, even more than an earthly father, has a purpose from the beginning that his people's understanding of his word should grow. His "meaning" all along is what we see at the end—ultimately at the consummation. At the same time, his meaning is already accessible earlier: we understand partially, but we do understand (1 Cor. 13:12).

We can use still another illustration. Imagine a person looking into a microscope at a thin section cut from a leaf. At first he sees only a blur. Then he turns the focus knob on the microscope, and the specimen comes into focus. He sees more and more detail. The specimen was there all the time, and in a sense he could see everything even before it was in focus. But he sees more details as he adjusts the focus. Likewise, God's plan for redemption is all there from the beginning, and 1 Samuel 22:1–2 among many other passages speaks about that plan. But it takes time, and more information, for the details to come into focus for us.

Perspectives on History

Any one deed or word enjoys a particular location in time, the time within which God brings it about. At the same time, it has a universal relevance, both because it fits into the universal, comprehensive plan of God for all time, and because it participates in and testifies to a forward motion toward Christ as goal. Christ is the goal both with respect to his first coming, in which he accomplished definitive and climactic redemption, once and for all, and with respect to his second coming, when he will bring to consummation the redemption that he has already accomplished.

For example, 1 Samuel 22:1–2 is a particular word that God gave at a particular time, perhaps at the time of Solomon. It also makes reference to the time of David's life. Both word and deed belong intrinsically to these two times, which are distinct times within the totality of history. Second, the message in 1 Samuel 22:1–2 has universal relevance, because it belongs within the total message of God for all times. Third, the message points forward to Christ, especially through the figure of

David as a foreshadowing of Christ. The same three observations hold not only with respect to the words of 1 Samuel 22:1–2, but also with respect to the underlying events described in 1 Samuel 22:1–2, events belonging to the life of David.

We can discern in these functions of God's words and deeds three perspectives. According to the particle perspective, each word and each deed is unique, both in what it is and in its location in time. According to the wave perspective, each word and each deed participates in the forward motion of history toward its goal. According to the field perspective, each word and each deed permanently enjoys its own meaning in relation to the totality of history, which God works out according to his plan.

As usual, these three perspectives interlock. We can understand the meaning of a word within the total plan of God only if we understand what it says in its uniqueness. Conversely, its uniqueness is crafted by God precisely in order to fit into his universal plan. Since God plans that his will should work out over time, in history, the forward thrust toward the goal belongs integrally within his universal plan. Conversely, when we examine the meaning of the forward thrust in history, God intends that we should perceive it as the working out of a plan from the foundation of the world.

Alternatively, we can look at the meaning of history from the normative, situational, and existential perspectives. The normative perspective leads to a focus on God's plan for history, because his plan is the norm for its meaning. The situational perspective leads to focusing on the events in history, both individual events and the totality of history, which together compose the environment for human beings. The existential perspective leads to a focus on persons. We can of course focus on ourselves, and endeavor to apply to ourselves the meanings that God gives us. Or we can focus on God, and especially on the person of Christ, who stands at the center of history through his life on earth, his death, his resurrection, and his ascension. He stands also as the goal of history, in whom God will "unite all things . . . , things in heaven and things on earth" (Eph. 1:10). Finally, he stands as the origin of history, because "by him all things were created" (Col. 1:16).

In sum, redemptive-historical interpretation involves meditation on *correlations* between the individual texts of Scripture. In this study of correlation, we meditate on the plan of God (normative), the totality of historical events (situational), and Christ the center (existential). We meditate on each event and word to see its unique purpose (particle perspective), its forward-pointing thrust (wave perspective), and its relationship to the entire plan of God with respect to the totality of history (field perspective). If we wish, we can sum up the process in a series of steps:

A. Observation
B. Elucidation
   1. One passage
   2. Topical correlation
   3. Redemptive-historical correlation
     *a. God's plan as source of meaning
     *b. Historical events (speaking and acting)
     *c. Christ as the center
C. Application

Each of the pieces can be further subdivided using the particle, wave, and field perspectives:

A. Observation
B. Elucidation
   1. One passage
   2. Topical correlation
   3. Redemptive-historical correlation
     a. God's plan as source of meaning
       *(1) Particle: God's plan for a unique word or deed
       *(2) Wave: God's plan for forward thrust of one word
       *(3) Field: God's plan for a fit into the total picture
     b. Historical events (speaking and acting)
       *(1) Particle: one word or deed located at one time
       *(2) Wave: forward thrust of one word
       *(3) Field: one word in relation to all of history
     c. Christ as the center
       *(1) Particle: one word or deed proclaiming Christ
       *(2) Wave: forward thrust to fulfillment in Christ
       *(3) Field: one word in relation to the glory of Christ in the beginning, end, center, and every point of history
C. Application

We could also turn our outline "inside out" by making the particle, wave, and field perspectives the primary categories for organizing the outline:

A. Observation
B. Elucidation
  1. One passage
  2. Topical correlation
  3. Redemptive-historical correlation
    *a. Particle: uniqueness of one word or deed
      (1) God's plan for the unique word
      (2) The word's unique location in time
      (3) The unique word proclaiming Christ
    *b. Wave: the forward thrust of a word or deed
      (1) God's plan for the unfolding in time
      (2) The movement of events in which the word participates
      (3) The word pointing forward to Christ
    *c. Field: a word or deed in *relation* to all of history
      (1) God's plan for the fit of the word into the totality
      (2) The word's relation to all of history
      (3) The word's relation to Christ as source, goal, and center
C. Application

Since we are dealing with perspectives, we need not treat either choice as a foundation for the other. We can use a two-dimensional grid (see table 21.1).

Table 21.1: Perspectives on God's Plan for History

	unique piece (particle)	development forward (wave)	In relationships (field)
God's plan (normative)	God's plan for a unique purpose	God's plan for development	God's plan for meaningful relationships
historical events (situational)	an event uniquely located in time	an event pointing forward	an event in relation to the totality of history
Christ's person (existential)	an event proclaiming Christ	an event pointing forward to Christ	an event making up a whole, displaying the comprehensive glory of Christ

Resources

Key analyses of the history of redemption:

Goldsworthy, Graeme. *Gospel and Kingdom: A Christian Interpretation of the Old Testament*. Exeter, England: Paternoster, 1981.

Vos, Geerhardus. *Biblical Theology: Old and New Testaments*. Edinburgh/Carlisle, PA: Banner of Truth Trust, 1975.

22

Christocentric Interpretation

Because of the centrality of Christ in redemptive history, and because of the challenges in understanding how the Old Testament points to Christ, we need to devote special attention to Christocentric interpretation of the Old Testament.

Several complementary perspectives can help us uncover relationships between the Old Testament and Christ. We will describe these perspectives and illustrate them.

Manner of Addressing the Future

Old Testament texts link themselves to the future redemption in Christ in several complementary ways. First, a text can directly predict the future coming of Christ. Some prophecies, like Isaiah 9:6–7, 11:1–5, Micah 5:2, and Zechariah 9:9, directly predict the coming of the righteous messianic king. Others, like Isaiah 40:1–11, 60:1–2, and Zechariah 14:1–3, predict the coming of God. Others predict the coming of great blessing, prosperity, and deliverance: Isaiah 44:3–5, 51:1–6, and 65:17–25. The focus on the Messiah, on the coming of God, and on the work of salvation can be combined, since ultimately God brings blessing and salvation through his Messiah. These direct predictions are important, because they help to give people a more definite picture to which they can relate other texts whose relation to the coming of Christ is more indirect.

Second, a text can set forth a general pattern or principle. For example, the book of Proverbs has general principles related to wisdom and to righteous living. Job and Ecclesiastes are also wisdom books. The book of Psalms contains writings like Psalm 18 that originated in particular circumstances (compare 2 Samuel 22), but by putting individual psalms such as this one in the book of Psalms, God is inviting Israel to see their general applicability. Israel is invited to sing and to meditate on the psalms throughout the ages, and the invitation then extends to us as heirs in union with Christ (Gal. 3:29). Because the principles are general, they apply not only to us but also to Christ, as fully human and representative for his people.

In fact, the principles apply *preeminently* to Christ, because in his humanity he represents what all humanity ought to be. He is, moreover, the pattern to which God will conform us:

> Thus it is written, "The first man Adam became a living being"; the last Adam became a life-giving spirit. But it is not the spiritual that is first but the natural, and then the spiritual. The first man was from the earth, a man of dust; the second man is from heaven. As was the man of dust, so also are those who are of the dust, and as is the man of heaven, so also are those who are of heaven. Just as we have borne the image of the man of dust, we shall also bear the image of the man of heaven. (1 Cor. 15:45–49)

> And we all, with unveiled face, beholding the glory of the Lord, are being transformed into the *same image* from one degree of glory to another. (2 Cor. 3:18)

> . . . until we all attain to the unity of the faith and of the knowledge of the Son of God, to *mature manhood, to the measure of the stature of the fullness of Christ.* (Eph. 4:13)

Christ is the wisdom of God (1 Cor. 1:30). So he fulfills the wisdom found in the Old Testament wisdom books. Christ is the righteousness of God (1 Cor. 1:30). So he fulfills the principles about the path of righteousness found in the book of Proverbs. Since he is our representative, his wisdom and righteousness are supposed to be reflected in us who are his people.

Third, a text can focus on a particular historical event or episode. First Samuel 22:1–2 and other historical texts use this manner of presentation. Each event in history is unique, but, as we have said, it also belongs to an overarching plan for history, and that history finds its climax in Christ. So these texts point to Christ. But they do so in a different manner than prophecy and wisdom books and Psalms.

Altogether, we have three main ways in which an Old Testament text can speak about time: (1) it can directly speak about the future; (2) it can speak about all times through a focus on general principles; and (3) it can speak about one specific time—but then this one specific time has relations to all the other times. These three ways of speaking are clearly distinguishable. But there are also sometimes combinations. Note that Psalm 18 comes from the life of David, and thus contains both a generalizable example of how to praise God (the focus on principle in pattern (2)) and references to specific times (the life of David, corresponding to pattern (3)). The end of the psalm also includes a more directly predictive element: "Great salvation he brings to his king, and shows steadfast love to his anointed, to David *and his offspring forever*" (Ps. 18:50). This predictive element illustrates pattern (1), the pattern of direct prediction.

We can also see that though the three patterns are distinguishable, each implies the others. Direct prediction (pattern (1)) points to a specific time in the future in which God will bring to pass what he has promised. So a predictive text also addresses a specific time (pattern (3)). The climactic fulfillment in Christ's earthly life belongs to a specific time, but also has implications for how people enter into salvation throughout history. So it embodies general principles about salvation and about our relationship to God (pattern (2)). Conversely, the general principles have specific embodiments in the life of Christ and thus belong to one particular time (pattern (3)). Principles in the Old Testament are also indirectly predictive (pattern (1)), because such principles must be embodied when the climactic salvation takes place.

Thus the three patterns are perspectivally related. Each in the end tacitly includes the others. Consider, for example, Matthew 11:13: "For all the Prophets and the Law *prophesied* until John." It is not so surprising to hear that the Prophets "prophesied," because this prophesying could take place through direct predictions within the prophetic books. But does the *Law* prophesy? Jesus says that it does. Some verses of the Law contain direct predictions (for example, Gen. 3:15; 49:10; Num. 24:17), but not many. Yet the whole Law does "prophesy." It points forward to Christ, but it does so not merely by direct prediction but by indirect prediction, such as when the animal sacrifices point to Christ's final sacrifice. "Prophesying," then, has become a perspective on the whole Old Testament.

We can see in the three patterns (prediction, general principle, and specific events) an instance of the particle, wave, and field perspectives. Direct prediction expresses linear time, corresponding to the wave perspective. A prediction made at one time points forward through intermediate times to the time of fulfillment. A general pattern expresses relationships between events at many times, corresponding to the field perspective, which highlights relationships. A text focusing on one event in one time corresponds to the particle perspective, which treats the event as a single, unified whole.

The Nature of Old Testament Promises

The first of these patterns, the pattern of prediction, might better be called the pattern of *promise*. The word *prediction* may suggest to some people three unfortunate connotations. First, it may suggest merely a human guess or a human estimate. A human weather forecaster may *predict* that there will be rain tomorrow. But such a prediction might prove false, because it has only human authority as its basis. By contrast, the predictions in the Old Testament have *God's* authority. They will definitely come to pass. The word *promise* better articulates this feature because a promise is not merely a prediction but a binding commitment from the person who is promising. In this case, God is the one who is committing himself to bring about the fulfillment of each promise that he makes.

Second, the word *prediction* may connote that the prediction depends only on foresight, not on power. A human prediction about the weather does not claim to *control* the weather, but only to foresee what will happen on the basis of atmospheric conditions and causal interactions among bodies of air outside the control of human observers. By contrast, God *controls* the future. He does not merely "predict" it by foreseeing something that will happen, as if things were beyond his control. The word *promise* better expresses this feature of God's predictions. God not only says what will happen but he also undertakes by his power to bring it about, at the time that he appoints.

Third, the word *prediction* can connote a manner of foretelling in which only the plainest, most prosaic description of the future is used. God frequently gives promises in poetic form. And they may have multiple stages of fulfillment. For example, God's initial promise of redemption in Genesis 3:15 has the poetic form of parallel lines:

> I will put enmity between you and the woman,
> and between your offspring and her offspring;
>
> he shall bruise your head,
> and you shall bruise his heel.

The climactic fulfillment of this promise takes place in Christ. Christ is the offspring of the woman. He bruises Satan's head by achieving the decisive defeat of Satan and evil in the cross (Col. 2:15). But in the Old Testament we also see many preliminary, temporary defeats of evil through "offspring" that God raises up. Noah defeats the evil around him through his righteousness and his trust in God. Joshua defeats the inhabitants of Jericho. Ehud defeats Eglon. David defeats Goliath. So the promise of God in Genesis 3:15 is richer in texture than a bare-bones newspaper report of a single event.

A Summary of the Perspectives of Promise, Principle, and Specific Event

If we integrate these perspectives into our overall outline, they fit within the subdivision for redemptive history:

A. Observation
B. Elucidation
   1. One passage
   2. Topical correlation
   3. Redemptive-historical correlation
      a. God's plan as source of meaning

  b. Historical events (speaking and acting)
  c. Christ as the center
   *(1) Wave: promises about Christ (prophecy)
   *(2) Field: general principles fulfilled in Christ
   *(3) Particle: particular times relating to Christ
 C. Application

Kinds of Relationships to Christ

Of the three types of patterns referring to Christ, the most challenging is the third, because it is less obvious *how* a particular event in the Old Testament points forward to Christ. We will concentrate on this challenge. But the ways we suggest for meeting the challenge are pertinent to other patterns in the Old Testament as well (see the examples in part VIII below).

So how does a particular episode like 1 Samuel 22:1–2 point to Christ? Each episode is unique, so no general recipe can cover everything. Yet we may suggest some general principles.[1]

First, an episode can relate to Christ by way of *analogy*. An *analogy* is any likeness between persons, or between places, events, relationships, etc. In 1 Samuel 22:1–2, David as commander and future king is like Christ the king. The people who gather to David are like the disciples who gather to Christ during his earthly life, or like the church that gathers spiritually to Christ during the gospel age, or, in the consummation, like all the nations that come to worship (Rev. 21:24–26). Christ is at the center of redemption, and so his leadership is at the center. But we can see in the case of David a broader principle that has many illustrations, with military leaders, family leaders, governmental leaders, and priestly leaders (Gen. 6:18; 7:7; 14:14; Ex. 17:10; Joshua 1; 1 Chronicles 23–27; Neh. 8:1–2).

It is easy to overlook the presence of analogies when they are of a fairly general and seemingly innocuous character. If we observe that there are many leaders, someone might reply, "So what?" But God created the world and sustains it in a regular way. There are many general patterns that take the form of analogies. These all serve to "hold his-

---

[1] For the discussion of analogy, symbolism, and typology, I am grateful for ideas from O. Palmer Robertson's teaching.

tory together." Human beings belong to many different cultures, but underneath they are the same—they are all human. They all bear the image of God; they are all sinners; they all need redemption; as sinners they all fight against God and evade him.

God's remedy for sin is fundamentally the same throughout history. He has mercy on sinners for the sake of Christ. As people place their faith in God and his promises (which look forward to Christ), they are united to Christ and God begins to transform them spiritually through the power of Christ in the Holy Spirit.

Thus analogies of even an "ordinary" kind have an integral relation to the meaning of redemption. We can identify with human beings described in the pages of the Bible because we are like them. We see the same God at work with them who is at work with us. The acts of redemption that God brought about in ancient times are fundamentally analogous to what he accomplished in Christ, and to what he still accomplishes today in the people in whom he is working out his salvation.

Future Orientation

We have spoken about analogies that "point forward to Christ." But someone may ask whether only *some* analogies have this forward-pointing thrust. Does David's leadership in 1 Samuel 22:1–2 actually "point forward"? Or is it just there, without any sense of a future thrust? The passage does not *say* in so many words that David's leadership has forward-pointing meaning.

In reply, we may observe that the larger literary context and then the context of later prophecies encourage us in this direction. David has been anointed as future king in 1 Samuel 16. He will eventually become the kingly leader of all Israel. He has also already been a military leader under Saul (1 Sam. 18:13–15). First Samuel 22:1–2 fits in with this pattern. Because of the promise inherent in Samuel's anointing of David, we can infer that 1 Samuel 22:1–2 looks forward to David's later role as king. David's kingship in turn looks forward to a line of kings (2 Sam. 7:8–16). This line of kings looks forward to a final, climactic kingship in the Messiah (Isa. 9:6–7; 11:1–9).

So is 1 Samuel 22:1–2 forward-pointing, or does it only *become* forward-pointing in retrospect, when we look at it in the light of other passages? That is a misframed question. The question presupposes that we can isolate the verses 22:1–2, and such isolation is artificial: it does not do justice to what the verses really are, by God's design. From the beginning, God designed those verses to be part of 1–2 Samuel as a whole book, and that whole book contains 1 Samuel 16, as well as a sustained attention to the issue of Israel's leadership, whether through Eli or Samuel or Saul or David. God designed 1 Samuel in turn to be part of the larger history in 1–2 Samuel and 1–2 Kings. And he designed that history to be linked to later prophecy that he would give, such as in Isaiah 9 and 11.

Moreover, a sensitive reader from Old Testament times could understand God's design, at least in general outline. The canon grows along with redemptive history. If a reader understands that 1–2 Samuel is God's word, and not merely human words, he can also infer that God is asking him to read it in the light of future revelation, not merely the past or the present. God's word in 1 Samuel 22:1–2 is incomplete; it is not the whole. And if it is not the whole, then God's intentions with 1 Samuel 22:1–2 are more expansive, and the reader ought to look forward to further words and deeds of God that build on what occurs in 1 Samuel 22:1–2.

Thus, *every passage* in the Old Testament, indeed every verse, is forward-pointing. Some passages, like Isaiah 9 and 11, are *more directly* forward-pointing, because they give direct predictions—they include God's promises concerning the future. Others are still forward-pointing in a fairly obvious way, because, like 1 Samuel 22:1–2, they are linked to themes like kingship, which in turn are linked to direct prophecies of the coming messianic king. Still others are not forward-pointing in an *obvious* way; they do not shout it out on the surface of the text. They are nevertheless forward-pointing, because all God's words and all God's deeds are so. He has a comprehensive plan.

Take, for example, 2 Samuel 8:16: "Joab the son of Zeruiah was over the army." It indicates Joab's military leadership. Is it forward-pointing? Not obviously. But every instance of leadership, good or bad or mixed, addresses challenges involving rule. The leader has to have the allegiance of the people under him. He has to be able to get them to participate in coordinated action within a group, and to do so in a way that leads to accomplishing larger tasks. Those tasks head forward to the consummation. The tasks are accomplished either in service to God or in disobedience to him. So failures and successes both have natural links with the climactic leadership of Christ. By accomplishing (or failing to accomplish) little tasks related to the consummation, these biblical instances of leadership tacitly point forward to the full history of all tasks, leading to the consummation. And within that full history, Christ's accomplishment of his task is central.

Symbols

In addition to ordinary analogies we can also observe *symbolism*. For example, in the Old Testament, animal sacrifices symbolize various aspects of the worshiper's relationship to God. The sin offering signifies and symbolizes God's forgiveness of sin on the basis of the offering of an innocent substitute. The peace offering signifies primarily thanksgiving and fellowship with God. The grain offering signifies primarily tribute offered to God in gratitude for his blessing in crops. The tabernacle of Moses signifies God's dwelling with his people Israel. These symbolic institutions point forward to Christ. The animal sacrifices point forward to Christ's final sacrifice for sin. The tabernacle of Moses points forward to Christ, whose body is the final temple of God: "he was speaking about the temple of his body" (John 2:21).

We have labeled these cases *symbolism* because they involve two levels of meaning rather than one. In animal sacrifice, the first level is the level of physical action, which involves killing an animal and offering it to God by burning all or part of it. The second level involves the *meaning* of the physical actions. They *signify* realities about God and his relation to his people. Similarly, the tabernacle is a physical structure on the first level, and it signifies God dwelling with his people on the second level. Symbolism could be viewed as one kind of analogy: we have an analogy between the physical actions on the one hand and the things they symbolize on the other. But the two-level structure distinguishes symbolism from ordinary analogy. The animals involved in sacrifice are analogous to any other animal. They are *not* analogous to Christ, on the same level. They are analogous by way of symbolism. In general, we can say that a *symbol* is a concrete representation of a divine truth.

Types

Now we can introduce another concept, the concept of a *type*. The word *type* here does not have its ordinary English meaning of a *kind* or *sort*, a particular class. It is a technical term, derived from the Greek word *tupos*, which signifies a visible impress, copy, or pattern.[2] The key instances of this usage of the word are found in three New Testament verses:

> . . . Adam, who was a *type* [*tupos*] of the one who was to come [Christ]. (Rom. 5:14)

> Now these things [in Israel's experiences in the wilderness] took place as *examples* [*tupoi*] for us, that we might not desire evil as they did. (1 Cor. 10:6)

> Now these things happened to them *as an example* [*tupikōs*, an adverbial form related to *tupos*], but they were written down for our instruction, on whom the end of the ages has come. (1 Cor. 10:11)[3]

Bible students have generalized from these verses and other New Testament verses that use the Old Testament in similar ways, though other verses do not happen to use the same key Greek word *tupos* (type). On the basis of the generalization, they have given us a modern technical term, *type*. A *type* is a symbol that points forward to a greater or climactic realization. The later realization of the symbol is customarily called the *antitype*. For example, animal sacrifices are *types* pointing to the final sacrifice of Christ, who is the *antitype*. The tabernacle is a *type* pointing to Christ as the final temple, the *antitype*. The prefix *anti-* may confuse some people, because they expect it to indicate opposition rather than continuity. But in this context the prefix *anti-* has a meaning closer to "corresponding to." The antitype is the reality that corresponds to the type.

In agreement with chapter 17, we should distinguish words and concepts. The Greek word *tupos* has a range of meaning, and even in the three verses quoted above, it means something like "example" or

---

[2] Walter Bauer, *A Greek-English Lexicon of the New Testament and Other Early Christian Literature* (2nd ed.; Chicago/London: University of Chicago Press, 1979).
[3] Note also Hebrews 9:24 and 1 Peter 3:21, which use the Greek word *antitupos* (ἀντίτυπος, cognate to the English word *antitype*).

"pattern"; it does not have the full technical meaning of the English word *type* as a technical term.

In modern discussions, the word *type* is sometimes used not only for forward-pointing *symbolism*, but for *any* forward-pointing element in the Old Testament that has a climactic realization in Christ or in his people. For example, it might be said that David in 1 Samuel 22:1–2 is a *type* for Christ as commander, and the men following David are a *type* for Christian disciples. The idea of *type* then includes all instances of forward-pointing analogies.

In fact, the New Testament examples with the Greek word *tupos* or its adverbial equivalent, from Romans 5:14, 1 Corinthians 10:6, and 1 Corinthians 10:11, all appear to be closer to a one-level analogy. In Romans 5:14 Adam as representative head of the human race is analogous to Christ, who as man is representative head for his people, the church. In 1 Corinthians 10:6 and 10:11, the experiences of the people of Israel are analogous to experiences that may come to people in the church, if they rebel against God.

But in a sense all analogies in the Old Testament are forward-pointing, because they are part of a larger redemptive history that moves forward to Christ. So this broad use of the word *type* to describe virtually any forward-pointing analogy may for some purposes be too broad. Of course it is up to us whether we want to use the word *type*. We can use it broadly or narrowly, as we wish. For the sake of clarity, we will use the word *type* more narrowly, for forward-pointing symbolism, which inherently involves two levels of meaning. We use the word *analogy* for likenesses that use only one level of meaning. One-level analogies may still come to their climactic realization in the life of Christ.

Preparatory History

In addition to analogies and types, we can see one other way in which a one-time event points forward to Christ. It points forward simply by being part of the overall historical process. In the providence of God, the entire process gradually leads to the point in time when Christ comes. It prepares the way.

Consider again 1 Samuel 22:1–2. David is an ancestor of Christ. So whatever happens to David constitutes one link in the total historical process that leads forward to Christ. David's life leads forward to Christ in the sense of genealogy. As an ancestor of Christ, David had to have a son who would carry on his line, and who would in turn have descendants in a long chain leading to Christ. If David had died prematurely, the chain would have been broken. But of course God was governing the life of David through his providence. The reader who understands God's purposes also understands beforehand that Saul would never succeed in killing David, because David had to survive to carry on his line.

The line forward involves not only genealogy but kingship. David establishes a pattern for Israel's kingship, and the later kings in his line conform to the pattern of David's good leadership—or they fail to conform. The ups and downs in Israelite kingship teach the people the nature of good and bad kingship, and increase the longing for the final good king, Christ.

The line forward in history involves not only David but the people of Israel as a whole. God preserves David partly so that David may lead the fight against the Philistines and protect Israel. God undertakes to preserve Israel, not only against the Philistines but also in the time of Rehoboam and even in the midst of their later experience of exile, so that there will be a people of God among whom Christ will live and to whom he will initially bring the message of God's saving kingdom (Matt. 10:5–6; 15:24). God preserves David in the cave of Adullam in 1 Samuel 22:1–2 as one small stage along the way to many historical developments, with David's descendants and with the people of Israel. When we focus on this sense of development and the role of 1 Samuel 22:1–2 in it, we may give our focus the label *preparatory history*.

The preparatory history involves the presence of God in Christ. God is merciful to sinners only on the basis of Christ's mediation. In the Old Testament times, Christ had not yet accomplished his work in his earthly life, death, resurrection, and ascension. But God mercifully made available the efficacy and benefits of Christ's work, reckoning beforehand what Christ was to accomplish. Christ was present as the divine Son, the second person of the Trinity, to mediate his benefits to human beings. David received protection from Achish and Saul and safety in the cave because Christ was present to give it to him and his followers.

Perspectives on Preparation

We now have three kinds of connection between Old Testament events and the New Testament: analogies, types, and preparatory history. These three are roughly distinguishable, but they can also function as perspectives on one another. As part of the *preparation* for the coming of the Messiah, God gave the people analogies and types. Conversely, the preparatory works of God have *analogies* with events at other stages of history.

For example, suppose we look at David as a leader. He is in some ways analogous to other leaders. Similarities in leadership offer one form of analogy. The analogies will be closest when we compare David to other leaders over the same group, the people of Israel. But more distant analogies exist even with pagan leaders. David's godly leadership contrasts with the ruthlessness of many pagan leaders in Assyria and Babylon and Egypt. But even the deficiencies of pagan leaders help to highlight by contrast what a good leader looks like. We can also focus on the people who benefit from David's leadership. The people under David are analogous to the people of Israel at other points in history, because of the continuity in the status of Israel as the special people of God (Ex. 19:5–6).

Is the distinction between one-level analogy and two-level symbolism a hard-and-fast distinction? No. It depends on what counts as a second level. Every event and person and institution in the Old Testament embodies the significance of God's plan for history. God's providential hand is always at work. So the presence of a second level of meaning is matter of degree.

We can take the case of David in 1 Samuel 22:1–2 as an illustration. In one sense, David as leader and Christ as leader are "on the same level," since David is human and Christ has a human nature. God works to bless his people through David and later through Christ. But David and Christ are not "on the same level" in every sense. Christ is God as well as man. He wages the climactic war against Satan and death, not merely against human enemies in the way that David did in his life. The engagement against Satan, and the finality of Christ's work, put his work on another, higher level than David's. So we could say *either* that David offers an *analogy* for

Christ *or* that he offers a *type* for Christ. The line between an analogy and a type is fluid.[4]

Aspects of Interpretation

We may summarize the perspectives for Christocentric interpretation in an outline:

    c. Christ as the center
        (1) Wave: promises about Christ (prophecy)
        (2) Field: general principles fulfilled in Christ
        (3) Particle: particular times relating to Christ
            *(a) Analogies
            *(b) Types (including symbols)
            *(c) Preparation

Resources

Clowney, Edmund P. *Preaching and Biblical Theology.* Grand Rapids, MI: Eerdmans, 1961.

———. *Preaching Christ in All of Scripture.* Wheaton, IL: Crossway, 2003.

———. *The Unfolding Mystery: Discovering Christ in the Old Testament.* Colorado Springs: NavPress, 1988.

Goldsworthy, Graeme. *Gospel and Kingdom: A Christian Interpretation of the Old Testament.* Exeter, England: Paternoster, 1981.

Johnson, Dennis E. *Him We Proclaim: Preaching Christ from All the Scriptures.* Phillipsburg, NJ: Presbyterian & Reformed, 2007.

Poythress, Vern S. *The Shadow of Christ in the Law of Moses.* Reprint. Phillipsburg, NJ: Presbyterian & Reformed, 1995.

---

[4] The three perspectives are implications from the particle, wave, and field perspectives, but in a complex way: see Vern S. Poythress, "Hierarchy in Discourse Analysis: A Revision of Tagmemics," *Semiotica* 40-1/2 (1982): 117–120, http://www.frame-poythress.org/wp-content/uploads/2012/08/semi.1982.40.1-2.107.pdf, DOI: 10.1515/semi.1982.40.1-2.107, accessed December 29, 2012.

23

Typology

How do we discern types and analogies in the Old Testament? The study of types, and how to discern them, is called *typology*. What can we say about principles for typology?

First, we should appreciate how details fit into the larger contexts: the literary context, historical and social context, and the context of redemptive history. Edmund P. Clowney developed a two-stage process to help people think it through.[1] In the first stage, we consider the meaning of a symbol in its immediate context in history. In the second stage, we travel forward to fulfillment in Christ.

Clowney's Triangle

Consider the case of the sin offering described in Leviticus 4. The sin offering has symbolic significance. In the first stage in Clowney's procedure, we ask what it symbolizes according to Leviticus 4. We take into account the rest of Leviticus, and the situation with Israel in the wilderness that Leviticus describes. The sin offering symbolizes God's forgiveness of sin. As usual, the symbol also *embodies* what it symbolizes. Worshipers who brought a sin offering in an attitude of faith could actually receive forgiveness from God. Forgiveness took place through the offering of the life of an animal. The animal substituted for the

---

[1] Edmund P. Clowney, *Preaching and Biblical Theology* (Grand Rapids, MI: Eerdmans, 1961), 110–112.

person, and bore the sin that the person had committed, as we see more explicitly in Leviticus 16:

> And Aaron shall lay both his hands on the head of the live goat, and confess over it all the iniquities of the people of Israel, and all their transgressions, all their sins. And he shall *put them* on the head of the goat and send it away into the wilderness by the hand of a man who is in readiness. The goat shall *bear all their iniquities on itself* to a remote area, and he shall let the goat go free in the wilderness. (Lev. 16:21–22)

Leviticus 16 as a whole gives instructions for a series of ceremonies for the annual Day of Atonement (Yom Kippur). Its instructions are very specific, and more elaborate than in the case of a normal sin offering. They involve not one goat but two, one of which is killed and the other of which bears away the iniquities. These two goats present complementary symbolic pictures concerning how God provides for atonement for sin. By contrast, the normal sin offering involves only a single animal that the worshiper presents to God at the tent of meeting and then kills (see Leviticus 4). But Leviticus invites us to see this simpler ceremony in the light of the more elaborate one.

Thus, the sin offering symbolizes atonement and forgiveness. It has this symbolic, spiritual significance within Leviticus, and its significance would make sense to an Israelite at the time that Leviticus was originally written.

As a second stage, Clowney advises Bible students to travel forward in time to fulfillment in Christ. The student begins with the truth about the sin offering in Leviticus. He then asks how this truth is realized in the work of Christ. And of course it *does* have such a realization. Christ himself is the final sacrifice, as the book of Hebrews makes clear:

> And every priest stands daily at his service, offering repeatedly the same sacrifices, which can never take away sins. But when Christ had offered for all time a single sacrifice for sins, he sat down at the right hand of God, . . . (Heb. 10:11–12; see also vv. 1–10)

We can say that the sin offering in Leviticus is a *type* of Christ. It is a concrete symbol that signifies divine truth, and that points forward to Christ.

Clowney has summarized his two-stage procedure in a diagram, which has become known as Clowney's triangle (fig. 23.1).[2]

Fig. 23.1: Clowney's Triangle

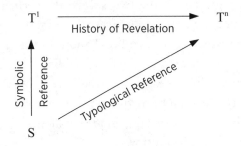

Stage one is represented by the vertical leg of the triangle. The student moves upward from the symbol S to the truth that it symbolizes, namely T^1 (truth to the first power, that is, initial truth). For the sin offering, S is the sin offering itself, and T^1 is the truth that God provides for atonement and forgiveness through the death of an innocent substitute. Clowney calls this movement in thought "Symbolic Reference," to indicate that the symbol S refers in its symbolic function to the truth T^1.

Stage two is represented by the horizontal leg of the triangle. Having grasped the truth T^1 as presented through the symbol, the student moves horizontally, through time, to the climactic truth T^n manifested in the work of Christ. This T^n s "truth to the n-th power," to indicate that it has a fullness not immediately visible to human beings during the Old Testament period. For the sin offering, T^n is the truth about Christ's sacrifice, as expounded by Hebrews 10 and other passages in the New Testament. Clowney calls this movement in stage two "History of Revelation," to indicate that the student is moving in his mind through history, from the time in the Old Testament to the time of fulfillment in Christ (Gal. 4:4). He is moving not only in history, but also through the history *of revelation*, since God purposed to reveal Leviticus 4 at the

---

[2] Clowney, *Preaching and Biblical Theology*, 110. Clowney cautions, "This diagram is of only limited usefulness" (ibid.). What he means, I suppose, is that the diagram is only a summary, and that it does not provide a mechanical formula that guarantees sound results. It will not substitute for communion with God, prayer, hard work, and knowledge of Scripture as a whole. It is nevertheless useful as a quick summary of the kind of process through which a student may develop a Christocentric interpretation of the Old Testament.

earlier historical time and Hebrews 10 at the later historical time. The history of revelation is an aspect of the history of redemption, a history that includes both words (word revelation) and deeds (which are also revelatory, but have to be interpreted through God's words).

Finally, as a result of moving through the two stages, the vertical stage and then the horizontal stage, the student arrives at a point where he has understood the relation between the symbol S and the truth in Christ, T^n. This relationship is represented by the diagonal line, which is the hypotenuse of the triangle. This line has the label "Typological Reference."[3] The *type*, namely the symbol S, functions as a type by referring to the truth about Christ, T^n. For example, the sin offering (S) as a type refers to Christ as the final sin offering (T^n).

When we apply the triangle to the case of the sin offering, we obtain fig. 23.2.

Fig. 23.2: Clowney's Triangle for the Sin Offering

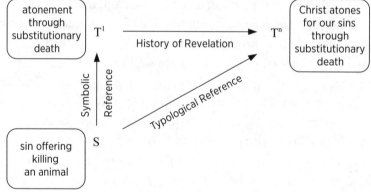

Application to David and His Men

As a further illustration, we may apply Clowney's procedure to the case of David and his men in 1 Samuel 22:1–2.

Stage one. Does David have a symbolic significance within the con-

---

[3] Clowney's original publication used the label "Typical Reference." The designation "Typical Reference" is technically correct; in this context, the word *typical* means "having to do with a type." But the word is likely to be misunderstood as having another meaning, "exhibiting the common characteristics of a group." For clarity, I have substituted the word *typological*.

text of the time of 1 Samuel? This case is not as easy as the case with the sin offering, because it is not so clear that there is a symbolic significance, or what that significance is. David as a human being and as a leader is analogous to other leaders, including Christ as the final king. But this analogy might be classified as an analogy and *not* a type. All human leaders are in a sense on the same "level." But David is not merely a human leader. As the future king of Israel, he is supposed to embody in his leadership the wisdom and justice and protection of God. So we could claim that there is, at least dimly, a symbolic significance. David symbolizes God's rule and care. He gives a haven or relief to the people who come to him, and in this sense he is a savior. If so, we have moved from David as a symbol (S) to a divine truth (T^1).

Stage two. Now we move forward in time in the history of revelation. How does Christ climactically embody the truth that we saw at the early point in time? To what truth (T^n) does God's rule and care through David point? It points to God's rule and care through Christ. And indeed this truth is a climactic embodiment. David's leadership and his kingly achievements were limited. He sinned and failed miserably in the episode with Bathsheba. Even at his best, David's achievements with respect to the Philistines resulted in triumph over an earthly enemy of a temporary sort.

Christ triumphed over Satan himself. David's leadership was temporary. Christ's rule is permanent. David provided temporary and limited relief for his men: he gave them relief from their distress, debt, and bitterness. David was a savior in a limited sense. Christ provides comprehensive and eternal relief. He is the final Savior. We experience his relief within this life when we are united to him by faith. We look forward to comprehensive relief and salvation in the new heavens and the new earth, of which Christ's resurrection is the first fruits.

When we have finished stage two, we have also understood how the situation with David in the Old Testament (S) has a "typological reference" (a reference as a type) to Christ as final King and Savior. We can sum up the movements using Clowney's triangle (fig. 23.3).

Justification for Clowney's Triangle

We can see that Clowney's triangle can be useful. But *why* is it useful? Is it justified? Do we really need to use it?

Fig. 23.3: Clowney's Triangle for David and His Men

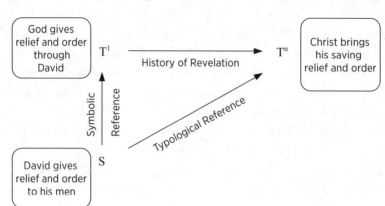

Clowney's triangle helps to express some important principles for understanding Scripture, especially the Old Testament. The horizontal line for stage two is rightly labeled "History of Revelation." We are dealing with God's plan, worked out successively in historical stages, and revealed successively in historical stages. Taking into account the organic unity of redemption helps us to put the details of the sin offering or of David's men in the context of a unified, comprehensive plan of God that works out in historical development. Stage two is asking us to think about God and his plan and his work and the unity of history under his control.

What about stage one? Stage one asks us to focus on the context in which an earlier revelation was given. God speaks to us in contexts. He controls the contexts as well as the words that he speaks. Because he is a God who affirms context, including also the eternal contexts of the relations among the persons of the Trinity, he speaks in a way that interacts with and takes account of contexts. Submission to his word includes submitting to his *way* of speaking. We should not arbitrarily rip his speech out of context. And that includes *temporal* contexts.

God also speaks in love to particular people at particular times. God showed mercy to Israelites back then and there. He was interested in them. He offered his word and his instruction to them. He is also speaking to us, but not in a way that eliminates his interest in other people who came before us. Thus we grow by asking, what was God's concern for Israelites in the wilderness, when he spoke Leviticus 4 and 16; or what was his concern for the Israelites when he spoke 1 Samuel 22:1–2? Because God's plan is one, and because there is only one way of redemption, his concern for them coheres with his concern for us now, when he speaks to us through Leviticus 4 and 1 Samuel 22:1–2. Thus the truth T^1 that God made available to Israelites coheres with the truth T^n that he makes known to us. We are privileged to know more, because we can look at the fullness of truth shown in Christ, T^n. But it was fundamentally the same truth that he made known in preliminary and shadowy form long ago, T^1.

Clowney's triangle helps us *positively* by encouraging us to think through the wise ways of God in redemptive history. But it also helps us *negatively*. When people try to do typological analysis of the Old Testament, sometimes they give their imaginations free rein, and gallop off to ideas that are merely their own and not according to the mind of God. They *impose* their ideas on an Old Testament text.

We illustrated the process earlier with an interpretation of 1 Samuel 22:1–2 imitating Philo of Alexandria. Philonic interpretation might claim, for example, that "David" stands for the soul as beloved. This interpretation ignores the context of 1 Samuel 22:1–2 and the way in which the passage would naturally communicate to earlier readers who were not privy to Platonic and Stoic philosophy. It is as if Philo assumed that everything in 1 Samuel is symbolic (S) and then jumped directly from the symbol S to a reference to philosophical truth about the soul (T). It is playing with its own meanings, rather than discerning the ways in which God positively uses context.

Christian interpreters do better when they have come to know Christ, because they know the one to whom the Old Testament is pointing. If they are spiritually healthy, they do not import Platonic or Stoic philosophy, or some modern existentialist or postmodernist analogue. They read the Old Testament knowing that it points to Christ as the center of history and as the one "in whom are hidden all the treasures of wisdom and knowledge" (Col. 2:3).

But if they are not sensitive to the principles that Clowney's triangle is representing, they may still sometimes travel into bypaths. In the first centuries of the Christian church, some interpreters thought that any mention of wood in the Old Testament pointed forward to the cross of Christ. It might be the acacia wood of the frames and furniture of the tabernacle, or the wood of the man gathering sticks on the Sabbath (Num. 15:32–33), or the wood of trees that were useful in war (Deut. 20:19–20). It did not matter—it was all about Christ.

Yes, it *is* all about Christ. But in what way? The interpreters who move from wood to Christ are right not only about the fundamental point of the centrality of Christ; they are right also about the centrality of the cross. They may preach a good, doctrinally sound sermon about the cross of Christ, based on the verse in Exodus 26:15, which says that the frames of the tabernacle should be made of acacia wood. Doctrinally speaking, the preachers are sound. And we should rejoice that they set forth Christ in his preeminence (Phil. 1:18). But might they do even better? Are they missing something?

One difficulty is that the sermon about the cross of Christ could be preached just as easily *without* Exodus 26:15. Exodus 26:15 is actually pretty tangential to the point. The main point is surely not that the cross of Christ was made of wood, but that Christ died there on our behalf, to atone for sins. So the preachers are really not using Exodus 26:15 effectively. They are overlaying Exodus 26:15 with other meanings, meanings that are doctrinally sound but that come from the New Testament teaching about the cross of Christ.

In addition, the preachers may then be missing some of the ways in which God is actually speaking to us in Exodus 26:15. Acacia wood suits the environmental context, because it was available in the wilderness. God is giving directions to Israel that interact with context. At the very least, this displays the wisdom of God and his pattern of using contexts. The frames of the tabernacle serve to hold up the curtains, and make the tabernacle into a tent house, which symbolizes God's dwelling with his people (Ex. 25:8). There actually is symbolic significance to the tabernacle, and to the frames as part of the tabernacle. But we see that significance when we pay attention to contexts, such as Exodus 25:8, which explicitly says that the tabernacle is to be "a sanctuary, that I may dwell in their midst." Acacia wood is useful as a functional part of the tabernacle. As an effective construction material, according to

God's design for creation and then for the tabernacle, the wood functions to hold up and brace the structure of God's dwelling place.

If we use Clowney's triangle, we can travel forward in redemptive history to the climax in Christ. Christ is the final dwelling place of God, as John 2:21 indicates: "he was speaking about the temple of his body." Christ's bones and sinews and the physical structure of his physical body give his body structural integrity, and enable his body to be the temple of God. The acacia wood points to Christ's body. The stability of the tabernacle as a physical structure points to the stability and faithfulness of God, who sustains the universe as well as the physical structure of the tabernacle. This stability and faithfulness of God is climactically manifested in Christ and his work.

According to the New Testament, we also as the church have become like a tabernacle. We "like living stones are being built up as a spiritual house, to be a holy priesthood" (1 Pet. 2:5). So the acacia wood points to us as well, who have become a temple through union with Christ. *We* become stable parts of the church through the faithfulness and stability of God in Christ. The preachers who see the cross in Exodus 26:15 fail not so much because of what they see, but because of what they fail to see when they overlay the text with something else.

We can feel the artificiality of the link between the acacia wood of the tabernacle and the wood of the cross. Both are wood. Yes, there *is* a connection. But by itself it does not lead anywhere. The wood does not function in the same way in the two contexts. Clowney's triangle asks us in stage one to pay attention to the context in Exodus. And in stage two it asks us at least implicitly to pay attention to the contexts in the life and work of Christ. The interpretation "wood = cross" fails to engage with stage one. It "leaps" directly from a specific text (S) to truth in Christ (T^n). It *claims* to find a typological reference, in which the acacia wood refers to the cross. Its endpoint is still in a good place, in the truth in Christ. But the claim about a typological reference misses genuine connections by replacing them with an artificial one.

The best interpreters through the ages have always understood the importance of contexts and of redemptive history. Many times their understanding of the principles has been largely tacit and intuitive, but nonetheless important in guiding their interpretation of particular texts.

They have absorbed sound principles because they have read and reread the Bible, and the Holy Spirit has taught them. They have grasped the importance of God's overall plan and its progressive working out in history. When they interpret particular texts, they reach sound results, because they are employing the equivalent of Clowney's triangle, even if they do not explicitly distinguish two stages in their own mind. The *explicit* use of Clowney's triangle is not necessary for rich and sound interpretation; but the *implicit* use of the principles that it embodies leads to fruitful interpretation.

Resources

The classic work on typology, still useful today, is:

Fairbairn, Patrick. *The Typology of Scripture*. Reprint. Grand Rapids, MI: Kregel, 1989. Originally published New York: Funk & Wagnalls, 1900.

24

Additional Stages
Reflecting on Typology

Can we add further stages that encourage reflection on typology?

Adding Application

Subsequent to the time when Edmund P. Clowney initially developed his triangle diagram for typology, someone suggested adding to it a line for application. Previously, we have included application as an entirely new step in the process of interpretation (the final step C). But the "steps" in interpretation are like perspectives, rather than isolatable, strictly successive steps. It is helpful to remind ourselves that types do have implications for application. Application can be fitted right into typological reasoning, because the truth in Christ always applies to us who are in Christ, that is, those of us who are united to Christ by faith.

Consequently, we may if we wish add to Clowney's triangle another line to represent a student who moves from truth in Christ (T^n) to application (A). The line can be a vertical line that goes downward from Christ to us. (See fig. 24.1.)

We can fill out the diagram for the case of the sin offering (fig. 24.2) or the case of David and his men (fig. 24.3).

Adding a line for application is a useful reminder that we need to apply the Bible's message to ourselves. But the arrow representing

Fig. 24.1: Clowney's Triangle with Application

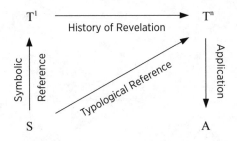

Fig. 24.2: Clowney's Triangle for the Sin Offering, with Application

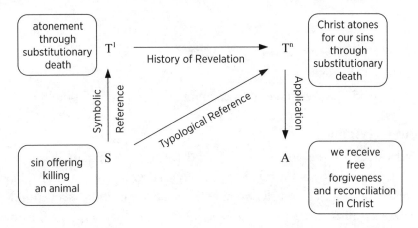

application should not be understood as representing something completely parallel to the earlier arrow, the vertical arrow for stage one representing symbolic reference. The arrow for symbolic reference ascends from a symbol (S) to the truth (T^1) that it symbolizes. The arrow for application does not descend from truth to symbol, but from truth (T^n) to us who are in Christ. We are people, not just symbols. We know the truth, and we experience it in our lives. Christ is in our lives through the indwelling of the Holy Spirit and through our personal fellowship with Christ. So the arrow for application should really go in another direction, perhaps in a third dimension, coming out of the page to point to the reader.

Fig. 24.3: Clowney's Triangle for David and His Men, with Application

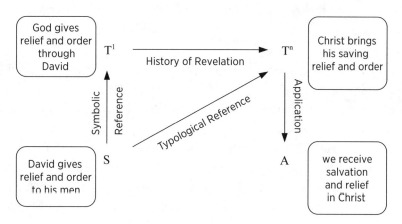

Adding More Stages

The substance of typology can be illumined by Clowney's two stages. But adding application helps us to think about the larger context in which a particular type is situated. If we like, we can label application as stage three, in a process that looks at the relation of a type to ourselves.

We can also explore still other questions, and add more stages. For example, we can ask how fulfillment in Christ adds significance that we might not easily discern if we had only the Old Testament. We have indicated that truth in Christ (T^n) expresses the same truth already expressed earlier (T^1). But the advance in redemptive history also includes an advance in revelation, and an advance in the richness of what we may understand. How does truth in Christ go beyond what Old Testament saints could easily discern? We can label this question as stage four.

For the sin offering, we see that Christ's sacrifice was once and for all and definitive, while the Old Testament sin offerings had to be repeated:

> And every priest stands daily at his service, offering *repeatedly* the same sacrifices, which can *never take away sins*. But when Christ had offered *for all time a single sacrifice* for sins, he sat down at the right hand of God, . . . (Heb. 10:11–12)

In the case of David and his men, what is new with the coming of Christ? Christ is the divine king as well as the final human king, and his rule and care over us bring a remedy at the level of spiritual reality, not merely temporal relief.

Next, we can ask whether our knowledge of fulfillment in Christ throws new light on what God said earlier. Does it lead us to notice details or aspects of earlier revelation that were there all along, but that we might not have noticed as easily? This question constitutes stage five.

For example, with the sin offering, we notice for the first time the role of blood in the description of the sin offering. Leviticus tells us that the blood stands for the life: "For the life of the flesh is in the blood, and I have given it for you on the altar to make atonement for your souls, for it is the blood that makes atonement by the life" (Lev. 17:11). The role of blood offers a prelude to what the New Testament says about Christ's blood, which represents his life and brings atonement:

> This cup that is poured out for you is the new covenant in my *blood*. (Luke 22:20)

> . . . the redemption that is in Christ Jesus, whom God put forward as a propitiation by his *blood*, . . . (Rom. 3:24–25)

What about the case with David and his men? We might not have noticed the details about what brought people to join David in 1 Samuel 22:1–2: "distress," "in debt," "bitter in soul." In the light of redemption in Christ, we understand that Christ's victory has brought about a remedy for every dimension of human need, and for the groaning of creation as well (Rom. 8:22). Both during his earthly life and as our reigning sympathetic high priest in heaven, Christ cares for every instance of physical and emotional suffering—distress, debt, bitterness.

But more obvious forms of suffering have their deeper spiritual analogues—distress over sin and separation from God; debt to God in the form of owing a payment for sins; bitterness in alienation from God; despair over the lack of ability to save oneself. The spiritual is not strictly separable from the physical and the emotional. We know, deep down, that all is not well with the world. Physical suffering is a reminder of this. And sometimes physical suffering is a direct consequence of sin.

How many of David's men were in distress or debt through no fault of their own, and how many were in distress or debt partly because of foolish and sinful decisions in their past?

The book of Job illustrates that sometimes physical suffering comes with no direct relation to particular sins. Yet even such distress reminds Job of the mysteries in his relation to God. So at a deeper level all human suffering belongs together. The reality of suffering has a connection with the reality of Christ's suffering, and that he *had to* suffer with us and for us (Heb. 5:7–10).

We can add a stage six in which we ask about the background of an Old Testament passage in the creation and fall, and how the passage has forward links not merely to the first coming of Christ but even to the consummation of all things.

For example, the sin offering has its roots in the fall, which brought about the alienation between God and man and the guiltiness of man to which the sin offering is a temporary answer. The alienation in the fall contrasts with the peace in the original creation situation. The sin offering, by offering reconciliation and restoration in the relationship with God, looks forward to the perfect relationship with mankind that God brings about in the new heaven and the new earth: ". . . his servants will worship him. They will see his face, and his name will be on their foreheads" (Rev. 22:3–4).

The case with David and his men has roots in the creation and fall of man, in that danger to David's life and distress among his men show the effects of the fall, and their contrast with the original good state of creation implies that we should seek a remedy. David's ability to lead has its foundation in the fact that God created man in his own image, with the ability to lead, imitating the archetypal ability of God. David's ability to lead also looks forward to the final triumph of God's rule over us in the new heaven and the new earth.

We can add a stage seven, in which we stand back and try to appreciate the uniqueness of any one passage within the Bible. David and his men are analogous to Christ and his disciples, but the two are not identical. God worked out the events in David's life in David's own time and place. David was uniquely David, and his story was never to be repeated. God illustrated redemption in a manner that suited (1) the individuality of David, (2) the role God had given him as anointed king, (3) the challenge of waiting, that is, David's having to wait and lead a small group in preparation for later kingship, and (4) the various distresses characterizing the time.

Outline for Interpretation

We can, if we like, add the details about Clowney's triangle to our outline for interpretation. The steps in Clowney's approach become subdivisions that naturally fall within our outline under the part of the outline devoted to types.

    c. Christ as the center
        (1) Wave: promises about Christ (prophecy)
        (2) Field: general principles fulfilled in Christ
        (3) Particle: particular times relating to Christ
            (a) Analogies
            (b) Types (including symbols)
                *((1)) Symbolic reference
                *((2)) Moving forward in history
                *((3)) Synthesis in typological reference
            (c) Preparation

25

Varieties of Analogies

A variety of *analogies* point forward to Christ. It is useful to classify some of the main kinds.

Christ as Mediator

We know that Christ in his incarnation is fully God (John 20:28) and fully man (Heb. 2:14–18). Even before his incarnation, he was God in eternal communion with the Father and the Spirit (John 1:1). So all the words and deeds of God in the Old Testament point forward to Christ as God.

Second, Christ not only is fully human; he also plays a representative role as the head of a new humanity formed in his image through the Spirit (1 Cor. 15:45–49). As a man, his experiences are analogous to the experiences of human beings throughout the Old Testament. At least at a general level, his humanity implies an analogy with every instance of human action in the Old Testament. He was like us except for sin:

> Therefore he had to be made like his brothers *in every respect*, so that he might become a merciful and faithful high priest in the service of God. (Heb. 2:17)

> For we do not have a high priest who is unable to sympathize with our weaknesses, but one who in every respect has been tempted as we are, yet *without sin*. (Heb. 4:15)

Third, Christ is the one *mediator* between God and men: "For there is one God, and there is one mediator between God and men, the man Christ Jesus, who gave himself as a ransom for all" (1 Tim. 2:5–6). Therefore, Christ is analogous to every mediatorial figure in the Old Testament.

These three truths about Christ lead to three perspectives on each Old Testament text. Concerning any Old Testament text, we can ask, "What is God doing?" "What are human beings doing?" and "What is a mediatorial figure doing?" Each question gives us a perspective on the text. Answers to each question lead to relations or analogies with respect to Christ. (See fig. 25.1.)

Fig. 25.1: Christ as Mediator

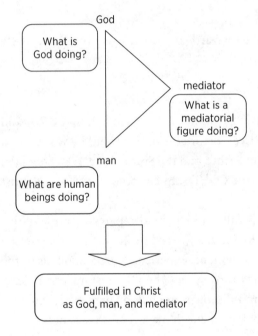

There are many dimensions to both our commonality with other human beings and our commonality with Christ as a human being. For example, God had an eternal plan for David and David's life. Then he chose David and raised him up as king. God's eternal plan included at its central focus the life of Christ on earth. God announced Christ's calling when he was baptized by John the Baptist (Matt. 3:17). We who belong to Christ have been chosen in Christ before the foundation of the world, according to God's eternal plan (Eph. 1:4). God then called us in time and raised us to new life with Christ. We now carry out the "good works, which God prepared beforehand, that we should walk in them" (Eph. 2:10).

We see another analogy when we look at human response to God's calling. We should respond by trusting in God's promises, committing our lives to him through Christ, and walking in his ways. David trusted in God during the time in which Saul was pursuing him. His trust is shown particularly when he refused the chance to take Saul's life (1 Sam. 24:4–7; 26:8–12). Christ supremely and perfectly trusted in God during his earthly life. We who are followers of Christ trust in him and in God the Father whom he has revealed.

Analogies Applied in 1 Samuel 22:1–2

We can illustrate how these perspectives work using 1 Samuel 22:1–2. First, ask what God is doing. The text does not explicitly mention God. But 1–2 Samuel as a whole invites us to see God at work providentially throughout the history it records. In addition, we remember that God instructed Samuel to anoint David as king (1 Samuel 16). God's anointing gives David a particular role in God's plan for his people Israel during this period in Israel's history. In the light of these general truths, we can see that God is providentially at work in protecting David from murderous plans that might arise from Achish king of Gath or from Saul. God's protection of David is simultaneously Christ's protection of David, because Christ is God in eternal fellowship with God the Father. The same Christ who protected David and took care of the details in his life now reigns in heaven and offers himself as a protector to all who trust in him.

Second, ask what human beings are doing. There are several human beings in the picture in 1 Samuel 22:1–2. We have David, his brothers, his father's house, and troubled people: "everyone who was in distress, and everyone who was in debt, and everyone who was bitter in soul" (v. 2). David's men had suffered in various ways. David himself suffered, both by living in a cave and from the mental and emotional uncertainty about what Saul would try to do against him.

Christ, when he came to earth, identified with human suffering. He had compassion on the multitudes and on those who were sick or lame or oppressed by demons. He himself suffered in the flesh (1 Pet. 4:1). As a man, he shared our lot, which included suffering. In fact, he suffered supremely in order to bear our sins (1 Pet. 2:23–24). His suffering was an aspect of his being our high priest:

> In the days of his flesh, Jesus offered up prayers and supplications, with loud cries and tears, to him who was able to save him from death, and he was heard because of his reverence. Although he was a son, he learned obedience through what he *suffered*. (Heb. 5:7–8)

> For we do not have a high priest who is unable to *sympathize* with our weaknesses, but one who in every respect has been tempted as we are, yet without sin. (Heb. 4:15)

Christ was the same person even before his earthly life, during the time of David. So we can infer that he sympathized with the sufferings of David and his brothers and his men. He had mercy on them on account of his sympathy. They had fellowship with him beforehand in his sufferings (compare Phil. 3:10). When Christ came to earth, his sufferings represented the climax for human suffering throughout history. So his sufferings were intrinsically linked with the sufferings of David and his men, as one instance of human suffering. We can see a closer link because Christ was like a refugee: "Foxes have holes, and birds of the air have nests, but the Son of Man has nowhere to lay his head" (Matt. 8:20). Christ's suffering has important implications when we ourselves undergo suffering. We can come to Christ in prayer, knowing that he is the sympathetic high priest.

David had to trust in God during the time when he was at the cave of Adullam. It was like a time of exile, because he was exiled from normal society. Christ supremely trusted in God during his time of figurative "exile" on earth. He trusted in God his Father. He trusted in God even in the time of being forsaken as he was bearing the sins of his people (Matt. 27:43, 46). We are called to trust in God during our time of "exile," as 1 Peter designates our time on earth (1 Pet. 1:1, 17; 2:11).

Finally, let us consider the perspective where we ask about what a mediator is doing. What is a *mediator*? In a broad sense, a mediator is someone who stands between two parties, and who serves to bring about a relationship or to express a relationship between the two. In the Western world, we are likely to think first of all of a mediator in a legal dispute, where the parties are fighting one another and the mediator's job is to try to reconcile them. But in an Asian context, a young man who is interested in pursuing a romantic relationship with a young woman may first send a trusted friend as a mediator, who will contact the young woman's best friend as a second mediator, in order to inquire whether the young woman might be interested. In principle, mediators can have many functions.

In the context of Christ the mediator, we are thinking especially of mediation between God and man. Mediation between man and man is secondary, though once we are reconciled to God we also have an obligation to seek reconciliation with one another, through Christ. Mediation between man and man can also serve as a symbolic representation of some of the meaning of mediation between God and man.

First Timothy 2:5 says that Christ is the "*one* mediator between God and men." He is the *only* mediator. So how can there be other mediatorial figures? In Exodus 19 Moses serves as a mediator. He goes up to Mount Sinai to meet with God, while the people stay at the bottom of the mountain. He comes down with the tablets in his hand, with "the writing of God" (Ex. 32:16). He serves to mediate the delivery of the tablets to the people. But since Christ is the one mediator, how can Moses be a mediator?

God is present in his holiness at the top of Mount Sinai. The people are present in their *unholiness* at the bottom of the mountain. Even after Moses consecrates them (Ex. 19:10), the people are not qualified to stand in God's immediate presence. "Take care not to go up into the mountain or touch the edge of it. Whoever touches the mountain shall be put to death" (Ex. 19:12). So how can Moses go up to the mountain? Relatively speaking, Moses is a specially qualified person. But he is not morally perfect. Moses himself needs a mediator. And that mediator is Christ.

In every case in the Old Testament where God shows mercy to sinners, we can infer the presence of mediation. There *must* be a mediator, because of God's majestic holiness and the offense of sin. "In his divine forbearance he [God] had passed over former sins" (Rom. 3:25). Romans 3:21–26 implies that he passed them over because there was to come a final "propitiation by his [Christ's] blood" (v. 25). In the time of the Old Testament, God reckoned backward on the basis of the propitiation and satisfaction that Christ was to achieve in the future. Christ's sacrifice, which was to come, was already the ultimate basis for God's mercy as shown in the Old Testament.

Thus Christ the mediator stands behind Moses, who is an imperfect mediatorial figure. Moses foreshadows Christ. More than that, Christ is already present to mediate Moses's ability to stand in God's presence at Mount Sinai. He must be present, or Moses would die because of his own sins. The same principle holds for all Old Testament mediatorial figures. All of them can function only because they foreshadow Christ's mediation, and also because they in one sense *embody* it. They themselves are benefiting from Christ's mediatorial work, or they would die under the impact of God's holiness coming to destroy sin. First Timothy 2:5 is right: there is only "one mediator between God and men, the man Christ Jesus."

So now we come back to 1 Samuel 22:1–2. Does the passage contain mediatorial figures, and if so what do they do? First Samuel 22:1–2 is God's word, which is holy with the holiness of God. So we must have Christ as mediator to enable us to receive it, through the Holy Spirit. That is true of all passages of Scripture. But we need also to ask whether 1 Samuel 22:1–2 describes a mediatorial figure who is active in the events. The obvious figure is David. David was earlier anointed by Samuel to be king (1 Sam. 16:1, 12–13). The king mediates the rule of God and the justice of God to the people—at least if he is acting in accord with God's instructions for kingship. The king is also responsible to lead men in fighting enemies who attack the people. David has been anointed king, but Saul still holds the office of king as long as he lives. So David is in a transitional period. Though he is not king over Israel, yet, he is "commander" over them, that is, over "about four hundred men." The story of Nabal shows that David and his men are beginning to take a role like that of a king and his men, because they protect Nabal (1 Sam. 25:15–16).

In leading his men, David brings them the benefits of God's rule and God's justice. David mediates God's rule. In addition, men who are suffering find relief. Relief and all good gifts come from God (James 1:17), but in this case David is a mediator of the gifts. So David points forward to Christ the mediator.

We can make an application of the passage to ourselves in more than one way. On the one hand, we can identify with the people under David. Like the people under David, we receive God's rule and his justice and his relief, but we receive them now through Christ the final mediator, the "one mediator." Second, we can identify with David himself. We are not Christ. But as part of Christ's body we can imitate Christ by bringing Christ's blessings to others. In a metaphorically extended sense, we can "mediate" God's rule and justice and gifts in situations where we have opportunity to bless others, either those in our own house or more distant neighbors. We bless them in the name of Christ, and we ask Christ to work through us to bless them and relieve them in their distresses and bitterness.

We can apply the passage in a third way. If we are trusting in Christ, we are not only like David's men who gathered around him. We are also like David's brothers. Hebrews indicates that Christ calls us brothers:

That is why he [Christ] is not ashamed to call them *brothers*, saying,

"I will tell of your name to *my brothers*; . . . (Heb. 2:11–12)

Therefore he had to be made like *his brothers* in every respect, so that he might become a merciful and faithful high priest in the service of God. (Heb. 2:17)

Just as David welcomed his brothers, had fellowship with them, and took care of them, so Christ welcomes us as brothers in the spiritual family, has fellowship with us, and takes care of us.

Prophet, King, and Priest

Mediation is a key idea in the Old Testament, partly because mediation between God and man has such a central role in redemption. Three main mediatorial offices appear in the Old Testament, namely the roles of prophet, king, and priest. A prophet mediates the word of God to others. A king mediates the rule of God. A priest mediates the presence of God and reconciliation with God, through overcoming sin.

At many times these three roles are relatively distinct. But Moses functions in all three ways. He brings the word of God, especially the Ten Commandments, thereby serving a prophetic role. He provides laws for governing the people, and he serves as judge in cases of dispute (Ex. 18:13, 26), thereby serving a kingly role. He offers sacrifices and consecrates Aaron, thereby serving a priestly role (Leviticus 8).

In a broader sense, all three of these roles serve as perspectives. When the word of God comes to the people, we see a prophetic mediation. But the word of God rules over the people, and God's rule expresses his kingly authority and his justice. So the prophetic role of bringing the word of God includes a kingly aspect. Conversely, an earthly king rules through laws and decrees, which are verbal. If he rules righteously, his words express the wisdom of God and express prophetic mediation. Since God is present in his word, God's word through a prophet also brings God near to the people, and brings the people into his presence, which represents a priestly function. The priests are supposed to instruct the people (Lev. 10:11; Mal. 2:7–9), and such instruction brings the word of God to the people, thus serving a prophetic function.

Christ is the final prophet, king, and priest. Hebrews 1:1–3 includes all three functions:

> [1] Long ago, at many times and in many ways, God spoke to our fathers by the prophets, [2] but in these last days he has spoken to us by his Son, whom he appointed the heir of all things, through whom also he created the world. [3] He is the radiance of the glory of God and the exact imprint of his nature, and he upholds the universe by the word of his power. After making purification for sins, he sat down at the right hand of the Majesty on high, . . .

The prophetic function comes to expression in God speaking through his Son (v. 2). The kingly function comes to expression in the fact that Christ "sat down at the right hand of the Majesty on high" (v. 3), which is the position of rule. We also see his rule in upholding "the universe by the word of his power" (v. 3). The priestly function comes to expression in the "purification for sins" (v. 3). The prophetic, kingly, and priestly functions offer three perspectives on Christ's work. Since Christ was present as the preincarnate Son of God in the Old Testament, he was already present in every instance of prophetic, kingly, and priestly mediation in the Old Testament. All these instances point forward to the great work of mediation when he became incarnate. (See fig. 25.2.)

Fig. 25.2: The Mediatorial Functions of Christ

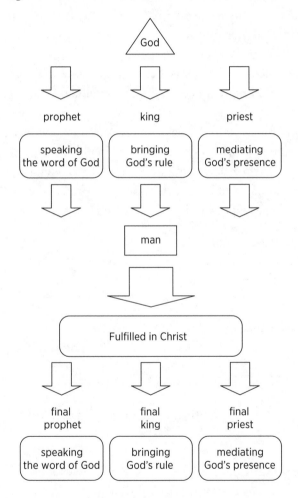

Concerning any passage in Scripture, we may ask how it brings to expression prophetic or kingly or priestly functions. These three form three perspectives on the passage. If we like, we can add wisdom as a fourth perspective. Wise men give counsel to others that reflects or mediates the wisdom of God. Since this kind of mediation is mostly verbal, it can also be considered as a variation on the prophetic function of bringing the word of God.

Consider 1 Samuel 22:1–2. Do we see a prophetic function in the passage? Not in an obvious way. But indirectly we can see a suggestion of such a function in the fact that David became "commander over them" (v. 2). A commander has to give verbal directions. If the directions are wise and godly, they manifest the benefits of God's wisdom, and so they serve faintly in a prophetic function.

Do we see a kingly function in the passage? David as anointed king and as commander serves a kingly function. His role points forward to Christ the king.

Do we see a priestly function in the passage? Again, not obviously. But we can infer that the men who were in distress, in debt, or embittered found some solace in their new community. They received partial healing, and this blessing has a link with the priestly blessing of communion with God. Note the responsibility of priests to bless the people, according to Numbers 6:22–27:

> The LORD spoke to Moses, saying, "Speak to Aaron and his sons, saying, Thus you shall bless the people of Israel: you shall say to them,
>
>> The LORD bless you and keep you;
>> the LORD make his face to shine upon you and be gracious to
>>   you;
>> the LORD lift up his countenance upon you and give you peace.
>
> "So shall they put my name upon the people of Israel, and I will bless them."

An Outline for Interpretation

We may add these perspectives on mediation to our outline for interpretation:

  c. Christ as the center
      (1) Wave: promises about Christ (prophecy)

(2) Field: general principles fulfilled in Christ
(3) Particle: particular times relating to Christ
    (a) Analogies
      *((1)) With God
      *((2)) With mediation
         *((a)) Prophetic
         *((b)) Kingly
         *((c)) Priestly
      *((3)) With humanity
    (b) Types (including symbols)
    (c) Preparation

26

Varieties of Types

In our terminology, *types* are forms of analogy that involve two levels. So everything that we have said about analogies applies in principle to types. But sometimes we need to make adjustments in the process. The two-level structure of types implies that not only persons but other, nonpersonal entities as well can serve as types pointing to Christ.

At an earlier point we mentioned the tabernacle. The tabernacle is a physical structure, a tent; it is not a person. It symbolizes God dwelling with his people. When Christ comes, God dwells with his people through the person of Christ, who is "Immanuel," "God with us" (Matt. 1:23). In the Old Testament it is also the case that persons, namely the priests, can mediate the presence of God, and signify that God is with his people. Thus it is possible for a variety of things to symbolize the same basic truth.

Kinds of Symbols

We may, if we wish, classify the kinds of types on the basis of the created order. God created different orders of creatures: human beings, animals, plants, and the nonliving world. Within a given context, God can use any of these things with additional symbolic significance. The animals in sin offerings signify the necessity of substitutionary death for sin. The crops that Israelites enjoy signify the blessing of God (Deut. 26:10–11; 28:3–4, 12). A rock can signify God's stability and faithfulness.

We may also use a cross-cutting classification in terms of kinds of structure. God has made a world in which there are three distinct kinds of structure: things, events, and relationships. Things include human beings, animals, plants, and nonliving things—the classification that we have just discussed. Things can signify divine truth. But so can events. In the actions of persons, events interlock with human intentions that involve goals. Needs or desires lead to plans and then to action to accomplish goals, and people reach their goals or fail to reach them. The little goals fit together into bigger goals, and the biggest goal is the consummation of all things. The word *plot* is the label that we can give for the structured sequence leading from an initial situation to a goal.

Plot

As a result, plots embody redemptive themes.[1] A central redemptive plot involves an instance where a person or people are literally redeemed from sin and rebellion and brought into a positive, saving relationship to God. God turns away his wrath and receives a person in mercy. Now there is "one mediator between God and men, the man Christ Jesus" (1 Tim. 2:5), who says that "I am the way, and the truth, and the life. No one comes to the Father except through me" (John 14:6). "And there is salvation in no one else, for there is no other name under heaven given among men by which we must be saved" (Acts 4:12).

If anyone becomes reconciled to God, it can only be on the basis of Christ and his work. This principle holds true in the Old Testament as well as the New. As Romans 3:25 indicates, the Old Testament proclaimed forgiveness on the basis of a future climax, which God reckons backward. Thus, *every* incident in which someone is saved involves Christ at the center. The Old Testament is full of Christ, because there is no other way to be saved.

The Bible contains many episodes in which people are delivered from physical distress. God delivers someone from a battle or a war, or from an enemy, or from sickness, or physical disability (lameness,

---

[1] On plot and redemption, see Vern S. Poythress, *In the Beginning Was the Word: Language—A God-Centered Approach* (Wheaton, IL: Crossway, 2009), chapters 24–26.

blindness), or poverty or famine or emotional distress or death. None of the people who receive deliverance deserve it. God has mercy.

The fact of physical deliverance does not imply by itself that the people whom God delivers are eternally saved. Yet physical deliverance and spiritual deliverance are symbolically related. The one signifies the other. And the final deliverance, in the consummation of all things, includes the resurrection of the body and eternal physical prosperity in the new heaven and the new earth. The physical well-being of the redeemed signifies their spiritual well-being. Every physical blessing is an expression of God's pleasure with his people, and the people receive these blessings as expressions that manifest God's love. They respond forever in gratitude.

We know that people were saved spiritually during Old Testament times, because Jesus indicates that Abraham, Isaac, Jacob, and all the prophets will be in the kingdom of God (Luke 13:28). But many of the particular histories in the Old Testament have much to do with physical distress, physical deliverance, and physical life and death. These things symbolize spiritual distress, spiritual deliverance, and spiritual life and death.

The symbolism is not arbitrary. God already established a symbolic relationship between physical life and his own divine life when he created life on earth. Physical life was a product and emblem of his archetypal divine life. The tree of life in the garden of Eden signified life with God, and thus had a spiritual dimension. When Adam and Eve rebelled against God, they suffered alienation from God, which is a spiritual death, and they became subject to physical death. God physically destroyed the people of Noah's day in the flood, because they had become spiritually corrupt.

At the climax of history, Jesus suffered, died, and rose, with all the physical dimensions belonging to his crucifixion, his physical death, and his physical resurrection. At the same time, his suffering, death, and resurrection had spiritual dimensions. He suffered for our sins, and he rose for our justification (Rom. 4:25).

The consummation, as we have seen, involves spiritual and physical prosperity, in which the one signifies the other, indeed embodies the other. We will *experience* God's spiritual blessing partly *through* our bodies, as we experience God's blessing concretely in the wonder of the new heaven and the new earth.

If, then, we see physical deliverances in the Old Testament, we need to see that in the purposes of God they go together organically with ultimate spiritual deliverance. God established relationships with Old Testament saints holistically. They received, as it were, a foretaste of the consummation. God blessed them both spiritually and physically. And when they were spiritually alert, they could understand, at least tacitly, that the physical blessings signified and embodied God's spiritual favor. Unbelievers, on the other hand, could receive benefits from God's common grace, but without genuine, saving spiritual communion with God through Christ as their saving mediator. Even benefits from common grace signify God's redemption in Christ in a broad sense, since they symbolize God's blessings, which are undeserved benefits that come to people by grace. But the unbelievers misunderstand and evade this signification.

Thus, biblical stories of physical deliverance are redemptive plots. Their plots offer analogies to the climactic events when Christ came and accomplished redemption through his death and resurrection. The relationship to Christ is a kind of *type*, since we have two levels. The story of physical deliverance has a focus on the physical level (though it also points to an underlying spiritual dimension), while the story of Christ's work has both a physical level (it is real history!) and a spiritual level: Christ bears sin, and in his resurrection accomplishes our justification.

The redemptive plots in the Bible are, however, not *merely* illustrations or symbols of something else. They describe real events in time and space. God is not only teaching us about redemption through symbols; he is also *accomplishing* redemption in the events themselves. To be sure, the small-scale redemption at any one point in time is limited in character. But it constitutes one step and one phase in the totality of history, every event of which leads forward to the consummation. Physical deliverance is significant, because it is a step toward the consummate physical deliverance of the consummation. All of these small-scale instances of redemption come by grace. And such grace is always based on the accomplishment of Christ, once for all, in his crucifixion and resurrection.

The Plots in 1 Samuel 22:1–2

How do these principles apply to a passage like 1 Samuel 22:1–2? We can see two overlapping plots. David is in danger, and he escapes to safety to the cave of Adullam. David receives physical deliverance from the danger of death. The second plot concerns people other than David. People in distress and in debt and bitter in soul gather to David and begin a new life. In their new life with David, they receive at least partial relief from their troubles. They receive physical or emotional deliverance. The description of David's experiences constitutes a redemptive plot, and so does the description of the experiences of David's men.

These redemptive plots signify redemption. God is ruling history. It is God who brings deliverance to David, and deliverance to his men. These deliverances point forward to the great redemption that Christ accomplished. Moreover, as we have said, Christ is already present as mediator in Old Testament times. David and his men receive deliverance from God through Christ the mediator, who embodies in his person the entire redemptive plot that he himself will accomplish when he comes to earth.

Relationships

The third kind of structure that we mentioned above is a relationship. It is not the same as a thing, such as an animal or a plant. Nor is it the same as an event. It is a relationship between two things, or between two events, or between a thing and an event, or between an event and a relationship, or between two relationships. Relationships can come in clusters.

A friendship between two people is a relationship. Human friendships can symbolize the friendship between God and man, because human beings are made in the image of God. Friendship between God and man becomes possible, of course, only through Christ. So friendship points to Christ. Love is a human relationship, and can symbolize God's love. God's love is expressed in Christ (Rom. 5:8).

In the Bible, a *covenant* is an important kind of relationship. The Mosaic covenant has a close relationship to the Ten Commandments, inscribed on stone. The stone tablets are things, in a creational classification. But the tablets signify and describe obligations pertaining to a relationship between God and the people of Israel. So the relationship is in focus. And this relationship points forward to the relationship that God will establish with the New Testament people of God through the new covenant (Luke 22:20). At the heart of the new covenant relationship is Christ, who establishes the new covenant in a covenant-making ceremony at the Last Supper.

The Last Supper is held as a Passover meal ("prepare the Passover"; Luke 22:8), so it picks up on the ceremonies involved in celebrating the Passover as an Old Testament covenantal meal remembering the exodus from Egypt and the covenant at Mount Sinai. At the same time, Jesus at the Last Supper speaks about "the new covenant in my blood" (Luke 22:20), indicating that he fulfills the Old Testament anticipations in Old Testament covenants. In Isaiah 42:6 and 49:8 God says that he is giving the servant "as a covenant," which virtually identifies the servant with the covenant. The servant in question is Christ, who *is* the covenant in its deepest meaning. Covenant in the Old Testament, which is a relationship, points forward to Christ, who is a person.

How do we apply this principle to 1 Samuel 22:1–2? We ask what relationships we see in the passage, and how these relationships may point to Christ. Two kinds of relationship stand out in the passage: the relationship between David and his brothers and other family members, and the relationship between David and the four hundred men for whom he was the commander. Being a commander over someone is a relationship. The men are also related to one another by being a group under a single commander, a group that must act cooperatively in order to function well.

We have already indicated that David's function as commander points forward to Christ's function as king and commander. Those under Christ's command are his people, the church. So the relationship of command points forward to the relationship between Christ and the church, or between Christ and each individual in the church.

We can also use the principle of mediation that we have already discussed. Christ is our commander, but he is also the mediator of God's kingly rule. In this perspective, God is the commander and king, and we are the subjects who receive his commands. The relationship of command between God and us is mediated through Christ, who is at the heart of the relationship. If we imitate the language about Christ being the covenant, we could say that Christ is the relationship of command. And what is God's command? To be in Christ and to be transformed into his image. Christ in a deep sense forms the content of the command as well as its channel.

The church in the New Testament is also the family of God. As a family, we are analogous to David's family relationships in 1 Samuel 22:1–2. Does this analogy make sense? David's brothers and his father's house received the benefit of David's protection and care when they came to him. They received family benefits through their relation to David. We receive family benefits through our relation to God as adopted sons. And what makes us sons? Our union with Christ the Son of God (Rom. 8:14–17, 29). Thus Christ is at the heart of our relation to God as members of his family.

Institutions

We now consider one more kind of structure. In human societies we find *institutions* such as marriage, the family, and civil government. Marriage, the family, and civil government are not "things" or creatures in the same way that people and animals and rocks are. Rather, they are semipermanent clusters of relationships that are recognized by society as integral wholes.[2] Many institutions remain whole even when the human participants gradually change. A family can add a member by birth or by adoption, or lose a member by death, and still be identifiable as a family. Employees can leave or be added to a business establishment, and the business as an institution, as a structural whole, remains in place.

Institutions can point forward to Christ. The church is an institution, which adds members by inward regeneration and outward baptism. Israel as the people of God in the Old Testament is an institution. It points forward to the church as the people of God in the New Testament, as the application of Old Testament language to the church implies:

> But you are a chosen race, a royal priesthood, a holy nation, a people for his own possession, that you may proclaim the excellencies of

---

[2] Vern S. Poythress, *Redeeming Sociology* (Wheaton, IL: Crossway, 2011), 199–200.

him who called you out of darkness into his marvelous light. Once you were not a people, but now you are *God's people*; once you had not received mercy, but now you have received mercy. (1 Pet. 2:9–10)

In the Old Testament, the Aaronic priesthood is an institution. So is the court of a king, or one of the twelve tribes of Israel, or an army, or a village or a city. There are many kinds of institutions, both in the ancient Near East and today.

When we identify institutions in a passage, we can ask how they point to Christ. In 1 Samuel 22:1–2 we see two institutions, the family of David and the band of four hundred men under David's command. We have already seen how both of these point forward to Christ.

Perspectives on Things, Events, and Relations

Institutions are partly like things, in that they have ongoing identity and stability. But they are also bundles of relationships, and may be classified as a kind of relationship. Thus we have three major kinds of structures: things, events, and relationships. These three are perspectivally related. We know about things because they are active in events and relationships. Events involve things that are active in relation to one another. Relationships are relationships between things and between events.

The three foci—things, events, and relationships—offer a particular kind of use of the three fundamental perspectives—the particle, wave, and field perspectives. The particle perspective leads to a focus on things, which are particle-like. The wave perspective leads to a focus on events. And the field perspective leads to a focus on relationships. These three interlock as a reflection of God, who is the archetype for these perspectives. God is present in our analysis. We depend on him at every moment. We can give thanks to him.

Aspects of Interpretation

We may add the classifications of this chapter to our previous outline for interpretation. In principle, the distinctions between things, events, and relationships apply to both analogies and types. But they apply

especially to types, where we make a transition between two levels. So
we choose to include them under the heading of types:

   c. Christ as the center
     (1) Wave: promises about Christ (prophecy)
     (2) Field: general principles fulfilled in Christ
     (3) Particle: particular times relating to Christ
       (a) Analogies
       (b) Types (including symbols)
         *((1)) Things
         *((2)) Events and plots
         *((3)) Relationships and institutions
       (c) Preparation

27

Antitypes

In view of Luke 24:25–27 and verses 44–48, we know that the Old Testament points to Christ. Specifically, "Thus it is written, that the Christ should suffer and on the third day rise from the dead, and that repentance and forgiveness of sins should be proclaimed in his name to all nations, beginning from Jerusalem" (Luke 24:46–47). We expect, then, that types will point to Christ as the antitype, the one who brings the fulfillment to which the type points. But the verses in Luke mention "all nations" as well. Do Old Testament patterns point not only to Christ but also to the nations?

Greg Beale's summary of principles for understanding the New Testament use of the Old Testament (discussed in chapter 21) includes principles that help us:

1. Corporate solidarity or representation is assumed. [An individual member within a group can be treated as represented by the group or vice versa.]
2. On the basis of point 1 above, Christ is viewed as representing the *true Israel* of the OT *and* the true Israel—the church—in the NT.[1]

We can thus expect that types in the Old Testament may point forward not only to Christ as an individual person, but also to Christ as a

---

[1] G. K. Beale, *Handbook on the New Testament Use of the Old Testament: Exegesis and Interpretation* (Grand Rapids, MI: Baker, 2012), 53.

representative. Christ as a representative represents "the true Israel—
the church—in the NT."

If so, the types in the Old Testament imply directly or indirectly
a fulfillment in which the work of Christ applies to the church as a
corporate body, and to each individual within the church. These applications do not exclude one another; on the contrary, they imply
one another. Fulfillment in Christ implies fulfillment in those whom
Christ represents, and vice versa. If Christ brought the climactic redemption—which he did—then he brought redemption *for someone.*
That someone includes Jews and Gentiles alike, and so the mention
of "all nations" in Luke 24:47 makes sense. "All nations" must also
include individuals within the nations—everyone who enjoys union
with Christ through faith. The intimacy with Christ and with God
that comes through the Holy Spirit includes intimacy with the church
as a community and also intimacy with individuals within the community. Galatians 4 uses both plurals and singulars to express these
two complementary truths:

> But when the fullness of time had come, God sent forth his Son, born
> of woman, born under the law, to redeem those [plural] who were
> under the law, so that we [plural] might receive adoption as sons
> [plural]. And because you [plural] are sons [plural], God has sent
> the Spirit of his Son into our [plural] hearts, crying, "Abba! Father!"
> So you [singular] are no longer a slave [singular], but a son [singu-
> lar], and if a son [singular], then an heir [singular] through God.
> (Gal. 4:4–7)

Church and Individual according to 1 Samuel 22:1–2

We can illustrate the process of application with 1 Samuel 22:1–2 as
our example. We have seen in our earlier reflections that David as leader
functions as an analogy or type for Christ. By bringing relief and protection to his brothers and his men, he prefigures the relief and protection
of Christ the final leader and king. But this redemption in Christ implies
that Christ leads, relieves, and protects someone—the church. Not only
is Christ an antitype for David; the church is an antitype for David's
men. Each individual within the church—you or I—receives the benefits
of Christ being our exalted leader and savior.

God designs from the beginning that the application to us should include both a corporate and an individual application. The passage addresses you if you are in distress or in debt or "bitter in soul." We should only stress that, in the Western world, where individualism is rampant, we should make a special effort to think through the corporate aspect of fulfillment. Relief and salvation comes not to individuals *in isolation*, but to individuals who are joined to Christ and therefore to each other in the community of the church. And the church is a community, not merely as a collection of individuals. It receives new communal life in its fellowship and its worship and its service. Conversely, if we are addressing a culture where communal thinking has submerged the individual into invisibility, we should make a special effort to think through the individual aspect of fulfillment: salvation comes to you, a person, not only to your tribe or your family.

In sum, for Old Testament types we may expect three distinct antitypes: in Christ, in the church, and in individuals who are saved. This analysis is pertinent to every aspect of the investigation of types. But it seems fitting, if we add it to our overall outline, to insert it under "B.3.c.(3).(b).((3)) Synthesis in typological reference," since this heading focuses on fulfillment rather than the earlier stages. Here is the pertinent portion of the outline for interpretation:

(b) Types (including symbols)
    ((1)) Symbolic reference
        ((a)) Things
        ((b)) Events and plots
        ((c)) Relationships and institutions
    ((2)) Moving forward in history
    ((3)) Synthesis in typological reference
        *((a)) Christ as a person
        *((b)) The church united to Christ
        *((c)) Individuals in Christ

Present and Future

Beale's principles for interpretation also include a specific principle that relates the present time to the future:

4. The age of *eschatological fulfillment* has come but has not been fully consummated in Christ.[2]

New Testament scholars have customarily spoken about "already" and "not yet" in fulfillment. Christ has accomplished redemption, in his death and resurrection, and so we *already* enjoy the benefits of redemption in him. When Beale's formulation says that *"eschatological fulfillment* has come," he announces the arrival of this fulfillment, the "already" aspect. In addition, during the present time, we wait for the resurrection of the body and full freedom from sin and death; such freedom has *not yet* come. In Beale's formulation, eschatological fulfillment "has not been fully consummated," which announces the "not yet" aspect. (I have sometimes taken up the suggestion that I heard from someone else—I do not know who—of using the label "yet to come" instead of "not yet." "Yet to come" highlights the positive aspect of our hope, rather than the negative aspect of what we do "not yet" have.)

According to Romans 8, we are already adopted by God as sons (8:15–17). We also await a future point of "adoption," when the creation is renewed: "And not only the creation, but we ourselves, who have the firstfruits of the Spirit, groan inwardly as we *wait eagerly* for adoption as sons, the redemption of our bodies" (8:23). Christ's resurrection was not merely a revivification of an untransformed body, but a transfiguration of his body to a new state, the state of resurrection life, indestructible life, which is the pattern for our future resurrection (1 Cor. 15:44–49). So his resurrection is the beginning of the new world order. But it is the "firstfruits" rather than the consummation. His own bodily resurrection has yet to lead to the full harvest in the form of bodily resurrection of those who belong to him.

We would expect, then, that many types in the Old Testament would find fulfillment in *both stages*, the "already" of the present age and the "not yet" of the new heavens and the new earth. Other types, of course, may find fulfillment primarily or exclusively in only *one* of the two stages. Both stages belong together in any case, because they are two stages in one unified process of redemption in Christ, begun in the achievement of Christ at his first coming, and to be consummated in the

---

[2] Beale, *Handbook on the New Testament Use of the Old Testament*, 53.

triumph of the second coming, when the fruits of his past accomplishment come to full realization.

Already and Not Yet in 1 Samuel 22:1–2

Can we apply this principle of "already" and "not yet" to 1 Samuel 22:1–2? First Samuel 22:1–2 has its own preliminary version of already and not yet. At the time when David is living in the cave of Adullam, he is *already* anointed to be the future king, but he is *not yet* enthroned. At a later point, he becomes king of Judah, the southern kingdom, but *not yet* over all Israel (2 Sam. 2:4). Finally, he becomes king over Israel as well (2 Sam. 5:1–5). David's role as leader shows analogous stages. When David is in the cave, he is "leader"—not yet king—over four hundred men (1 Sam. 22:2). Not only is the quantity of his followers limited, but his own resources for helping them are also limited. He cannot relieve his men from all physical hardships, as is clear from the fact that they are living in the cave and perhaps also around it. *Already* David shows capable leadership and provides relief and protection. *Not yet* does his leadership reach its full potential for providing for those under him.

Now we can ask how David's leadership points forward to Christ. Does it point forward only to Christ's first coming or only to his second coming or to both? We could perhaps see some degree of parallel between the stages in David's leadership and the stages in Christ's greater leadership. The early stage, with four hundred men, reminds us of Jesus on earth with his band of disciples. The stage where David is king of Judah reminds us of the present stage, this age, where Christ is already king but his kingship is not universally acknowledged among human beings. David's kingship over all Israel then corresponds to the consummation, when Christ's kingship will be universally acknowledged. The parallels are not perfect, since David's kingship over all Israel was not *consummated*: it may still have left a few disgruntled people who did not submit, and his kingship over all Israel included still going out to war against the Philistines.

In any case, we can see organic continuity between Christ's kingship at his first coming and his second coming. The latter is the full realization of what is already implicit in the former. So, yes, if David's leadership points forward to Christ at all, it includes in principle a picture that is pertinent to both the first coming and the second coming of Christ. The incompleteness in David's leadership in the earlier stage of 1 Samuel 22:1–2 nevertheless suggests a closer parallel with the first coming of Christ. We might even discriminate between the time of Christ's life on earth, when the kingdom of God and climactic salvation are *dawning*, and the time between Pentecost and the second coming, when the kingdom of God and salvation are robustly manifested in full flower, but still short of consummation. So then we have three periods in which the kingdom of God comes to realization: Christ's earthly life (the "dawn"); the new covenant age (from Pentecost to the second coming of Christ ("already"); and the consummation ("yet to come").[3]

If we like, we can add this twofold or threefold differentiation to our overall outline for interpretation:

(b) Types (including symbols)
   ((1)) Symbolic reference
      ((a)) Things
      ((b)) Events and plots
      ((c)) Relationships and institutions
   ((2)) Moving forward in history
   ((3)) Synthesis in typological reference
      *((a)) Christ's earthly life
      *((b)) The new covenant (already)
      *((c)) The consummation (not yet)

This division in terms of time cuts across the earlier division in terms of individual and community. We can represent the interaction of these two dimensions by further subdivisions:

   ((3)) Synthesis in typological reference
      *((a)) Christ's earthly life
         *a1. Christ
         *a2. The church
         *a3. The individual
      *((b)) The new covenant (already)

---

[3] Premillennialists will want to add a fourth stage, namely the millennial period between the second coming and the consummation.

           *b1. Christ
           *b2. The church
           *b3. The individual
   *((c)) The consummation (not yet)
           *c1. Christ
           *c2. The church
           *c3. The individual

Or we can represent the interaction of the two dimensions by a two-dimensional grid (table 27.1).

Table 27.1 Applications to Individual and Community,
Now and in the Future

	Christ's earthly life	New covenant (already)	Consummation (not yet)
Christ	State of humiliation	Present reign	Consummate presence
The church	Disciples	Post-Pentecost church	All nations
The individual	Peter, John, James	present-day individuals	Individuals enjoying the consummation

28

Themes

The Bible as a whole and the Old Testament in particular have major themes that run through them. As we would expect, the themes come to their climactic realization in Christ. So almost any major theme helps us to think through the way in which the Old Testament points to Christ.

Major Old Testament Themes

We have already touched on major themes of the Old Testament as we discussed some of the fruitful analogies and types in the Old Testament. Among them are the themes of God, man, and mediator (chapter 25). Among the mediatorial figures are prophets, kings, priests, and wise men. In addition, people who are not officially labeled as prophets, kings, priests, or wise men may temporarily function to mediate God's word or God's rule to others. Thus we need to be on the alert to broader manifestations of the theme of mediation. All the Old Testament instances of mediation point forward to Christ, who is the final mediator (1 Tim. 2:5).

For each passage in the Old Testament, such as 1 Samuel 22:1–2, we may ask how it illustrates these larger themes. Some of the themes will not be visible in any direct way. For example, the theme of wisdom is not obviously present in 1 Samuel 22:1–2, though we might infer that David would need wisdom to lead his men well. We need to respect the individual texture of each text, and not "force" a theme onto a text that does not really evoke the theme. But whether we find a theme present in an obvious way, or faintly, or only by implication or suggestion, it helps us to ask a multitude of questions. We are then more likely to notice themes that we otherwise might neglect.

In addition, we may think about institutions and things that perform mediatorial functions. God's covenants with Israel have a prophetic aspect, because each covenant contains the word of God to his people. At the same time, the covenants have a kingly aspect, because they make promises that require an exercise of God's kingly sovereignty, and they may contain stipulations that bind the people to obey God's will. By their obedience the people submit to God's kingship. The covenants may also express the intimacy between God and his people, and in this way they embody the theme of God's presence and his priestly mediation.

Closely associated with the priesthood are the themes of sacrifice and temple. Christ offers himself as the final sacrifice (Heb. 7:27). His body is the final temple (John 2:21). The church has now become a temple (1 Cor. 3:16), and the body of an individual Christian has become a temple (1 Cor. 6:19), because the Spirit of Christ dwells there. In the Old Testament, the temple theme includes not only Solomon's temple but also the tabernacle of Moses, and in addition "sanctuaries" without an obvious physical structure. For example, through Ezekiel God says to the exiles that he has "been a *sanctuary* to them for a while in the countries where they have gone" (Ezek. 11:16). No physical structure is present in the countries of exile, but the spiritual reality of a sanctuary is still there. The garden of Eden functions as a sanctuary, the "garden of God" (Ezek. 28:13; cf. Isa. 51:3). And at the consummation, the final dwelling of God with his people is reminiscent of the garden of Eden (Rev. 22:1–3).

Closely associated with covenant we have the themes belonging to God's covenantal promises: the promise of land and offspring. Promise belongs to a three-stage history: (1) promise, (2) development and call to trust, and (3) fulfillment. The promises of God come to realization in Christ (2 Cor. 1:20). Redemptive covenants disclose God's gracious initiative, and they call for a response of faith. Faith looks forward to the promised Redeemer, who is Christ. Reconciliation with God comprises many benefits: atonement, forgiveness, acceptance, love, peace, blessing, and the presence of God himself (especially through the Holy Spirit). These benefits come through Christ.

We must also pay attention to redemptive plots. These can be either plots with happy endings (redemption properly speaking) or plots with unhappy endings (plots ending in curse and judgment). Under this heading we should include the repeated pattern of sin, then suffering, then glory (reversal of suffering). Jesus alludes to this pattern when he interprets the Old Testament in connection with his own suffering and glory:

> "O foolish ones, and slow of heart to believe all that the prophets
> have spoken! Was it not necessary that the Christ should *suffer* these
> things and enter into his *glory*?" And beginning with Moses and all
> the Prophets, he interpreted to them in all the Scriptures the things
> concerning himself. (Luke 24:25–27)

Christ did not suffer for his own sins, because he had none (Heb. 4:15). But the pattern of sin followed by suffering is still present, because he identified with the sins of the people and suffered on their behalf.

We may add to these themes other major themes related to God's character: omnipotence, omniscience, holiness, righteousness, goodness, love, wisdom, faithfulness, truthfulness, patience, wrath, mercy, grace. Jesus perfectly and climactically expresses the character of God.

To all these themes we can add John Frame's perspectives, which can serve as themes: the authority, control, and presence of the Lord are themes closely related to kingship; the normative, situational, and existential perspectives are themes related to ethics and to God's requirements.

Other Themes

David Murray's book about Christ in the Old Testament brings together a large number of ways in which the Old Testament points to Christ.[1] Graeme Goldsworthy's book on hermeneutics also offers a useful list of major themes and connections.[2] In addition to what we have mentioned

[1] David Murray, *Jesus on Every Page: Discovering and Enjoying Christ in the Old Testament* (Nashville/Dallas/Mexico City/Rio de Janeiro: Thomas Nelson, 2013).
[2] Graeme Goldsworthy, *Gospel-Centered Hermeneutics: Foundations and Principles of Evangelical Biblical Interpretation* (Downers Grove, IL: InterVarsity Press, 2006), 253–256.

above, we may list some more themes, with some overlap with themes, analogies, and types already discussed:

(1) Christ is mediator of creation, and therefore of redemptive re-creation (John 1:1–5; Col. 1:15–17). The world was made in God's wisdom so that it has many analogies built in that can illustrate redemption. For example, physical light illustrates that Christ brings the light of redemption (John 1:4–5; 8:12). Physical vines illustrate Christ who is the true vine (John 15:1).

(2) Christ is active in sustaining Old Testament persons. He sustains them physically, and those who are saved receive their salvation through him. They receive his mercy; they believe in him through believing in God's promises that pointed to his coming.

(3) As God, Christ is the giver of the Old Testament. Those who sin against God's commandments also sin against him.

(4) Since Christ is fully human, every human character acting righteously reflects his perfect righteousness, while every sinning human character shows by contrast his distinctive perfection.

(5) Suffering saints in the Old Testament anticipate Jesus's final, climactic suffering.

(6) Glory given to God by Old Testament events and persons is also glory given to Jesus as God.

(7) Jesus is present in Old Testament appearances of God ("theophanies"), since all divine revelation is mediated through him (Matt. 11:27). Theophanies include "the angel of the Lord" (when this "angel" or "messenger" is divine) and appearances in cloud and fire.

(8) Old Testament law reveals God's righteousness, which was perfectly fulfilled in Christ (1 Cor. 1:30).

(9) Old Testament law as well as Old Testament events reveal the just punishment of sin. This punishment was fulfilled in Christ when he bore our sin (1 Pet. 2:24).

(10) The Old Testament laws addressing community life reflect Jesus's work to establish moral purity in the new community, the new humanity begun in the church.

(11) Old Testament law in its goodness and wisdom reflects the goodness and wisdom of God in Christ.

(12) The law's purity convicts us of sin, and shows the need for Christ as Savior.

(13) Jesus as perfect man learned the contents of the Old Testament as he grew up (Luke 2:46–47, 52).

(14) The Old Testament is the record of Israel as the people of God among whom Jesus grew up, and also the record of Jesus's personal ancestry (Matt. 1:1–17).

(15) Jesus's life-purpose on earth was to fulfill the Old Testament (Matt. 26:54; Luke 24:26–27).

(16) The Old Testament informed Jesus's human moral life, as he resisted temptation (Matt. 4:1–11).

(17) Jesus drew on the Old Testament in his teaching.

(18) Jesus sang the songs of the Old Testament (Matt. 26:30; Heb. 2:12).

(19) In analogy with Israel as "son" of God (Ex. 4:22; Deut. 8:5), Jesus is the obedient son, the true Son, and the true Israel, who succeeds in all respects where Old Testament Israel repeatedly failed.

(20) Whereas Israel suffered as punishment for her sins, Jesus suffered as punishment for the sins of his people (1 Pet. 2:24).

(21) Hopes for future climactic salvation are fulfilled in Jesus (Mark 1:15).

(22) God's kingly reign over his people is fulfilled in Jesus's reign as king.

Themes in Individual Old Testament Books

In addition, each book of the Old Testament has its own major themes. For example, 1 Samuel has a focus on the transition in Israel from the period of the judges to the period of kingship. First Samuel records that Eli "judged Israel forty years" (1 Sam. 4:18), but his sons fail abysmally to continue in faithfulness (1 Sam. 2:22–36). Samuel functions as the last judge (1 Sam. 7:15–17).

Saul and David, the first two kings of Israel, offer a study in contrasts. Kingship is a major theme, enriched by the contrasts between Saul, the king who mirrors the people's waywardness in relation to God, and David, the king "after his [God's] own heart" (1 Sam. 13:14; cf. Acts 13:22). The king is a key leader as Israel struggles with troubles: (1) the temptations toward idolatry and false worship; (2) the need for justice internally (1 Sam. 8:3; 12:3); and (3) the need for safety against foreign attacks, particularly the Philistines.

In the book of 1 Samuel, Samuel is a prophet. The theme of prophets and of the fulfillment of God's prophetic word runs through 1–2 Samuel and 1–2 Kings. Overarching the entire narrative is the theme of God's kingship, including his providential care and his righteous judgments, both over Israel and over the judges and kings. At the same time he shows mercy (1 Sam. 12:22–23).

Finally, when we study a particular passage, such as 1 Samuel 22:1–2, we want to ask how it is related thematically to other passages, not only through major themes but through any minor themes that crop up distinctively within the passage.

Themes Applied to 1 Samuel 22:1–2

How does this concern for themes have relevance to 1 Samuel 22:1–2? We want to be aware of how 1 Samuel 22:1–2 is related to the rest of the Bible. Since God has already chosen David to succeed Saul as king, the broad theme of kingship is linked to 1 Samuel 22:1–2. The theme of prophetic mediation is related to the passage indirectly, because Samuel as a prophet has revealed God's plan that David would become king. Since the prophetic word cannot be broken, we know that David will escape any attempts of Saul or of Achish king of Gath against his life. David's preservation also expresses the theme of covenant, since God's word of promise through Samuel is covenantal in nature. God has made a verbal commitment.

First Samuel, together with 2 Samuel and 1–2 Kings, covers the ups and downs of kingship during the beginnings of the monarchy up until its demise at the time of the exile. One central issue is whether the king follows God and his ways, as expressed through the law. Or, does he turn to trust in false gods or false worship or military might or foreign alliances? The king as a representative also has a big influence on the people under him. In many ways, as goes the king, so goes the nation under him. This representative role, in its failures as well as its partial successes, points forward to Christ the final king and representative. In 1 Samuel 22:1–2 David has not yet been acknowledged as king, but he is "king-elect," and we see him as having a representative function toward those under him. They prosper because of his leadership.

We have considered many of these connections earlier, as we have investigated how 1 Samuel 22:1–2 points forward to Christ. It is worthwhile looking at thematic connections, as we are now doing, because they offer another perspective that leads to the same results.

In addition to human kingship, David Tsumura mentions two other major themes that occur in 1 Samuel: the sovereignty of God and the reversal of fortunes.[3] The sovereignty of God is evident at many points throughout the narrative. It is evident in 1 Samuel 22:1–2 in that God providentially provides for David and his men. God protects the life of David, in accordance with his sovereign choice to establish David as the next king (1 Sam. 16:7, 12). The theme of reversal of fortunes is introduced in Hannah's prayer in 1 Samuel 2:1–10. Samuel is raised up while Eli's sons are put down. David is selected as the anointed one even though he is the youngest among his brothers (1 Sam. 16:6–13). David is raised up while Saul, after an initial favorable start, is put down. When we reach 1 Samuel 22:1–2, David is in an unfavorable situation, but God is with him, and eventually his situation will be reversed. The supreme reversal, of course, takes place with Christ, in the transition from his humiliation in the cross to his exaltation (Phil. 2:8–11).

We may notice one more thematic connection that concerns a minor

---

[3] David Toshio Tsumura, *The First Book of Samuel* (Grand Rapids, MI: Eerdmans, 2007), 68–73.

theme in 1 Samuel 22:1–2. First Samuel 22:2 has a kind of ironic parallel in 1 Samuel 14:52:[4]

> There was hard fighting against the Philistines all the days of Saul. And when Saul saw any strong man, or any valiant man, he attached him to himself.

Saul is a leader of fighting men. So is David. So the two men are partially parallel. But other things are antiparallel. Saul takes the initiative. He looks out for suitable men, and attaches them "to himself." David, on the other hand, is not described as looking out to invite people to join him. Rather, they come to him on *their* initiative. (Of course, behind the scenes God is the one who draws them to David.) We also see a contrast in the type of people that come. Saul gets "any strong man, or any valiant man." David gets "everyone who was in distress, and everyone who was in debt, and everyone who was bitter in soul." David's people have problems, and we do not hear of anything indicating that they have outstanding skills in war. Saul gets the elite from the people around him. David gets the refuse, the outcasts.

Is this relationship accidental? We might think so, but 1 Samuel as a whole sets up an elaborate contrast between Saul and David, and Saul consciously sees David as a competitor and then as an enemy (1 Sam. 18:7–11). The global contrast invites us to consider contrasts in detail, such as between these two verses, 14:52 and 22:2. Moreover, the two verses are only a few chapters distant from one another. And they are among the few verses that describe what processes led to the gathering of followers.

The contrasts suggest that Saul and David fit into a larger theme of reversal, such as is articulated by Hannah (1 Sam. 2:4–8) and later by Mary (Luke 1:48–53). The strong are brought down while the weak are lifted up. It is God's purpose to show mercy to those who do not deserve it and have no "qualifications." He delights to show his power by confounding the strong (1 Cor. 1:18–31), "that no human being might boast in the presence of God" (1 Cor. 1:29). This reversal finds its fulfillment in Christ, who "was crucified in weakness, but lives by the power of God" (2 Cor. 13:4).

---

[4] My son Justin drew my attention to this ironic parallel.

Adding Themes to the Outline for Interpretation

We have already discussed many of the themes in connection with earlier chapters. The themes are most relevant when we focus on correlation, both topical correlation and redemptive-historical correlation. We will add our list of themes under topical correlation, partly to remind ourselves that we can focus on thematic unity through all times (topical unity) as well as the development of themes from seed to flower to fruit as history moves forward (redemptive-historical correlation). So our outline might look as follows:

   A. Observation
      1. Read
      2. Continue to observe, using questions
   B. Elucidation
      1. One passage
      2. Topical correlation
         *a. God
            *(1) Lordship
               *(a) Authority
               *(b) Control
               *(c) Presence
            *(2) Character of God: omnipotence, omniscience, holiness, righteousness, goodness, love, wisdom, faithfulness, truthfulness, patience, wrath, mercy, grace
            *(3) Ethics
               *(a) Normative perspective
               *(b) Situational perspective
               *(c) Existential perspective
       *b. Man
       *c. Mediators
          *(1) Prophets
          *(2) Kings
          *(3) Priests
             *(a) Sacrifices
             *(b) Temple
          *(4) Wise men
       *d. Covenants

            *(1) Promises
                *(a) Land
                *(b) Offspring
            *(2) Promise, development, and fulfillment
          *e. Redemptive plots
            *(1) Positive redemption
            *(2) Curse
            *(3) Sin, suffering, and glory
         *f. Themes of individual books
      3. Redemptive-historical correlation
   C. Application

Resources

Goldsworthy, Graeme. *Gospel-Centered Hermeneutics: Foundations and Principles of Evangelical Biblical Interpretation.* Downers Grove, IL: InterVarsity Press, 2006.
Murray, David. *Jesus on Every Page: Discovering and Enjoying Christ in the Old Testament.* Nashville/Dallas/Mexico City/Rio de Janeiro: Thomas Nelson, 2013.

Part VII

ASSESSMENT

29

Hermeneutics Outline in Detail

We may now sum up all the ground that we have covered, by offering a detailed outline that includes the various perspectives discussed in earlier parts of the book. Within the outline, some of the headings include references to previous chapters. These references indicate the chapter within which the heading is broken down into smaller subdivisions.

An Overall Outline
(Chapter 4)

    I. Pray
   II. Look at the rest of the book
  III. Use the three steps (chapter 4)
     A. Observation
       1. Read
       2. Continue to observe, using questions
     B. Elucidation (chapter 6)
       1. One passage
         a. The literary context (chapter 7)
         b. The transmission context (chapter 7)
           (1) God writes through a human author
             (a) Author: God through human author
             (b) Text: autograph of 1–2 Samuel
             (c) Reader: Israelites

      (2) God providentially supervises the text's voyage,
           that is, the transmission in the middle period

        (a) Authors: scribes

        (b) Text: scribal copies

        (c) Readers: later scribes

      (3) God sees to it that I receive what he says

        (a) Author: ESV translation team

        (b) Text: ESV of 1 Samuel

        (c) Reader: me (and others)

  c. The text (chapter 8)

    (1) The text as act of communication (chapter 9)

      (a) Authorial intention (chapter 10)

        ((1)) Divine intention

        ((2)) Mediatorial intention

        ((3)) Human intention

      (b) Textual expression (chapter 12)

        ((1)) Units (chapter 14)

          ((a)) Contrast (chapter 15)

            a1. Meaning

            a2. Impact

            a3. Import

          ((b)) Variation

          ((c)) Distribution (and genre,
             chapter 19)

            c1. In substitution class

            c2. In sequence

            c3. In system

        ((2)) Hierarchies (chapter 18)

          ((a)) Discourse flow

          ((b)) Discourse topics

          ((c)) Discourse figures (chapter 16)

        ((3)) Systemic linguistic contexts (chapter 12)

          ((a)) Referential subsystem

          ((b)) Grammatical subsystem

          ((c)) Graphological subsystem

      (c) Readers' impression

    (2) The social contexts

    (3) The historical contexts

    (d. Consult exegetical commentaries
    (chapter 20))
 2. Topical correlation (chapter 28)
  a. God
   (1) Lordship
    (a) Authority
    (b) Control
    (c) Presence
   (2) Character of God: omnipotence, omniscience,
    holiness, righteousness, goodness, love, wisdom,
    faithfulness, truthfulness, patience, wrath, mercy,
    grace
   (3) Ethics
    (a) Normative perspective
    (b) Situational perspective
    (c) Existential perspective
  b. Man
  c. Mediators
   (1) Prophets
   (2) Kings
   (3) Priests
    (a) Sacrifices
    (b) Temple
   (4) Wise men
  d. Covenants
   (1) Promises
    (a) Land
    (b) Offspring
   (2) Promise, development, and fulfillment
  e. Redemptive plots
   (1) Positive redemption
   (2) Curse
   (3) Sin, suffering, and glory
  f. Themes of individual books
 3. Redemptive-historical correlation (chapter 21)
  a. God's plan as source of meaning
  b. Historical events (speaking and acting)
  c. Christ as the center (chapter 22)

(1) Wave: promises about Christ (prophecy)

(2) Field: general principles fulfilled in Christ

(3) Particle: particular times relating to Christ

    (a) Analogies (chapter 25)

        ((1)) With God

        ((2)) With mediation

           ((a)) Prophetic

           ((b)) Kingly

           ((c)) Priestly

        ((3)) With humanity

    (b) Types (including symbols) (chapter 23)

        ((1)) Symbolic reference (chapter 26)

           ((a)) Things

           ((b)) Events and plots

           ((c)) Relationships and institutions

        ((2)) Moving forward in history

        ((3)) Synthesis in typological reference (chapter 25)

           ((a)) Christ as a person

               a1. Earthly life of Christ

               a2. New covenant (already)

               a3. Consummation (not yet)

           ((b)) The church united to Christ

               b1. Earthly life of Christ

               b2. New covenant (already)

               b3. Consummation (not yet)

           ((c)) Individuals in Christ

               c1. Earthly life of Christ

               c2. New covenant (already)

               c3. Consummation (not yet)

    (c) Preparation

C. Application

Complexity and Simplicity

Having such a complex and detailed outline may seem intimidating. Does this outline suggest that a person can understand a passage of the Old Testament only by elaborately traveling through each of over a hundred subdivisions or steps? No. A human being within this world never understands the Bible *exhaustively*. But God has designed the Bible to be clear in its central message, and we can learn from God enough to live for him.

We can learn by praying and by going through the simple three steps of observation, elucidation, and application. Or, since these three "steps" are each a perspective on the whole, we can learn by using only one step. That step could be labeled "observation" (a simple process of reading) or "elucidation." As a perspective, either of these tacitly includes application. If we do not focus explicitly on application at some point, we run the danger of not doing our duty before God: "be doers of the word, and not hearers only" (James 1:22). But if our hearts are sensitive, and if the Holy Spirit works within us, it is also possible that we may include application without ever explicitly and self-consciously *focusing* on it and saying, "Now let me make sure that I focus on application." Likewise, if we have read other parts of the Bible, we may automatically do some correlation when we read 1 Samuel 22:1–2.

Perspectively speaking, all interpretive interaction with the Bible should include *implicitly* all the subdivisions in our detailed outline. For example, when reading 1 Samuel 22:1–2, readers who have become informed about the Bible know that there is a larger context in 1 Samuel, and in 2 Samuel and 1–2 Kings as well. They know that 1–2 Samuel was originally written long before the New Testament; that God designed it to address earlier readers as well as us; that it points forward to redemption in Christ; and so on. Precisely because knowledge of this kind forms an implicit environment for reading 1 Samuel 22:1–2, it need not necessarily be made explicit in order for it to have an influence and inform a reader's understanding of 1 Samuel 22:1–2. A sensitive, spiritual reader automatically knows that God is addressing him and applying the text to him in the light of the full scope of his plan for all history.

The detailed outline is therefore an *aid* to interpreting, but it is not necessary to use it in the form of explicit steps. The other side of the coin is that the principles expressed in the outline are significant as a *tacit background of knowledge* when we read an individual text.

Noticing

The details in the outline are also significant because sometimes we as interpreters are negligent or evade what God is saying. We fall victim to sins. And sometimes we are stumped. The Bible student asks himself, "What do I do now?" He has run out of ideas for asking more questions, and he finds himself just staring at the page and the words. No new insights are coming. A detailed outline such as what we have offered gives us ways to get going again, and to ask fruitful questions.

And, if we have a pronounced tendency to evade some aspects of Scripture, the outline can remind us to pay attention in new ways. One person consistently evades application. Another consistently evades paying attention to the details of the text (avoiding observation), and lets the text serve primarily as a springboard for his own imagination. Another sees the Old Testament as offering moral examples but does not notice how it points to Christ. By paying attention to an outline, we can push ourselves to overcome deficiencies in the habits with which we approach the study of the Bible.

30

Alternate Paths of Interpretation

The Old Testament offers challenges for interpretation because, super-ficially, it seems to address us less directly and less relevantly. Not only was it originally written within a cultural setting vastly different from the modern West, but that original communication took place within a redemptive-historical epoch preceding the coming of Christ. It is antici-patory rather than final, and accordingly the New Testament directly indicates that some of the Mosaic ceremonies have become obsolete (Mark 7:19; Heb. 8:13; 9:10).

Should we conclude that the Old Testament has become irrelevant? Romans 15:4 indicates that God still intends to instruct us through it:

> For *whatever* was written in former days was written for our in-struction, that through endurance and through the encouragement of the Scriptures we might have hope.

The many instances where the New Testament quotes from or alludes to the Old Testament confirm this principle.

The Old Testament speaks to us, but how? Bible interpreters through the centuries have explored a number of paths or routes for maintain-ing the relevance of the Old Testament. But not all have been equally effective or equally sound. We will now look at some of these routes, to compare them with the redemptive-historical, Christocentric interpreta-tion that we have set out in preceding chapters.

The Approach of Historical Lecture

Some interpreters offer *historical lectures* on Old Testament passages. This approach begins with the question of what happened in the past and how we are to understand it. After retrieving information about the past, the interpreter offers his historical lecture to inform his audience. He tells his audience about what was happening historically back then and there, and what the passage communicated to an ancient readership at the time when it was first written. But the lecture stops there. It offers no indication about how this historical information might be relevant to modern times.

For 1 Samuel 22:1–2, a historical lecture might provide information about two times, the time when 1–2 Samuel was written and the time in David's life when he escaped to the cave of Adullam. It would recount the events that 1 Samuel 22:1–2 mentions, and perhaps comment on the setting. It might suggest reasons why David's life might be endangered from Achish, king of Gath, and Saul, king of Israel. It might also try to sketch (from admittedly limited information) how the social and economic situation might leave some people in distress or in debt. Moving to the time when 1–2 Samuel was written, it would comment on how 1–2 Samuel might give hope to later Israelites concerning God's continued faithfulness and his regard for David and his descendants.

In the history of the West, the approach of historical lecture appeared most prominently in connection with the classical historical-critical approach that developed in the seventeenth through the nineteenth centuries in Europe. The historical-critical approach regarded the Bible as a purely human document, and therefore the Old Testament was not the voice of God but only a human record recounting events of its time, and including what various people of the time believed that God was doing. If this approach were correct, one conclusion might be that the Old Testament is not intrinsically relevant to modern times, except as a source of historical information about events and about what people were saying and believing. Given these assumptions, modern academic use of the Bible naturally inclined toward historical lecture.

In theory, this approach is also available to people who believe that the Old Testament is the word of God. The Old Testament could still be treated in practice merely as a historical source. And if the interpreter brings God into the picture, it may be only to talk about what God was saying to people long ago. In principle, the interpreter may avoid saying anything about the present. In that respect, his presentation is still in the style of historical lecture.

Fortunately, this approach has not been common among people who believe the Bible. Romans 15:4 and other passages make it plain that a modern interpreter has the obligation eventually to think about how God instructs, encourages, and gives hope to us. Even apart from the principles in Romans 15:4, an interpreter who knows that God is speaking knows tacitly that his speech will be relevant, because of who God is. In addition, there is a practical issue. Preachers who adopt the style of historical lecture are likely to receive complaints and gradually lose their parishioners, who find the style boring and irrelevant.

We may summarize the strengths and weaknesses of the historical lecture:

Strengths
  • Sustained focus on the text, including details.
  • Ability to affirm details in meaning.
  • Recognition of setting in time and in culture.
  • Emphasis on what it said then.

Weaknesses
  • No modern relevance.
  • Bored audience.
  • May neglect the presence of God speaking in the text.
  • Bypasses the principles of Romans 15:4.
  • Bypasses Luke 24 and the centrality of Christ.
  • No gospel message, announcing Christ's victory and inviting people to respond.

The Exemplary Approach

A second path, the *exemplary* approach, uses the text as a moral example. It begins with the question of what parallels we can see between human characters in ancient times and ourselves in our situation today. Then it draws moral lessons from the parallels. In principle, this use can encompass both positive and negative examples. King Saul in some of his failings could serve as a negative example or warning to a modern audience. The Bible interpreter then exhorts people to learn and not to be like Saul. David too had his failures, but in many passages he may serve as a positive moral example. The interpreter exhorts the modern audience to be like David and to imitate him.

This exhortation could focus wholly on one human being's relationships to other human beings and to his environment, without bringing God into the picture. For example, an interpreter could use 1 Samuel 22:1 to exhort people to imitate David's wisdom in avoiding threats from his enemies. He could then use verse 2 to exhort his hearers to imitate David's leadership, partly by welcoming all who come, both family and those in distress. Or the interpreter could use David's relationship to God as the example. He exhorts his hearers to trust in God as David did, and rely on God's providence even when the situation is difficult.

A steady diet of this type of preaching means that the people will hear moralism. The overall message is to "be good." Even if the interpreter brings God into the picture, the advice amounts to saying, "Be good in your relationship to God." But what has the preacher offered to people who in fact are *not* good, who repeatedly fail to measure up to God's standards? Is he merely implying, "Do better next time"? He ends up implying that people should try to save themselves by moral effort.

The exemplary approach has the following strengths and weaknesses:

Strengths
- Relevant to the audience.
- Potentially engaging and convicting.
- Easy to find and understand the parallels.

Weaknesses
- Temptation to read in and then read out human motivations that the text does not really specify.
- Does not work well with morally mixed examples.
- Man-centered.
- Moralism or legalism.

- No Christ.
- No gospel.

In spite of its weaknesses, this approach tends to be fairly common. Perhaps that is partly because it is relatively easy to draw moral parallels. It has an appeal both to the preacher and to his audience, because we instinctively have a tendency to identify with the characters in a story. Why not make this identification the central link in the treatment of the passage?

The Approach Focusing on Revelation of God's Character

Interpreters who recognize the weaknesses of the exemplary approach may turn away from a focus on man and begin to focus on God. They have an approach that concerns *the revelation of God's character*. They ask not about the parallels between human beings now and then, but about the parallels due to the unchanging character of God. If God was faithful back then, we can trust him to be faithful now.

When they apply this approach to a passage like 1 Samuel 22:1–2, they look for what God is doing in the passage. Since the passage does not directly mention God, they ask what God is doing behind the scenes. He is providentially caring for David and his men, against the background of his previous promise to David that David would become king. The passage therefore illustrates God's faithfulness to his word and his promises, his faithfulness to people like David, his wisdom, his providential control of circumstances, and his compassion on those in distress (David's men). It also illustrates God's knowledge of the future, since God has plans that will lead to David becoming king.

By being God-centered, this approach helps people to take their eyes off a sinful focus on self, or a depressing focus on their troubles. Instead, they should look upward to God. It is clearly a partial counterbalance to the exemplary approach. Here are its strengths and weaknesses:

Strengths
- God-centered.
- Relevant to the present because of the unchangeability of God.
- Encourages reflection on the character of God and trust in him.

Weaknesses

- Could wash out the particularity of single events. All events are treated as if they were no more than illustrations of a general principle, namely the unchangeable character of God.
- Emphasis on God could still seem remote from the sweat and grime of human struggles.
- Where is Christ? An interpretation can be God-centered and still not be Christ-centered.
- Where is the gospel announcing the victory of Christ and calling for response?

The Approach through Preparation

Next, we consider an approach that focuses on the path of redemptive-historical *preparation* for the coming of Christ. The whole Old Testament sets forth the period of preparation for the coming of Christ. Israel as God's people is the historical community enduring through the ages until Christ comes. The line of David is the line of descendants that God preserves through the generations until Christ comes. The land of Palestine is the land to which Christ will eventually come. The preparation approach asks the question, "What was God doing in this text, and in the events recorded in the text, that served as one step forward in a long history, a history that in God's providence and according to his plan led eventually to the coming of Christ?"[1]

How does this approach apply to a passage like 1 Samuel 22:1–2? Mentally, the approach draws a timeline that goes from creation to consummation. Development in time is in focus. The approach then places the passage at the appropriate point on the timeline. In the case of 1 Samuel 22:1–2, there are two points, the point in David's life and

---

[1] This approach has also been called "redemptive-historical" preaching. Sidney Greidanus wrote an important study of a twentieth-century controversy in the Netherlands about preaching (*Sola Scriptura: Problems and Principles in Preaching Historical Texts* [Toronto: Wedge, 1970]). The controversy involved a polarization between "exemplary" preaching that was more man-centered, and "redemptive-historical" preaching that focused on God's work in history. The exemplary preaching of that time was similar to what we have described as the exemplary approach. What Greidanus calls "redemptive-historical" preaching is close to what we have described as the *preparation approach* (though there may be significant variations in the Netherlands; we are simplifying our description in order to consider a "pure" version of a preparation approach). The expression "redemptive-historical" preaching, which was used amid the controversy, aptly describes the characteristic focus on the question of how a given passage fits into the total history of redemption. However, we have already introduced the expression *redemptive history* in a broader context. As we shall see, the approach through preparation is in fact only *one* of several approaches that endeavor to reckon with redemptive-historical context. Thus we have avoided using Greidanus's label in our own description.

the point when 1–2 Samuel is produced to write down the record of David's life. Both points in time have an integral function in the history of redemption.

First Samuel 22:1–2 describes a particular point within David's life, and that point in time must be appreciated. It is in between the point when Samuel anoints David as future king (1 Samuel 16) and when David becomes king of Judah and then all Israel (2 Samuel 2; 5). God works to preserve David's life and his trust in God during a time of suffering and trouble. David's kingship serves as the foundation for a line of kings that will lead forward to Christ. So God's preservation of David is a necessary step along the way. God shows his faithfulness to us by working in history through all the steps necessary for Christ to come to earth and then accomplish our salvation. The timeline extends to us, who live in the age of the new covenant and receive the gospel. We receive the benefits of Christ's accomplished work and his reign at the right hand of the Father.

The approach through preparation thus tries to do justice to the uniqueness of each event, like the event when David arrives at the cave of Adullam, and at the same time to indicate how this one event forms one link in a chain in time that stretches out over the history of redemption. By stretching out, it comes to Christ and then eventually embraces us who live our own unique lives, each in his own time and place.

We can see the following strengths and weaknesses in this approach:

Strengths
- Focus on unique, unrepeatable events.
- Focus on history.
- Sensitivity to the timeline of redemptive history.
- God-centered: God rules history according to his plan.
- Somewhat Christ-centered, in that history prepares for Christ.

Weaknesses
- Can become a redemptive-historical lecture that never manages to come to the point of application. Even when application is included, it may appear exclusively at the end, when the audience has been somewhat wearied by a long discourse that discusses exclusively past times.

- Some awkwardness when applied to books of the Bible that have no obvious date (Psalms; Job; Joel).
- Can tempt an interpreter to focus almost wholly on the events behind the text rather than on what God is saying in the text.
- Not wholly Christ-centered. In some forms of the preparation approach, Christ appears only at the end of the timeline. In a sense this is correct, since the incarnation took place at a single point in time. But God the Son was active as the second person of the Trinity during the Old Testament. In addition, the benefits of Christ's work to come were already being applied, and God gave types and shadows that prefigured Christ's work, and through which the people could exercise faith.

The Typological Approach

Next, we consider the *typological* approach. As the name suggests, this approach asks how an Old Testament text shows us types of Christ (and then perhaps also types of the church and of the individual believer). The word *type* can also be used more broadly to cover many kinds of analogies that point forward to Christ. So a typological approach looks for types in the narrower sense, types that involve two levels of meaning, and in addition analogies that involve only one level of meaning. (But, as indicated in chapter 22, the line between types and analogies is fluid.) This approach is closest to the one that we have developed in preceding chapters.

We can sum up its strengths and weaknesses:

Strengths

- Christ-centered.
- Proclaiming the gospel.
- Taking account of redemptive history and organic unity of redemption.

Weaknesses

- More challenging for a preacher to develop.
- More challenging to communicate (because it intrinsically involves complexities—the presence of symbolism and a focus on three distinct times: the Old Testament time, the time of Christ's

life, and the time of the hearer to whom the message is now applied).

- May tempt the interpreter to neglect application. (The preacher may draw the line pointing to Christ but never discuss the implications for the people in his audience.)
- May tempt the interpreter to neglect or suppress ways in which the type *differs* from the antitype.
- May result in "forced" analogies and neglect the original historical context. (The text becomes merely a springboard for a New Testament sermon.)
- May seem arbitrary.

In previous chapters I have advocated something similar to a typological approach. But at this point I have tried to be honest about its weaknesses. The first two "weaknesses" are really challenges. The typological approach is not so easy. But it is worth it, because its strengths honor God's intentions in Scripture. The last four weaknesses are *potential* problems into which practitioners may fall, rather than weaknesses inherent in the approach. So they do not disqualify the approach; they serve as cautions.

Interrogating the Typological Approach

The typological approach has a long history in the church. One can observe its use among interpreters going back to the second century. And of course these interpreters built on typological examples in the New Testament, which encouraged them to proceed by way of imitation. In the nineteenth and twentieth centuries, however, typology lost popularity among biblical scholars, partly because the scholars increasingly adopted a tradition that focused wholly or almost wholly on human meaning (see appendix A). In the twenty-first century, we still live with the ongoing effects of scholarly suspicion and caution. So I believe that the typological approach needs vigorous embrace and practical adoption.

Past centuries of typological interpretation have sometimes fallen victim to one of the weaknesses: the interpreter may neglect or suppress ways in which the type *differs* from the antitype. This danger bears further reflection.

Christ accomplished *climactic* redemption. His work was not just "another case," another instance. We can hear the note of climax in the description from Hebrews 1:

> Long ago, at many times and in many ways, God spoke to our fathers by the prophets, but in these *last* days he has spoken to us by his *Son*, whom he appointed the heir of *all* things, through whom also he created the world. He is the radiance of the glory of God and the *exact imprint* of his nature, and he upholds the universe by the word of his power. After making *purification for sins*, he *sat down* at the right hand of the Majesty on high, having become as *much superior* to angels as the name he has inherited is *more excellent* than theirs. (Heb. 1:1–4)

The Old Testament persons, events, and institutions are inferior to Christ. This inferiority is a built-in feature. It is not something that a typological interpreter should suppress or about which he should feel embarrassment. Precisely by their insufficiency, the Old Testament types proclaim that "this is not the endpoint" and "more is to come; the climax is still to come." The discontinuities between a type and its antitype have a *positive* function in Scripture. So we should use them rather than discard them.

For example, in 1 Samuel 22:1–2 David is a type of Christ, but he is limited in this regard. He is human, not divine. He offers relief of a sort to his family and his men, but that relief is inevitably limited in scope. His relief is temporary. His relief cannot reach the depth of the heart or the depths of sin. He cannot overcome the power of Satan and death. To be sure, the verses 22:1–2 are moving toward times in which David will have more power and more scope to exercise his leadership—he will become king. But a sensitive reader can see, even at this early point, the two sides. David will achieve great things, but those great things can never achieve the full redemption that we honestly need, in view of the direct and indirect effects of sin on ourselves and on the world. The passage proclaims not only that David is a type, but that he is a type that contains within itself indications of its own insufficiency in comparison with the antitype.

In past generations of the church, typological interpreters have sometimes delighted in multiplying the parallels between a type and its antitype. The preacher announces, perhaps, that he will preach about fifty ways in which Joseph (the son of Jacob) is a type of Christ. And indeed maybe there are fifty ways, or more! But Joseph is still not Christ, nor could he be. Once we recognize that simple fact, it should open the way to recognize Joseph in his historical uniqueness, and to be unembarrassed about ways in which he does not completely correspond with Christ.

Resources

Greidanus, Sidney. Sola Scriptura: *Problems and Principles in Preaching Historical Texts.* Toronto: Wedge, 1970.

31

The Fulfillment Approach

We would therefore propose still another kind of approach, the *fulfillment* approach. The fulfillment approach includes the typological approach, plus the acknowledgment of Christ's superiority as the "Son, whom he appointed the heir of all things" (Heb. 1:2). It explicitly asks not only how Christ is like a type in the Old Testament, but how he is unlike the type.

The word *fulfillment* is appropriate, because it suggests two sides. First, the fulfillment in the New Testament corresponds organically to something in the Old Testament that it fulfills. The earlier stage is a type, pointing to the fulfillment stage. Second, the word *fulfillment* indicates the superiority of what has come in Christ. Christ's work *achieved* everlasting salvation. It is the climax of history. The earlier works only *foreshadowed* it.

At their best, practitioners of the typological approach have always known about this superiority and climactic character of Christ's fulfillment. People's definitions of "types" may even include explicitly the note that the antitype surpasses the type. But it is worth stressing that this element of "surpassing" means not only that the antitype is *more than* the type, by way of escalation, but also that it is *other than* the type, by way of exclusion. The type proclaims its own insufficiency. It is *not* the real thing, but signifies beforehand the real thing. Since it is not the real thing, it has features that are *unlike* the antitype to which it points. Such features are not dispensable and are not accidental within God's plan.

Even this is not the whole story, however, because we must also continue to reckon with the fact that the benefits of Christ's work, and his presence as Redeemer, belong to the Old Testament types, when these are received by faith. The Old Testament worshipers did receive real forgiveness of sins when they offered animal sacrifices. But they did so, not because these sacrifices were sufficient in and of themselves, but because God was reckoning beforehand the benefits of Christ's future sacrifice, and he was reckoning those benefits to those who placed their faith in God's promises and the future redemption to which those promises pointed forward. The type, we might say, is *not* the real thing, but Christ, who *is* the real thing, is present in the type for the benefit of those who come to God in faith.

Similar principles hold in the case of David and his men in 1 Samuel 22:1–2. David as type is not Christ, but he signifies Christ beforehand precisely by means of his insufficiency, as well as his positive achievements. But through David, Christ can also be present and can minister both spiritually and materially to the needs of David's family and David's men. They experience God's providential mercy and care and leadership, not merely David's mercy. And how do they deserve God's mercy and care? Are they worthy? No, they receive mercy by virtue of Christ's sacrifice and his resurrection, reckoned backward to their time, through David their representative, who functions as a type of Christ. And this reckoning backward is not merely a kind of "mental" operation on God's part; it takes place through the actual *presence* of Christ as the eternal Son through the Spirit, in anticipation of his incarnation and death. The presence of Christ is necessary because mediation is necessary between holy God and sinful man.

These reflections mean that we do not have to "escape," as it were, from David and from his time in order to find Christ as antitype at the end of the period leading up to his first coming. The realities of redemption are already present. But they are, as always in the Old Testament, present by way of type and anticipation, *preparing for* Christ's coming in time and space at a future point.

Since the fulfillment approach incorporates the typological approach, it has strengths and weaknesses similar to those of the typological approach:

Strengths

- Christ-centered.
- Proclaiming the gospel.
- Taking account of redemptive history and the organic unity of redemption.

Weaknesses

- More challenging for a preacher to develop.
- More challenging to communicate.

We have omitted the last four of the weaknesses of the typological approach. Let us consider these weaknesses one by one.

In the first weakness, an interpreter neglected application. Fulfillment takes place preeminently in Christ, once and for all. He alone can die as a substitute for sins and accomplish salvation. But then a kind of fulfillment takes place in the people whom Christ saves. They receive the benefits of Christ's accomplishment. Moreover, the Old Testament has types, analogies, and prophecies that include within their scope the benefits of salvation that come to God's people. So in this way fulfillment includes application. Therefore, rightly understood, the fulfillment approach includes application. (But still, an individual preacher may accidentally forget this aspect, so the omission is still a potential danger.)

The second weakness of the typological approach involved neglecting *differences* between type and antitype. We have built into our description of fulfillment an attention to these differences.

The third weakness involved neglecting historical context. The fulfillment approach encourages attention to historical context, because this context reinforces the point that the type belongs to a different context, and does not represent the climax.

The fourth weakness of the typological approach involved the appearance of arbitrariness. This weakness is at least diminished in the fulfillment approach, because the fulfillment approach encourages the interpreter to acknowledge discontinuities between the type and the antitype. The open acknowledgment of discontinuities helps the interpreter not to "force" more analogies than he can reasonably justify. He does not merely try to increase the length of his list of continuities and parallels. Increasing the list runs the danger of including parallels that look artificial or arbitrary.

We can illustrate using 1 Samuel 22:1–2. Suppose we are using a typological approach in a narrow and rigid way, and not paying attention to the principles of fulfillment. If we are trying to lengthen the list of parallels, we can be tempted to try to line up a kind of one-to-one correlation. So we start listing possible parallels. David is a type of Christ the king and leader. David's brothers correspond to those in the New Testament who are already in the church, whom Christ calls brothers (Heb. 2:11). David's "father's house" corresponds to the Jews, who belong to God the Father's community in the Old Testament. David's "men" correspond to the Gentiles, who start outside God's family. The fact that all of these people come to David corresponds to the fact that the gospel goes out to all nations, calling both Jew and Gentile to Christ.

What do we think about this attempt? Are these parallels exact? No. The correspondences do not all work on the same level. In 1 Samuel 22:1–2 David's brothers and his father's house really belong together, on essentially the same level, because they represent the company of blood relatives. In the alleged typological correspondence, one group, the brothers, stands for people already inside the church, while the other, "his father's house," stands for Jews who are still outside but invited inside. We sense an artificiality.

Yes, we can see some vague correspondences, but we can also see that within the two stories, of David and of Christ, the roles of the various parties are not thoroughly parallel. We could confirm our feeling of uneasiness by using Clowney's triangle. David's family, his father's house, and the larger group of people in distress do not in any clear way have distinct symbolic significances that strongly distinguish them from each other within the context of 1 Samuel. Without such distinct symbolic significances, we cannot complete the horizontal leg of Clowney's triangle in a way that would nonartificially lead to distinct groups within the age of the new covenant. Hence, using Clowney's triangle tells us that we are better off if we drop this claim about a detailed correspondence.

We can still say that, in a general way, David was a blessing to several kinds of people—those who were naturally closer to him by blood and those who had no special claim to a relationship. Through David, God showed mercy to both. In a loose way, this range of blessing does correspond to the blessings in the gospel that come both to those who are "near" and to those who are "far off" (Eph. 2:17). Provided we do not press for *exact* parallels, we can still see expressions of general principles about God's salvation and his mercy. We can explain to others that both in David and in Christ we see instances of God's mercy to those who have no earthly claim or special privilege. We can say that much without claiming that there is some tight and exact parallel between the various subgroups among David's followers and the various subgroups within the church.

The fulfillment approach, at its best, helps to steer us away from artificial correspondences by enabling us to relax about David and his men being *different* from Christ and his disciples. God was doing something for David and his men in their own day. He was redemptively at work, but it did not correspond completely to Christ's work. If it had, David would virtually *be* Christ, which he is not, and his redemption would *be* Christian redemption, which it is not. The antitype exceeds the type, and is *other than* the type.

Combining Approaches

The fulfillment approach is a *perspective*. If we use it expansively as a perspective, it can encompass all the positive aspects of the alternative approaches that we have mentioned in the previous chapter. Let us see how.

First, consider the historical-lecture approach. Its strength lies in focusing on what happened back then and there, and the meaning that it had at the time. The fulfillment approach encompasses in principle this focus on the past, since the idea of fulfillment explicitly includes the idea of an earlier time, the time before fulfillment, that points forward to the fulfillment. The fulfillment approach or the typological approach must only make sure that it does not too quickly pass over the details of past time in eagerness to arrive at the time of fulfillment. Thus, for 1 Samuel 22:1–2, we need to take time to understand what is happening to David, and how it fits into 1–2 Samuel. We do not immediately decide that, because David is a type of Christ, all we need is to study Christ and not David. Studying Christ is of course an excellent and edifying practice, but our study of Christ need not leave David out. The Old Testament and not merely the New proclaims Christ, as Luke 24 indicates. If we are studying 1 Samuel 22:1–2, we need to study the Old Testament passage itself and not only the New Testament.

Second, consider the exemplary approach. The exemplary approach has its strength in drawing lines of comparison between human beings in Old Testament times and ourselves as human beings in our own time. Yes, there will certainly be many analogies, because human beings in some ways are all alike. We are all made in the image of God, all except for Christ are fallen and sinful, and all except for Christ are in need of redemption from sin.

We can incorporate this approach within the fulfillment approach if we notice that one aspect of fulfillment lies in the fact that Christ is representative of his people. He is fully human. He is of course one human being among many, but he is more, in his representative capacity. He represents his people as their high priest who intercedes in the presence of God. He is also the pattern for what humanity *should* be like, and so his life has pertinence even to unbelievers. For one thing, he shows them by contrast how they fall short.

Christ as a representative human being is connected with every human character in the Old Testament. He sums up whatever is good about them, and at the same time he surpasses them. We as followers of Christ are called on to become like him (2 Cor. 3:18). The Holy Spirit empowers us in this imitation, so that our imitation is not an achievement for which we can take credit. Or, to put it another way, Christ is a moral example for us (1 Pet. 2:21), but not merely an example. He accomplished our salvation. His power saves us. He did not merely set forth an example so that we might accomplish our own salvation by ourselves and in our own power!

In imitating Christ, we are also imitating whatever is good in Old Testament personages. And we are avoiding the bad moral examples in the Old Testament, all of which show by contrast the deficiencies of fallen humanity in comparison to Christ.

Thus from the perspective of fulfillment we can see that the good and bad moral examples in the Old Testament are indeed moral examples for us to imitate or avoid. But a deeper analysis shows that they are so in a way that puts Christ in the center, as the principal example and representative. We can sum up the relationship in a diagram (fig. 31.1).

Fig. 31.1: Fulfilling Old Testament Examples

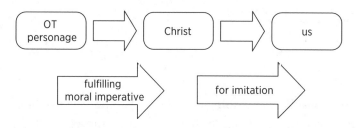

Third, consider the preparation approach. The preparation approach draws a line in time from the time in the Old Testament to Christ. Fulfillment affirms this timeline. Fulfillment means fulfillment after a passage of time. The earlier event, the passage of time, and the fulfillment itself all unfold according to the wisdom of God's plan.

Fourth, consider the approach through God's character. Its strength lies in the fact that God is indeed the same God at all times. We can therefore depend on him now in a way similar to the way that people could depend on him long ago.

God reveals his character supremely in Christ (John 14:9; Heb. 1:2–3). The general principles that we can find in describing the character of God are summed up in Christ. For example, in focusing on God's character we may argue that God cared providentially for David and his men. He is the same God now, and so he is able to care for you. But God's providential care came to a climax in Christ. God the Father cared for Christ during his earthly life, and Christ as God in the flesh cared for those around him. The life of Christ offers the supreme announcement and exemplification of God's care. And so we can say not only that God is *able* to care for you, but that he *will* care for you as you commit yourself to him in Christ.

We can sum up the revelation of God's character in a diagram (fig. 31.2).

Fig. 31.2: Fulfillment and God's Character

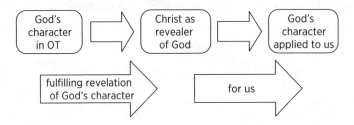

Finally, we consider the typological approach. Since the fulfillment approach represents a refinement of the typological approach, it obviously includes the typological approach.

All in all, the fulfillment approach can encompass the positive points in the other approaches. All the approaches can be seen in the light of fulfillment in Christ. Earlier history is real, as sovereignly controlled by the Father, the Son, and the Holy Spirit (the historical lecture approach). Christ is the climactic moral example, the standard for living our lives. He is also the one who empowers us to new life through the Holy Spirit (the exemplary approach). Of course, Christ is not *merely* our example, or *merely* the one who empowers us. He is also the one who brought forgiveness and justifying righteousness to us, through his work on the cross. We are saying that Christ has relevance to the exemplary approach, in addition to many other ways in which he is the foundation for our salvation. Christ represents the climax for which Old Testament history prepares and toward which it moves (the preparation approach). Christ supremely reveals the character of God (God's-character approach). Christ is the center toward which Old Testament analogies and types point (the typological approach).

Examples in the New Testament

From time to time the New Testament uses the Old Testament in ways that resemble all the approaches that we have cataloged. Our argument for the centrality of the fulfillment approach results in affirming positive points about the other approaches, and thus enables us to understand why we can find in the New Testament places that are similar to each of the other approaches. Let us consider some examples.

The historical-lecture approach is the most distant from the New Testament, because the New Testament is never using the Old Testament in *merely* an antiquarian way, *merely* as a source of bits of information about the past. There is always some practical point. But in some New Testament examples the element of information about the past is quite prominent. We can see at least that the New Testament presupposes the reality of history and the reality of the past given in the Old Testament. Consider Stephen's speech in Acts 7:2–53. Stephen rehearses a lot of Old Testament history and provides a lot of "information" before he reveals the practical point in 7:51–53. Likewise Paul in Acts 13:16–41 goes over Old Testament history.

For an exemplary approach, consider James 5:16–18, where Elijah serves as an example for us.

Something similar to a preparation approach can be seen in Stephen's (Acts 7:2–53) and Paul's (Acts 13:16–41) speeches in Acts, which we just mentioned.

What about the approach through God's character? An emphasis on God's character can be found in Hebrews 13:5–6.

For illustrations of the typological approach, we can observe that the New Testament uses types and analogies at many points. Among the most well known is 1 Corinthians 10:1–11, which actually uses Greek words from which we get the English word *type*.

Other Approaches as Perspectives

In sum, the fulfillment approach affirms and even encompasses positive points from the other approaches. But taken by themselves, the other approaches have some deficiencies. Some of the deficiencies have already come out as we talked in the previous chapter about the weaknesses of each approach. I would advise students for the sake of simplicity to prefer the fulfillment approach.

Yet it is also true, when we think in terms of perspectives, that each approach can be seen as a perspective that opens up larger vistas and that tacitly leads to the other approaches.

To begin with, the historical-lecture approach focuses on the time when the Old Testament was originally written, and the times in history to which these texts refer. God was active in these times. God in speaking to people then and there also intended, even at that time, that his words would also speak to us here and now. He also intended that the words and events would point forward to Christ. So when we reckon with the significance of God's work at an earlier time, it requires us to reckon with his whole plan for history, and we move toward the fulfillment perspective.

Next, consider the exemplary approach as a perspective. The exemplary approach focuses on the constancy of human nature, which leads to analogies between human beings like David and ourselves today. Christ has a human nature. So the same principle ought to lead to paying attention to the relation between David and Christ. Moreover, human beings like David and his men have the same problem of sin and the same need for redemption as do all human beings. Accordingly, they need redemption in Christ. And if they experienced the offer of redemption and the power of redemption in their own lives, that experience was a foretaste of the redemption that Christ would accomplish when he came to earth. Thus, we once again find ourselves reckoning with everything belonging to the fulfillment perspective.

Next, consider the preparation approach. The preparation approach focuses on the fact that what happened long ago was on a timeline leading to Christ. That is, it leads to Christ who is the fulfillment. And if he accomplishes fulfillment, his fulfillment has a multitude of connections with previous history. One such connection is the linear, temporal connection: Christ's fulfillment comes at the end of a timeline. But there are other, enriching connections because of the unity of God's redemption and the unity of his plan. So we find ourselves using the fulfillment perspective.

Next, consider the approach through God's character. Since Christ and Christ's work supremely reveal God's character, examining God's character includes examining Christ and his work, which includes the fulfillment perspective.

Next, consider the typological approach. Since Christ and those whom he represents are the antitype, and since the antitype surpasses

The Fulfillment Approach 333

the type, we must also reckon with the discontinuities between type and antitype, and so we include the fulfillment approach.

In sum, all the other approaches can be expanded into perspectives so that they lead to the fulfillment approach. However, though this expansion is possible in theory, it is easy for practitioners to use the other approaches in a one-dimensional and restricted way. They forget about some of the dimensions of fulfillment. To avoid these difficulties, I am recommending the use of the fulfillment perspective as the primary one.

32

Boundaries for Interpretation

We may now undertake some further evaluation of the fulfillment approach to Old Testament interpretation. The fulfillment approach, we have said, is challenging. Some of the potential weaknesses of typological interpretation can be mitigated by enriching typological interpretation and moving to fulfillment interpretation as a kind of enhancement. But there remains still on the list of "weaknesses" the fact that the typological approach and the fulfillment approach are challenging in practice.

By contrast, the exemplary approach in some ways is easy. The exemplary approach says, "Just focus on some human being in the past, and use that human being as a moral example." The exemplary approach seems to crop up frequently in preaching. Why? We might suspect that both the relative ease of the approach and the naturalness of the way in which we identify with human beings in a story contribute to its popularity.

In one sense the historical-lecture approach is not easy, because we may have to do extensive historical research to try to reconstruct in our minds the times in which ancient people lived. And we might find it impossible to do a reconstruction in a solid way, because evidence concerning the past is always limited. But in another sense the historical-lecture approach is still easy with respect to its *method*. The idea of finding out about the past is a straightforward idea.[1]

---

[1] But there are different views of history (Vern S. Poythress, *Inerrancy and Worldview: Answering Modern Challenges to the Bible* [Wheaton, IL: Crossway, 2012], chapters 5–7). So it is not nearly as easy as it looks!

Limiting the Field to New Testament Types

By contrast, the fulfillment approach and the typological approach to which it is akin have complexities in method. What does it mean for something to be a type, if it does not wear a sign on its shirt, saying explicitly, "I am a type"? Some interpreters would advise us, for the sake of safety, to find types in the Old Testament only when the New Testament clearly identifies something as a type.

Even this recipe has its difficulties, because it may not always be clear when the New Testament is using Old Testament material as a type or in some other way. In James 5:16–18, is Elijah a "type" for Christian prayer, or just an example? We have refused to draw a sharp, definitive line between types and analogies, and this fluidity may trouble us when we consider New Testament uses of the Old Testament. Hebrews 11 has a catalog of people of faith, whose faith is analogous to Christian faith today. In a kind of partial inversion of Hebrews 11, Stephen's speech in Acts 7 has something like a catalog of Israelite unbelief and rejection of the prophets: "Which of the prophets did your fathers not persecute?" (7:52). Both Hebrews 11 and Acts 7 show us analogies, but of a somewhat loose kind. What do we make of them?

Even if we could achieve a perfect clarity with respect to New Testament use of Old Testament types, would that be enough? The Old Testament contains many passages, including 1 Samuel 22:1–2, on which the New Testament does not directly comment. What do we do with such passages? Luke 24 tells us that the whole Old Testament, not just a few prophecies here and there, moves forward to Christ and points to him. The New Testament provides not only particular examples of types from the Old Testament, but broader principles as well. Among those principles is the central one that God has a redemptive plan that encompasses all of history. Another is that this plan has come to climactic realization in Christ. Beale's principles, cited earlier (chapter 21), come into play. They encourage us to see the whole Old Testament, not simply the passages actually quoted in the New Testament, as Christ-centered in texture.

Our interpretations are fallible even when we have the direct guidance of a New Testament quotation from the Old Testament. Even in such a case, we still have to understand and interpret what the New Testament is doing. We are all the more fallible when we interpret the Old

Testament without having a direct New Testament quotation. So how can we be confident and still avoid a kind of prideful overconfidence?

Clowney's Triangle Again

Clowney's triangle and its two-stage reasoning helps. The first stage gives us guidance that we use in the second stage when we move forward to Christ. If we do our reasoning responsibly, we anchor our interpretation in what God symbolized within the earlier period of time. Then we explore how fulfillment in Christ is organically connected with this earlier symbolization. So we avoid the feeling of arbitrariness that can sometimes crop up when people attempt a typological or allegorical interpretation. Arbitrariness comes in when people give free rein to their imaginations and ignore the literary and historical context.

Clowney's triangle is useful. But where does its usefulness end? Where do we stop? When we consider the sin offering described in Leviticus 4, we have confidence that it offers a type of Christ, because the New Testament indicates in various ways that Christ offered the final sacrifice for sins (Heb. 10:12). Likewise, we know from Old Testament prophecies as well as from the New Testament that David is the beginning of a line of kings leading to Christ the messianic king. So we can confidently conclude that David is a type of Christ, at least in some of the passages dealing with his life. But what happens when we confront looser, vaguer connections and analogies than these? What about even a passage like 1 Samuel 22:1–2, which involves David but where David is not yet king? Does it still have any connection with Christ the king? If David is "leader" over his four hundred men, is that enough to establish a connection?

Well, with a case like 1 Samuel 22:1–2 it helps to consider that the context of 1–2 Samuel deals with the larger theme of kingship, the kingship of God as well as the kingship of Saul and then David. First Samuel 22:1–2 might seem a doubtful passage with which to deal if we had no context, but when we have a context like 1–2 Samuel, our doubts dissipate.

Overall Principles

But then what do we do with a passage whose connections forward toward the New Testament are more obscure? What we have said in previous chapters about themes, plots, and analogies all has relevance. We can especially bear in mind the principle of mediation, because all instances of mediation in the Old Testament depend on Christ who is the one mediator (1 Tim. 2:5). We can bear in mind the pattern of redemptive plots, because all cases of mini-redemptions depend on the one redemption that Christ accomplished: "And there is salvation in no one else, for there is no other name under heaven given among men by which we must be saved" (Acts 4:12). These principles help. But we are going to have to deal with cases where we move forward with less confidence.

We always have to rely on God and who he is. We always have to rely on general truths that we have learned from Scripture. For instance, we should be praying for illumination from the Lord. We should be growing in knowledge of the Bible as a whole. There is no substitute for this general knowledge, because the more we know Scripture and the ways of God that it reveals, the more sense we have, often intuitive (and, we trust, Spirit-guided), about how one passage fits into the larger whole. We become more sensitive to important but sometimes subtle themes in Scripture. And, we hope, we become more humble. Humility is what leads us to submit to what God is saying rather than simply letting our imaginations run wild and imposing on a text whatever comes into our head. We seek to please God and not our own fancy. All this takes time, and sanctification takes time. The budding preacher who is twenty-five years old cannot expect that he will preach with the wisdom and spiritual maturity of a sixty-year-old veteran saint.

Taking an Audience into Account

We may also reflect on the corporate dimensions of our understanding of Scripture. We can be encouraged ourselves if others besides us confirm our understanding in some cases. If we have received a responsibility that involves preaching or communicating to others, we also have to bear in mind their capacity. Even if we ourselves are confident in our own understanding of a passage, can we communicate our conclusions to our audience in a manner that enables them to understand and agree? If our audience consists of non-Christians or of people with limited understanding, that has to be taken into account. A person may be convinced in his own mind about a typological connection, and yet wisely decide, based on limits in time or limits in the audience, to keep his convictions to himself.

Since the authority of Scripture depends on God, and not ultimately on the human authority of the preacher, we must try to bring to bear our convictions about God's word based on his word, not on our own human claims. Our audience, like the Bereans, should be encouraged to be "examining the Scriptures daily to see if these things were so" (Acts 17:11). They should not accept what we say about a type simply because we say it. On the other hand, Bible students who are highly analytic by nature sometimes underestimate the ability of ordinary people to grasp a typological connection on the basis of a short explanation. Once Christian people have digested a good deal of Scripture and they understand its principles, they do not demand extensive and labored proofs in order to see a type for what it is. On the pages of the New Testament we see that New Testament writers do not always provide extensive reasoning, but expect their readers to get the point once a type or analogy is pointed out.

Looser Connections

But questions remain about how we handle looser and more tangential connections between the Old Testament and the New, or between two or more different passages in the Old Testament. When do we acknowledge a connection, and when do we not?

First, the meaning of a passage taken more or less by itself offers a perspective on the meaning—or rather, the import—of a passage in the context of the whole Bible. We can think about meaning in a narrower sense. We can ask ourselves, "What does 1 Samuel 22:1–2 say on an obvious level?" It says that David departed from there, that is, from Gath, and escaped. We can recite the passage out loud, or paraphrase it in several ways, and we are giving "the meaning" in a narrow sense. But by itself that does not get us very far. God's plan is comprehensive, and according to his plan the Scripture as canon is a single whole. It is all the word of God, and it belongs together. All the connections as well as all the individual passages are his doing, and they have his endorsement. Any connection that we see, however remote, does not take God by surprise. He knew it before we knew.

Even twisted and distorted uses of Scripture, that is, uses for heresy or uses governed by human pride, do not take God by surprise. He does not endorse such uses, of course. But he uses even the twisting of Scripture for his own righteous purposes, to bring judgment on the pride of those who twist the Scripture. They end up being trapped in their own pride and blinded to the truth, and that is a judgment from God. Second Thessalonians 2 describes an extreme case that, because of its extremity, can serve as analogy for less extreme cases:

> The coming of the lawless one is by the activity of Satan with all power and false signs and wonders, and with all wicked deception for those who are perishing, because they *refused to love the truth* and so be saved. Therefore God sends them *a strong delusion*, so that they may believe what is *false*, in order that all may be *condemned* who did not believe the truth but had pleasure in unrighteousness. (2 Thess. 2:9–12)

The fact that someone's imagination has given him an idea does not mean that God endorses the idea. We need to be critical and continually return to Scripture. But God does establish connections between Scriptures. All human beings share humanity. And that already results in a connection between modern readers and the characters in the Bible. All share the need of redemption. All human beings face the reality that Christ is the only Savior. Repetitions of ideas, and subordinately, repetitions of words, result in connections of at least a loose sort. These connections go on and on. There is no end to them. If we focus on the mind of God, we know that the mind of God is infinite. Any one individual passage offers an opening to his mind. And that one opening leads naturally to thinking about *everything* in his mind—all of his character and all of his plan.

I suggest, then, that the study of analogies and types has no clear, sharp boundary beyond which we could make the bold claim, "These are all the connections there are, and all that there is to learn." It is *never* all. I suggest rather that we understand that there is a spectrum of connections. Some analogies and types are clear. They represent salient connections, important connections. Sometimes a large number of similarities line up and reinforce one another. But then there are also more minor connections, or distant connections, or weaker connections, as we might label them. And then there are multistage connections.

For example, the judges in the book of Judges contrast with Saul, the first king, and Saul contrasts with David, the king, and thoughts of David lead to the promise in 2 Samuel 7:8–16 about the Davidic dynasty, and the Davidic dynasty leads to Christ, and Christ leads to thoughts about the Old Testament prophecies concerning a coming messianic king, and the prophecies lead to prophecies about the coming of God as king. And the coming of God as king leads to thoughts about the coming of God as savior and judge and bringer of a new creation (Isa. 65:17). Where do we stop? All these things are related in God's plan. The coming of Christ in his first coming makes plainer the details about *how* they are all related. But they were related already before his coming in the plan of God, and many of the relations were dimly visible, at least, to spiritually keen Old Testament readers.

The connections do not come to an end. Moreover, salient connections fade off into distant connections that are nevertheless connections. We need a sense of proportion as to what is important and what stands out. We do not need an arbitrary boundary, beyond which we turn our minds off and refuse to recognize connections that are there. Not everything is equally important. Not everything is an equally strong connection, nor an equally significant connection within the total purpose of God in Scripture. And that leads us back to affirming the importance of knowing God in Christ, through knowing Scripture as a whole.

Allegorical Interpretation

What then do we say about allegorical interpretation? In its simplest meaning, "allegorical interpretation" means interpretation on two levels. And some passages of Scripture obviously invite such interpretation. Luke 15:3–6, the parable of the lost sheep, has two levels. On the first level, we have a shepherd, one hundred sheep, one lost sheep, the shepherd finding the lost sheep, and the shepherd rejoicing. On a second level, we have God the shepherd and Jesus the shepherd going after lost sinners, and the rejoicing when a lost sinner is "found." Jesus endorses this interpretation in verse 7. The parable asks for allegorical interpretation (and more as well, because it has connections with the whole of redemption). Like many of Jesus's parables, the parable of the lost sheep is challenging to the audience, not merely a re-expression of truths already shared. It differs in this way from *some* allegories. But other allegories, like Judges 9:7–15, contain both shared information and a challenge. The parable of the lost sheep differs by offering us more, not less, than an allegory that merely illustrates known truths.

In a second meaning, "allegorical interpretation" can denote a theoretical framework that an interpreter brings to all of Scripture. When the interpreter comes to any passage of Scripture whatsoever, he has a formula for interpretation. The formula says that he should look for a second level. And typically, it specifies the *kind* of thing he should expect to find on the second level. Here we meet one of the problems with Philonic interpretation. Philo, as we said earlier, was heavily influenced by Platonic and Stoic philosophy. He went to Scripture expecting that the second level would contain lessons about intellectual and spiritual purification through right philosophy. And he found what he was looking for, because his allegorical method enabled him to find it. What he did not realize is that he was looking at the reflection of his own assumptions, as it were in a mirror. He got no new message, only the message that he already had from philosophy. Unfortunately, the message was not only not new, but wrong. Philosophical redemption through right thinking and through moralistic action in accord with that thinking is not only distinct from Christian redemption, but antithetical to it. It invites people to save themselves through their minds and their understanding of philosophy, rather than to come to God through Christ for salvation by pure grace.

Allegorical interpretation *as a total framework* has several deficiencies. First, it tempts its readers to read in messages that actually go against Scripture. Second, it tempts them to ignore what God is actually saying. Third, it flattens out Scripture by suggesting that all Scripture is the same kind of genre, the same kind of literature, namely a two-level allegory that is asking for a corresponding two-level interpretation. Fourth, in some of its uses it invites the reader to find basically the *same* message, again and again, as the contents of the second level.

So allegorical interpretation as a total framework is a mistake.

Two-Level Interpretation as a Possibility

The expression "allegorical interpretation" has yet another sense. Critics can use it to denounce or criticize any typological interpretation of which they do not approve. So we have to be careful to ask about the meaning of the expression "allegorical." And when the expression is used in criticism, we have to ask whether the criticism is sound.

Consider. Any interpreter who finds a symbol or a type might use two levels in examining the symbol. For example, he interprets an animal sacrifice both as an animal that dies and as a symbol of the truth that reconciliation to God takes place through an innocent substitute. But suppose he does not insist on using the same two-level framework for each and every passage. What do we say then?

It depends on the passage and on the interpretation. A critic may always label a two-level interpretation as "allegorical," intending that label to indicate that the interpretation is mistaken. But in a broad sense, any interpretation that employs two levels is "allegorical." That does not make it wrong. Old Testament sin offerings are dead animals on one level, and symbols for atonement on a second level. The Bible contains many such things. The word "allegorical" is not very helpful if it sometimes describes the mere existence of two levels and at other times is used to denounce an interpretation with which a critic does not agree. Since the word "allegorical" has unfortunately become pejorative in some circles, we may use the less prejudicial term "typological." There can still be good and bad forms of typological interpretation.

So what is the critic complaining about? Some critics may complain that typological interpretation ignores history. But this complaint is not necessarily correct. Most typological interpreters believe that the history really happened. They see themselves as dealing with a second level of meaning, not as denying the first.

Critics may also complain that a typological interpretation is "artificial." But what seems artificial to one person will not seem so to another. Clearly the typological interpreters themselves think that their interpretations make sense.

I think that many of the criticisms of typological interpretation boil down to issues on which we have already touched. Suppose that a typological interpretation "leaps" to typology directly, using the hypotenuse of Clowney's triangle, without going through Clowney's two-stage reasoning. The interpretation ignores the historical context and the symbolism present at the time when God spoke to the original audience. It may seem "unhistorical" and "artificial" because it does not relate organically to what God said to an audience back then and there. But at times an interpretation that does not explicitly *discuss* the two legs in Clowney's triangle may nevertheless be *based on* the full triangle, including the legs, or may be compatible with a conclusion reached by using both legs.

We have to look and see. If we are going to criticize someone else's interpretation, there is no substitute for first listening carefully and respectfully to the interpretation, to see whether it is compatible with symbolism already present when the passage was first given by God. And we must wrestle ourselves with what the passage means. We should not hastily reject someone else's interpretation without having a better one, which we think does more justice to what God says and what he plans.

In addition, a critic may be complaining when a typological approach confines itself to lining up parallels and ignores the dissimilarities, the disanalogies, and the way in which the antitype surpasses the type.

I fear, however, that this kind of criticism can be abused. If a critic fails to specify what is really the matter, and instead uses vague labels like "unhistorical," "artificial," and "allegorizing," these labels can become weapons to discourage any but the most obvious typological interpretations.

As we observed earlier, we live in a time in which the mainstream of biblical scholarship has been influenced by bad assumptions about meaning and about history. Within this atmosphere, some scholars may be tempted to suppress the multidimensional character of God's word in favor of a superficial reading that asks only about human meaning or only about surface-level facts. The label "allegorizing" then offers itself as a means to denounce any interpretations that move beyond the surface.

Fourfold Interpretation

In the medieval church in the West, fourfold interpretation became popular. Fourfold interpretation expects to find four distinct meanings in any text: a literal meaning, a moral meaning (sometimes called "tropical meaning"), an allegorical meaning, and an anagogical meaning.

The literal meaning focuses on the text in its most obvious dimensions. For a historical text, it means a focus on the events and their contribution to ordinary history. David departed from Gath and came to the cave of Adullam. Others joined him. It happened back then and there.

The moral meaning focuses on moral lessons to be drawn from the text. This meaning could take the form of a moral example. "Be a leader like David and help those in distress." Or, "trust in God's care, as illustrated in David's life." Another moralistic interpreter could treat texts as allegories about the spiritual state of the individual soul. In the case of 1 Samuel 22:1–2, we might get a moralistic allegory akin to our earlier example of Philonic interpretation: David stands for the soul of man. Achish stands for worldliness. David escapes from worldliness. The cave stands for asceticism that renounces worldly pleasures and disciplines the body with hardness. Technically, this kind of interpretation is "allegorical" in displaying two levels of meaning. But it should still be classified as looking for moral meaning—the second out of four kinds of meaning. The fourfold approach in the medieval church meant something different when it treated "allegorical meaning" as the third among four kinds of meaning.

In the medieval system, the allegorical meaning consists in a two-level interpretation applying the passage to Christ and the church. David stands for Christ, and the people around him stand for the church. The church comes to Christ to be rescued from distress spiritually.

Finally, the fourth kind of meaning, the anagogical meaning, consists in an application to the new Jerusalem, or the new heaven and new earth. So David and his men stand for Christ and the new humanity, once they are freed from distress.

Modern times have seen much criticism and mockery of fourfold interpretation. But a close look shows that it has some grains of truth. The literal level of meaning is similar to what we have called the historical-lecture approach. This approach by itself is insufficient. And it is wrong if it confines itself to an allegedly merely human meaning. But attention to the historical setting is valuable and can be combined with other insights.

The moral meaning is similar to the exemplary approach. The allegorical meaning is similar to the typological approach. And the anagogical meaning is similar to the not-yet aspect of typology. We expect a fuller fulfillment in the new heaven and the new earth than what we have now.

So the fourfold approach appropriates at least some of the strengths of other approaches. We may briefly list its strengths and weaknesses.

Strengths

- Encourages attention to the strengths of four approaches: historical-lecture, exemplary, typological, and typological applied to the not-yet aspect.
- Encourages looking at the text from multiple perspectives.
- May be Christ-centered in the typological approach.
- Includes application in the exemplary approach.

Weaknesses

- Fourfold interpretation may leave little sense of apparent unity between the four so-called "meanings."
- Application (moral meaning) is detached from Christ (typological meaning)
- The idea of a uniform fourfold method applied to all texts undermines respect for the distinctive genres of different texts in Scripture.
- The need for four meanings can lead interpreters to "force" a meaning when the text does not lend itself to one of the uses.
- Lack of stress on historical and literary context for the nonliteral meanings can lead to reading in meanings that belong to tradition rather than Scripture.
- The formula for seeking four meanings easily leads interpreters to neglect connections lying outside of the four directions that they have been taught to explore.

By contrast, the fulfillment approach intrinsically unites the strengths of the four foci—literal, moral, typological, and anagogical. And the fulfillment approach, rightly understood, is not merely a "formula" that automatically dictates beforehand how a passage will most saliently and forcefully point to Christ.

Preaching the Gospel

We should also ask how we evaluate a case where a preacher preaches the gospel from the Old Testament, but where his preaching seems to ignore the way the passage functioned back then and there. If we want an example, we can take the case that interprets 1 Samuel 22:1–2 with David standing for Christ, David's brothers for the church, David's father's house for the Jews, and the people in distress for the Gentiles.

In evaluation, we can see strengths and weaknesses. First, the gospel is being preached, and for that we should rejoice. Paul set an example of rejoicing when some people were preaching the gospel, even though they did it "from envy and rivalry" (Phil. 1:15). Surely we should rejoice even more when people proclaim the gospel in true good will, albeit from texts that do not fully support the way they use them.

Second, it may be that a sermon that at first looks like it is disconnected from historical context is more connected than it looks. The preacher may have actually thought through Clowney's triangle, or tacitly done something equivalent to the triangle, and yet not have spelled out all his reasoning.

Third, a genuine connection often exists between the major thrust of passages, because of common themes, such as the theme of mediation or a redemptive plot. In the case of David and his men, David's king-like leadership does have connections with the larger context, even though the detailed breakdown into church, Jews, and Gentiles does not connect to the immediate context in a completely harmonious way. So a sermon of this type may be justified in its major thrust, even though it is doubtful in some details.

Fourth, a typological sermon sets a good example by indicating that we should seek to understand how the Old Testament points to Christ. Simultaneously, however, it may also set a bad example by suggesting to hearers that they, like the sermon, are justified in taking arbitrary leaps, as long as they end up with Christ. When it thus becomes a bad example, we should see that the problem is not primarily with the meanings that it does find. It finds the gospel, and that is a primary message of the Bible as a whole, a message to which every passage leads when we follow the connections far enough, with enough understanding. Rather, the problem lies primarily in the way in which bad interpretation tends to close off further exploration of good interpretation. Once satisfied with a "solution" that preaches the gospel, the interpreter stops asking more questions and stops probing for deeper understanding, and so misses the opportunity to grow by further discovery.

Finally, note that an interpreter who uses an Old Testament passage analogically or typologically for the sake of proclaiming the gospel is at the very least using the passage as a kind of illustration for the gospel. Every preacher knows that illustrations are valuable. An illustration that happens to use the Bible itself is likewise still valuable even though it may run the danger of being understood as *more than* an illustration, and as a direct claim that the preacher's message is the "meaning" of the text. A lot depends on how people understand the communication.

We may sum up strengths and weaknesses of using the Old Testament to illustrate the gospel:

Strengths
- Preaching the gospel.
- May be a sound typological use that the critic does not appreciate.
- May use the Old Testament effectively as an illustration.
- Encourages people to look for Christ in the Old Testament.

Weaknesses
- Hearers may see it as an endorsement for fanciful typologizing.
- Hearers may stop with the gospel as offered, but be discouraged from examining the text any further for implications not already visible.

Strictures from Scholars

I mentioned earlier the danger of loosely using labels like "unhistorical," "arbitrary," or "allegorizing" to discourage typological interpretation. In my experience, this danger arises most among scholars. Many ordinary people happily engage in typological interpretation and do not worry. They sometimes overdo it, perhaps, by preaching the gospel in a way that is disconnected from what God was saying back then and there. But at least they are preaching the gospel. Scholars have an opposite problem. It is easy for some of them to think that anything that does not meet their standards of rigor is not legitimate. But it is impossible to combine a desire for a certain mechanical kind of rigor with seeking God and the depth of his mind. Growth comes by the grace of God, through the Holy Spirit, by humbly submitting to God speaking. Connections need not be salient and obvious in order to exist. Every truth eventually points to every other truth, because God's mind and God's plan unite them all.

I therefore have two final concerns. First, a number of times I have heard scholars speak critically about people who seek for Christ "under every rock and tree" in the Old Testament. The motive of these scholars, I hope, is to steer people away from fanciful, noncontextual interpretation. I have my sympathies with this motive, as I hope the preceding chapters have shown. But are the scholars also despising these simple people? And are they saying that the people are wrong about the goal?

The scholars want interpretation to pay attention to context. But contexts are of more than one kind. The historical and literary contexts are there, but so is the context of the reality of fulfillment in Christ. So also is the context formed by the fact that God did have mercy on people and did save people in the Old Testament era. Whenever he did so, he acted on the basis of the work of Christ who was to come, and who even then was present as the eternal Son in fellowship with the Father. We also have a context formed by the reality that God is speaking to us here and now, in the power of the resurrected Christ through the Holy Spirit.

The ordinary people about whom I am concerned may live and interpret Scripture in ways that use these contexts. If they do, they begin to see things that they ought to see, because they receive sound instruction through God who speaks to them. Are the scholars aware of what happens through the Spirit in ordinary people?

I do not want to force a choice between ancient contexts or modern contexts, or between nitty-gritty details of history and the presence of redemption in Christ in the midst of that history. Both are there; both are ordained by God; both need our attention if we want to understand God in intimate fellowship. I am for both. But I am concerned to issue a warning lest we who are scholars miss those contexts to which our scholarly training has not attuned us.

I am concerned also because I believe that, at the end of the day, Christ *is* "under every rock and tree." The scholars are wrong if they reject the goal. He is there, everywhere, even though we may not have the knowledge or maturity to understand or articulate how. He is there because, theologically, that is the only way in which history can exist and move forward at all:

> He is the radiance of the glory of God and the exact imprint of his nature, and he *upholds the universe by the word of his power.* (Heb. 1:3)

He is there, interpretively, because in the end his Spirit is the chief interpreter, because interpretation is a unified operation, and because meaning in the mind of God coheres with the entire plan of God. The world of modern biblical scholarship needs redemption in the light of these realities (see appendix A).

Love

Let us, in sum, listen with respect to Saint Augustine's observations about the process of interpretation:

> A great variety of interpretations, many of them legitimate, confronts our exploring minds as we search among these words [of Genesis 1:1–2] to discover your will. . . .
>
> But when they contend that Moses did not mean what I say, but what they say, I reject their claim and have no time for it, because even if what they say is correct, so reckless an assertion is a mark of presumption, not of knowledge; it is the fruit of no vision but of conceit.
>
> This is why we must tremble before your judgments, O Lord, for your Truth is not mine, nor his, nor hers, but belongs to all of us whom you call to share it in communion with him, at the same time giving us the terrible warning not to arrogate truth to ourselves as private property, lest we find ourselves deprived of it. For anyone

who appropriates what you provide for all to enjoy, and claims as his own what belongs to all, is cast out from this commonwealth, cast out to what is truly his own, which is to say from the truth to a lie; for anyone who lies is speaking from what is his own. . . .

"If we both see that what you say is true, and we both see that what I say is true, where do we see it? I certainly do not see it in you, nor do you in me; we both see it in the immutable truth itself which towers above our minds. Since, then, we do not argue about that light of the Lord our God, why should we argue about the thought in the mind of our neighbor? . . . Unless we believe that Moses meant whatever he did mean in his books with an eye to those twin commandments of charity, we shall make the Lord out to be a liar, by attributing to our fellow-servant [Moses] a purpose which is at odds with the Lord's teaching. Since, then, so rich a variety of highly plausible interpretations can be culled from those words [in Genesis 1], consider how foolish it is rashly to assert that Moses intended one particular meaning rather than any of the others. If we engage in hurtful strife as we attempt to expound his words, we offend against the very charity for the sake of which he said all those things."[2]

---

[2] Saint Augustine, *The Confessions*, 12.33–35, trans. Maria Boulding, The Works of Saint Augustine, A Translation for the 21st Century (Hyde Park, NY: New City Press, 1997).

Part VIII

EXAMPLES

33

Proverbs 10:1

So far, we have illustrated the process of interpretation mostly using the passage 1 Samuel 22:1–2. We now fill out the picture with some other examples. By choosing verses from some other kinds of passages, we confirm that the same process can be used, with appropriate adjustments, for all kinds of passages.[1]

Our first passage is Proverbs 10:1:

The proverbs of Solomon.

> A wise son makes a glad father,
>> but a foolish son is a sorrow to his mother.

Since we have already been through the entire process of interpretation with 1 Samuel 22:1–2, and have discussed general principles as well, our study of Proverbs 10:1 can be somewhat abbreviated by comparison. We will discuss explicitly only some out of the total number of steps.

Three Steps in Interpretation

We may proceed to use the steps of observation, elucidation, and application in the way discussed in chapter 4.

We pray and read the passage, with some context (the whole book

---

[1] I have not included within the next three chapters any illustration using a passage from the law of Moses. I thought that it was less necessary, since I have written a book about the law (*The Shadow of Christ in the Law of Moses* [reprint; Phillipsburg, NJ: Presbyterian & Reformed, 1995]).

of Proverbs is a pertinent context). Then we observe, elucidate, and apply. In the process we may develop questions such as the following:

Observation

1. What is the topic?
2. What persons are mentioned?
3. Is the saying general or particular?
4. How do the persons relate to one another?
5. "Son" is masculine. Why?

Elucidation

1. What is a "proverb"?
2. What is the significance of the word "Solomon"? Does it imply that Solomon authored the proverbs, or maybe that he collected them, or that he and his men (scribes, perhaps) collected them, or that they come from the time of Solomon, or all of these?
3. How does the expression "The proverbs of Solomon" function in relation to the rest of the verse?
4. What is the relation between the two lines beginning with "A wise son . . ." and "but a foolish son"?
5. What is wisdom, and how does it relate to folly?
6. How does the verse picture the relation between a son and his parents?
7. Why might parents react strongly to what their son does?
8. How do the principles of this verse relate to daughters?
9. Do the principles have any exceptions? Why or why not?
10. How do similar principles apply in personal relationships other than a parent-child relationship?
11. How do the principles relate to God as father?
12. How do the principles relate to Jesus as the Son of God?

Application

1. In what ways do I consider myself wise or foolish?
2. In what ways do my character and my actions affect my parents? Other people with relationships to me?
3. How can I show respect to my parents?
4. In what ways does God evaluate me?

5. How can I grow in wisdom and avoid folly?
6. How might I use this verse in guiding others younger in age?
7. How does the wisdom of Jesus provide illumination for my life?

Introducing Detail

We can now proceed as we did in the main part of the book to consider elucidation in greater detail.

B.1.a. The Literary Context

What is the literary context for Proverbs 10:1?

In the canonical form in which God has provided it, the book of Proverbs is a unified book, consisting of proverbs and instruction in wisdom. It might seem at first that Proverbs 1:1 functions as a heading for the whole book: "The proverbs of Solomon, son of David, king of Israel." But there are other headings later on:[2]

The proverbs of Solomon. (10:1)

These also are sayings of the wise. (24:23)

These also are proverbs of Solomon which the men of Hezekiah king of Judah copied. (25:1)

The words of Agur son of Jakeh. The oracle. (30:1)

The words of King Lemuel. An oracle that his mother taught him. (31:1)

So the initial heading in 1:1 may belong especially to the section 1:1–9:18, or, on the other hand, it may be serving as the title for the entire book. Derek Kidner points out that if 1:1 were merely a title for the first section, we would expect that the second section would have begun in 10:1 with a title, "These *also* are proverbs of Solomon," in a manner parallel to 24:23 and 25:1.[3] Thus, it is probable that 1:1 is the title for the whole book.

---

[2] See the extended discussion of structure in Bruce K. Waltke, *The Book of Proverbs: Chapters 1–15* (Grand Rapids, MI: Eerdmans, 2004), 9–28.
[3] Derek Kidner, *The Proverbs: An Introduction and Commentary* (Downers Grove, IL/London: InterVarsity Press, 1964), 22.

The initial section, 1:1–9:18, is distinctive in comparison with the rest of Proverbs. It has some distinctive unified themes and some longer sections, such as the warning against the seduction of the adulteress (7:1–27) and the invitation of wisdom and folly (8:1–9:18). Following Proverbs 1–9, the heading in Proverbs 10:1 covers all the central material, perhaps as far as Proverbs 24:22. In 1:1–9:18 the father speaks in the first person to the son in the second-person form ("you"), while the central material from 10:1 onward to 22:16 is characteristically in the third person. Then, Proverbs 22:17 and the following verses shift back to the predominance of second-person pronouns. This shift marks the beginning of a separate section.

This difference in the use of pronouns produces a subtle difference in flavor in the sections as a whole. By using second-person address, 1:1–9:18 is more directly hortatory, and more directly challenges the reader to seek wisdom and wise living. The section 10:1–22:16 implies lessons for living. But it has a complementary function, by inviting more meditative reflection on the patterns of human living rather than by urging the reader immediately to leap into action. In terms of total impact, the two kinds of communication are not that far apart. The direct exhortation in 1:1–9:18 implies the importance of reflection, while the reflective material in 10:1–22:16 calls for appropriate action in response.

Within the central section, 10:1–22:16, neighboring verses sometimes show unified themes, such as the theme of diligence versus laziness in 10:4–5, and the theme of prosperity versus lack, which extends through 10:2–5. But the overall impression is of a string of short proverbs, arranged like beads on a string. Each "bead" has its own shape and color, and needs to be examined for its own beauty. At the same time, some beads lie together in natural groups. And all the beads together function to make up a "necklace" displaying the nature of wisdom and folly, and giving wise instruction about human conduct.

Thus, when we come to consider verse 10:1 in detail, we have several useful orientations. (1) The first line (a) of verse 10:1, "The proverbs of Solomon," belongs to the whole section and not just to the next two lines. (2) The next two lines (b and c) are one bead on the necklace of proverbs. We can therefore focus on them alone, with the goal of appreciating their beauty and their unique contribution. (3) At the same time, the rest of Proverbs provides a context that contains the theme of proverbial wisdom. Into this context fits the one "bead," 10:1b–c.

We may also note that, in accordance with Hebrew poetic parallelism, many of the individual proverbs, including the proverb 10:1b–c, are two-part proverbs, where the second line contrasts with or supplements the first. In our case, the relation is contrastive: a wise son contrasts with a foolish son.

B.1.b. The Transmission Context

How was Proverbs 10:1 transmitted down to us?

The history of transmission depends as usual on whether we are accessing the English text of Proverbs 10:1 or the original Hebrew. Those who have access to the Hebrew may ignore the further complexity involved in considering the process of translation. The evidence of the Hebrew manuscripts agrees. We have today the same text as the autograph.

There is one minor difficulty with respect to the heading in line a: "The proverbs of Solomon." By consulting *Biblia Hebraica Stuttgartensia*, we find that the heading does not occur in the ancient Greek or Syriac translations or in some manuscripts of the Vulgate (Latin). It may have been omitted by a scribe who thought that it was an accidental duplication of 1:1. Scribes tend to smooth out perceived difficulties. So it is more likely that it was omitted in transmission than that it was inserted in the original Hebrew. The Hebrew manuscripts all include it, which confirms its originality. It makes little difference in meaning, since, if it should be omitted, the heading in 1:1 would extend directly through the middle section and lead to nearly the same results.

B.1.c. The Text

B.1.c.(1).(a) Authorial Intention

What did the author intend?

When we consider authorial intention, we should include the divine author, namely God; the human author; and the mediatorial role by which Christ brings fellowship between God and the human author. We have been considering the divine author through the whole course of our study. So let us consider the human author. Solomon is in one sense the main human author.[4] But the later heading in 25:1 mentions the involvement of "the men of Hezekiah king of Judah" in copying. Scribes would have done the physical job of writing out the text. We know that at least part of the text of Proverbs that we now have goes back to an autograph from the time of Hezekiah or later, rather than to the time of Solomon, because it reflects the involvement of Hezekiah's men (25:1). What "the men of Hezekiah" copied is identified as "proverbs of Solomon," so the authorship was much earlier. But Hezekiah or his men or both would have made the decision to include either all or only a selection of proverbs that they found or collected. It does not matter. God's inspiration controlled and superintended ordinary actions in compilation, decision making, and copying, as well as more extraordinary actions involved in the creation of proverbial sayings.

Moreover, Solomon could be an "author" in more than one way. First Kings 4:32 says that he "*spoke* 3,000 proverbs," which probably means that he composed or invented them. It is possible that he may also have collected sayings that were already in circulation, when he saw that they were wise. He may in some cases have reworded or reworked sayings in circulation, in order to enhance them or correct deficiencies. The details do not matter. Whatever the exact process, God's inspiration of the final product is the significant point.

In the nature of the case, proverbial sayings are preeminently sayings "in circulation." When they circulate in oral form, many of them do not identify a specific human author. Solomon composed proverbs, and when he did this he designed them for circulation. The quality of the saying rather than the human author would be the prominent factor in their circulation. When a proverbial saying is truly wise, the real ultimate source for it is God, who is the fount of all wisdom (Prov. 8:22). That does not mean that an ordinary proverbial saying within any culture has absolute divine authority. Unlike the Bible, such sayings are all subject to human fallibility. At the same time, ordinary human proverbial sayings may exhibit the effects of common grace. To the degree to which they reflect God's divine wisdom, they do point to the transcendent authority of God.

When God caused a saying to be included in his inspired word in the

---

[4] Waltke, *Book of Proverbs: Chapters 1–15*, 31–37.

book of Proverbs, he assured us that this particular saying has divine authority. God as the source of wisdom stands as the preeminent author. The human author fades into the background. Solomon is important in one main way: he is a classic symbol of supreme human wisdom, and a symbol of the wise king, from whom wisdom flows to a whole kingdom.

In addition, the issue of human authorship does not matter much because we know little about the personality of Solomon, and less about the scribes who may have been involved. Concerning Solomon, we know what the historical books 1 Kings and 2 Chronicles tell us, but it is almost all "external history" rather than direct discussion of Solomon's character. We know that later in life Solomon fell into false worship (1 Kings 11:1–8), in spite of his earlier wisdom (1 Kings 4:29). So Solomon's wisdom, in and of itself, did not guarantee that everything he said possessed divinely authoritative wisdom. Only God's authorship guarantees that. Solomon as a human contributor cooperated with God, but this cooperation is mysterious. In the end, our interpretation of the Bible ought to take shape from our knowledge of the divine author. And we should reckon also with the mediation of Christ. His work of salvation has resulted in God's mercy to us, and this mercy includes the provision of wisdom through the book of Proverbs.

B.1.c.(1).(b).((1)) Textual Expression: Units

What linguistic units do we meet in Proverbs 10:1?

We have already decided that there are three lines in the verse, the first of which functions as the heading for the entire section 10:1–22:16 (or perhaps for 10:1–24:22):

> [Line a:] The proverbs of Solomon.
> [Line b:] A wise son makes a glad father,
> [Line c:] but a foolish son is a sorrow to his mother.

Each of the two lines *b* and *c* is a single clause. In Hebrew, each line (b and c) is four words. Rendered woodenly, it would come out as,

> Son wise gladdens father
> And-son fool sorrow-of his-mother.

The connecting conjunction that introduces line c in Hebrew is *waw* (וֹ). It is translated woodenly by "and," and in the ESV with "but." In fact, it is a very common coordinating conjunction, whose functions include both simple coordination ("and") and contrast ("but"). (This broad range is a display of linguistic variation.) The lines *b* and *c* obviously contrast, so "but" is an appropriate link in English.

The sequence of two words "son fool" in line *c* needs some attention. The Hebrew word underlying the English *son* is *bēn* (בֵּן), in the absolute state, not the construct state.[5] So we have a sequence of two words *bēn kəsîl* (בֵּן כְּסִיל), both in the absolute state ("son fool"). What is the effect of having the two in succession? Such a question can be answered by looking up the issue in the standard Hebrew grammar by Gesenius.[6] A student may begin by consulting the table of contents to locate the section on "Syntax." Or, if he already suspects that he is seeing here an appositional relationship, he may search in the "Index of Subjects" under "apposition." Gesenius's grammar confirms that in such a construction the second term is naturally construed as in *apposition* to the first (§131b).[7] The son is a son who is further defined as a fool. So the translation "foolish son" is appropriate.

In the phrase "sorrow-of his-mother," sorrow (*tūgat*, תּוּגַת) is in the construct state. The construct links "sorrow" to "his mother," but how? Gesenius indicates that it can express a relationship of *objective genitive* ("sorrow to") (§130h).[8] These interpretations are not difficult, and may easily have been achieved even without explicitly searching out an answer in Gesenius.

B.1.c.(1).(b).((1)).((c)) Genre

What is the genre of Proverbs 10:1?

The genre of lines *b-c* is a proverb. The clauses have the crispness and condensation characteristic of a proverb. The crispness enhances the aesthetic attraction and invites a reader's contemplation. Proverbs

---

[5] The construct state in Hebrew typically signifies that the word in the construct state is closely linked to and modified by the immediately following word. The absolute state is typically used where no such linkage exists.

[6] Wilhelm Gesenius, *Gesenius' Hebrew Grammar*, 2nd English ed., rev. E. Kautzsch and A. E. Cowley (Oxford: Clarendon, 1980).

[7] Also Bruce K. Waltke and M. O'Connor, *An Introduction to Hebrew Syntax* (Winona Lake, IN: Eisenbrauns, 1989), §12.3b.

[8] Also ibid., §9.5.2c, "genitive of effect."

do not necessarily express universal truths that have no exceptions. This particular proverb would obviously have an exception if the father or mother had already died. It might also have an exception when the father and mother were themselves wicked or foolish, and did not delight in wisdom.

The proverb nevertheless expresses a general truth. Even parents who are not very wise themselves would usually find it easy to evaluate their son's conduct, because people are frequently more able to tell the difference when they are evaluating someone else, not themselves. The fruit of wisdom or folly in the son's life, in the form of prosperity or disaster, would often be undeniable, and would evoke evaluations from his parents.

A proverb by its genre invites reflection. It does not carry all of its implications on the surface. It is crisp and sparse, and so it does not explicitly mention possible exceptions. It does not explicitly draw out its implications. Instead, it invites a process of reflection, in which the reader turns it over in his mind, and thinks about the relation of a wise or foolish son to other things that he knows from Proverbs and from his own observations of life.

B.1.c.(1).(b).((2)) Hierarchies (and Discourse)

Now we consider how 10:1 fits together as a discourse with smaller parts embedded in larger ones. It is not too difficult. 10:1a, as we have said, functions as a heading, and as such connects itself to 10:1b–22:16 as a whole. 10:1b and 10:1c are both single clauses and single propositions, which together make up a coherent larger unit, a single proverb. The relation between the two is one of contrasting sides of a single larger pattern, the pattern of appropriate happiness or sorrow from parents as they look at their son. This one proverb, 10:1b–c, is connected in turn to the rest of the proverbs in the entire section 10:1b–22:16. It is one bead on the necklace.

This particular proverb, 10:1b–c, has its place at the beginning of this section of Proverbs, right after the initial section of the book, 1:1–9:18. By virtue of its place, it resonates strongly with one of the themes of 1:1–9:18, namely the theme of a father instructing his son and urging the son to gain wisdom. As the first bead-like proverb in the section, it serves as a transition to the whole section. In this observation, we are not only using our sense of linear flow in the text, but also noticing thematic connections that are independent of the written order. They both work together in making 10:1b–c a transitional proverb.

We do not know whether the human author self-consciously reasoned out that this proverb would make a good transition and introduction to 10:1b–22:16. It does not matter, because the human author intended to be a spokesman for divine wisdom, and thus directly or indirectly a spokesman for divine inspiration. His intention was to affirm the divine intention. The divine intention includes the intention to have 10:1b–c relate forward and backward to the surrounding texts in just the manner that we have observed.

In considering discourse structure, we should consider topical and figural relationships, as well as the relationships in linear flow on which we have already focused. Topically, the two lines have clear relationships that draw them together: the son and the parents, wisdom versus folly, and gladness versus sorrow. All of these topics or themes run through Proverbs as a whole. We are invited to see how the relation of son to parents forms one aspect of a total picture of wisdom in relation to folly, positive versus negative results in life, and consequent gladness or sorrow.

This proverb along with others indicates how one person's life affects others around him. Our wisdom or folly, our righteousness or sin, is not confined to ourselves alone but spreads to others in the form of consequences. The son affects his father and mother. As we have seen, 10:1b–c has a relationship to the preceding section 1:1–9:18, in which a father instructs his son and urges him to get wisdom. In the light of this relationship, we may say that 10:1b–c suggests that the father has something to do. He should be diligent in instructing his son in wisdom, with the hope that the son will give him gladness in return. His own actions have an effect on the son, and this reality of effects lies behind the effects that 10:1b indicates concerning the son's effects on his father.

At the same time, in keeping with the theme of 1:1–9:18, the primary focus of 10:1b–c is on the need for the son to gain wisdom. He should do so not only for the sake of his own life but for the sake of honoring his parents. The fact that his actions have effects on his parents supplies a further motivation for applying himself to gain wisdom.

The mother (or the father) may experience sorrow from a foolish son, not only because she is saddened by seeing a person that she loves go astray, but because the son reflects on her. He brings honor or dishonor to his mother through his behavior. In the world of the ancient Near East, and in some cultures today, family reputation means a lot. The parents suffer social shame if their son is acting foolishly, and his foolishness reflects on the reputation of the entire family. In addition, parents may experience regret or guilt over the fact that their own failings have played a role in influencing the life of their son. They are in that respect living with the consequences of their own sins, and that adds to the sorrow.

Literarily, the son is a synecdoche for a child of either gender. The proverb includes daughters by implication. The verse focuses on the relationship between human parents and their human son, but the principle is extendable by analogy. Masters or employers or kings or others in positions of authority and responsibility may have similar experiences in relation to those subject to them. A wise student gladdens a teacher, but a foolish student brings him sorrow. A wise employee gladdens his employer, but a foolish employee brings sorrow to him. The word *sorrow* is perhaps not equally apt in this connection. The mother suffers emotional pain from reports about her foolish son. The employer suffers financially from a foolish employee, and may bear the burden of straightening out parts of his business that the employee has wittingly or unwittingly disrupted.

God is a father to his people. In relation to God, his people function in the role of sons:

> Know then in your heart that, as a man disciplines his *son*, the LORD your God disciplines you. (Deut. 8:5)

> As a *father* shows compassion to his *children*,
>   so the LORD shows compassion to those who fear him. (Ps. 103:13)

> For the LORD reproves him whom he loves,
>   as a *father* the *son* in whom he delights. (Prov. 3:12)

The role of God as father implies that Proverbs 10:1 serves to illustrate by analogy the ways in which God evaluates the thoughts and actions of his human "sons." He rejoices in their wisdom, and has sorrow for their folly. God is our father rather than our mother. But Scripture does use figures of speech in which the people of God as a whole function like a spiritual mother: Isaiah 54:1; Galatians 4:26–27. Thus, by focusing on the figurative dimension of Proverbs 10:1b–c, we have moved out in a perspectival way into an exploration of topical and redemptive-historical correlations. We will return to this point when we take up the study of the correlations of Proverbs 10:1 with other biblical texts.

B.1.c.(1).(b).((3)) Systemic Linguistic Contexts

All the way through our discussion, we have been constantly using grammatical and lexical information. We have relied on the interlocking between grammatical and referential subsystems. We need not devote explicit focus to the subsystems, but we should acknowledge our dependence on God, who has richly provided for verbal communication even in ways to which we seldom explicitly attend.

B.1.c.(1).(c) Readers' Impression

How should Proverbs 10:1 be received by readers?

We have already considered the invitation to readers to reflect and turn over in their minds the significance of a proverb. The proverb also urges them to apply it to their lives. This principle applies to ancient readers and to modern ones—you and me. Thus, we have a perspective on application.

B.1.c.(2) The Social Contexts

What are the main social contexts surrounding Proverbs 10:1?

When we consult the introductory sections of commentaries on Proverbs, we find that wisdom had a close association with kingship. Solomon recognized that he needed wisdom for ruling (1 Kings 3:9). Wise men functioned as counselors to the king (e.g., Daniel 1; 2; 5). The ups and downs of the monarchial period in Israelite history show the influence of wise and foolish decisions by the kings. The book of Proverbs might serve as a way of instructing the king's son, in preparation for the time when the son will become king.

So in Proverbs 1–9, is the "father" the king and is the "son" the future king? The association established in Proverbs 1:1 between the proverbs and King Solomon certainly invites this use, as one possible use. But I believe that the language of father and son in Proverbs should also be taken at face value as universally relevant.[9] The instruction in Proverbs and the wisdom embodied in proverbs are relevant both for a future king's instruction and for any father teaching any son. In fact, by implication they are relevant for anyone seeking wisdom. In content, Proverbs points us outward to the entire experience of social and economic life among the people of Israel. And from there we easily see that it has implications for all the peoples of the world. At some level, everyone wants to live well. But our lives are marred and ruined by sin. So what does good living look like? Not the self-indulgence and seeking after short-term pleasure to which we are tempted.

We should also take into account that within Israelite culture family bonds mattered a good deal, and questions of honor and shame mattered. The behavior of a son reflects on his family. If the son is wise, it brings honor to the family, and to the father in particular. The father is glad partly because the neighbors see the son's wisdom and it increases the family honor.

If the son is foolish, it brings shame to the family. An ill-behaved son, even when he is physically an adult, dishonors his parents and brings the family name into disgrace. The neighbors see what the son is. They may even remark about it. The mother's sorrow is increased by the fact that she knows she has been disgraced in the eyes of society.

B.1.c.(3) The Historical Contexts

What are the main historical contexts for the origin of Proverbs 10:1?

Proverbs shows two prominent historical contexts, one in the time of Solomon, the other in the time when the book of Proverbs took its present form, which may have been during the reign of Hezekiah (25:1) but possibly later. Yet Proverbs by nature is not strongly tied to any historical period in an exclusive way. Proverbs is proverbial, not only in containing individual proverbs but in having the kinds of contents that

---

[9] Bruce Waltke distinguishes helpfully between the "Setting of Composition," which would be the kingly court, and the "Setting of Dissemination," which would be primarily the family (Waltke, *Book of Proverbs: Chapters 1–15*, 58–63).

God has indicated are relevant for all times. Of course Proverbs includes some culturally specialized information. For example, its references to a king presuppose a situation of monarchial government. But even such particular references have implications for other cultures.

In the end, it matters little what were the details of what was happening in the time of Solomon or the time of Hezekiah. Solomon matters as a classical exemplar of wisdom, and the associations with Solomon function to underline rather than undermine the universal relevance of wisdom. On the other hand, it *does* matter that Solomon belongs among the line of Davidic kings leading forward to the Messiah. But this observation fits more properly under other headings in our outline—B.3.c.(3).(a).((2)).((b)) and B.3.c.(3).(b).((3)).((a)). We will not, however, develop further a focus on Solomon as an individual figure living at a particular time. Proverbs invites us to focus primarily on general principles for living.

B.2. Topical Correlation

What topical correlations does Proverbs 10:1 have with other parts of Proverbs and with the rest of Scripture?

The topical correlations are many, as is characteristic of proverbs. First, what do we see about God? Proverbs 10:1 does not explicitly mention God. But God is presupposed, as the ruler of the world. He rules not only over the broad sweep of history but over each individual's life and over society and social relationships. "The LORD does not let the righteous go hungry, but he thwarts the craving of the wicked" (Prov. 10:3). God established the family.

What do we see about mankind? Proverbs 10:1b–c is about mankind—specifically, about a father, a mother, and a son, and in the end about two kinds of sons. Like the other proverbs, it is about human life with its ups and downs. Proverbs lends itself in this respect to correlations characteristic of exemplary preaching. Each of us is like the father or the mother or the son—really like all three, in different respects.

We can also see a hint of the theme of mediator. Solomon serves in the mediatorial role of kingship, and in a broad sense every wise man mediates wisdom to others.

What about covenant? Proverbs does not have on its surface a reference to God's specific covenants with Israel. It does, however, indicate the foundational role of "the fear of the LORD" (Prov. 1:7). Underlying the English term "the LORD" is the Hebrew tetragrammaton, *YHWH*, the special covenantal name that has connection with God's covenants with Israel (see Ex. 3:13–17; 34:5–7). So Proverbs does link itself to the covenants. In addition, it implicitly relies on the universal covenantal structure established between God and creation, and between God and man, by virtue of creation. The reference to King Solomon provides a link between truths pertaining to the universal scope of creation and truths given more particularly to Israel among the nations.

What about redemptive plots? By their nature, proverbs are not extended stories. But many of them contain mini-stories, and the mini-stories have mini-plots. Proverbs 10:1b–c has two contrasting stories. In the first, the son attains wisdom, and as a result gladdens his father. In the second, the son falls into folly, and as a result brings sorrow to his mother. These are "quest" stories, with either reward or punishment, depending on whether the quest is successful. In this way, they express by analogy the repeated quests and successes and failures that each of us experiences in his individual life, and that social groups experience in their corporate stories.

Among the significant topical correlations in Proverbs are the correlations arising from common themes in Proverbs. So the wisdom and folly in 10:1b–c correlate with the theme of wisdom and folly all the way through Proverbs. The theme of wisdom and folly crops up elsewhere in the Old Testament as well, not merely when the words occur but in every historical example of wisdom or folly or a mixture of both, and in every case where instructions or precepts show wisdom.

This contrast between the way of wisdom and the way of folly is also a contrast between the way of life and the way of death (8:35, versus 8:36 and 9:18; 10:2b). Given the close relation of wisdom to fearing the Lord (1:7), the contrast is also a contrast between the way of life in serving the Lord and the way of disobedience in rebellion against the Lord. This contrast goes back to the original rebellion of Adam and Eve in Eden.

Gladness and sorrow characterize human life as described in Proverbs, but also throughout the Old Testament. The division between gladness and sorrow traces back ultimately to Adam and Eve, who brought sorrow on themselves and on the race by their folly and disobedience. Since then we all labor in situations of mixed gladness and sorrow. The sorrow comes ultimately as a result of the fall, but Job's story tells us to resist the temptation to see in every case of disaster a punishment for some specific sin. Gladness goes back ultimately to the grace of God, who gives us good things in spite of our not deserving them.

B.3.a. and B.3.b. Redemptive-Historical Correlation: God's Plan and History

How does Proverbs 10:1 fit into the history of redemption?

God's plan is the final source for meaning, not only for the grand sweep of historical development but for each human life. Each wise or foolish son has a life in accordance with God's decrees. Christ as God rules over life, including the life of Israelite sons and your life and my life today. Whether we live wisely or foolishly depends on his rule.

B.3.c. Christ as the Center

How does Proverbs 10:1 point forward to Christ?

B.3.c.(1). and B.3.c.(2) Promises and Principles

What promises and principles in Proverbs 10:1 point forward to Christ?

The Old Testament may point forward by promises (direct prediction), or by expression of general principles that are to be fulfilled in Christ. Proverbs 10:1 is not a direct prediction, but it does express the general principle of wisdom (in contrast to folly). Christ is the wisdom of God:

> . . . Christ Jesus, who became to us *wisdom* from God, righteousness and sanctification and redemption. (1 Cor. 1:30)

> . . . Christ, in whom are hidden all the treasures of *wisdom* and knowledge. (Col. 2:3)

The New Testament also indicates the fulfillment of wisdom in Christ in less direct ways. "And Jesus increased in *wisdom* and in stature and in favor with God and man" (Luke 2:52). In a situation in which people looked askance at Jesus's behavior, he said, "Yet *wisdom* is justified by all her children" (Luke 7:35; compare Matt. 11:19). Jesus also compares himself to Solomon:

> The queen of the South [Sheba] will rise up at the judgment with this generation and condemn it, for she came from the ends of the earth to hear the *wisdom* of Solomon, and behold, something greater than Solomon is here. (Matt. 12:42)

Jesus also gives an invitation to "take his yoke," similar to the invitation that Jews associated with wisdom:

> Come to me, all who labor and are heavy laden, and I will give you rest. Take my yoke upon you, and learn from me, for I am gentle and lowly in heart, and you will find rest for your souls. For my yoke is easy, and my burden is light. (Matt. 11:28–30)

B.3.c.(3).(a) Redemptive-Historical Correlation: Analogies

We should consider how Proverbs 10:1 contains *analogies* that point forward to Christ.

Christ serves as kingly mediator, and as such he mediates wisdom to those who come to him. As we have hinted, this mediatorial work is analogous to the Solomonic and kingly mediation of wisdom in the Old Testament. Christ, in fact, is the descendant of Solomon (Matt. 1:6–7). All the Davidic kings look forward to Christ. When they embodied righteousness or wisdom, they encouraged people to look forward to the final righteous and wise king in the line of David. When they failed, they pointed by their failure to the need for a king who was their opposite.

Every instance where a wise father instructs his son looks forward to the final instruction through Christ. Christ's mediation of wisdom is analogous to the father's mediation of wisdom to his son. In particular, Christ supplies the wisdom that leads to the gladness of the father described in Proverbs 10:1.

Christ as a human being also embodies wisdom in his own living. Thus, he is analogous to the wise son in Proverbs 10:1.

B.3.c.(3).(b) Types

Now consider how Proverbs 10:1 may function in a *typological* manner.

The Old Testament in general and Proverbs in particular already recognize an analogy between God and a human father (Prov. 3:12). Human fathers in relation to their sons reflect transcendent truths about God. Therefore, the mention of father and son in Proverbs 10:1b has potentially a symbolic depth. This depth is activated when we bring 10:1b into relation to 3:12:

> For the LORD reproves him whom he loves,
>   as a *father* the *son* in whom he delights.

We have also discussed the principle that truths in the Old Testament point forward to fuller realizations of truth in the New Testament. In the case of Proverbs 10:1b–c, this forward-pointing function is present. The character of father and son point forward respectively to God as Father and Christ as Son. The redemptive plot of obtaining wisdom points forward to Christ's growth in wisdom (Luke 2:52). Of course, the Old Testament also includes plots in which people fail to attain wisdom or fall into folly and suffer for it. Even these plots, by setting forth a contrast with wisdom, point forward to Christ as the wise person who *does* succeed in wisdom. Christ receives his reward for wisdom when he is raised from the dead and exalted to the right hand of the Father, where his wisdom gladdens the heart of the Father. The human relationships within an earthly family point forward, by way of either positive or negative example, to the fullest realization of familial love in the love between the Father and the Son.

In addition, God as creator functions in a kind of fatherly relation to his human creatures—though this relation has been broken by the fall. All of humanity has in a sense become a foolish son, whose actions are shameful and dishonor God who made him. Humanity is restored only by union with Christ, who is the supremely wise son.

The passage applies not only to Christ but also to his people. The people of God in the New Testament are united to Christ (1 Cor. 1:30). We are adopted into God's family (Gal. 4:4–5), and we become wise through the instruction of the Holy Spirit in the gospel (John 16:13; 1 Cor. 2:10–16). We learn to act wisely in the Spirit (Gal. 5:25) and to please God (1 Thess. 4:1). God is pleased with our good works, not because they are sinlessly perfect but because their defects are covered by Christ's blood. In the future we look forward to a "new heavens and a new earth in which righteousness dwells" (2 Pet. 3:13). If righteousness dwells there, wisdom also dwells there, because the Lamb is there (Rev. 7:17; 21:22–23; 22:1–5). Human fathers will be glad to see their wise sons in their company. The heavenly Father will be glad to see all his wise sons in the company, because of the wisdom of the one unique Son.

And why, we might ask, did God make a world in which there were fathers, and why did he make the fathers so that wise sons would gladden them? Man is made in the image of God (Gen. 1:26). The fathers reflect on the level of the creature the relation of wisdom and gladness and love between the eternal Father and his one eternal Son, through the fellowship and indwelling of the Holy Spirit.

Proverbs 10:1 is not an accident or a trivial observation. It has deep roots in the wisdom of God.

B.3.c.(3).(c) Preparation

We may now consider how Proverbs 10:1 functions as part of the timeline of *preparation* leading to Christ.

The whole Old Testament period represents a preparation where people experience pieces of the wisdom of God, but not the fullness of wisdom. Proverbs instructs the people in wisdom. Its instruction gives genuine wisdom. But genuine wisdom includes longing for more wisdom, to "seek it like silver and search for it as for hidden treasures" (Prov. 2:4). The treasure arrives when Colossians 2:3 announces that "in [Christ] are hidden all the treasures of wisdom and knowledge." In the meantime, the wisdom that Solomon received, and the wisdom that each human father succeeds in communicating to his son, are small portions and foretastes. These foretastes are provided only through the presence of the Son of God, the mediator. He is present already in Old Testament times. He is present in blessing a father who endeavors to bless his son with wisdom, and present with the wise son who in turn blesses the father. The blessing derives from God in Christ, not merely from the son (James 1:17).

C. Application

How does Proverbs 10:1b–c *apply* to us?

The main obvious applications for Proverbs 10:1b–c would be in praising God for his wisdom in Christ, in asking that his wisdom be embodied in us through the power of the Spirit, and consequently in living lives of wisdom, especially as parents and children. Fathers and mothers should be both encouraged and warned by this proverb to teach their children diligently in the ways of the Lord (Deut. 6:7–9), to pray for them to be saved (which for the children is the beginning of the fear of the Lord and therefore of wisdom; Prov. 1:7), and to pray for them to grow in wisdom. Moreover, parents should not only give verbal instruction but live exemplary lives. Parents need the spiritual power of Christ in their own lives first, if they are to live in the way of wisdom.

Sons and daughters, in turn, need to reject the worldly wisdom that despises and disrespects parents, often by favoring the peer group or modern passing fashions. Children need to listen to the wisdom of their parents. A son or daughter who first gets a driver's license may ignore parental instructions and words of caution, and speed carelessly into an accident that results in months of work in physical rehabilitation, or even in death. Both parents and child have sorrow. The examples could be multiplied. The focal examples in family life illustrate larger principles of wisdom and folly that apply to every segment of life, personal and social.

34

Psalm 4:8

Our next passage for interpretation is Psalm 4:8:

> In peace I will both lie down and sleep;
>> for you alone, O LORD, make me dwell in safety.

Since we have traveled through the steps of interpretation in somewhat more detail in dealing with 1 Samuel 22:1–2 and Proverbs 10:1, we will confine ourselves to a few highlighted areas in dealing with Psalm 4:8.

B.1.a. Literary Context

What is the literary context for Psalm 4:8?

The immediate context of verse 8 is the rest of Psalm 4. Psalm 4 in turn falls within the first of the five "books" making up the book of Psalms as a whole: Psalms 1–41, 42–72, 73–89, 90–106, and 107–150. It appears that there is some degree of subtle organization in the grouping into five books, and in the internal arrangements of psalms within any one book. Many of the psalms of David appear in the first book. The second book begins with some "maskils" of the sons of Korah. Psalms 120–134 are "songs of ascent." A number of psalms of praise occur at the end of the fifth book. Psalms 1 and 150 are suitable "book-end" psalms to open and close the entire collection.

These signs of organization reinforce the overall unity of the collection. But the signs are subtle. The main point is surely that this is the official, God-inspired hymnbook and prayer book for his people Israel. Each psalm is a relatively complete literary whole.

Psalm 4 as a whole expresses both distress (vv. 1, 2) and confidence (vv. 3, 5, 7–8). The psalmist appears to be in distress partly because of the verbal attacks of others (v. 2). One of the difficulties, expressed also in other psalms, such as Psalm 73, involves the fact that wicked people prosper and do not immediately experience God's judgment on their wickedness. The righteous, by contrast, may experience distress. The closing two verses of Psalm 4 respond to these difficulties by finding inward joy in the Lord (v. 7) and confidence in the Lord's protection (v. 8).

Scholars have observed that Psalm 1 is a fitting opening for the whole book of Psalms, through its thematic introduction of the righteous man and the wicked. Psalm 2 introduces the theme of the Davidic king, and looks forward to the final messianic king. After these two Psalms, it may be that Psalm 3 and Psalm 4 come next because they were used as a morning prayer (Ps. 3:5) and an evening prayer (Ps. 4:8), respectively. This thematic suitability makes sense, though of course Psalm 3 and Psalm 4 have broader applications.

Psalm 3 and Psalm 4 both have a dominant mood of confidence. They are psalms of trust. But they both contain in addition some elements of lament and petition.

B.1.b. Transmission Context

How was Psalm 4 transmitted to us?

As a collection, the book of Psalms doubtless has a complicated history leading up to the complete book that we now have. Psalm 18 is almost identical to 2 Samuel 22, which David wrote during his lifetime (2 Sam. 22:1). Psalm 137 appears to have been written during the exile, and Psalm 126 after the exile. The final collection into 150 psalms would therefore have taken place after the exile. As usual, this final collection is the book that belongs to the canon, the word of God, that he intended permanently for the edification of his people. We need not worry ourselves that we do not know the details concerning the process of collection. God superintended the process in such a way that the book we now have is his infallible word.

In Hebrew, Psalm 4:8 (numbered verse 9 in the Hebrew) shows only minor difficulty in text criticism. A few manuscripts have a variation in the Hebrew underlying the English word *alone* (ləbadəkā, לְבַדְּךָ, instead of ləbādād, לְבָדָד).[1] This variation is hard to translate, because the meaning is essentially the same.

B.1.c.(1).(a) The Text: Authorial Intention

Now let us focus on the author.

Who is the human author? The superscription runs, "To the choirmaster: with stringed instruments. A Psalm of David." We need not enter into the complex discussions concerning these superscriptions.[2] Because the superscriptions are not always the same in the Septuagint and in other ancient translations as they are in the Hebrew,[3] some scholars wonder whether the superscriptions were autographic or whether they belong to a later stage. Even if they belong to a later stage, they may be historically accurate.

But there is debate about the meaning as well. The expression "A Psalm of David" may mean that Psalm 4 was written by David, but the Hebrew could also mean, "written in honor of David," or "written with David in mind." This range of possible meanings cannot easily be represented in an English translation. The most common Hebrew construction that we normally translate in English with the word "of" consists in a sequence of two nouns in Hebrew, the first of which is in the "construct state." The expressions "The words of Amos" (Amos 1:1) and "the vision of Isaiah the son of Amoz" (Isa. 1:1) are of this kind. The expression at the beginning of Psalm 4 (and elsewhere in the Psalm superscriptions) is not the same. Literally, it is "psalm to/for/belonging to David" (lədāwid, לְדָוִד). So is the meaning broader?

Note that Psalm 18 has a superscription using the key expression "of David," clearly stating that David wrote it. The superscription further identifies David as the one "who addressed the words of this song to the

---

[1] In addition, the notes in *Biblia Hebraica Stuttgartensia* suggest that the Hebrew for "Lord" should be omitted for metrical reasons. But this suggestion has no support in the manuscripts, and is to be rejected.

[2] For an up-to-date discussion, see Willem A. Vangemeren and Jason Stanghelle, "A Critical-Realistic Reading of the Psalm Titles: Authenticity, Inspiration, and Evangelicals," in *Do Historical Matters Matter to Faith? A Critical Appraisal of Modern and Postmodern Approaches to Scripture*, ed. James K. Hoffmeier and Dennis R. Magary (Wheaton, IL: Crossway, 2012), 281–301.

[3] In addition, manuscripts of the psalms at Qumran show variation in the titles (cf. ibid., 285–287).

Lord . . ." The authorship for Psalm 18 is confirmed by 2 Samuel 22:1. This one clear instance clarifies by implication the other occurrences of similar expressions in the Psalter.[4]

The inclusion of a prayer or song within the Psalter places the original human author in the background. The prayer as we have it belongs primarily to the Psalter, not to the earlier individual situation in which a private person wrote it. Its inclusion guarantees its divine authorship, and we should receive it as such. We are no longer supposed to focus primarily on questions about what was going on in David's mind and what were the circumstances in his life. We receive the prayer as a model prayer for God's people to pray and sing, as God enables them.

B.1.c.(1).(b).((1)) Textual Expression: Units

What textual units do we find in Psalm 4:8?

In Hebrew, there are only a few basic interpretive problems. First, there is a possible ambiguity with respect to the Hebrew word for *alone* (*ləbādād*, לְבָדָד). Does the word describe the psalmist or the Lord? It could possibly mean, "O Lord, you make me dwell alone in safety" (cf. Mic. 7:14). The word order in Hebrew, which places "alone" right after "O Lord," argues in favor of the ESV rendering, "you alone, O Lord, make me dwell in safety" (cf. Ps. 62:1, 5; 72:18; 83:18; 86:10; 136:4; etc.).

In addition, it is possible to break the second line in the middle, leading to a somewhat different meaning:

> In peace I will both lie down and sleep;
>   for you alone are the Lord; you make me dwell in safety.[5]

This rendering is possible, but less likely. The fact that the God of Israel is the Lord provides the ultimate reason for the psalmist's security and

---

[4] See Derek Kidner, *Psalms 1–72: An Introduction and Commentary on Books I and II of the Psalms* (Downers Grove, IL/London: InterVarsity Press, 1973), 33, who makes a broader argument in favor of authenticity (32–35). Nevertheless, other people could argue that the expression "to David" is *always* broader in the meaning, and that the clarification in Psalm 18 comes only through the added information, "who addressed the words . . . ," not from the expression "to David." Note also Psalm 72:1, "Of Solomon" (i.e., to/for/belonging to Solomon). The contents of Psalm 72 suggest that it might have been written as reflection about Solomon, not necessarily written *by* Solomon.

[5] So John Goldingay, *Psalms: Volume 1: Psalms 1–41* (Grand Rapids, MI: Baker, 2006), 123; Peter C. Craigie, *Psalms 1–50*, Word Biblical Commentary, vol. 19, 2nd ed. with supplement by Marvin E. Tate (n.l.: Nelson, 2004), 77.

safety. But standing as it does, the statement "you alone are the Lord" remains somewhat disconnected from the rest. By contrast, "you alone make me dwell in safety" offers a contextually appropriate connection (so ESV, NKJV, NIV, NASB). The contextual fit argues that this latter rendering is the correct meaning.

There is also a minor challenge concerning the tense of the verbs. In Hebrew all three verbs are in the imperfect tense. The imperfect can be used either to describe a repeated or customary pattern or to describe a future event. The translation into English could therefore use either the present tense in English, to express a general pattern, or the future tense to denote a future event:

> In peace I both lie down and sleep;
>> for you alone, O LORD, make me dwell in safety.

or

> In peace I will both lie down and sleep;
>> for you alone, O LORD, will make me dwell in safety.

Since the second line gives a reason, it is more likely to express a general principle, and so is more aptly expressed by a present tense in English: "for you alone, O LORD, make me dwell in safety." The rest of Psalm 4 seems to focus at least to some extent on a specific situation in which the psalmist is in distress: "Answer me when I call"; "be gracious to me and hear my prayer!" (4:1). Accordingly, it is slightly more suitable to take the first part of verse 8 as future. But it makes little difference to the overall thrust of verse 8 and the psalm as a whole, since a single instance of sleep expresses a general principle, and conversely the general principle will in the course of time be embodied in specific instances.

B.1.c.(1).(b).((2)) *Textual Expression: Hierarchies*

What is the hierarchical organization into which Psalm 4:8 fits?

Psalm 4:8 consists of two lines,

> [Line 1:] In peace I will both lie down and sleep;
> [Line 2:] for you alone, O LORD, make me dwell in safety.

Like the book of Proverbs, the poetry of the psalms uses poetic parallelism. But the two (or sometimes three) lines in parallel need not use simple repetition ("synonymous parallelism") or simple contrast ("antithetical parallelism"). There can be more complex relationships. In this case, each line in English consists of a single clause, though the first clause has a compound verbal structure ("lie down and sleep"). Line 2 provides a cause and a reason for the speaker to enjoy peace: the Lord provides safety.

Verse 8 is the final verse of the psalm, and as such provides a relatively peaceful culmination. Earlier in the psalm we can see tension. The psalmist is "in distress" (v. 1) and calls to the Lord for help. In verse 7 it appears by implication that he lacks abundant food and external security. Men oppose him, either by bringing distress upon him or by ungodly words (vv. 2, 6, 7). So his expression of confidence in verse 8 is in spite of distress. The confidence is therefore all the more striking. The expression of confidence comes in spite of the fact that ungodly men temporarily prosper (vv. 2, 7).

What topics appear in verse 8? One main topic is the psalmist in his situation, and then we must include the topics of security, peace, sleep, and the Lord's help. The topic of distress is there by implication, since it provides the background for verse 8.

What figural dimensions belong to the verse? Sleep can serve as a metaphor for death (Ps. 13:3, "lest I sleep the sleep of death"). In the neighboring Psalm 3, the psalmist indicates in verse 5 that he might not have awakened from sleep, because his foes might have killed him (vv. 1–2, 6). Sleep is analogous to death, because in both cases one surrenders control over one's body and one ceases to interact consciously with the surrounding physical world. To "lie down" (4:8) is analogically like facing the imminent approach of death, and determining to lay down one's life.

The psalmist commits his life to the Lord's safety as he lies down to physical sleep. But is there something more? The Lord promises to be the God of his people. In so promising, he gives a promise that is deeper than just a concern for physical sustenance, because God himself is deeper than that. Fellowship with God is at the heart of real living. So by figural analogy, the verse suggests a relationship between lying down for physical sleep and committing oneself to God when one faces "the sleep of death," and when the safety in question must therefore mean safety on the other side of death.

B.1.c.(1).(c) Readers' Impression
What impact does Psalm 4:8 have on readers?

The psalms are designed for people to pray over and sing. God invites each person who reads or sings Psalm 4:8 to appropriate it to his own life. Entrust your life to the Lord. Believe that the Lord makes you dwell in safety. Entrust both your physical sleep and your future "sleep in death" to the Lord. You should particularly take the verse to heart if you, like the psalmist, are beset by enemies or by those who have attacked with words, and if the ungodly are prospering (v. 7).

B.1.c.(2) The Social Contexts
To what social contexts does Psalm 4:8 belong?

The social contexts for the book of Psalms are the Israelite contexts of worship, prayer, and singing, through the centuries. The Levites were commissioned to sing as part of the temple service, and they sang psalms (1 Chronicles 16; 25). The book of Psalms also has a strong anchorage in the Davidic kingship. David was culturally well known as "the sweet psalmist of Israel" (2 Sam. 23:1). David himself wrote psalms and a lament over Saul and Jonathan (2 Sam. 1:17–27). The king is the representative for all Israel. So the psalms are psalms that the king is to pray and sing as a representative. One psalm is explicitly addressed to the king (Ps. 45:1), and several are about the king (Psalms 2, 72, 110). But there is a wider atmosphere of kingship, because of the role of David as a psalm writer and the king as representative of the nation.

B.1.c.(3) The Historical Contexts
To what historical contexts does Psalm 4:8 belong?

The book of Psalms is raised above any particular historical event or historical period by being a collection of poems written under varied circumstances and in a span of historical periods. Some superscriptions, like the one for Psalm 3, indicate a background in a particular historical event: "A Psalm of David, when he fled from Absalom his son" (referring to the events of 2 Samuel 15–16). But a superscription of this kind is an exception. And the contents even of Psalm 3 can be applied to many individuals and many circumstances. The contents do not contain historical particulars. Psalm 4 shows the same pattern. There are no historical particulars that would enable us to identify one particular incident in the life of David that served as the stimulus for this psalm. This lack of detail is a part of God's wise design. God invites us to see the patterns of prayer and praise, and apply them to ourselves, just as the Israelites would have applied them in their times of worship and on other occasions in their personal lives.

B.2. Topical Correlation

What topical correlations do we find with various topics and themes?

First, what is God doing? God is of course the primary author of the psalm. But he is also a participant in verse 8. The Lord makes "me dwell in safety."

What is man doing? Man is present in the voice of the psalm, who looks for sleep and safety and commits his life to the Lord.

What mediatorial functions are present? The Lord often mediates safety through intermediates. The righteous king provides safety and security for his people. And, as we indicated, the psalms live with kingship always in the background. If we are to survive when confronting the sleep of death, we need mediatorial mercy.

Is the divine covenant present as a theme? No specific covenant is mentioned, but the verse presupposes that God has committed himself to providing safety for those who seek him and fear him. He says so explicitly in covenantal promises, from Abraham onward.

Is a redemptive plot present? Yes, the issue in the psalm is safety or abandonment, and that implies a plot. The psalmist's situation goes downward as the threat increases, and comes up in victory when the Lord grants safety. There are many such small plots in the lives of the saints, but also a bigger plot, in the sense that all of life on earth contains threats, the last of which is death. The promise of redemption is ultimately a promise of victory over death, which intruded through the fall.

The theme of safety and refuge, as provided by the Lord, runs through the book of Psalms.

B.3.c.(3) Redemptive-Historical Correlation:
Christ in Particular Events

How does Psalm 4:8 fit into the history of redemption?

Psalm 4:8, as we have seen, is both about an individual who slept in the Lord's safety, and about a general pattern that Israelite readers are to appropriate for themselves. The individual and the kingly representative point forward to Christ, who is the final king. Christ is not only mediator, but a man. He, like other Israelites, appropriates the psalm to himself. But of course he is not just one Israelite among many. He is the unique Son, the focal Israelite, the uniquely qualified representative. So the psalm applies *especially* and uniquely to him. In fact, God, who plans history, had it written for Christ and about him. It was also about those Israelite readers. We do not have to choose between the alternatives, as if they excluded each other, because God included both aspects in his purposes.

Christ experienced the safety of God the Father every time he slept. We may recall especially that he slept while he and his disciples were in the midst of a storm (Matt. 8:23–27). He called his disciples "you of little faith" (v. 26), which makes us reflect on the fact that they did not in faith take to heart Psalm 4:8 as thoroughly as they could have. The parallel passage in Mark 4:39 includes the detail that Jesus said, "Peace! Be still!" We might imagine that "peace" in Mark 4:39 echoes "peace" in Psalm 4:8, but in the original languages there is no direct verbal correspondence. The correspondence is only the general thematic correspondence between two instances where the Lord brings peace.

We can ask whether there is a typological correspondence. In Psalm 4:8, physical sleep is emblematic of the posture of trust and commitment to the Lord. Thus, it is also emblematic of commitment in the face of the sleep of death. This theme moves forward into the New Testament, and finds fulfillment ultimately in Jesus's victory over death in his resurrection. In peace, Jesus lay down and slept:

> "Father, into your hands I commit my spirit!" And having said this
> he breathed his last. (Luke 23:46)

In so laying down his life, Jesus trusted that the Lord alone would make him dwell in safety. And it proved true.

The final safety is not merely safety within temporary human existence. It cannot be, since earthly safety is always threatened by death at last, and threatened in many ways before the last, in the form of sickness, poverty, war, famine, economic loss, and hatred. Final safety lies in the new heavens and the new earth, "in which righteousness dwells" (2 Pet. 3:13). Jesus Christ laid the firm foundation for that final safety by his own resurrection from the dead, because of which he "will never die again; death no longer has dominion over him" (Rom. 6:9). What is true for him also becomes true for those who come to him in faith and are united to him: "So you also must consider yourselves dead to sin and alive to God in Christ Jesus" (Rom. 6:11).

God has made Christ dwell in safety forever through his resurrection. He sits and rules at God's right hand. He has also made *us* who are in Christ to dwell in safety—we are "seated . . . with him in the heavenly places in Christ Jesus" (Eph. 2:6). We already have spiritual safety. But we also have, as what is yet to come, the firm expectation of consummate safety in our own future transfiguration in a resurrection body like his (1 Cor. 15:44–49):

> "Death is swallowed up in victory."
> "O death, where is your victory?
>   O death, where is your sting?"

> The sting of death is sin, and the power of sin is the law. But thanks be to God, who gives us the victory through our Lord Jesus Christ. (1 Cor. 15:54–57)

Each of us who trusts in Christ may therefore lie down and sleep the sleep of death in peace, because God has firmly founded our safety in Christ. The promise applies, of course, to the church as a whole. The whole church may look forward to its transfiguration in the new world.

B.3.c.(3).(c) Preparation

How does Psalm 4:8 function as part of the timeline preparing for Christ?

Throughout the ages, the Old Testament saints committed themselves to the Lord for safety. But the Old Testament saw not only many enemies but many apostasies, even among or sometimes especially among the Israelite kings who should have been prime examples of trusting in the Lord. Precisely through the limitations in human trust, the Old Testament stirs up longing for the coming of a final manifestation of trust as it should be—the faithfulness of the messianic Son of David:

> There shall come forth a shoot from the stump of Jesse,
>   and a branch from his roots shall bear fruit.
> And the Spirit of the LORD shall rest upon him,
>   the Spirit of wisdom and understanding,
>   the Spirit of counsel and might,
>   the Spirit of knowledge and the *fear* of the LORD.
> And his delight shall be in the *fear* of the LORD. (Isa. 11:1–3)

In its theme of faithfulness and safety, Psalm 4:8 leads forward to the final safety of the new heavens and the new earth. It also leads backward to the original security of the garden of Eden, in which God secured Adam and Eve's safety while they continued to trust in him. And it leads to reflecting on God's faithfulness in the whole created order, to which we should respond in faithfulness and trust. Christ's work as the second Adam fulfills faithfulness, whereas Adam and all of us who are his posterity have failed.

In the middle of history, the psalmist experiences the protection and safety of God amid trials. He receives protection not because he is ultimately deserving but because the Son of God is present as mediator to grant undeserved benefit, as a foretaste of the safety in Christ's present reign at the right hand of the Father, and the future reign of the Lamb on the throne (Rev. 22:1, 3).

C. Application

How do we apply Psalm 4:8?

The principal fulfillment comes in the death and resurrection of Christ. But the passage also applies to each one of us. We are to commit ourselves to trust in God amid each trial. We are to be patient when the enemies of God seem to prosper. David lies before us as an encouraging example, as do all the saints who sang and prayed Psalm 4:8 in ages before us. But our supreme exemplar is Christ, who is not only an example but our empowerer and guarantee:

> Therefore, since we are surrounded by so great a cloud of witnesses, let us also lay aside every weight, and sin which clings so closely, and let us run with endurance the race that is set before us, looking to Jesus, the founder and perfecter of our faith, who for the joy that was set before him endured the cross, despising the shame, and is seated at the right hand of the throne of God. (Heb. 12:1–2)

35

Amos 1:3

Finally, we consider the interpretation of Amos 1:3. In the English Standard Version the verse runs,

Thus says the Lord:

> For three transgressions of Damascus,
>   and for four, I will not revoke the punishment,
> because they have threshed Gilead
>   with threshing sledges of iron.

B.1.a. Literary Context

How does Amos 1:3 fit into its literary context? Amos 1:1 identifies the prophet Amos and the historical setting of his ministry. It serves as a heading for the whole book. Amos 1:2 draws the reader's attention to the majesty and solemnity of God's word, and thus serves as an introduction to the rest of the book, which sets forth God's words through Amos.

Amos 1:3–2:8 contains a clear organization into sections or stanzas. In succession, the Lord gives indictments against Damascus (1:3–5), Gaza (1:6–8), Tyre (1:9–10), Edom (1:11–12), the Ammonites (1:13–15), Moab (2:1–3), Judah (2:4–5), and Israel (2:6–8). Each section begins with "Thus says the Lord," and some end with "says the Lord" as well. After each opening line, "Thus says the Lord," comes a stereotyped pair of lines:

> For three transgressions of X,
>   and for four, I will not revoke the punishment,

Then comes a specification of crimes, introduced by "because" (Hebrew *'al*, עַל). In every section except the last (2:6–8), there follows also a specification of the punishment that will come (in English, introduced by "So . . ."). The punishment for Israel, corresponding to the indictment in 2:6–8, probably has its specification in the section 2:9–16, especially in verses 13–16. But this section is longer than the sections that specify the punishment for other nations. The increase in length suits the fact that the principal focus for the book as a whole is on the northern kingdom of Israel.

The rest of the book of Amos, from 3:1 onward, has a looser organization. It focuses mostly on divine indictment and prophesies divine punishment for Israel. Finally, at the end, God prophesies restoration and blessing (9:9–15). Almost the whole book is poetry.

B.1.b. Transmission Context

How did Amos 1:3 come from its original autograph to us? It came as part of the book of Amos. We do not know whether the book of Amos was written down by Amos himself or by later disciples, after Amos fulfilled his commission to deliver his message orally (Amos 7:10–17). As usual, the details of the process do not matter; what matters is that the product, by divine providence, determination, and inspiration, is the word of God.

Amos 1:3 does not display any text-critical difficulties. We have the same text that God caused to be written in the days of Amos.

B.1.c.(1).(a) The Text: Authorial Intention

As usual, we have two authors: God the divine author and Amos the human author. In addition, if Amos's disciples were involved in the final compilation of the book as we now have it, they were in a sense scribal authors. Under the inspiration of God (2 Pet. 1:21), the scribal intention was to set forth the intention of Amos. And the intention of Amos was to set forth the message of God. The first part of the heading, "The words of Amos" (1:1) simply identifies the human source, and does not itself indicate the status of Amos's words. But it continues with "which he *saw*," which is an expression indicating prophetic inspiration (compare Isa. 1:1). The repeated refrain, "Thus says the LORD," puts direct emphasis on divine speech and divine authority for the speech.

Amos is only a spokesman for the Lord. He is not speaking out of his human imagination. A merely human imagination could conceivably infer from a knowledge of God's justice and his mercy that God would judge the sins of the nations, including Israel, and that he might eventually in his mercy restore Israel, because of his promises to Abraham and to David. But the details are not within human competence to know. Amos is saying, "Not I, but the Lord: the Lord is the real source for my message." The autobiographical note in Amos 7:14–15 indicates that Amos was self-consciously aware of being a divine spokesman, and specifically underlines the humble, secondary role that he himself takes:

> Then Amos answered and said to Amaziah, "I was no prophet, nor a prophet's son, but I was a herdsman and a dresser of sycamore figs. But the LORD took me from following the flock, and the LORD said to me, 'Go, prophesy to my people Israel.'"

The Lord invites us to read the book of Amos as a book conveying the Lord's message. Only in a secondary sense is it the book of Amos, the human spokesman. God raised him up and called him so that he would announce the *Lord's* word, not his own.

B.1.c.(1).(b).((1)) Textual Expression: Units

How is the text organized into units?

The text is fairly straightforward, in Hebrew and in English. Only a few details need our remarks.

First, underlying the word *says* in the introductory line, "Thus *says* the LORD," is a Hebrew word in the perfect tense. (The word occurs in the same form in the subsequent sections.) It is a standard form in prophetic address. The tense implies that the Lord has spoken (as a completed act). What he says is a firm, established fact. As such, his word continues to address the people of Israel. So, in the context of prophetic communication, the translation "says" is appropriate.

Second, consider the English expression "I will not revoke the punishment." The Hebrew would translate woodenly as "I will not turn it back," as a footnote in the ESV indicates. "I will not turn it back" is succinct and somewhat cryptic. "It" in context must be the punishment, which is specifically announced in verses 4–5. In this context, "turn back" means to turn back the punishment before it arrives, i.e., to "revoke" it.

The Hebrew word for "threshing sledges" is not common in the Hebrew Bible, but given the context there is no doubt about its meaning.

B.1.c.(1).(b).((2)).((a)) Hierarchies: Discourse Flow

How is the text organized hierarchically?

Consider first the textual flow. How do the smaller units fit together in 1:3 and in 1:3–5? Verse 3 divides into four poetic lines:

[Line A:] Thus says the LORD:

[Line B:] For three transgressions of Damascus,
[Line C:] and for four, I will not revoke the punishment,
[Line D:] because they have threshed Gilead with threshing sledges
    of iron.

Line A introduces the rest of the section, 3b–5, which is the contents of what the Lord says.

Lines B and C are parallel, as is evident from the expressions, "for three" and "for four." But how many transgressions are there, three or four or more? Only one is actually mentioned in line D. The structure with "three" and "four" has a figural dimension, as would be expected in poetry. Hebrew poetry works largely by parallel lines. And the parallel lines often contain parallel words or phrases. "Wise son" and "foolish son" are parallel in Proverbs 10:1, and so are "father" and "his mother." Since a number cannot be strictly parallel to anything except itself, Hebrew customarily puts within the second parallel line the next higher number:

There are *six* things that the LORD hates,
    seven that are an abomination to him: . . . (Prov. 6:16)

The leech has *two* daughters:
    Give and Give.

Three things are never satisfied;
> *four* never say, "Enough": . . . (Prov. 30:15)

Three things are too wonderful for me;
> *four* I do not understand: . . . (Prov. 30:18)

Under *three* things the earth trembles;
> under *four* it cannot bear up: . . . (Prov. 30:21)

As is often the case with Hebrew poetry, the second line has an ascending emphasis. "Three, and yes, one more: four."

Amos 1:3d lists only one transgression of Damascus, but there could be a longer list. And it could be extended from three to four (or more).

Line *D* is the transgression on the basis of which punishment will come. It is the reason for lines *B–C*.

We should also consider the relation of 1:3b–d to the larger context. 1:4–5 describes the punishment that the Lord will bring on the king and kingdom of Syria, on account of the transgressions on 1:3b–4. The section 1:3–5 lies alongside the indictments and punishments in the other sections from 1:6 to 2:8 (and up to 2:16).

The last section (2:6–8) is climactic and shocking. The previous sections make their way around the various nations surrounding Israel, most of whom are traditional enemies of Israel. The next-to-last section (2:4–5) comes to Judah, the southern kingdom, with whom the northern kingdom had fights and tensions, but who shared with them the religious heritage of the Mosaic covenant and an ancestry tracing back to Jacob. In 2:4–5 the Lord's indictments are coming close to home. In 2:6–8 they reach home—the northern kingdom of Israel, where Amos had been sent with the Lord's message (7:10–15). So the passage 1:3–5, where our verse lies, is the first step in a buildup to 2:6–8. Amos 2:6–8 in turn leads to the rest of the book, which largely concerns the sins of Israel and the punishments that the Lord will bring as a consequence.

B.1.c.(1).(b).((2)).((b)) Hierarchies: Discourse Topics

Next, consider topical connections. Line *A* contains the theme of God's speech. Lines *B-C* both contain the theme of transgression and God's evaluation. Line *D* contains the theme of God's specification of transgression.

These themes recur in the subsequent sections, leading to the climax in 2:6–8. The general themes of sin, God's evaluation, and God's judgment run throughout Amos.

B.1.c.(1).(b).((2)).((c)) Hierarchies: Discourse Figures

We also need to consider figural elements in verse 3. The parallelism between "three transgressions" and "four" is figural, since the text does not actually count three distinct transgressions. We have already discussed how "three" and "four" function in parallel.

"Damascus" as the capital of Syria functions as a synecdoche (part for whole) standing for the kingdom of Syria and its ruling houses, Hazael and Ben-hadad (Amos 1:4; see 2 Kings 8:7–15).

In verse 1:3d the mention of "threshing" is figural. For what exactly is it a figure? It is not immediately clear. We could begin by looking up information about threshing and threshing sledges in either a Bible dictionary or a general encyclopedia. A threshing sledge in the ancient world was an agricultural implement consisting of a flat platform, from the bottom of which projected sharp edges, of flint or iron or another hard substance. The sledge was driven over grain in order to cut it into small pieces so that the chaff could then be separated from the grain. Iron was a durable metal, and the mention of iron probably points to the durability of the sledge and therefore the thoroughness of its results.

What then does it mean to "thresh Gilead"? There is an obvious comparison between the threshing process in agriculture and the work that Syria did against the people of Israel inhabiting Gilead. But what is the point of comparison? And what exactly did Syria do? When we come to consider the historical context below, we can gather some information about the Syrian oppression of Israel. The text of 1:3d does not enter into details. It suggests that the Syrians cut the people of Gilead into small pieces. This act might include cutting soldiers literally to pieces. But it probably implies cutting the society to pieces. The people were destroyed, and their property was harvested, in analogy with the role of threshing in agricultural harvests. The picture might even suggest that Syrian actions were like driving a threshing sledge literally over human captives, as a form of torture. In that case, the picture underscores the cruelty and ruthlessness of Syrian oppression.

However, the details of Syrian aggression do not come into the picture, since the book of Amos as a whole is not about Syria but about Israel. The point is that God as a God of justice has rendered judgment against Syria for her transgressions against Israel. The injustice in Syrian actions is depicted vividly by using an agricultural picture. The result is a heightened emotional engagement of the readers, which leads to our next focus, the focus on the readers.

B.1.c.(1).(c) Readers' Impression

The text would engage the original readers, because Syria was a traditional enemy of Israel. The Israelite readers would rejoice to hear of God's judgment against Syria and other enemies, one by one. They would rejoice in God's justice, and they would agree with the integrity of his justice. This agreement would "set them up for a fall," so to speak, when they came to the climax in 2:6–8. It is as if the text said, "You want God's justice when it comes to injustices against you. And you are right to celebrate this justice. Then you must also admit that God's justice will lead to your own punishment, and that you will suffer just as they have. You condemn yourself!"

B.1.c.(2) The Social Contexts

What are the social contexts for Amos 1:3?

The social contexts of the northern kingdom of Israel during Amos's time included numerous forms of injustice, as we know from the indictments scattered throughout Amos (e.g., 2:6–8, 12; 3:10; 4:1; 5:7, 10–12; 6:1, 4–7). The rich were fattening themselves (4:1; 6:4–7), and the poor were oppressed under them (4:1; 5:11–12). Social and economic oppressions and false worship (4:4; 5:5) are seen and judged by the Lord, and so the Lord announces coming judgment. Verse 1:3 fits into this picture as a picture of the Lord's just judgment, serving as a counterpoint to the judgments that he will issue against Israel.

B.1.c.(3) The Historical Contexts

What are the historical contexts for Amos 1:3?

The book of Amos specifically identifies a historical setting in verse 1:1. Amos prophesied during the reign of Uzziah king of Judah and

Jeroboam II king of Israel (about 780 to 740 BC, according to standard extrabiblical chronologies). The book would probably have been put together by Amos or his disciples. It could have been assembled piece by piece during the course of his ministry, or all at once shortly after the end of his career as a prophet. Even if, in the providence of God, he caused the final product to be put together somewhat later, God intends for us to focus on the time period comprised by the reigns of Uzziah and Jeroboam. But by making the book a canonical document, he also indicates that it is for the profit of the people of God in all future generations (Rom. 15:4).

As we have already mentioned, Syria had a history of conflict against Israel, as one can see from some of the instances mentioned in 1–2 Kings: 1 Kings 20; 22; 2 Kings 6:8–7:15; 8:12. Syria was the most prominent nearby enemy at the time of Amos. It is natural that the indictments against the nations would begin with Syria. Amos 1:3 may have in mind one of these encounters in particular. But it is likely that its indictment extends by implication to the whole history of the Syrian conflict. The principle that the Lord will judge oppression and punish the enemies of his people is a broad one. That broader principle is one bridge by which the words of God have relevance for his people, not simply for the whole Syrian conflict but for subsequent generations. But it goes together with the principle in the later parts of Amos, that God's justice also leads to punishment falling on the people of God when they go astray in disobedience and practice injustice.

B.2. Topical Correlation

What topical correlations exist in Amos 1:3?

Several topics link Amos 1:3 with the rest of the Bible. God speaks. God sees injustice. God threatens and then brings punishment. God judges the enemies of his people. But—later in Amos—he also judges his people for their injustices and rebellion. We as human beings are in some ways like the human beings mentioned in the text. And we must consider the relationship between the human beings in Amos 1:3 and Christ as a human being.

Without such topical correlations, a modern reader can still be left with a feeling of complacency about the text, because he can tell himself that he is not there—he is not the Israel of Amos's time. No, but God intends to speak to us as well. We see in Amos 1:3 a display of God's justice. We must take it to heart, and ask ourselves whether we are like Israel, or even like Syria.

Amos 1:3 also enjoys a connection with covenant. In covenants, God holds human beings responsible. He promises blessings for obedience and curses for disobedience. Syria does not participate in the particular covenant that God made with Abraham and his descendants, but it does participate in the covenant with Noah and the generic covenantal structure that exists for all humanity by virtue of creation and the continued presence of God as a God of justice and judgment.

Amos 1:3 also exemplifies a redemptive plot in reverse form. Redemption goes from sin upward to rescue. Judgment reverses this pattern by going from sin downward to judgment. But judgment against sin and injustice is necessary if the human race is to be delivered. Israel as the people of God is delivered partly through the judgments against her enemies. Ultimately Christ delivers us from sin and death and Satan by God's passing judgment against them, in the crucifixion and resurrection of Christ (Col. 2:15) and then finally in the last judgment (Rev. 20:14).

B.3. Redemptive-Historical Correlation

What redemptive-historical correlations does the passage exhibit?

There are several. In line *A* God speaks his word. Amos serves as prophetic mediator of the word. His mediation points forward to the final mediation of Christ: "Long ago, at many times and in many ways, God spoke to our fathers by the *prophets*, but in these last days he has spoken to us by his Son" (Heb. 1:1–2).

Lines *B–C* have the theme of transgression and punishment for transgression. Line *D* makes it clear that the transgression takes the specific form of oppressing Israel, the people of God (Gilead). Lines *B* and *C* together provide a connotation of heaping up or multiplying transgression. Ultimately, attacks against the people of God go back to the initial attack by the serpent in the garden of Eden. And they extend through all of history up to the consummation. Over time, the attacks multiply, as they did at the time of Noah (Gen. 6:5) and the time of

Israel's sojourn in Egypt. The climax of wickedness comes with those who put to death the true Israel, Jesus Christ the Messiah.

In response to this wickedness, God eventually brings judgment—the flood of Noah, the destruction of the Egyptian army in the Red Sea, the conquest of Canaan. The resurrection of Jesus Christ is his vindication and therefore a judgment against his earthly enemies. At the same time, it also accomplishes judgment against the satanic powers who were behind them: "He disarmed the rulers and authorities and put them to open shame, by triumphing over them in him" (Col. 2:15). The climactic judgment is then worked out in consummate form at the last judgment:

> And the devil who had deceived them was thrown into the lake of fire and sulfur where the beast and the false prophet were, and they will be tormented day and night forever and ever. (Rev. 20:10)

The oppression of Israel "with threshing sledges of iron" shows a particularly cruel and thorough oppression. It has a climactic analogical parallel when Christ's enemies oppress him. It extends to the scourging he received, which made cuts in his body.

In reflecting on redemptive-historical correlations, we should take into account the role that Amos 1:3 plays in the larger context of Amos. Amos 1:3–5 and the other early sections in Amos lead up to an announcement of judgment against Israel in 2:6–8. Amos announces that Israel will receive judgment for her sins. When Christ the true Israel comes, he has no sin; but through his identification with the sinful people whom he has come to save, he becomes their sin-bearer and suffers on their behalf. So the climactic judgment against Israel in Amos has an even more climactic typological parallel in the judgment executed on Christ, the true Israel, for the sins of God's people (2 Cor. 5:21; 1 Pet. 2:24).

Christ suffers injustice from the hands of God's enemies, in analogy with Syrian unjust oppression of Israel. At the same time, Christ suffers as sin-bearer under the weight of God's justice, in analogy with the punishment announced against Israel in Amos. How can both be true? It is the mystery of the cross. God brings good out of evil. He uses the supreme crime in human history, the crucifixion of Christ, to establish victory over death and over all sins and crimes. This victory is truly a fulfillment, because it surpasses all the Old Testament instances of evil and all the instances of preliminary blessings. The "threshing" of Christ by his enemies becomes simultaneously the beginning of the harvest of final righteousness, peace, and prosperity. Concerning his own ministry, Christ says, "Truly, truly, I say to you, unless a grain of wheat falls into the earth and dies, it remains alone; but if it dies, it bears much fruit" (John 12:24).

This victory also takes the form, "Thus says the LORD." Christ is the eternal Word of God, come from heaven (John 1:1). During his earthly life he announces in person the beginning of the saving reign of God. And through the power of his Spirit, after his resurrection, he sends out the message of victory through his messengers (Acts 1:8; 2:33). The message is a message of salvation from all the Syrias of this world. At the same time, it is a message announcing judgment:

> The times of ignorance God overlooked, but now he commands all people everywhere to repent, because he has fixed a day on which he will judge the world in righteousness by a man whom he has appointed; and of this he has given assurance to all by raising him from the dead. (Acts 17:30–31)

This message of victory and judgment is based on God's action in Christ's crucifixion and resurrection. Christ's work is the fulcrum for history. It expresses at the definitive central moment the principles of God's justice and victory manifested in creation, fall, redemption, and consummation. These principles are also expressed in the particulars of one moment, the moment where Israel in Amos's time stands in relation to enemy nations around her.

B.3.c.(3).(b).((3)).((b)) Types Pointing to the Church

Does Amos 1:3 point forward to the church as well as to Christ?

The principle of suffering and vindication has preeminent embodiment in Christ, but it also applies subordinately to those who are in Christ. We who place our hope in Christ are united to him and have become partakers in Israel. As such, we may expect to suffer, both corporately as a church and individually as believers, while waiting for vindication. God is a righteous judge, as demonstrated in Christ.

B.3.c.(3).(c) Preparation

How does Amos 1:3 function as part of the timeline preparing for the coming of Christ?

The transgressions and punishments mount up through time in the Old Testament. The people ask, "How long?" until the Messiah comes. In the meantime, Christ as the divine Son mediates patience and ministers compassionately in sustaining his people amid suffering and oppression, including the Syrian oppression. Judgment in history, including judgments against Syria (Amos 1:4–5), come from the Father, the Son, and the Spirit, paving a long and painful path forward to climactic judgment. The same justice of God that we see manifested in the cross was in measure given beforehand in judgment on Syria, and even in judgment on Israel herself.

C. Application

To what applications does Amos 1:3 naturally lead?

Applications can move in the direction of perseverance under suffering, as we compare ourselves with the sufferings of Old Testament Israel and the sufferings of Christ (Phil. 3:10; see John 15:20–21). God is a God of justice and will act on our behalf (Luke 18:1–8; Rom. 12:18–21). Applications can also move in the direction of taking seriously God's judgments against sin, including the sins of his own people.

Conclusion

We may conclude where we began, with the great commandment, to "love the Lord your God with all your heart and with all your soul and with all your mind" (Matt. 22:37). The inclusion of "your mind" encourages us to think and think again about what we are reading in the Bible, to engage in serious study, and to use perspectives such as we have developed in this book. Intellectual gifts are valuable for the body of Christ, and when used in a godly way they promote not only the sanctification of the individual but the growth and health of the body of Christ.

At the same time, the emphasis on love implies not only loving God but loving our neighbor and loving fellow Christians: "And this commandment we have from him: whoever loves God must also love his brother" (1 John 4:21). If we love, we will also respect every member of the body of Christ. The Lord may give spiritual insights to people who have not traveled through explicit steps of reasoning, but who use their knowledge of Scripture as a whole as the tacit background for their reading. The Holy Spirit teaches these people.

Loving the Lord with our minds means continuing to study and to thirst for a deeper knowledge of God and his word. It means applying ourselves intellectually. At the same time, we know that loving is more than having facts. The commandment challenges us to engage our hearts with our minds, and to grow as whole people into the image of Christ. We grow partly through the growth of the body of Christ as a whole (Eph. 4:11–16). The challenge is multidimensional.

Since Christ reigns at the right hand of God, may he continue to supply this growth in our lives, according to his power and wisdom:

. . . the working of his great might that he worked in Christ when he raised him from the dead and seated him at his right hand in the heavenly places, far above all rule and authority and power and dominion, and above every name that is named, not only in this age but also in the one to come. And he put all things under his feet and gave him as head over all things *to the church*, which is his body, the fullness of him who fills all in all. (Eph. 1:19–23)

APPENDICES

Appendix A

Redeeming How We Interpret

In this book we are proposing an approach that differs from the mainstream of biblical scholarship and even from a good deal of evangelical scholarship. We are radically recasting how we understand the process of interpreting texts, and how we go about it. For the sake of brevity and clarity, this book provides an outline, a handbook. Other books fill in details and provide fuller reasons.[1]

Why does interpretation need recasting? God needs to work in us, in the power of Christ through the Holy Spirit, to redeem how we interpret texts, and especially how we interpret the Bible.

The Spiritual Antithesis

The Bible indicates that we need the Holy Spirit in order to understand rightly:

> . . . no one comprehends the thoughts of God except the Spirit of God. Now we have received not the spirit of the world, but the Spirit who is from God, that we might understand the things freely given us by God. . . .

---

[1] For similar concerns, see Graeme Goldsworthy, *Gospel-Centered Hermeneutics: Foundations and Principles of Evangelical Biblical Interpretation* (Downers Grove, IL: InterVarsity Press, 2006); Vern S. Poythress, "God's Lordship in Interpretation," *Westminster Theological Journal* 50 (1988): 27–64; Poythress, "Christ the Only Savior of Interpretation," *Westminster Theological Journal* 50 (1988): 305–321; Poythress, *God-Centered Biblical Interpretation* (Phillipsburg, NJ: Presbyterian & Reformed, 1999). In a broader sense, nearly everything that I have written serves as background for the present book (see the bibliography).

The natural person does not accept the things of the Spirit of God, for they are folly to him, and he is not able to understand them because they are spiritually discerned. The spiritual person judges all things, but is himself to be judged by no one. "For who has understood the mind of the Lord so as to instruct him?" But we have the mind of Christ. (1 Cor. 2:11–12, 14–16)

This passage talks about "the things freely given us by God" (v. 12) and "the things of the Spirit of God" (v. 14). Given the preceding context in 1 Corinthians 1 about the foolishness of the gospel, these "things" consist in the truths of the gospel, which believers receive through the Holy Spirit. Unbelievers, by contrast, consider the gospel "folly." A sharp contrast or *antithesis* exists between believers and unbelievers in their understanding.[2] Believers have come to understand, because they have the Holy Spirit dwelling in them. Unbelievers do not understand, because they do not have the Holy Spirit.

When the passage speaks about "the spiritual person," it does not mean someone who is especially advanced or sanctified in Christian living; nor does it have in mind a person who keeps his head in the clouds and seems to be untouched by ordinary events. "The spiritual person" has the Holy Spirit dwelling in him—he is "spiritual" because of the *Holy Spirit*'s presence and work. He has been born again by the work of the Spirit as described in John 3:1–8. Conversely, "the natural person" does not have the Holy Spirit dwelling in him but remains in a fallen state of rebellion against God. He has not been born again.

Some interpreters have drawn the conclusion that the antithesis between believers and unbelievers arises only with respect to a narrow area of "spiritual" knowledge. According to this viewpoint, unbelievers can indeed understand ordinary things, such as 2 + 2 = 4 or the life of Napoleon, but they are unable to accept or understand *spiritual* things.

First Corinthians 1–2 does show that the antithesis comes to a climax when people accept or do not accept the gospel. But the principle of antithesis is broader. The early part of the key passage in 1 Corinthians 2:11–16 talks about the Holy Spirit comprehending the thoughts

---

[2] On antithesis, see Cornelius Van Til, *The Defense of the Faith*, ed. K. Scott Oliphint, 4th ed. (Phillipsburg, NJ: Presbyterian & Reformed, 2008).

of God (v. 11). All truth resides first of all in God's mind. Whatever we know, we know in communion with him. Even "ordinary" truths like 2 + 2 = 4 are truths that we know because God has given us knowledge (Job 32:8; Ps. 94:10). When unbelievers rebel against God, they disrupt their entire relationship with God. They suppress the fact that God has given them the knowledge that 2 + 2 = 4. In suppressing God's role and suppressing the origin of truth in God, they distort the truth. They do not know anything at all in the way that they ought to.

So how do they know that 2 + 2 = 4? God is gracious to them, even though they do not deserve it. He makes himself known (Rom. 1:18–25) and he makes the truth known. Theologians have called this graciousness of God *common grace*—"common" because it comes to unbelievers, in distinction from the special grace of God that saves believers. It is "grace" because neither believers nor unbelievers deserve it.[3]

Thus, common grace explains how unbelievers know many truths. But they do not know in the way that they ought to know, because they evade communion with God, who is the source of truth and the fountain of truth.

Abraham Kuyper understood the same principle by reflecting on the lordship of Christ:

> No single piece of our mental world is to be hermetically sealed off from the rest, and there is not a square inch in the whole domain of our human existence over which Christ, who is Sovereign over *all*, does not cry: "Mine!"[4]

Accordingly, Kuyper called Christian believers to rethink every area of life on the basis of their distinctively Christian understanding of God and their relation to him. His book *Lectures on Calvinism* has chapters on the implications for politics, science, and art; and further chapters could have been added with respect to other subjects.[5]

---

[3] Vern S. Poythress, *Redeeming Philosophy: A God-Centered Approach to the Big Questions* (Wheaton, IL: Crossway, 2014), chapter 2.

[4] Abraham Kuyper, "Sphere Sovereignty," in *Abraham Kuyper: A Centennial Reader*, ed. James D. Bratt (Grand Rapids, MI: Eerdmans; Carlisle, PA: Paternoster, 1998), 488. The quote was originally part of Kuyper's speech at the inauguration of the Free University of Amsterdam in 1880. Kuyper's declaration about Christ's lordship can be seen as exemplifying the biblical theme of exclusive loyalty to God: Exodus 20:3; 1 Kings 18:21.

[5] Abraham Kuyper, *Lectures on Calvinism: Six Lectures Delivered at Princeton University Under Auspices of the L. P. Stone Foundation* (Grand Rapids, MI: Eerdmans, 1931); see also Cornelius Van Til, *Essays on Christian Education* (Phillipsburg, NJ: Presbyterian & Reformed, 1979).

Could he have added a chapter on interpretation? Yes. His principle applies universally, because Christ rules as Lord universally (Matt. 28:18; Eph. 1:21). Our procedures, goals, and rules for interpreting texts must conform to Christ's lordship. Kuyper's implications hold true especially for interpreting the Bible, because of its key status as the word of God. But they apply also in interpreting any text whatsoever. No area of study or reflection is religiously neutral; the antithesis affects them all. Christ rules as Lord over all.

Then why do many people, including Christian believers, think that no reform is needed in the arena of textual interpretation? They see many truths and attractive methods in the ways in which the world approaches the task of interpretation. They look with admiration, because by common grace God has given unbelievers many insights. But common grace always occurs amid a deeper antithesis. We ought not to accept the ideas of unbelievers uncritically, as if they were religiously neutral, as if belief or unbelief made no difference—as if God and his presence made no difference.

Effective and thorough appropriation of insights from common grace actually depends on the recognition of antithesis:

> Their minds [the minds of unbelievers], in spite of having spurned the knowledge of the only wise God, accomplish remarkable feats. To the extent that they make intellectual progress, however, they do so only on "borrowed capital," that is, by taking advantage of the very truths that contradict their most basic commitments. Van Til's approach, then, while radically antithetical, does not at all lead to contempt for human accomplishments but makes possible our appreciation of them.[6]

We should indeed appropriate all the insights that we find among unbelievers. But we ought not to appropriate them uncritically. We must assess the distortions that have crept in because of unbelief.

---

[6] Moisés Silva, "The Case for Calvinistic Hermeneutics," in Walter C. Kaiser, Jr., and Moisés Silva, *An Introduction to Biblical Hermeneutics: The Search for Meaning*, rev. and expanded ed. (Grand Rapids, MI: Zondervan, 2007), 295–318 [301]; reprinted with minor changes in *Revelation and Reason: New Essays in Reformed Apologetics*, ed. K. Scott Oliphint and Lane G. Tipton (Phillipsburg, NJ: Presbyterian & Reformed, 2007), 74–94 [81].

Interpretation in the Twentieth and Twenty-First Centuries

Concern grows when we look at the discussions of hermeneutics (principles for interpretation) from the Enlightenment onward. The Enlightenment championed the use of *reason*. And reason is a gift from God (by common grace, again). But the Enlightenment twisted this good gift into *rationalism*, which meant making human reason into a final arbiter. It made reason into a god. At one point in the French Revolution, officials conducted a ceremony in which Reason (represented by a well-known French actress) was enthroned as a goddess in the Notre Dame Cathedral in Paris. That ceremony symbolized the exaltation of human reason as an ultimate arbiter. Or, looking at it another way, we could say that the Enlightenment wanted to allow each of us to be his own god, to be autonomous.

The nineteenth century saw the triumph of antisupernaturalistic historical-critical method among scholars in the mainstream of biblical interpretation.[7] Orthodox scholars as well as orthodox believers as a whole became more and more a cultural backwater. They clung to belief in supernatural miracles and the supernatural origin of the Bible. But mainstream biblical scholars and mainstream intellectuals in the secular arena paid less and less attention to them, except to criticize their backwardness.

The last half of the twentieth (and early twenty-first) century has seen enormous growth in discussions of hermeneutics in the Western world. Secular concerns have driven the growth. With few exceptions, Bible believers have not contributed creatively. Rather, they have either criticized and rejected the world or gradually appropriated pieces out of the world.

At least in the English-speaking world, fundamentalists and evangelicals have become the main groups who believe in the decisiveness of being born again. If they believe in new birth, do they also believe that it has intellectual effects? Do they take seriously the antithesis that we described above? Do they see the antithesis at work in biblical studies?

Post-Enlightenment developments in hermeneutics represent a

---

[7] Vern S. Poythress, *Inerrancy and Worldview: Answering Modern Challenges to the Bible* (Wheaton, IL: Crossway, 2012), chapters 5–6. A short sketch of the history can be found in Louis Berkhof, *Principles of Biblical Interpretation: (Sacred Hermeneutics)* (Grand Rapids, MI: Baker, 1950), 31–39. The story is told in greater detail by many other works, from various points of view.

temptation to evangelical biblical scholars: either use the developments or be left behind. No intellectual wants to be left behind. Believers with intellectual gifts understand that they must use their gifts, and if they use them it seems to follow that they too must "keep up." They find it difficult, even impossible, to keep up with the volume of scholarly writing even within their own specialty. Moreover, as biblical specialists they may not care to think about religious presuppositions, influences of worldviews, assumptions behind current methods, and spiritual antithesis. These matters belong to other specialties—perhaps to apologetics or to systematic theology or to philosophy.

Evangelical biblical scholars may still reject scholarly arguments that depend on blatant antisupernaturalism, or that obviously contradict central elements of the gospel, but they may not ask hard questions about the operation of antithesis all the way across their field of study. Moisés Silva warns,

> Calvin's approach [of appropriating benefits of common grace] must be distinguished from that of many evangelical scholars who make free use of critical methods that have been developed without consideration of (sometimes in opposition to) biblical faith. The issue here is not whether such methods should be used, but whether it is appropriate to use them without careful reflection on their theological implications. To put it differently, one seldom sees an attempt to integrate the principles of critical scholarship with the distinctives of evangelical thought. The impression one usually gets is that, unless a specific conclusion of scholarship explicitly contradicts a tenet of "conservative" theology, we should freely appropriate the work of "liberal" critics.
>
> This attitude, however, can only undermine the integrity of evangelicalism. For one thing, the very coherence of the evangelical faith is likely to be crippled as potentially incompatible elements are adopted without critical evaluation. In addition, the approach does not sit well with nonevangelical scholars, who argue, with some justification, that the credibility of conservative thinking becomes suspect. In short, the desire to gain intellectual respectability backfires.[8]

---

[8] Silva, "Case for Calvinistic Hermeneutics," 299 (in Oliphint and Tipton, *Revelation and Reason*, 79).

In accepting uncritically the methods of mainstream scholarship, evangelical scholars ignore the antithesis in heart commitments and the antithesis in presuppositions.

Silva issued his warning in 1994,[9] and repeated it in another form in his presidential address to the Evangelical Theological Society in 1997.[10] Have we improved since then? Perhaps some people have taken Silva's concern to heart. But I suspect that in some respects the situation has deteriorated since 1997 rather than improved.

We now see people with evangelical roots becoming restless about the idea of inerrancy, and either abandoning it or redefining it.[11] Silva's concern speaks to their situation. He wanted evangelicals to avoid either uncritically rejecting mainstream biblical scholarship because of its roots, or uncritically accepting it because of its plausibility, or picking and choosing items of scholarship that happen to support conservative positions. Rather, we need to inspect presuppositions, reckoning with antithesis and common grace. This reckoning gets neglected when scholars simply go about "business as usual" and no longer ask deeper questions about the foundations for their field and its procedures. Or even if they ask the deep questions, they ask without seeing how the teaching of the Bible informs the answers.

Motives

Evangelical scholars also need to reckon with motives. We have spoken of the antithesis between believers and unbelievers. But believers themselves are not free from sins, including intellectual sins. Sins contaminate the mind and bias our study of Scripture. Bias appears in an obvious way when we resist the teaching of Scripture, or twist its teaching in favor of our pet ideas, or make our own behavior an exception to biblical ethical principles. But subtler forms of sin also creep in. Perhaps we desire acceptance or at least recognition by the mainstream of scholarship. Or perhaps we desire admiration from our own "crowd" for our strong stance *against* the mainstream. Or perhaps as teachers

[9] Moisés Silva, "The Case for Calvinistic Hermeneutics," in Walter C. Kaiser, Jr., and Moisés Silva, *An Introduction to Biblical Hermeneutics: The Search for Meaning* (Grand Rapids, MI: Zondervan, 1994), 255. Earlier quotes have come from the second, expanded edition of this work.
[10] Moisés Silva, "'Can Two Walk Together Unless They Be Agreed?' Evangelical Theology and Biblical Scholarship," *Journal of the Evangelical Theological Society* 41 (1998): 3–16.
[11] Poythress, *Inerrancy and Worldview*, 13–14.

we love to have students hanging on our words. Pride comes in many forms, and it does not easily disappear in the course of sanctification.

I want to turn attention to still another kind of temptation, a temptation that may increase with scholarly specialization. Many of the famous biblical commentators up until the time of the Reformation served as preachers and pastors. They may have had good knowledge of languages and history, measured by the standards of their day, but they were also worshiping the Lord and serving the church in their studies, and their studies led to preaching sermons as well as writing commentaries that would serve the people of God. Today, biblical scholars may preach occasionally, but specialization has had its effect, and most biblical scholars identify with the guild of scholarly specialists in the Bible. Specialization promises deeper penetration of a certain kind. But only of a certain kind. Do we know God more intimately? Not necessarily.

Desire for Mastery

Moreover, the triumphs of modern science, together with the growth of academia, tempt intellectuals to follow what Herman Dooyeweerd calls "the science ideal," the ideal of mastering the world and mastering knowledge in a particular sphere. The historical-critical method, as understood by the mainstream, was supposed to promote mastery of the biblical text and the associated history. Mastery would allegedly come by using reason. The historical-critical method promoted "objectivity," which was supposed to be independent of religious dogma. Religiously speaking, this desire for mastery has an attractive side, because it represents a distorted form of the cultural mandate to exercise "dominion" (Gen. 1:26, 28). Unfortunately, it also has an idolatrous side, because it aspires to be like God in its mastery. The method functions in service of would-be autonomous reason.

Many evangelical scholars would say that they reject the antisupernaturalist bias in the historical-critical method. But do they also reject its desire for mastery through religiously neutral reason? Or do they rather engage in the same study, with the same "ground rules" of neutrality, in the hope of convincing the skeptics?

The word *method* in the expression *historical-critical method* already conceals danger. What does the word mean? The principle of antithesis suggests that it has at least two meanings, if not more. In one meaning we serve God and in another we do not: we serve autonomy, the desire to be master. In the second meaning, which has in fact crept into uses of the historical-critical method, "method" in hermeneutics parallels method in science. By sticking with an objectively defined set of procedures, we exclude all personal bias, including religious and dogmatic bias, in order to arrive at the facts and arrive at the truth. Method implies control. If all goes well, over time it means increasing control, leading to mastery. We subdue the text under our gaze, like a butterfly pinned to an entomological display case, with its genus and species name printed underneath. And if the information currently available does not lead to a single fixed and well-established conclusion, then objectivity supposedly means that we assign probabilities to a spectrum of options. The butterfly could be this species or that. We do not yet know, but we know that it belongs to some species or other, and knowledge means this kind of determination.

For method to function with this kind of goal, it has to have certain strictures. Method requires that personal biases have no intrinsic relation to the subject matter, and then that the biases be set aside for the sake of objectivity. If we study the text, we must isolate the study from our personal involvement and our spiritual life and our evaluation of the text's claims. We must also isolate it from God, since God is unmasterable.

Physical scientists ideally perform an experiment on a physically isolated system, so that they can assure themselves that the effects that they see belong to the system in question, rather than being produced by light or sound or vibration from the environment. Some people think that this method extends by analogy to biblical studies. Biblical interpreters, like scientists, must endeavor to isolate a text from world history and from the multitude of third- and fourth-degree associations in meaning and grammar generated by the full multidimensional complexity of actual language use. The immediate cultural and historical and linguistic environments of a text come into play, of course, but the traditional goal is to determine *the meaning* of a word or a sentence or a paragraph. This goal includes an assumption about the isolatability of meaning, because only through a kind of isolation can we achieve "the meaning" with a kind of fixity equivalent to pinning the butter-fly to the display case. If postmodernism convinces some scholars that such a meaning does not exist or is permanently inaccessible, scholars can set as a goal the contemplation of multiple meanings—the play of meanings, indefinitely prolonging itself. I believe that both the modern-ist isolation of meaning and the postmodernist play of meanings are distortions.

Or we engage in historical study. We search to find out the history of the text, how it evolved from its past. The goal is to describe a determi-nate path, or if the available information proves insufficient, to describe the probabilities associated with multiple possible paths. Or, if we lis-ten to postmodernism, we play with multiple paths and rejoice in the indeterminacy. Once again, we have involved ourselves in distortions arising from assumptions about the isolatability or nonisolatability of one piece of history.

It is vanity. And we as evangelical biblical scholars have appropri-ated too much of it.

Evaluation

I have taught New Testament for more than thirty-nine years at West-minster Theological Seminary. Over the course of my career, I have tried to analyze not only my own motives but also the assumptions and presuppositions of *methods* typically in use for biblical interpreta-tion. I have grown increasingly discontent. Within the typical methods that are considered common to the "guild" of biblical scholarship, the motives are wrong, the goal is wrong, and the specific techniques we use under the guidance of motives and goal fundamentally distort the nature of the Bible.

So I will say it boldly: I am giving up on unrevised "methods." Silva spoke of the need to inspect presuppositions underlying the methods. I stand close to him. But I am willing to use more radical language. I am not talking about revising these "methods," to make them harmonize with the nature of God and God's world. I am talking about overthrow-ing them and rebuilding from the ground up. Let us reckon with the antithesis and, as best we can, drive the sword of the Spirit, which is the word of God, and which embodies the principle of antithesis, right through the middle of the methods. I believe in common grace. I appreciate Silva's point. But I think we need to engage in recasting the entire program of biblical interpretation.

We cannot do it without recasting how we interpret texts in general (that is, texts other than the Bible). And we cannot do that latter task thoroughly without recasting as well academic disciplines that impinge on interpretation: metaphysics,[12] epistemology,[13] ethics,[14] logic,[15] theory of language (including linguistics),[16] sociology and social anthropology,[17] philosophy of history and historiography,[18] psychology,[19] and literary criticism.[20] We should add natural science[21] to the list as well, since natural science as an admirable example of achievement (or, in the eyes of some, an example to be avoided) has an atmospheric influence on other disciplines, and in addition has a dominant influence on what modern interpreters think they can believe when they read texts belonging to prescientific cultures. It is a formidable list, and a formidable challenge to rethink foundations. But faithfulness to God requires it.

Some evangelical biblical scholars may not want to talk about using "the historical-critical method" or its tools in a positive way. We might talk instead about "grammatical-historical method." Maybe this expression denotes historical-critical method, cleansed of its antisupernaturalist biases. Yes, I think we need to be aware of antisupernaturalist biases. But we also need to become aware of mistaken presuppositions less obvious and more difficult to uproot—like the idea of a method as a way to master meaning, and the idea that a method can easily stand free from the presuppositional influences of modern life and the academic disciplines listed above.

12 Poythress, *Redeeming Philosophy*.
13 John M. Frame, *The Doctrine of the Knowledge of God* (Phillipsburg, NJ: Presbyterian & Reformed, 1987).
14 John M. Frame, *The Doctrine of the Christian Life* (Phillipsburg, NJ: Presbyterian & Reformed, 2008).
15 Vern S. Poythress, *Logic: A God-Centered Approach to the Foundation of Western Thought* (Wheaton, IL: Crossway, 2013).
16 Vern S. Poythress, *In the Beginning Was the Word: Language—A God-Centered Approach* (Wheaton, IL: Crossway, 2009).
17 Vern S. Poythress, *Redeeming Sociology: A God-Centered Approach* (Wheaton, IL: Crossway, 2011).
18 Poythress, *Inerrancy and Worldview*, chapters 5–6.
19 Ibid., chapters 19–21.
20 Vern S. Poythress, "A Framework for Discourse Analysis: The Components of a Discourse, from a Tagmemic Viewpoint," *Semiotica* 38-3/4 (1982): 277–298, http://www.frame-poythress.org/wp-content/uploads/2012/08/semi.1982.38.3-4.277.pdf, DOI: 10.1515/semi.1982.38.3-4.277, accessed December 29, 2012; Poythress, *In the Beginning Was the Word*, chapters 20–29.
21 Vern S. Poythress, *Redeeming Science: A God-Centered Approach* (Wheaton, IL: Crossway, 2006).

So what am I proposing positively? It takes a while to say, because I question things that many biblical scholars take for granted. I am not advocating "grammatical-historical method" in anything like the usual sense.[22] For one thing, "grammatical-historical method" is not a single object. The label papers over differences. The label tempts us as biblical scholars to fall into the attitude of "business as usual." As scholars, we have been raised on grammatical-historical method as our bread and butter. Precisely because of our unthinking devotion to it, it is in danger of becoming a golden calf. And if it is a golden calf, which protects our little idolatries of mastery and of neutral, presuppositionless method, let it be slaughtered with the sword of the Spirit. We need to reject the ideal of mastery, the ideal of mastering the meaning of each text in isolation, the ideal of mastering cultural setting, and the ideal of mastering a piece of history, isolated so that it is small enough to digest.

So let us love God and submit to him. And if we do, we will find that any grain of truth in worldly "methods" will find a place as a perspective, that is, a moment of focus on one aspect of the infinity of God in his communication to us. We will find insights that harmonize with God's own purposes for his communication and for us, rather than falling into a pattern of truncating the fullness of communication in order to isolate a piece.

The Relevance of Perspectives

I am a multiperspectivalist.[23] Decades ago, I started down the road of using multiple perspectives partly because it was heuristically useful. But along the way I have become more aware that finiteness always involves perspectives. And God's own infinitude also involves the incomprehensible triad of perspectives of the three persons of the Trinity. Because of sin, we have a pervasive temptation to absolutize some method or methods. We are tempted to pretend that some methods will provide a final stability and a platform for mastery in research, rather

---

[22] In the early part of my career, I wrote some pieces that adopted the expression "grammatical-historical interpretation" without offering as many cautions. For the benefit of readers who wonder, let me say that without radically changing the main point of such pieces, I would today rewrite things in order to note dangers more clearly.

[23] Vern S. Poythress, *Symphonic Theology; The Validity of Multiple Perspectives in Theology* (reprint; Phillipsburg, NJ: Presbyterian & Reformed, 2001).

than admit that we as finite beings can perfectly stabilize and master neither our own minds nor our methods nor our language nor what we perceive to be our knowledge of the world. The only absolute rock of stability is God himself, in his Trinitarian character. He gives us access to his stability through Scripture. By contrast, the whole of modern scholarship gets subtly corrupted by a false, utopian ideal of stable, scientific, neutral, "objective" research using methods whose perspectival character is concealed for the sake of human exaltation.[24]

And, in my mind, that means that the *whole* of scholarship has to be recast. In reality, there are no "methods," in the sense that scholarship defined in the modernist, Enlightenment mode thinks of them. There is only one God, and many human beings in their marvelous and unfathomable diversity. Human beings serve God with the gifts that he himself has given in the body of Christ. And then there are also marvelously created human beings still in rebellion against God, casting up insights and blessings in spite of themselves, blaspheming God right in the midst of displaying God's glory.

I have tried to underscore this point about lack of "methods" by writing this book in an overtly perspectival fashion. Each chapter offers perspectives on the whole. There is nothing here except perspectives. There is no "method" in a modernist sense, not in any chapter or any subsection of any chapter. No perspective *is* the whole, nor does any one perspective offer us unmediated access to the rock of stability that is God himself. Each perspective exists in perspectival relation to all the others. The perspectives are coinherent, with a coinherence derivative from the incomprehensible coinherence of the persons of the Trinity.

Any one perspective gives access to the truth. Each of the three persons of the Trinity knows all the truth of God. Moreover, human persons have access to the truth. Because God reveals himself to human beings, they have access to the truth as they use one perspective or many. The Bible by its teaching contradicts all forms of relativism. But by teaching the distinction between Creator and creature, and by

---

[24] Or some inhabitants of the universities, with postmodernist leanings, reject "objectivity" in favor of the subjectivity of playing with multiple options. The one thing they still have in common with the ideal of modernist objectivity is the love of autonomy: they think that, no matter what, you should not subject yourself to specific divine claims, for that would lead to oppressive tyranny and the destruction of human nature at the deepest level.

teaching the doctrine of the Trinity, the Bible also teaches that human knowledge of the truth always involves mystery.

What kind of scholarship can put up with this kind of mystery and unmasterability? Not modernism. Not postmodernism either, because postmodernism rejects the reality of God's clear revelation just as vigorously as modernism does. In contrast to both of these stances, the infinite God provides real knowledge to finite human beings. By the grace of God in Christ through the Spirit, each perspective provides mediated access to the perfect stability of the knowledge of God in Christ.

Appendix B

Secular Views of Meaning

Many secular views of meaning appear on the market nowadays. Within a short compass we cannot consider all of them. But we may usefully look at a few, in order to appreciate the difference between secular views and an approach that studies Scripture in the presence of God. Even with the few that we consider, we must simplify and suggest only a sketch of what might result from a thorough interaction.

In our interaction and evaluation, we use as background assumptions the principle of antithesis and the principle of common grace (see appendix A). According to the principle of antithesis, every person is serving either Christ or some other master (Luke 16:13). Since Christ is Lord of all of life, a person's fundamental commitment has pervasive effects—some obvious and some subtle. We must critically sift the products of secular thinking. Yes, we must even sift the products of Christian thinking, because all Christians on earth suffer from the contaminating influence of remaining sins.

The principle of common grace says that God blesses non-Christians with insights. As a result, much can be learned from non-Christian sources.

The interaction of the two principles, antithesis and common grace, means that analysis is challenging and delicate. It would be an immense labor to conduct a thorough analysis of even one thinker with respect to even one subject he addresses. Given this complexity, in this and the following appendices we must content ourselves with mere sketches.

We may roughly classify secular views of meaning in terms of their foci on author, text, or reader. Some secular views locate meaning primarily or exclusively in the intention of the author. Other views locate meaning in the text, and still others in readers or in the larger situation surrounding readers. We may begin with the third type, views that focus on the reader. We consider first the views of Hans Georg Gadamer and then the views of Stanley Fish.[1]

Hans Georg Gadamer

Hans Georg Gadamer chooses to focus his reflections on *understanding* rather than on *meaning*.[2] He offers a form of reader orientation, since understanding or attempts at understanding take place among readers. Gadamer says that he is setting himself to describe what is the case rather than what *ought* to be the case. Others may argue about what ought to be the proper goal of interpretation, and what ought to be the methods and paths that readers take to try to arrive at the goal. Gadamer will focus not on these arguments but on what actually takes place among readers, both the good and the bad.

Understanding, Gadamer observes, is a process affected not only by the text and the information that readers have about the author of the text, but by presuppositions or prejudices or a whole spectrum of assumptions about life and truth that readers may bring to the text. Their previous assumptions may serve at times to block understanding as well as to aid it. Readers aware of a previous history of interpretation of the text are also affected by that history. The history helps orient the picture that they already have of what the text says and the questions that they bring to the text. Readers in any one period and culture contribute in their turn to the tradition of interpretation, and this tradition passes to the next generation of readers.

Gadamer also observes that readers themselves can change as they receive influence and ideas from a text. They do not necessarily stay the

---

[1] For a brief critique of deconstruction as still another current approach to meaning, see Vern S. Poythress, *In the Beginning Was the Word: Language—A God-Centered Approach* (Wheaton, IL: Crossway, 2009), appendix I.
[2] Hans-Georg Gadamer, *Truth and Method* (New York: Crossroad, 1989).

same. They may change their lives by adopting ideas or views of life that they receive from a text. Or they may even change in a kind of reverse direction in reaction to a text with which they violently disagree.

Gadamer's observations contain some positive insights about changes in readers. Jesus says, "You must be born again" (John 3:7). The Holy Spirit works a radical change to bring people to new birth. The Holy Spirit is the agent at work, but 1 Peter 1 indicates that the word of God has a role: "you have been born again, not of perishable seed but of imperishable, through the living and abiding *word of God*" (1 Pet. 1:23). The reader of Scripture changes *radically* when the Holy Spirit works regeneration. Subsequently, changes of a less radical kind continue to take place as the word of God serves as an instrument for sanctification:

Sanctify them in the truth; *your word* is truth." (John 17:17)

The law of the LORD is perfect,
    reviving the soul;
the testimony of the LORD is sure,
    making wise the simple. (Ps. 19:7)

Through your precepts I get understanding;
    therefore I hate every false way. (Ps. 119:104)

We are not neutral scientific observers of Scripture. Moreover, assumptions and commitments that we already have affect whether we are open or closed to the teaching of Scripture. Isaiah 6:9–10 talks about the blind eyes and deaf ears of those who refuse to listen.

So Gadamer provides a useful reminder of influences that affect readers. His approach has affinities to what we have called *impact*, changes effected by reading. However, because he focuses on what is the case rather than what ought to be the case, many people have been disappointed by his reflections. They want an answer about how to distinguish between good and bad interpretation, responsible and irresponsible interpretation. Does Gadamer provide norms by which we may discriminate? The answer is basically no. That is not his purpose. But the result is that his analysis sounds relativistic. And indeed it becomes relativistic if a person thinks of it as the whole story. A person can use it as an excuse to lapse into an attitude of "Every reader for himself." There are no boundaries. I think this use of Gadamer is something of a misuse, because it treats Gadamer's reflections as if they were the whole answer, rather than a limited focus. But, be that as it may, the idea of readers' freedom to treat the text as they wish has become a popular one. If meaning boils down only to whatever is in a reader's mind, we do have a thoroughly relativistic view of interpretation.

Stanley Fish

Stanley Fish represents a second reader-oriented approach to meaning.[3] Briefly, Fish says that readers create meaning from texts. There is no meaning in a text, but only in the reader. And the meaning that the reader creates depends on the group to which he belongs. A group of readers brings a reading strategy to the text, and the reading strategy creates a meaning common to the group. Fish assures people that this does not mean that anything goes with interpretation, because any one group has standards for how one approaches texts.

Fish, like Gadamer, offers some positive insights. The focus on the group is useful, because groups do indeed have an influence on what their members see in texts. We may think, for instance, of the way in which, at the time of the Reformation, Roman Catholic tradition tended to control many readers' perceptions of what the biblical text meant. The same applies in principle even to Protestant groups. Tradition is present when leaders from one generation teach the next generation. The next generation comes to the Bible with assumptions about what it means. And they may have good and useful assumptions, if the teaching of the preceding generation has been good. Tradition can be a help as well as a hindrance. The Reformers protested, not against the mere presence of tradition, but against the way in which the Roman Catholic defenders of tradition obscured the meaning of Scripture by appeal to tradition.

But Fish's approach has an obvious deficiency. Taken by itself, it does not have a way of judging one group's tradition to be superior to another group's tradition. The result is relativism, if we affirm in

---

[3] Stanley Fish, *Is There a Text in This Class?: The Authority of Interpretive Communities* (Cambridge, MA: Harvard University Press, 1980).

democratic fashion the equal validity of all groups. Or it leads to oppression, if one group tries not only to claim that it is right and others are wrong, but also to use power to crush opposing groups. If God does not exist, or if God is absent, there is no political solution to relativism on the one hand and oppression on the other. The Reformers claimed—rightly, I believe—that Scripture is clear and God is present, speaking in Scripture, to guide his people into the truth (John 16:13). The presence of God in the power of the Holy Spirit provides an answer that Fish's approach does not contemplate. Of course it is an answer that requires patience—ultimately a patience that waits for the day of judgment. Until then, God may require us to live with disagreements about Scripture. We try to persuade others, and they try to persuade us, in order that the body of Christ may grow (Eph. 4:12–16). We believe that God can work to soften opponents' hearts—and to soften our own! But we should avoid using state power to enforce conformity in belief.

Textual Meaning

A second approach to meaning locates meaning primarily in texts. One such approach came into prominence with "the New Criticism." William Wimsatt and Monroe Beardsley, advocates of the new criticism, wrote in their landmark book, *The Verbal Icon*,[4] that literary analysis should proceed to analyze texts more or less in isolation from their authors. They contributed a positive insight by warning against psychologizing. They observed that speculations about the psychology of the author, and speculative attempts to reconstruct the influences that led to the author's production of a text, should not replace analysis of the text. The meaning is found in what the text says, not in the history of its origin.

But their point of view also has deficiencies. A text detached from any author and detached from any historical environment is capable of sponsoring more than one meaning. As a simple example, consider a text message passed from one person to another, with only the message "Yes." The meaning, we could say, is affirmation. But affirmation of what? The full meaning can be recovered only when we know

---

[4] William K. Wimsatt, Jr., and Monroe C. Beardsley, *The Verbal Icon: Studies in the Meaning of Poetry* (Lexington: University of Kentucky Press, 1954).

something about the environment—in this case, to what question the answer is responding. Literary texts, and especially self-standing poems, to which Wimsatt and Beardsley directed their focus, have often been framed and crafted by an author so that they are not highly dependent on special information about the author or the circumstances. In this respect, their mode of communication and their literary structure provide greater stability of meaning, loosening them a bit from ties with the immediate environment.

Alongside self-standing poems we may add legal documents and technical scientific documents. Both legal documents and technical scientific documents are often crafted so that they function well when viewed as anonymous. They achieve an impressive precision and stability in meaning. But how do they do it? Legal documents lean on a voluminous legal tradition, a tradition that has imparted special technical meanings to various legal terms. This tradition has accumulated standard ways of dealing with potential ambiguities that arise when judges and lawyers attempt to apply legal texts in dealing with real-life disputes. Even then, a clever lawyer may be able to find loopholes. And a judge with creative agenda may find clever ways of reinterpreting the law in order to make it go in a direction that he subjectively prefers.

Technical scientific documents depend on a massive surrounding tradition in science, and often they explicitly cite many other papers, which help to structure the environment in which the reader can understand the contribution and the thrust of the new document. Thus, legal and scientific documents do not have their meaning completely "inside" them, though superficially it might appear so.

In addition, even a text with carefully crafted internal stability can be radically changed in meaning by reading it as an ironic statement rather than a straightforward statement. Jorge Borges imagines a more subtle form of reframing of a text when he discusses what it would be like to find a text authored by Pierre Menard that was word for word the same as Miguel Cervantes's work *Don Quixote*.[5] Borges—or rather

---

[5] Jorge Borges, "Pierre Menard, Author of the *Quixote*," first published in Spanish in *Sur* (May 1939), now available online both in Spanish (http://www.literatura.us/borges/pierre.html, accessed December 24, 2012) and in English (http://www.coldbacon.com/writing/borges-quixote.html, accessed December 24, 2012). Borges adds layers of delight and playfulness by having his "reviewer" reveal that Pierre Menard left his work "unfinished." It "consists of the ninth and thirty-eighth chapters of the first part of *Don Quixote* and a fragment of chapter twenty-two."

the "voice" of the fictional reviewer that Borges creates to review Menard's "new" work—suggests, rightly I think, that its meaning would not be the same as the original.

When we apply Wimsatt and Beardsley's text-centered approach to the Bible, its result is not satisfactory. It clearly does matter to Christians that God is the divine author of the biblical text. Otherwise it would not have divine authority, and we would not receive it in the same way. Moreover, we interpret the meaning of the text against the background of what we know about God. We may make mistakes, because of defective knowledge of God. Nevertheless, the principle of taking God into account is not only valid but vital for doing full justice to what he says.

E. D. Hirsch

Finally, we consider the approach of E. D. Hirsch, who focuses on authorial intention.[6] Hirsch wants to avoid the relativism inherent in reader-centered approaches, and he is aware of the instabilities that arise when a text is detached from its author, as the New Criticism wants. He wants a stable goal for interpretation. And that goal is the meaning, which he further identifies as the intention of the author.

Many evangelical biblical scholars are attracted to his position, because it appears to offer the obvious alternative to relativism. I want to counsel us, "Not so fast." Just because Hirsch has avoided the deficiencies of major competing views, we should not naively assume that his view has avoided deficiencies of other kinds.

We need first to understand three refinements that Hirsch makes in giving further explanations of the nature of meaning.

First, Hirsch says that meaning is a *type*. (This meaning of the word *type* is quite distinct from the meaning with respect to types and antitypes in Scripture.) In Hirsch's terminology, a *type* is an abstract idea, which can be embodied in any number of *tokens*. The *tokens* are the many specific texts specifying the same meaning. The *type* is the one common meaning expressed by any one of the texts. For example, "Man is mortal" and "all human beings are subject to death" are two sentences that are tokens expressing the same type, namely the common

---

[6] E. D. Hirsch, Jr., *Validity in Interpretation* (New Haven, CT: Yale University Press, 1967); Hirsch, *The Aims of Interpretation* (Chicago: University of Chicago Press, 1976).

meaning, the assertion of human mortality. In a parallel manner, all occurrences of the letter *A* in print are tokens of the same type, namely the abstract or generic idea of the letter *A*. This distinction between type and token enables Hirsch to say that two interpreters who faithfully interpret a text, and expound its meaning in two different discourses, may both represent the same meaning. The meaning is common, though the two discourses as tokens of meaning are distinct.

Second, Hirsch distinguishes meaning from significance. Meaning is what the author intended. Significance is what the reader *does* with the meaning, by way of application. The reader draws out relationships between the meaning and other ideas, or between the meaning and his own life, as he appropriates the meaning for himself. Hirsch thinks that it is certainly legitimate for readers to explore significances, and that there are multiple significances, depending on the reader and depending on the particular thing to which the reader relates the meaning. There is only *one* meaning, but the one meaning has *many* significances, because the meaning has many relationships with many other ideas and many other persons.

Third, Hirsch indicates that he includes in authorial intention *unconscious* intention. Meaning includes not only intentions that an author consciously entertained, but also what he would include as valid implications of his conscious intentions and the expressions in his discourse. For example, suppose an inquirer wants to know about Romans 1:16, "it [the gospel] is the power of God for salvation to everyone who believes, to the Jew first and also to the Greek." The inquirer asks the apostle Paul, "Did you intend to include the Scythians as potential believers?" The apostle might answer, "Well, I was not consciously thinking about the Scythians in particular when I wrote that sentence, but I intended to include them along with all the rest of the Gentiles." Thus Paul intended to include them without necessarily having explicitly thought about them as a distinct group.

This kind of intention is a form of what Hirsch calls *unconscious intention*. Hirsch understands that authors always include more than they say explicitly, and more than they explicitly, consciously entertain. An interpreter would fall into a kind of unfruitful psychologizing if he included within meaning only those intentions that an author consciously had in mind. He would have left out a good deal that the author actually desired him to understand by way of implication. He would also be engaging in speculation, since it is impossible to tell from a text alone how much was conscious and explicit. When Paul was writing Romans 1:16, he may or may not have thought explicitly about the Scythians, the Lydians, the Cyrenians, the Ethiopians, or many other groups. There is no way to tell. And it is not necessary to know, because we can see from the text and its context that he intended to include all the subgroups among the Gentiles.

Insights and Difficulties

Hirsch's approach contains positive insights. Certainly the inclusion of unconscious intention represents an insight about how authors characteristically write texts, and how they expect readers to respond. The difficulty here is that the outer *boundaries* of "unconscious intention" are not transparently clear. Authors imply more than they say explicitly. But how much more? Do they include everything that they themselves believe, even if they did not set it down in the text? That would seem to be too expansive. But then are authors necessarily complete masters of what they imply?

We can also see both insights and difficulties in the two other clarifications of Hirsch's idea of meaning. Consider the idea of a type. This idea has an obvious connection with the insight that we can re-express a meaning by paraphrase. We can say the same thing, or at least roughly the same thing, using two different utterances. So do two paraphrases mean exactly the same thing? Maybe, and maybe not. We may sometimes be able to see that two paraphrases have in common many "core" elements of meaning, while differing in nuances. They differ in point of view, or tone, or emotional overtones, or more fine-grained connotations. So do they represent the "same" meaning or not? It depends on how fussy we are. And we may notice that many of the most penetrating interpretations of texts are not paraphrases that merely substitute equivalent expressions in various places. Rather, they dig beneath the surface and excavate significant and powerful implications. But were the implications unconsciously intended?

Hirsch seems to maintain that the author is the final arbiter for what implications are validly part of "the meaning." His recipe is, "Ask the author, if you have doubts." But an author may himself not know for sure. Suppose we imagine asking the apostle Paul whether all of what he says in Ephesians is part of the implications of what he wrote in Romans. In other words, is Ephesians part of the "unconscious intention" of Romans? The reply from the apostle might conceivably be,

> I believe that what I wrote in Ephesians is true, and I already believed it all when I wrote Romans. But I am not sure how much of Ephesians is actually implied by what I wrote earlier in Romans. I said some more things in Ephesians that I did not say explicitly in Romans. I am not sure whether some of these new things were already implied by the earlier writing in Romans.

A human author does not necessarily know in a precise way what are the "outer boundaries" of the implications of what he wrote.

Finally, consider the difference between meaning and significance. Again, we can appreciate a positive insight in Hirsch's distinction. The kind of meaning that we express with a close paraphrase is not the same as the kind of significance that a reader may find by an extended personal application. But is the distinction between meaning and significance a sharp one, as Hirsch's exposition seems to suggest? Do not authors *intend* that their works should be applied by readers? Do they not invite readers to see relationships between the text and other things, relationships that the authors may not have consciously intended and yet might welcome? And if so, are not the applications part of the intention, and thus part of the meaning?

The distinction between meaning and significance becomes particularly problematic when we consider the divine intention in a passage of Scripture. God intends that Scripture be applied. Not only so, but in his omniscience he foresees all possible applications. Those applications that he endorses are clearly part of his intention. But even those applications that distort the text represent divine judgments on the person who produces the distorted interpretation. So, in a broad sense, the distortions are also part of God's intention, though not a part of what he morally *approves*. Thus all application and all significance are part of the meaning. It is so because God's knowledge is unlimited.

Accordingly, we took the view earlier that meaning and application belong together, and that meaning and "import" belong together, as perspectives on one another. Hirsch has not really considered how a perspectival approach might be an alternative to his own.

Systematic Difficulties

Are these difficulties mere peccadilloes? It might seem so, but I think they are symptomatic of deeper difficulties. In trying to establish a theory of meaning and interpretation, Hirsch has not reckoned with the power and presence of God. Instead, he has avoided dealing with God, because he wants to have a theory of meaning that would be neutral among religious viewpoints. He wants a secular view of meaning. Consequently, he must tacitly have a secular view of language, a secular view of human nature, a secular view of authorship, and a secular view of the nature of communication.

After establishing his theory of meaning, Hirsch does consider at one point what it would mean to interpret a text like the Bible that claims to have a divine author. But all of this is too late. His view of divine authorship results in two meanings for the same text, based on two distinct intentionalities, namely the intention of the divine author and the intention of the human author. This result is of course fully consistent with his starting point, which attempts to ground the theory itself in a neutral arena.

The result is that divine intentionality is grafted on as an afterthought to a theory that is secular at the core. Within the context of this grafting, divine and human intentionality in the Bible do not function as perspectives on each other, through the mediation of Christ, but simply sit side by side. Divine intention never touches human intentionality, because the theory demands in principle that human intentionality retain an integrity. And this integrity, at bottom, is the integrity of a would-be autonomous human mind. Hirsch's model cannot deal with interpenetrating perspectives, because the model makes each meaning a monolith: each meaning is a type.

Hirsch's intentions may be good in some respects. And he may help us through the insights that we have already mentioned. But the essentially secular character of the theory as a whole does injustice to the presence of God in the whole world. No theory that eliminates God does justice to the reality of authors, meanings, intentions, language, and communication. To eliminate God is not to fall into a peccadillo, but to distort radically the nature of reality.

Let us be specific. If someone says that a human author controls meaning thoroughly, and draws precise lines in principle between unconscious intention and what is not within intention, he makes the author into a god who has godlike control. Human beings simply do not have this kind of control. They do not perfectly control either the language they use, or the process of choice in writing, or the depths of their unconscious, or their knowledge of implications. Only God has absolute control, and only God, not man, can serve as the final adjudicator as to whether interpretation is faithful. Hirsch's theory, taken as a secular theory, has a mistaken conception of human authorship, and it fails to reckon with the reality that any human author can only be an author by imitating the creativity of the divine author, by virtue of common or special grace received from God.

The theory also fails in its psychology of authorship because it pictures the author's mind as within his autonomous control, rather than in fellowship with God and other human beings, and subject to influence from angels and demons as well. In fact, human authors are conflicted. As human beings made in the image of God, they cannot escape the knowledge of God. As sinners, they do seek to escape God and make themselves autonomous. They do not write with one mind, a sound mind, but as spiritual schizophrenics. Human intention is not completely unified.

The theory also has difficulty with its theory of meaning as a type. A type that can be perfectly distinguished from its tokens is akin to a Platonic form or else an Aristotelian form, both of which are monolithic, impersonal abstractions. This view of meaning does not take into account the interpenetration of meaning and significance, or meaning, impact, and import. And I believe that it goes astray into an untenable metaphysics. The theory of type and token makes the type, as a unity, logically prior to and more fundamental than the tokens that express the unity through a diversity of discourse forms. This priority of unity over diversity is fundamentally at odds with a metaphysics based on the

Trinity, according to which unity and diversity are equally ultimate. We cannot enter into a full discussion here, but the underlying assumptions about unity and diversity need rethinking.[7]

A secular theory of meaning also needs a secular theory of language, a theory that views language in isolation from God and his presence. Such a view suppresses the revelation of the glory of God in language, which reflects the archetype of God's speech.[8]

In sum, an approach to biblical interpretation that has its starting point in a secular theory of meaning has already corrupted its starting point. We need to rethink the meaning of meanings, authors, language, and communication from a Christian point of view if we are to do justice to who God is. And this we must do, if we love him.

---

[7] Vern S. Poythress, *Redeeming Philosophy: A God-Centered Approach to the Big Questions* (Wheaton, IL: Crossway, 2014), chapter 6.
[8] Poythress, *In the Beginning Was the Word.*

Appendix C

Interpreting Human Texts

In this book we have devoted our attention to the question of how we interpret the Bible. We have not focused on how we should interpret noninspired human texts from noninspired human authors. Does our approach to the Bible have any implications for interpreting such human texts?

The Influence of Autonomy

The Enlightenment brought into prominence a desire that has been present ever since the fall of man into sin, namely the desire for autonomy. According to Enlightenment thinking, each person through the use of reason should be his own law and should judge according to the universal standards of reason, standards independent of all religious commitments. This desire implies among other things rational autonomy in interpreting texts. According to Enlightenment thinking, all texts whatsoever should be interpreted according to human reason. That principle implies excluding the revelation of God and the presence of God. Techniques that the Enlightenment developed for interpreting human texts are then applied to the Bible as merely another human text.

There is a grain of truth in this approach, since the Bible is fully human as well as fully divine. But the Enlightenment recipe results in suppressing the divine claims of the biblical text. That is to say, the divine authorship of the Bible is ignored. Moreover, the approach from the Enlightenment distorts its view of the human authors of Scripture as well. It tends to suppress the human authors' desire to speak in fellowship with God, empowered by the Spirit of God. As we have argued in chapter 10, the human authors in the Bible intend tacitly to affirm what God says. The Enlightenment recipe of reading the Bible "like any other book" tends to ignore this aspect of *human* intention. Instead, it pictures a human author who may indeed have *wanted* to speak for God, but whose intentions are in fact merely *private* intentions, merely human.

More broadly still, the Enlightenment distorts its view of every human author whatsoever, because it suppresses the presence of God. In doing so, it suppresses the fact that every human being lives inescapably in the presence of God, is continually sustained by God, and is continually responding to God.

The Enlightenment recipe says that we should read the Bible like any other book. This recipe needs not only to be repudiated but also to be turned around: we should read *all other books* in the light of what the Bible says about God and man and redemption and all the other topics that it addresses.

The Nature of Mankind

In particular, we may ask about the nature of mankind. God made man in the image of God, so God himself is the archetype, or original, from which we should understand man. In addition, the destiny of redeemed mankind is to be conformed to the image of Christ: "Just as we have borne the image of the man of dust [Adam], we shall also bear the image of the man of heaven [Christ]" (1 Cor. 15:49).

We may bring these truths into relation to the Holy Spirit. As God, Christ is filled with the Holy Spirit from all eternity. As man, Christ was filled with the Spirit for the purpose of accomplishing the work of redemption:

> For he whom God has sent utters the words of God, for he gives the Spirit without measure. (John 3:34)

> The Spirit of the Lord is upon me,
>   because he has anointed me
>   to proclaim good news to the poor.

He has sent me to proclaim liberty to the captives
>and recovering of sight to the blind,
>to set at liberty those who are oppressed,
to proclaim the year of the Lord's favor. (Luke 4:18–19)

Since Christ is the model for what we should be in the fulfillment of true humanity, we should all be filled with the Holy Spirit. This filling takes place at a lower level than with Christ, and is based on his accomplishment (Acts 2:32–33; Eph. 5:18).

The human authors of Scripture were filled with the Spirit in a special way in order to write the very words of God (2 Pet. 1:21). We in our day are not given the same task—the task of producing more books to add to the existing canon of Scripture—but God still gives the Holy Spirit to his people, in order to empower them for the tasks that he gives them. According to Ephesians 5:18, we should all be filled with the Spirit. The words that the authors of Scripture speak are infallible, because they have full divine authority. By contrast, the words that we speak are fallible. But when we are filled with the Spirit, our words will edify others because they express the truth and wisdom of God in Christ (Col. 3:16).

We must always remember the distinct role that the Bible plays as the infallible word of God. Yet because of the pouring out of the Spirit, all God's people become prophets in a subordinate sense (Acts 2:17–18). What we say when we are filled with the Spirit carries the Spirit's wisdom, and not merely our own. Consequently, our words need to be interpreted in a manner that acknowledges the presence of the Spirit. Interpreters need to take into account God's presence.

That means that nearly everything that we have said about interpreting God's word in Scripture carries over into principles for interpreting the communication of God's Spirit-filled people. It carries over, that is, by way of analogy, not identity. We who are indwelt by the Spirit remain fallible, and that fallibility qualifies what we say. Still, we are privileged through the Holy Spirit to be carriers of the word of God:

Let the *word of Christ* dwell in you richly, teaching and admonishing one another in all wisdom, singing psalms and hymns and spiritual songs, with thankfulness in your hearts to God. (Col. 3:16)

Frequently that Spirit-filled communication may take place by actually quoting from Scripture texts that address the needs and struggles of others. But it may also take the form of rephrasing the meaning of Scripture using other words.

And now let us consider other human beings. What about Christians who are temporarily caught in sin and are grieving the Spirit (Eph. 4:30)? What about non-Christians, who do not have saving fellowship with Christ and the Spirit? What we have said is pertinent to non-Christians. The destiny of Spirit-filled mankind offers a model to them as well, by indicating what they *should* be. The truly human destiny is Spirit-filled humanity. The non-Christian form of humanity is a corrupted, fallen, distorted form, which we understand only in relation to what it should be. Non-Christians, as we observed in the previous appendix, are in conflict with themselves. They are created in the image of God, and made for fellowship with God, but they continually suppress and evade the purpose for which they were created.

In addition, non-Christians enjoy common grace. They do not deserve the benefits that God gives them, so the benefits are by grace rather than by deserving. If so, such benefits come through Christ and the Spirit, though the benefits fall short of leading to salvation. Thus, in interpreting the works of non-Christians, we need to pay attention both to what the Spirit gives and to distortions that take place because of sin. God through the Spirit is present in common grace even with non-Christians. Proper interpretation takes into account the divine presence (in order to understand rightly the human life of a non-Christian). Thus, our principles for interpreting the Bible in the presence of God apply even to the writings of non-Christians, once we have made important adjustments to reckon with the conflicted character of non-Christian existence.

The Enlightenment tells us to interpret the Bible like any other text. To the contrary, now we are saying that we need to interpret all other texts in the light of biblical teaching. Because of the presence of God, we must deal with God, not only with man; and we must deal with mystery, the mystery of his infinite purposes being worked out even in the lives and writings of non-Christians.

Appendix D

Redeemed Analogues to Critical Methods

This handbook has not made direct reference to the traditional critical methods employed in the mainstream historical-critical method.[1] Why not? The mainstream method, as often understood, includes a bias against the supernatural, and in addition ignores the divine authorship of the Bible. In my judgment, both of these moves are ghastly mistakes, which distort the process of interpretation. Moreover, because of its academic dominance, the historical-critical method has often had adverse effects on the methods of evangelicals as well.

Evangelical scholars believe in the supernatural and in the divine authorship of the Bible, but they feel the pull from the mainstream of scholarship. Mainstream scholarship includes insights from common grace, and these insights are often not easily detachable from a context of distorted beliefs and worldviews. When evangelicals appropriate insights from the mainstream, they can unwittingly bring along distorted assumptions. Belief in the supernatural and in the divine authorship of the Bible can become nonfunctional when evangelicals imitate the mainstream. Or there can be subtler adverse effects (appendices A–C).

This handbook has accordingly treated divine authorship and divine

---

[1] Text criticism is an exception (see chapter 7).

presence as key themes that run through the entire process of interpretation. In doing so, we have emphasized the antithesis between the methods of the mainstream of scholarship and an approach that honors and loves God in the process of interpretation.

In addition, at the end of appendix A we have discussed corruptions that have entered the world of scholarship in the very conception of how a "method" should work. "Methods" can easily be corrupted by the desire for autonomous mastery and the avoidance of mystery.

It is nevertheless right to point out that there exist within the mainstream instances of common grace. There are similarities between prominent critical methods and our approach. Accordingly, we now point out how some of the critical methods have analogues in this handbook.

The main classical critical methods of the nineteenth and twentieth centuries were text criticism, source criticism (often a part of a larger project, "higher criticism"), form criticism, and redaction criticism. The late twentieth century has seen further additions to the list, but we will begin with these.

Text Criticism

Text criticism is the study of ancient manuscripts that are copies of an original. It has the purpose of organizing and understanding the variations between manuscripts and then trying to reconstruct the original from which the manuscripts descended.

Text criticism is useful for evangelicals as it is for everyone else. It has a comparatively minor role, because, in comparison with virtually all other ancient texts, the text of the Bible has been well preserved over the centuries and the variations are comparatively minor. We have touched on text criticism in chapter 7. We have not entered into details, because text criticism is a technical area. Those who want to pursue it can consult textbooks devoted to it.

Belief in the supernatural nature of Scripture goes together with the conviction of God's providential control over all events whatsoever, whether "supernatural" or "natural." God's providential control includes his control over text transmission, as described in chapter 7. The Westminster Confession of Faith sums it up:

The Old Testament in Hebrew . . . and the New Testament in Greek . . . , being immediately inspired by God, and *by his singular care and providence kept pure in all ages*, are therefore authentical. (1.8)

God's providential care gives us confidence that we have today substantially the same text as the original. There are small variations in the manuscripts, here and there, but they do not prevent us from understanding the doctrine of salvation and the way we must live to please God.

Study of text criticism should therefore proceed both with confidence and with gratitude to God for his providential care. Text criticism as conducted by mainstream scholarship has a different existential attitude and commitment. But in many ways it has adjusted itself to the reality of God's providence, though it may not use the same descriptive label. Thus an evangelical interpreter interested in text criticism can learn a lot from the technical details in mainstream discussions.

Source Criticism

The next "tool" of historical criticism is source criticism. Source criticism analyzes the written sources used by the human author of a particular book of the Bible. For example, with respect to the Gospels, it is often supposed that Matthew and Luke used Mark as a source. But although that is the most common view among scholars, it is uncertain.[2] First and Second Chronicles apparently used 1–2 Kings as a source. First and Second Kings in turn refer explicitly to books that may have served as sources: "the Book of the Chronicles of the Kings of Israel" (1 Kings 14:19; etc.), "the Book of the Chronicles of the Kings of Judah" (1 Kings 14:29; etc.), "the Book of Jashar" (2 Sam. 1:18), and "the Book of the Acts of Solomon" (1 Kings 11:41). These earlier books have all perished. The doctrine of inspiration is quite compatible with a process in which God and the human author used sources. The doctrine of inspiration says that the product, the finished text, has divine authority; it leaves open the question of what processes took place in leading to the finished product.

---

[2] Vern S. Poythress, *Inerrancy and the Gospels: A God-Centered Approach to the Challenges of Harmonization* (Wheaton, IL: Crossway, 2012), chapter 16.

In most other cases we know nothing explicit about sources. Trying to reconstruct sources involves speculation. Moreover, each book of the Bible has its own integrity, and needs to be received for what it says, not for what its sources may have said. Source criticism can respond to human curiosity about sources, but has almost nothing to contribute to understanding the meaning of the texts that we have.[3] For this reason we have not included it within our overall outline. If someone wishes to include it, it would fall under B.1.c., as part of "transmission."

Form Criticism

The next traditional critical tool is *form criticism*. Form criticism tries to reconstruct oral sources behind the written sources. It does so by using clues from the "form" or genre of embedded pieces within the books of the Bible. The genre of these pieces, such as miracle stories or parables within the Gospels, might provide clues as to the circumstances in which oral stories were told at earlier stages. The difficulties with source criticism apply also to form criticism, because it is speculative and because earlier stages, even if properly reconstructed, do not tell us the meaning of the texts that we have before us.

We have accordingly not included it in our overall outline.

Redaction Criticism

The next critical tool is *redaction criticism*. Redaction criticism began as a study of the changes that a "redactor" or final editor added to earlier sources as he put together the final product. These changes, it was hoped, would reveal his purposes. But, granted that the redactor used sources, what he left the same is just as revealing of his purposes as what he changed. Redaction criticism draws attention to what is distinctive about a text, and it may thus reveal something about theological or personal emphases that an author included. But these emphases are there whether or not the author used an earlier source. It is possible to study the particular emphases of a text without worrying about which text used another text as a source. This kind of study of the emphases of the final text is sometimes given the same label, "redaction criticism."

---

[3] Ibid.

But to use the same label for the two kinds of study is confusing. The second kind of study is really quite different; it is a study of the finished text according to topics (chapter 18).

In the case of 1–2 Chronicles, one of the earlier sources is available to us, namely 1–2 Samuel and 1–2 Kings together. First–Second Chronicles was written considerably later than Samuel and Kings, so it can take advantage of the fact that its readers already know Samuel and Kings. This previous knowledge can allow readers to notice what is new or different in 1–2 Chronicles. So taking into account the sources can help us to perceive how God intended 1–2 Chronicles to be received by its readers. But even here the differences can be exaggerated. Chronicles affirms what remains the same from Kings, as well as what is different. As a complete communication, it has its own integrity.

Moreover, 1–2 Chronicles is an exception, because 1–2 Kings was probably already acknowledged to be part of the canon of Scripture at the time Chronicles was written. Samuel and Kings would already have functioned as a fixed point in readers' knowledge. That is a different situation from cases where scholars guess that other books of the Bible used sources that were less widely known.

Thus redaction criticism, if understood as a study of changes made by a redactor from previous texts, has many of the difficulties that we have already seen in source criticism and form criticism. Except in the case of 1–2 Chronicles, where one main source (Samuel and Kings together) is prominently available, redaction criticism is speculative. And it obscures the integrity of the finished text as a text having its own meaning, distinct from the meaning of whatever sources it may have used.

We have not included it in our overall outline. Instead, we have included kinds of focus that study the finished text, such as analysis of topics (chapter 18, B.1.c.(1).(b).((2)).((b)).) and genre (chapter 19, B.1.c.(1).(b).((1)).((c)).).[4]

---

[4] Thus I downplay source criticism, form criticism, and redaction criticism as virtually irrelevant to meaning. May I suggest that the development of the three forms of criticism was influenced by an ideology? In the nineteenth-century Western world, the idea took hold that explaining anything at all took place by explaining the history of its origin. Historical explanation became the preeminent mode of intellectual explanation for human meaning, and in Darwinism it became the preeminent mode for explaining biological organisms. I do not deny that historical explanation can address certain types of interesting questions. But it is completely inadequate as a route to verbal meaning. Biblical scholarship got itself onto a fruitless sidetrack. It was all the more fruitless because the dominant ideal for history excluded the presence of God.

More Recent Additions

The late twentieth century and opening years of the twenty-first century have seen a proliferation of types of approach, so that it is difficult to categorize them all. Genre criticism is similar to our discussion of genre in chapter 19. *Tradition criticism* analyzes the growth of "traditions." It is similar to our analysis of growth of themes in the context of redemptive history (B.3.) as well as topical correlations (B.2.). But sometimes tradition criticism is understood in a way that "levels" all traditions and does not recognize the uniqueness of divine authorship.

Rhetorical criticism is a form of discourse analysis (chapter 18), with a certain focus on formal (grammatical and phonological) techniques. *Literary criticism* has been applied mostly to narrative, and is a form of analysis of discourse (chapter 18, especially B.1.c.(1).(b).((2)).((a)), B.2.e., and B.3.c.(3).(b).((1)).((b)).).

We have touched on reader-response approaches in chapter 9, section B.1.c.(1).(c). *Deconstruction* can be included as a special kind of reader-response approach,[5] as can *Marxist* and *feminist criticism*.[6] All kinds of critical methods can be influenced by antibiblical assumptions. But reader-response approaches are especially vulnerable, since they may explicitly permit a heavy influence from readers and the assumptions that readers carry with them.

Because of the perspectival nature of the points within the overall outline, any of them is capable of being perspectivally expanded to include further topics on which human ingenuity may undertake to focus.

---

[5] Vern S. Poythress, *In the Beginning Was the Word: Language—A God-Centered Approach* (Wheaton, IL: Crossway, 2009), appendix I.
[6] Vern S. Poythress, *Inerrancy and Worldview: Answering Modern Challenges to the Bible* (Wheaton, IL: Crossway, 2012), chapter 18.

Appendix E

Philosophical Hermeneutics

The critical methods associated with the historical-critical method, which are discussed in the preceding appendix, grew up during the nineteenth and twentieth centuries. The same period saw a growth in interest in philosophical hermeneutics, with contributions from a host of luminaries. We might start with Friedrich Schleiermacher, and go through Wilhelm Dilthey to Martin Heidegger, Rudolf Bultmann, Emilio Betti, Ludwig Wittgenstein, Hans-Georg Gadamer, Ernst Fuchs, Gerhard Ebeling, Paul Ricoeur, Hans Robert Jauss, Karl-Otto Apel, Jürgen Habermas, Richard Rorty, Jacques Derrida, Stanley Fish, and others. A full discussion would take volumes.[1] We cannot do that here. We confine ourselves to some elementary observations.

Major Themes

One of the most obvious major themes in modern philosophical hermeneutics is the theme of human *finiteness*. How do we obtain knowledge

---

[1] Helpful analysis is found especially in a number of contributions by Anthony C. Thiselton and Kevin J. Vanhoozer: Anthony C. Thiselton, *The Two Horizons: New Testament Hermeneutics and Philosophical Description with Special Reference to Heidegger, Bultmann, Gadamer, and Wittgenstein* (Grand Rapids, MI: Eerdmans, 1980); Thiselton, *New Horizons in Hermeneutics* (Grand Rapids, MI: Eerdmans, 1992); Thiselton, *Interpreting God and the Postmodern Self: On Meaning, Manipulation, and Promise* (Grand Rapids, MI: Eerdmans, 1995); Thiselton, *Hermeneutics: An Introduction* (Grand Rapids, MI: Eerdmans, 2009); Kevin J. Vanhoozer, *Is There a Meaning in This Text?: The Bible, the Reader, and the Morality of Literary Knowledge* (Grand Rapids, MI: Zondervan, 1998); Vanhoozer, *First Theology: God, Scripture, and Hermeneutics* (Downers Grove, IL: InterVarsity/Leicester, England: Apollos, 2002). My concerns about the questions of philosophical hermeneutics are expressed primarily in Vern S. Poythress, "Christ the Only Savior of Interpretation," *Westminster Theological Journal* 50/2 (1988): 305–321; and subordinately, "God's Lordship in Interpretation," *Westminster Theological Journal* 50/1 (1988): 27–64.

amid the limitations of our own horizon, including the limitations of language and culture? The theme of finiteness is indeed a most important theme with which to reckon when we engage in interpretation. And the tradition of philosophical hermeneutics offers many insights by virtue of common grace. But this philosophical tradition, like Western philosophy as a whole, suffers under the burden of a sinful fundamental commitment. Philosophical hermeneutics has decided to conduct its inquiry as a general intellectual problem, a problem that it aspires to address without submitting to God's instruction in the Bible.[2] But how can one hope to understand in a proper way the issue of human finiteness while ignoring God the infinite person with reference to whom finiteness makes sense? In particular, how can we understand the human ability to talk about finiteness, in a way that transcends the immediate environment, without recognizing that human beings as creatures imitate on their own level the archetypal transcendence of God? And how can we hope to understand the human condition without reference to God having created man in his image, with the design that man should be in communion with God?

Philosophical hermeneutics does not want to confront in depth the problem posed by sin when a person seeks access to God.[3] But without fellowship with God, including propositional knowledge of God, the philosopher loses the transcendent reference point necessary for understanding both the nature of finiteness and the unity and diversity in human nature that characterizes humanity. This break with God results in a failure properly to access transcendent truth. There are no culture-transcending truths available without transcendence, and philosophical hermeneutics in its very foundation has decided against the only route to fellowship with the transcendent God, namely Christ himself.[4]

A second theme in modern philosophical hermeneutics is the theme

---

[2] On the general problem of philosophy, see Vern S. Poythress, *Redeeming Philosophy: A God-Centered Approach to the Big Questions* (Wheaton, IL: Crossway, 2014), chapter 3.

[3] Philosophers may speak about God. They may discuss how to have access to God. But usually they do not proceed to enjoy and use such access when they are putting their philosophizing into writing. That is, they do not use in their writings the only way that God has provided, namely through Christ and the Bible as the word of God. When a person ignores the one way given in Christ, access to God is corrupted.

[4] Is this evaluation too harsh? Could not some practitioners of philosophical hermeneutics remain neutral or uncommitted, rather than actually deciding *against* Christ? No. "Whoever is not with me is against me" (Luke 11:23). The person who wants to be neutral seems in his own eyes to be playing it safe and to be genuinely "noncommittal." But he is relying on himself rather than admitting his need for salvation in the hermeneutical sphere. And he is tacitly refusing to do what Christ demands, namely to submit to Christ's claims and his authority (Matt. 28:18).

of *historicality* of understanding. As human beings we are *historical* creatures. We change over time. We grow and change in the course of interacting with and trying to understand communication and texts. But how can one hope to understand growth and change without understanding God as Lord of history, and the purposes with which God governs history and individual human lives? In this book, we have addressed historicality through the wave perspective and the transmission perspective.

A third theme is the theme of *sympathy*: readers need to read sympathetically in interacting with a text and its author. In this book we have addressed it under another label, namely the theme of love. We ought to love God, and to love our neighbor as ourselves. Loving God includes the desire to hear what he says. Loving our neighbor includes the desire to hear what the neighbor says. In both cases, how can we understand love as we ought to, unless we have communion with God and are instructed by him?

A fourth theme is the theme of *suspicion*. We ought to be suspicious of human communicative moves because human beings can have sinister and manipulative motives, and can use oral, written, and imagistic forms of communication as part of programs to gain power. We have addressed this theme with another label, namely the label of *sin*. How can philosophical hermeneutics hope to understand sin when it conducts its discussion without reference to God? At its root, sin is rebellion against God and includes violation of God's standards.

Biblically Based Answers

The Bible in its instruction provides a rich field for reflection on all these themes. We may acknowledge insights from common grace from philosophical hermeneutics. But the antithesis between serving God and rebelling against him requires that we rethink such insights and endeavor to understand hermeneutics in a way that is thoroughly informed by a biblical worldview. This goal is not easily attained. We have begun the process in this book. (And other books to which we have referred also engage in the process.) Our discussions look different from philosophical hermeneutics, because they interact with the teaching of the Bible and begin to think through its implications.

We need to reckon with the presence of God. And that means not only growing in knowing God, but growing in knowledge of his salvation in Christ. It is Christ who through the Holy Spirit rescues us from the power and guilt of sin. That rescue leads to effects in the renewal of our minds: "Do not be conformed to this world, but be transformed by *the renewal of your mind*, that by testing you may discern what is the will of God, what is good and acceptable and perfect" (Rom. 12:2). Renewal of our mind includes renewal in how we study and understand the Bible. And in the long run the effects spill over into all areas of life, including how we understand other communications besides the Bible.

Bibliography

Augustine. *The Confessions*. Translated by Maria Boulding. The Works of Saint Augustine, A Translation for the 21st Century. Hyde Park, NY: New City Press, 1997.

Baldwin, Joyce G. *1 and 2 Samuel: An Introduction and Commentary*. Downers Grove, IL/ Leicester, England: InterVarsity Press, 1988.

Barr, James. *The Semantics of Biblical Language*. London: Oxford University Press, 1961.

Bauer, Walter. *A Greek-English Lexicon of the New Testament and Other Early Christian Literature*. Translated by William F. Arndt and F. Wilbur Gingrich. 2nd English ed., rev. and augmented by F. Wilbur Gingrich and Frederick W. Danker. Chicago: University of Chicago Press, 1979.

Beale, Gregory K. *Handbook on the New Testament Use of the Old Testament: Exegesis and Interpretation*. Grand Rapids, MI: Baker, 2012.

Beale, Gregory K., and D. A. Carson, eds. *Commentary on the New Testament Use of the Old Testament*. Grand Rapids, MI: Baker/Nottingham, England: Apollos, 2007.

Beekman, John, and John Callow. *Translating the Word of God*. With Scripture and topical indexes. Grand Rapids, MI: Zondervan, 1974.

Berkhof, Louis. *Principles of Biblical Interpretation: (Sacred Hermeneutics)*. Grand Rapids, MI: Baker, 1950.

Biblia Hebraica Stuttgartensia. Stuttgart: Deutsche Bibelstiftung, 1977.

Blomberg, Craig L., with Jennifer Foutz Markley. *A Handbook of New Testament Exegesis*. Grand Rapids, MI: Baker, 2010.

Borges, Jorge. "Pierre Menard, Author of the *Quixote*." First published in Spanish in *Sur* (May 1939). Now available online both in Spanish (http://www.literatura.us/borges /pierre.html, accessed December 24, 2012) and in English (http://www.coldbacon.com /writing/borges-quixote.html, accessed December 24, 2012).

Borowski, Oded. *Daily Life in Biblical Times*. Atlanta: Society of Biblical Literature, 2003.

Bowald, Mark Alan. *Rendering the Word in Theological Hermeneutics: Mapping Divine and Human Agency*. Aldershot, England/Burlington, VT: Ashgate, 2007.

Bromiley, Geoffrey W., ed. *The International Standard Bible Encyclopedia*. 4 vols. Rev. ed. Grand Rapids, MI: Eerdmans, 1995.

Brown, Francis, S. R. Driver, and Charles A. Briggs. *A Hebrew and English Lexicon of the Old Testament with an Appendix Containing the Biblical Aramaic*. With corrections. Oxford: Oxford University Press, 1953.

Bruce, F. F. *New Testament History*. Garden City, NY: Doubleday, 1980.

Burton, Ernest DeWitt. *Syntax of the Moods and Tenses in New Testament Greek*. Reprint of the 3rd ed. (1900). Grand Rapids, MI: Kregel, 1976.

Carson, D. A. *Exegetical Fallacies*. 2nd ed. Grand Rapids, MI: Baker, 1996.

———. *New Testament Commentary Survey*. Grand Rapids, MI: Baker, 2007.

Clowney, Edmund P. *Preaching and Biblical Theology*. Grand Rapids, MI: Eerdmans, 1961.

———. *Preaching Christ in All of Scripture*. Wheaton, IL: Crossway, 2003.

———. *The Unfolding Mystery: Discovering Christ in the Old Testament*. Colorado Springs: NavPress, 1988.

Craigie, Peter C. *Psalms 1–50*. Word Biblical Commentary. Vol. 19. 2nd ed. With 2004 Supplement by Marvin E. Tate. n.l.: Nelson, 2004.

Currid, John D., and David P. Barrett. *Crossway ESV Bible Atlas*. Wheaton, IL: Crossway, 2010.

Danker, Frederick William, ed. *A Greek-English Lexicon of the New Testament and Other Early Christian Literature*. Chicago: University of Chicago Press, 2000. This third English edition is inferior in some ways to the second edition, authored by Walter Bauer and translated by Arndt and Gingrich.

Doriani, Daniel M. *Getting the Message: A Plan for Interpreting and Applying the Bible*. Phillipsburg, NJ: Presbyterian & Reformed, 1996.

———. *Putting the Truth to Work: The Theory and Practice of Biblical Application*. Phillipsburg, NJ: Presbyterian & Reformed, 2001.

Fairbairn, Patrick. *The Typology of Scripture*. Reprint. Grand Rapids, MI: Kregel, 1989. Originally published New York: Funk & Wagnalls, 1900.

Fee, Gordon D., and Douglas Stuart. *How to Read the Bible for All Its Worth*. Grand Rapids, MI: Zondervan, 2003.

Ferguson, Everett. *Backgrounds of Early Christianity*. 3rd ed. Grand Rapids, MI: Eerdmans, 2003.

Fish, Stanley. *Is There a Text in This Class?: The Authority of Interpretive Communities*. Cambridge, MA: Harvard University Press, 1980.

Frame, John M. *Apologetics to the Glory of God: An Introduction*. Phillipsburg, NJ: Presbyterian & Reformed, 1994.

———. "Backgrounds to My Thought." In *Speaking the Truth in Love: The Theology of John M. Frame*. Edited by John J. Hughes. Phillipsburg, NJ: Presbyterian & Reformed, 2009. Pp. 9–30.

———. "Bibliography." In *Speaking the Truth in Love: The Theology of John M. Frame*. Edited by John J. Hughes. Phillipsburg, NJ: Presbyterian & Reformed, 2009. Pp. 1029–1063.

———. *Cornelius Van Til: An Analysis of His Thought*. Phillipsburg, NJ: Presbyterian & Reformed, 1995.

———. *The Doctrine of the Christian Life*. Phillipsburg, NJ: Presbyterian & Reformed, 2008.

———. *The Doctrine of God*. Phillipsburg, NJ: Presbyterian & Reformed, 2002.

———. *The Doctrine of the Knowledge of God*. Phillipsburg, NJ: Presbyterian & Reformed, 1987.

———. *The Doctrine of the Word of God*. Phillipsburg, NJ: Presbyterian & Reformed, 2010.

———. "Greeks Bearing Gifts." In *Revolutions in Worldview: Understanding the Flow of Western Thought*. Edited by W. Andrew Hoffecker. Phillipsburg, NJ: Presbyterian & Reformed, 2007. Pp. 1–36.

———. *A History of Western Philosophy and Theology: Spiritual Warfare in the Life of the Mind*. Phillipsburg, NJ: Presbyterian & Reformed, 2015.

———. *Perspectives on the Word of God: An Introduction to Christian Ethics*. Eugene, OR: Wipf & Stock, 1999.

———. "A Primer on Perspectivalism." 2008. Internet publication, http://www.frame-poythress.org/frame_articles/2008Primer.htm, accessed January 26, 2012.

———. "Recommended Resources." In *Speaking the Truth in Love: The Theology of John M. Frame*. Edited by John J. Hughes. Phillipsburg, NJ: Presbyterian & Reformed, 2009. Pp. 1063–1070.

———. "Review of Esther Meek's *Longing to Know*," *Presbyterion* 29/2 (Fall 2003), http://www.frame-poythress.org/review-of-esther-meeks-longing-to-know/.

———. *Salvation Belongs to the Lord: An Introduction to Systematic Theology*. Phillipsburg, NJ: Presbyterian & Reformed, 2006.

———. *Systematic Theology*. Phillipsburg, NJ: Presbyterian & Reformed, 2013.

———. *Van Til the Theologian*. Phillipsburg, NJ: Pilgrim, 1976.

Gadamer, Hans-Georg. *Truth and Method*. New York: Crossroad, 1989.

Gesenius, Wilhelm. *Gesenius' Hebrew Grammar*. 2nd English ed. Rev. E. Kautzsch and A. E. Cowley. Oxford: Clarendon, 1980.

Goldsworthy, Graeme. *The Goldsworthy Trilogy*. Milton Keynes, UK/Colorado Springs/Hyderabad: Paternoster, 2000.

———. *Gospel and Kingdom: A Christian Interpretation of the Old Testament*. Exeter, England: Paternoster, 1981.

———. *Gospel and Wisdom: Israel's Wisdom Literature in the Christian Life*. Exeter, England: Paternoster, 1987.

———. *Gospel-Centered Hermeneutics: Foundations and Principles of Evangelical Biblical Interpretation*. Downers Grove, IL: InterVarsity Press, 2006.

———. *Preaching the Whole Bible as Christian Scripture: The Application of Biblical Theology to Expository Preaching*. Grand Rapids, MI: Eerdmans, 2000.

Greidanus, Sidney. *The Modern Preacher and the Ancient Text: Interpreting and Preaching Biblical Literature*. Grand Rapids, MI: Eerdmans/Leicester, England: InterVarsity Press, 1988.

———. *Preaching Christ from the Old Testament: A Contemporary Hermeneutical Method*. Grand Rapids, MI: Eerdmans, 1999.

———. *Sola Scriptura: Problems and Principles in Preaching Historical Texts*. Toronto: Wedge, 1970.

Hirsch, E. D., Jr. *The Aims of Interpretation*. Chicago: University of Chicago Press, 1976.

———. *Validity in Interpretation*. New Haven, CT: Yale University Press, 1967.

Hughes, John J. "The Heart of John Frame's Theology." In *Speaking the Truth in Love: The Theology of John M. Frame*. Edited by John J. Hughes. Phillipsburg, NJ: Presbyterian & Reformed, 2009. Pp. 31–74.

Hughes, John J., ed. *Speaking the Truth in Love: The Theology of John M. Frame*. Phillipsburg, NJ: Presbyterian & Reformed, 2009.

Johnson, Dennis E. *Him We Proclaim: Preaching Christ from All the Scriptures*. Phillipsburg, NJ: Presbyterian & Reformed, 2007.

Joy, Charles R. *Harper's Topical Concordance of the Bible*. New York: HarperCollins, 1989.

Kaiser, Walter C., Jr., and Moisés Silva. *An Introduction to Biblical Hermeneutics: The Search for Meaning*. Grand Rapids, MI: Zondervan, 1994.

———. *An Introduction to Biblical Hermeneutics: The Search for Meaning*. Rev. and expanded ed. Grand Rapids, MI: Zondervan, 2007.

Kidner, Derek. *The Proverbs: An Introduction and Commentary*. Downers Grove, IL/London: InterVarsity Press, 1964.

———. *Psalms 1–72: An Introduction and Commentary on Books I and II of the Psalms.* Downers Grove, IL/London: InterVarsity Press, 1973.

Klein, Ralph W. *1 Samuel.* Word Biblical Commentary. Vol. 10. Waco, TX: Word, 1983.

Klein, William W., Craig L. Blomberg, and Robert L. Hubbard, Jr. *Introduction to Biblical Interpretation.* Rev. and expanded ed. Nashville/Dallas/Mexico City/Rio de Janeiro: Nelson, 2004.

Kline, Meredith G. *The Structure of Biblical Authority.* Grand Rapids, MI: Eerdmans, 1972.

Koehler, Ludwig, and Walter Baumgartner. *The Hebrew and Aramaic Lexicon of the Old Testament.* Rev. Walter Baumgartner and Johann Jakob Stamm. Leiden/New York: Brill, 1994–2000.

Kohlenberger, John R., III. *Zondervan NIV Nave's Topical Bible.* Grand Rapids, MI: Zondervan, 1992.

Kruger, Michael J. *Canon Revisited: Establishing the Origins and Authority of the New Testament Books.* Wheaton, IL: Crossway, 2012.

Kuhatschek, Jack, and Cindy Bunch. *How to Lead a LifeGuide Bible Study.* 3rd ed. Downers Grove, IL: InterVarsity Press, 2003.

Kuyper, Abraham. *Lectures on Calvinism: Six Lectures Delivered at Princeton University Under Auspices of the L. P. Stone Foundation.* Grand Rapids, MI: Eerdmans, 1931.

———. "Sphere Sovereignty." In *Abraham Kuyper: A Centennial Reader.* Edited by James D. Bratt. Grand Rapids, MI: Eerdmans/Carlisle, PA: Paternoster, 1998. Pp. 463–490.

Leithart, Peter J. *Deep Exegesis: The Mystery of Reading Scripture.* Waco, TX: Baylor University Press, 2009.

Liddell, Henry George, Robert Scott, Henry Stuart Jones, and Robert McKenzie. *A Greek-English Lexicon.* 9th ed. With a rev. supplement. Oxford: Oxford University Press, 1996.

Longman, Tremper, III. *Old Testament Commentary Survey.* Grand Rapids, MI: Baker, 2007.

Marshall, I. Howard, A. R. Millard, J. I. Packer, and D. J. Wiseman, eds. *New Bible Dictionary.* 3rd ed. Downers Grove, IL: InterVarsity Press, 1996.

McCartney, Dan G., and Charles Clayton. *Let the Reader Understand: A Guide to Interpreting and Applying the Bible.* 2nd ed. Phillipsburg, NJ: Presbyterian & Reformed, 2002.

Merrill, Eugene H. *Kingdom of Priests: A History of Old Testament Israel.* 2nd ed. Grand Rapids, MI: Baker, 2008.

Murray, David. *Jesus on Every Page: Discovering and Enjoying Christ in the Old Testament.* Nashville/Dallas/Mexico City/Rio de Janeiro: Thomas Nelson, 2013.

Novum Testamentum Graece: Nestle-Aland. Institute for New Testament Textual Research. German Bible Society, 2012.

Oliphint, K. Scott, and Lane G. Tipton, eds. *Revelation and Reason: New Essays in Reformed Apologetics.* Phillipsburg, NJ: Presbyterian & Reformed, 2007.

Osborne, Grant R. *The Hermeneutical Spiral: A Comprehensive Introduction to Biblical Interpretation.* Rev. and expanded ed. Downers Grove, IL: InterVarsity Press, 2006.

Packer, J. I. *"Fundamentalism" and the Word of God: Some Evangelical Principles.* Grand Rapids, MI: Eerdmans, 1958.

———. *Knowing God.* Downers Grove, IL: InterVarsity Press, 1993.

Pike, Kenneth L. *Linguistic Concepts: An Introduction to Tagmemics.* Lincoln/London: University of Nebraska Press, 1982.

Piper, John. *Biblical Exegesis: Discovering the Meaning of Scriptural Texts.* Internet publication, http://www.desiringgod.org/resource-library/seminars/biblical-exegesis, accessed December 27, 2012.

Polanyi, Michael. *Personal Knowledge: Towards a Post-Critical Philosophy.* Chicago: University of Chicago Press, 1964.

———. *The Tacit Dimension.* Garden City, NY: Anchor, 1967.

Poythress, Vern S. "Christ the Only Savior of Interpretation," *Westminster Theological Journal* 50 (1988): 305–321.

———. "Divine Meaning of Scripture," *Westminster Theological Journal* 48 (1986): 241–279.

———. "Extended Definitions in the Third Edition of Bauer's Greek-English Lexicon." *Journal of the Evangelical Theological Society* 45/1 (2001): 125–131. http://www.frame -poythress.org/extended-definitions-in-the-third-edition-of-bauers-greek-english-lexicon/, accessed January 1, 2013.

———. "A Framework for Discourse Analysis: The Components of a Discourse, from a Tagmemic Viewpoint," *Semiotica* 38–3/4 (1982): 277–298. http://www.frame-poythress.org /wp-content/uploads/2012/08/semi.1982.38.3-4.277.pdf, DOI: 10.1515/semi.1982.38.3-4.277, accessed December 29, 2012.

———. *God-Centered Biblical Interpretation.* Phillipsburg, NJ: Presbyterian & Reformed, 1999.

———. "God's Lordship in Interpretation," *Westminster Theological Journal* 50 (1988): 27–64.

———. "Hierarchy in Discourse Analysis: A Revision of Tagmemics," *Semiotica* 40-1/2 (1982): 107–137. http://www.frame-poythress.org/wp-content/uploads/2012/08/semi.1982.40.1 -2.107.pdf, DOI: 10.1515/semi.1982.40.1-2.107, accessed December 29, 2012.

———. "How Have Inclusiveness and Tolerance Affected the Bauer-Danker Greek Lexicon of the New Testament (BDAG)?" *Journal of the Evangelical Theological Society* 46/4 (2003): 577–588. http://www.frame-poythress.org/how-have-inclusiveness-and-tolerance -affected-the-bauer-danker-greek-lexicon-of-the-new-testament-bdag, accessed January 1, 2013.

———. *In the Beginning Was the Word: Language—A God-Centered Approach.* Wheaton, IL: Crossway, 2009.

———. *Inerrancy and the Gospels: A God-Centered Approach to the Challenges of Harmonization.* Wheaton, IL: Crossway, 2012.

———. *Inerrancy and Worldview: Answering Modern Challenges to the Bible.* Wheaton, IL: Crossway, 2012.

———. *Logic: A God-Centered Approach to the Foundation of Western Thought.* Wheaton, IL: Crossway, 2013.

———. "Multiperspectivalism and the Reformed Faith." In *Speaking the Truth in Love: The Theology of John M. Frame.* Edited by John J. Hughes. Phillipsburg, NJ: Presbyterian & Reformed, 2009. Pp. 173–200; online at http://www.frame-poythress.org/poythress _articles/AMultiperspectivalism.pdf, accessed January 26, 2012.

———. "The Presence of God Qualifying Our Notions of Grammatical-Historical Interpretation." *Journal of the Evangelical Theological Society* 50 (2007): 87–103.

———. "Propositional Relations." In *The New Testament Student and His Field.* Vol. 5 of *The New Testament Student.* Edited by John H. Skilton and Curtiss A. Ladley. Phillipsburg, NJ: Presbyterian & Reformed, 1982. Pp. 159–212.

———. *Redeeming Philosophy: A God-Centered Approach to the Big Questions.* Wheaton, IL: Crossway, 2014.

———. *Redeeming Science: A God-Centered Approach.* Wheaton, IL: Crossway, 2006.

———. *Redeeming Sociology: A God-Centered Approach.* Wheaton, IL: Crossway, 2011.

———. *The Returning King: A Guide to the Book of Revelation.* Phillipsburg, NJ: Presbyterian & Reformed, 2000.

———. *Science and Hermeneutics: Implications of Scientific Method for Biblical Interpretation.* Grand Rapids, MI: Zondervan, 1988.

———. *The Shadow of Christ in the Law of Moses.* Reprint. Phillipsburg, NJ: Presbyterian & Reformed, 1995.

———. *Symphonic Theology: The Validity of Multiple Perspectives in Theology.* Reprint. Phillipsburg, NJ: Presbyterian & Reformed, 2001.

———. *Understanding Dispensationalists.* 2nd ed. With postscript. Phillipsburg, NJ: Presbyterian & Reformed, 1994.

Poythress, Vern S., and Wayne A. Grudem. *The TNIV and the Gender-Neutral Bible Controversy.* Nashville: Broadman & Holman, 2004.

Ridderbos, Herman. *Redemptive History and the New Testament Scriptures.* Phillipsburg, NJ: Presbyterian & Reformed, 1988.

Rosenthal, Franz. *A Grammar of Biblical Aramaic.* Wiesbaden: Harrassowitz, 1995.

Ryken, Leland. *How to Read the Bible as Literature.* Grand Rapids, MI: Zondervan, 1984.

Ryken, Leland, James C. Wilhoit, and Tremper Longman, III, eds. *Dictionary of Biblical Imagery.* Downers Grove, IL: InterVarsity Press, 1998.

Silva, Moisés. *Biblical Words and Their Meaning: An Introduction to Lexical Semantics.* Grand Rapids, MI: Zondervan, 1994.

———. "'Can Two Walk Together Unless They Be Agreed?' Evangelical Theology and Biblical Scholarship." *Journal of the Evangelical Theological Society* 41 (1998): 3–16.

———. "The Case for Calvinistic Hermeneutics." In Walter C. Kaiser, Jr., and Moisés Silva, *An Introduction to Biblical Hermeneutics: The Search for Meaning.* Rev. and expanded ed. Grand Rapids, MI: Zondervan, 2007. Pp. 295–318. (First edition, 1994, pp. 251–269.) Reprinted with minor changes in *Revelation and Reason: New Essays in Reformed Apologetics.* Edited by K. Scott Oliphint and Lane G. Tipton. Phillipsburg, NJ: Presbyterian & Reformed, 2007. Pp. 74–94.

———. *Has the Church Misread the Bible?* Grand Rapids, MI: Zondervan, 1987.

Sterrett, T. Norton, and Richard L. Schultz. *How to Understand Your Bible.* Downers Grove, IL: InterVarsity Press, 2010.

Thayer, Joseph H. *Greek-English Lexicon of the New Testament.* Peabody, MA: Hendrickson, 1995.

Thiselton, Anthony C. *Hermeneutics: An Introduction.* Grand Rapids, MI: Eerdmans, 2009.

———. *The Hermeneutics of Doctrine.* Grand Rapids, MI: Eerdmans, 2007.

———. *Interpreting God and the Postmodern Self: On Meaning, Manipulation, and Promise.* Grand Rapids, MI: Eerdmans, 1995.

———. *New Horizons in Hermeneutics.* Grand Rapids, MI: Eerdmans, 1992.

———. *The Two Horizons: New Testament Hermeneutics and Philosophical Description with Special Reference to Heidegger, Bultmann, Gadamer, and Wittgenstein.* Grand Rapids, MI: Eerdmans, 1980.

Traina, Robert. *Methodical Bible Study.* Grand Rapids, MI: Zondervan, 2002. (A revision of a 1952 precursor to flow analysis and "arcing.")

Tsumura, David Toshio. *The First Book of Samuel.* Grand Rapids, MI: Eerdmans, 2007.

Van Til, Cornelius. *The Defense of the Faith.* Edited by K. Scott Oliphint. 4th ed. Phillipsburg, NJ: Presbyterian & Reformed, 2008.

———. *Essays on Christian Education.* Phillipsburg, NJ: Presbyterian & Reformed, 1979.

Vangemeren, Willem A., and Jason Stanghelle. "A Critical-Realistic Reading of the Psalm Titles: Authenticity, Inspiration, and Evangelicals." In *Do Historical Matters Matter to Faith? A Critical Appraisal of Modern and Postmodern Approaches to Scripture.* Edited by James K. Hoffmeier and Dennis R. Magary. Wheaton, IL: Crossway, 2012. 281–301.

Vanhoozer, Kevin J. *First Theology: God, Scripture, and Hermeneutics.* Downers Grove, IL: InterVarsity/Leicester, England: Apollos, 2002.

———. *Is there a Meaning in This Text?: The Bible, the Reader, and the Morality of Literary Knowledge.* Grand Rapids, MI: Zondervan, 1998.

Vos, Geerhardus. *Biblical Theology: Old and New Testaments.* Edinburgh/Carlisle, PA: Banner of Truth Trust, 1975.

Wald, Oletta. *The New Joy of Discovery in Bible Study.* Rev. ed. Minneapolis: Augsburg-Fortress, 2002.

———. *The New Joy of Teaching Discovery.* Minneapolis: Augsburg Fortress, 2002.

Wallace, Daniel B. *Greek Grammar Beyond the Basics: An Exegetical Syntax of the New Testament.* Grand Rapids, MI: Zondervan, 1996.

Waltke, Bruce K. *The Book of Proverbs: Chapters 1–15.* Grand Rapids, MI: Eerdmans, 2004.

Waltke, Bruce K., and M. O'Connor. *An Introduction to Biblical Hebrew Syntax.* Winona Lake, IN: Eisenbrauns, 1989.

Warfield, Benjamin Breckinridge. *The Inspiration and Authority of the Bible.* Edited by Samuel G. Craig. With an introduction by Cornelius Van Til. Philadelphia: Presbyterian & Reformed, 1948.

Wegner, Paul D. *A Student's Guide to Textual Criticism of the Bible: Its History, Methods, and Results.* Downers Grove, IL: InterVarsity Press, 2006.

Whitney, Donald S. *Spiritual Disciplines for the Christian Life.* Colorado Springs: NavPress, 1991.

Wimsatt, William K., Jr., and Monroe C. Beardsley. *The Verbal Icon: Studies in the Meaning of Poetry.* Lexington: University of Kentucky Press, 1954.

General Index

suffering. *See* distress
symbolism/symbols, 179, 241; and the involvement of two levels of meaning rather than one, 241; symbolism as a kind of analogy, 241; symbols as concrete representations of divine truths, 241

tabernacle, the, 241, 294
tagmemics, 132n1
temple, the, 294
text criticism, 81, 435n1, 436–437
themes, 293; in 1 Samuel, 298; in 1 Samuel 22:1–2, 298–300; major Old Testament themes, 293–295; Old Testament themes that point to Christ, 295–297
theology, 36; systematic theology, 36n9, 41, 42
theophanies, 28, 296
Thiselton, Anthony C., 441n1
tolerance, 37
tradition, 38
tradition criticism, 440
translation, 144
transmission, 80–82; and the author, text, and reader perspectival triad, 76–77; and the context of transmission, 78–79; and copies and translations, 81, 84, 84n6; the focus of divine authority on the originals, 84; and literary context, 77–78; and original documents (autographs), 81, 84; outline of the process, 81; and plot structure (planning and initiation, work toward the goal, achievement), 80; stages of, 80; and uncertainties, 82
Trinity, the, 18–20; acting of in respect to contexts, 127–128; and linguistic subsystems, 143–144, 145; mutual indwelling (coinherence) of, 22–23, 68–69, 76; mystery of, 21, 69; and original communication, 103–104; and thought and speech, 193; and the three aspects of God's speech, 29; *Trinity* as a word and a concept, 185, 185n6
Tsumura, David, 90, 204n3, 299
typology/types, 179, 242–243, 275; the early church's use of wood in the Old Testament as

pointing forward to Christ, 254–255; events as types (*see* redemptive plots); and Greek *tupos*, 242, 242–243; institutions as types (*see also* church, the, as a type), 281–282; and the things, events, and relationships perspectival triad, 282; things as types, 275, 276; types as symbols that point forward to a greater or climactic realization, 242. *See also* Clowney's triangle; interpretation, typological approach to; typology/types, and antitypes; typology/types, relationships as types
typology/types, and antitypes, 243, 285–286; already/not yet, 287–289, 291 (table); already/not yet in 1 Samuel 22:1–2, 289–290; church and individual in 1 Samuel 22:1–2, 286–287; and Greek *antitupos*, 242n3
typology/types, relationships as types, 276; friendships, 279. *See also* covenants

Van Til, Cornelius, 404n2
Vangemeren, Willem A., 377n2
Vanhoozer, Kevin J., 441n1

Waltke, Bruce K., 357n2, 367n9
Warfield, Benjamin Breckinridge, 19n5
Westminster Confession of Faith, 82, 123, 173, 436–437
Westminster Larger Catechism, 39
Wimsatt, William, 421–422
Wittgenstein, Ludwig, 441
words and concepts: concepts as units of thought, 193; and "dispute about words" (Greek *logomachia*), 195; distinctions between words and concepts, 192–194; distinguishing between words and concepts when studying Scripture, 191; Hebrew, Aramaic, and Greek words and concepts, 191–192; relations between words and concepts, 194–195; and systematic language contexts, 193; and the unit, hierarchy, and context perspectival triad, 193; words as units of language, 193

Scripture Index

The Case for Biblical Inerrancy

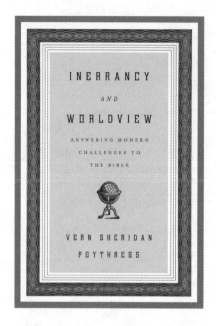

"This book gets deeper into the question of inerrancy than any other book I know."

JOHN M. FRAME, J. D. Trimble Chair of Systematic Theology and Philosophy, Reformed Theological Seminary

"Every Christian student at every secular university should read and absorb the arguments in this book."

WAYNE GRUDEM, Research Professor of Bible and Theology, Phoenix Seminary

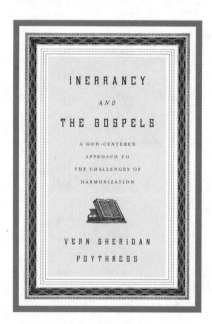

"Clear, convincing, accessible, and practical, Inerrancy and the Gospels *is everything we need in a book on this topic."*

C. D. "JIMMY" AGAN III, Associate Professor of New Testament and Director of Homiletics, Covenant Theological Seminary

"This is a study well worth reading and considering."

DARRELL L. BOCK, Executive Director of Cultural Engagement and Senior Research Professor of New Testament Studies, Dallas Theological Seminary

Available at crossway.org